SAP S/4HANA Financial Accounting Configuration

Learn Configuration and Development on an S/4 System

Second Edition

Andrew Okungbowa

Apress®

SAP S/4HANA Financial Accounting Configuration: Learn Configuration and Development on an S/4 System

Andrew Okungbowa
New Addington, UK

ISBN-13 (pbk): 978-1-4842-8956-3   ISBN-13 (electronic): 978-1-4842-8957-0
https://doi.org/10.1007/978-1-4842-8957-0

Managing Director, Apress Media LLC: Welmoed Spahr
Acquisitions Editor: Divya Modi
Development Editor:Laura Berendson
Coordinating Editor: Divya Modi

Cover designed by eStudioCalamar

Cover image designed by Pixabay

Distributed to the book trade worldwide by Springer Science+Business Media New York, 1 New York Plaza, New York, NY 10004. Phone 1-800-SPRINGER, fax (201) 348-4505, e-mail orders-ny@springer-sbm.com, or visit www.springeronline.com. Apress Media, LLC is a California LLC and the sole member (owner) is Springer Science + Business Media Finance Inc (SSBM Finance Inc). SSBM Finance Inc is a **Delaware** corporation.

For information on translations, please e-mail booktranslations@springernature.com; for reprint, paperback, or audio rights, please e-mail bookpermissions@springernature.com.

Apress titles may be purchased in bulk for academic, corporate, or promotional use. eBook versions and licenses are also available for most titles. For more information, reference our Print and eBook Bulk Sales web page at http://www.apress.com/bulk-sales.

Any source code or other supplementary material referenced by the author in this book is available to readers on GitHub via the book's product page, located at www.apress.com/9781484289563. For more detailed information, please visit http://www.apress.com/source-code.

Printed on acid-free paper

This book is dedicated to God Almighty who made it possible for me to complete this book despite all odds.

Table of Contents

About the Author

Andrew Okungbowa is an accountant and a business advisor with 20+ years of experience solving complex business issues. He is an acclaimed author of several books in accounting and finance. He also co-founded Spoxio App, a sports app designed for sports professionals, sports enthusiasts, and fans to network on a mobile app.

Andrew is a qualified accountant. He holds a combined bachelor's degree in accounting and IT, a master's degree in Investment and Finance. He has over 15 years of experience in SAP FI/CO consulting and over 20 years of accounting and finance experience in a number of FTSE 100/250 companies in the UK and abroad.

Andrew has sat on the board of several companies in the UK, such as Spoxio Ltd, Changing Lives Housing Trust, and Twenty-Fifth Avenue Ltd.

About the Technical Reviewer

Dr. Ravi Surya Subrahmanyam has a Doctorate in Finance. He has been working as an Architect on various SAP S/4HANA Conversion & SAP S/4HANA Upgrade projects in India and the United States. He has been a Visiting Instructor for SAP S/4HANA for SAP Education, SAP India, and SAP Indonesia. He has been a speaker, blogger, and an author. He has conducted the SAP TDI program at the *University of Indonesia* on behalf of SAP Education -SAP Indonesia. He has been a technical and financial writer and his articles have been published in National and International journals.

Acknowledgments

I would like to start first by acknowledging Divya Modi, the acquisition editor, who encouraged me to write a second edition of my first book (SAP ERP Financial Accounting) with Apress Publishing and set me on my toes to make sure the book was completed and published within six months. Your support and encouragement was of immense value and highly appreciated. I also want to thank the Apress editorial team, who contributed to the success of this book.

Secondly, I want to thank Dr. Ravi Surya Subrahmanyam, the technical reviewer for working with me on this book. Dr. Ravi, I appreciate your contributions and the way you professionally coordinated this book project. I also want to thank the developmental editorial team, for their professional editing skills and for painstakingly editing this book line-by-line, page-by-page, and chapter-by-chapter to get it in the finest state. Others whose names have not been mentioned who have contributed one way or another to the success of this book, without you, I don't think this book would have been completed professionally. My thanks also go to Shonmirin P.A, the production editor and technical reviewers of this book and for converting the manuscript into this book.

Finally, I will not forget to say a big God bless to my beautiful daughter Zoe-Chelsea and to my lovely wife Hephzibah for the moral support while I was working on this book.

Introduction

What is SAP?

SAP (Systems, Applications, and Products in Data Processing) is the leading ERP (Enterprise Resource Planning) business application software on the market today and provides a unified platform that allows business processes integration. SAP was developed by SAP AG, a German software company founded in 1972 by five ex-IBM employees. SAP is headquartered in Walldorf, Baden-Württemberg, Germany, with regional offices around the world.

The SAP system is used by major Fortune 500 companies worldwide as a preferred business solution for processing their operations and for generating reports real-time, which aids all aspects of management levels in decision making and enables them to manage their business processes effectively and efficiently.

What is SAP HANA?

SAP HANA (High-performance Analytic Appliance) is a multi-model database that stores data in its memory instead of keeping it on a disk. The column-oriented in-memory database design allows you to run advanced analytics alongside high-speed transactions – in a single system. Why is this so important? Because it lets companies process massive amounts of data with near-zero latency, query data in an instant, and become truly data-driven. By storing data in column-based tables in the main memory and bringing online analytical processing (OLAP) and online transactional processing (OLTP) together, SAP HANA is unique – and significantly faster than other database management systems (DBMS) on the market today.

Launched in 2010, SAP HANA is a modern and mature solution used by tens of thousands of customers around the world. But SAP HANA is much more than a database. In addition to acting as a database server, storing and retrieving data requested by applications, SAP HANA offers advanced search, analytics, and data integration capabilities for all types of data – structured and unstructured. It also functions as an application server and helps companies build smart, insight-driven applications based on real-time data, in-memory computing, and machine learning technology. These capabilities are available both in the cloud and on premise.

By combining multiple data management capabilities – and making all types of data instantly available from a single system – SAP HANA simplifies IT, helps businesses innovate, and knocks down barriers to digital transformation (Source SAP).

What is SAP FI?

FICO is an acronym for Financial (FI). This is a core module in SAP to help organizations capture financial business transactions, maintain efficient financial records, and generate financial reports for both external and internal reports for efficient decision making and strategic planning.

Financial (FI)

FI Module is a business process designed specifically for organizations to maintain their financial records efficiently on a daily basis, for management to be able to ascertain their financial position, and to generate financial statutory reports for external purposes to meet the needs of various stakeholders real time.

The FI module consists of other sub-modules, which include General Ledger (G/L), Accounts Receivable (AR), Accounts Payable (AP), Bank Accounting, Asset Accounting, Special Purpose Ledger, Travel Management, etc.

FI is integrated with other modules like Controlling (CO), Asset Accounting (FI-AA), Sale and Distribution (SD), and Material management (MM). Postings made in these modules with financial implication are posted real time to FI.

Easy Access

The Easy Access menu is a user-specific point of entry into the SAP system. It is the first screen that comes up when you log on to SAP. It is designed as a tree structure containing a list of several key items, which allow you to navigate the system and perform tasks and business processes. For example, you can perform transactions, generate reports, and access web addresses (where you can access documents from a remote Internet server).

IMG

The IMG is a generic tool that you can use to customize business processes and requirements to meet specific needs of an organization. You are presented with three implementation variants in SAP:

- SAP Reference IMG. A standard structured hierarchical tool in the R/3 system (real-time three-tier architecture) that contains the procedure for customizing various country settings and application modules.

- Project IMG. The configuration process can be very daunting. To help manage the complexity involved in customizing when using the reference IMG, you can create each implementation project based on specific functions needed for business processes and the project requirements. For example, you can reduce the project scope to specific objects such as countries.

- Project View IMG. You choose certain properties by specific criteria in order to generate views to organize your project activities. For example, a project view could hold each activity required in a project IMG.

Matchcodes

Matchcodes are user-friendly search functions designed specifically to help you look up or retrieve data records stored in the system. They provide an efficient way of looking for records stored in the system when you do not remember the key.

Who should use this book?

This book is written for SAP FI, MM, SD and FI-AA functional consultants, application consultants, FI business analysts, accountants, FI project management teams, and FI accountants.

A Quick Review of the Book's Content

Each chapter provides a sequence to be followed in customizing SAP FICO from start to finish. The sequence has been arranged to give you the opportunity to work through a complete FICO customizing lifecycle progressively. Each chapter includes all the configuration concepts or activities necessary for your customizing or draws on a previous chapter.

Chapter 1 sets the scene by looking at organizational structure and explains how to create various objects in SAPR/3. This includes how to create company codes, business areas, segments, country-specific settings, and so forth.

Chapter 2 explains and defines the Master Record, including how to edit the Chart of Accounts and how to assign a company code to the Chart of Accounts. It further explores how to define the Account Group and Retained Earnings account.

Chapter 3 looks at the purpose of document control and various forms of document types in the SAP S4 system. It also looks at the steps involved in defining number ranges and setting field status variants. It emphasizes the various principles along with the importance of posting keys, normal and special posting periods, and how to create variants for posting periods.

Chapter 4 explores posting authorizations by discussing the purpose of posting authorization, defining tolerance groups for G/L accounts and employees, assigning users to defined tolerance groups, and creating accounts for clearing differences.

Chapter 5 takes a look at the general ledger and its sub ledgers. It covers when to use line items and open item management, how to create G/L accounts, and how to set other objects settings to consider when creating G/L accounts.

Chapter 6 discusses clearing open items and various types of open-item clearing issues. It covers configuring automatic open item clearing, maximum exchange rate difference settings, the importance of foreign currency valuation, foreign currency balance sheet accounts, and G/L account balances managed on an open-item basis. It also looks at types of exchange rates and how open items are valued in foreign currency.

Chapter 7 explains how to define local and foreign currencies for company codes, maintain the relationship between currencies per currency type, and the purpose of exchange rates. It also explores how to maintain the various exchange rate types and how to define translation ratios for currency transactions.

Chapter 8 explores how to define GR/IR (Goods Receipt/Invoice Receipt) and how to configure GR/IR settings in the SAP R/3 system.

Chapter 9 deals with the House Bank and how master records are created in it. It explains using the House Bank ID and account ID, bank statements supported by SAP, creating global settings for electronic bank statements, configuring manual bank statements, defining posting keys and posting rules for check deposit, and defining variants for check deposit.

Chapter 10 looks at taxes on sales and purchases, including VAT. It covers how to create sale and purchase taxes in SAP R/3, how to specify the tax category in the G/L accounts to which taxes are posted, how to assign the basic tax code for sales and purchases, how to specify the accounts to which different tax types are posted, and how to assign tax codes for non-taxable transactions.

Chapter 11 covers the cash journal by explaining what it is and explaining which items are defined when setting up a new cash journal. It identifies the document types for cash journal items, explains how to create G/L accounts for cash journals, and how to set up the cash journal.

Chapter 12 explains the Financial Statement Versions (FSV). The chapter looks at how to create an FSV from scratch, covers the specifications to be conducted when defining FSV, how to call up FSV hierarchy nodes, and how to assign appropriate G/L accounts.

Chapter 13 explores the Integration of FI with other modules in SAP R/3. This includes automatic postings of material to FI using the valuation class of material as the key to which the G/L account materials are posted, the settings for automatic posting configuration, how to create inventory accounts using the BSX transaction key, how to create corresponding credit accounts for GR/IR clearing accounts using the WRX transaction key, how integration of FI and SD works, and how to prepare revenue account determination.

Chapter 14 deals with Accounts Receivable and Accounts Payable by looking at what is Accounts Payable/Receivable, the steps involved in creating Payable/Receivable, what is Account Group and the function of Account of Account Group, how to enter Accounting Clerk name under an Identification code (ID), Create Number Range for Vendor/Customer, how to resolve Number Range overlaps, Assign number range to Customer/Vendor group, define account group with screen layout. The use of Payment terms in SAP, Assignment of Payment Terms to business partners, the purpose of defining payment terms in SAP, how to create an Installment Plan. How to configure Cash Discount Taken/Granted, Define Payment Block Reasons and process payment manually, how to Maintain Tolerance groups for Employees, Customers/Vendors, and GL Accounts. Finally, how to Maintain Automatic Outing Payment to allow the system to make multiple payments of open item invoices.

Chapter 15 looks at the various levels involved in defining dunning and the specification of Special GL transactions to allow the system to dun Special GL transactions.

Chapter 16 looks at why it is important to disclose Special GL transactions separately by using alternative reconciliation accounts. An explanation of Special GL Transactions includes Guarantees (Automatic Offsetting Entry (Statistical)) and Down Payments (Free Offsetting Entry). The Configuration of Special GL Transactions, What is Down Payment, Down Payment Made, Received and Requested and how to Define Tax Clearing Account for Down Payments

Chapter 17 looks at ledgers in SAP S4 HANA and the types of ledgers presented in S4, such as standard ledgers and extended ledger, and defines accounting principles that form part of parallel accounting. It also looks at how to define ledger groups, ledger settings for ledgers and currency types, and how to assign accounting principles to ledger groups.

CHAPTER 1

Customizing Financial Accounting Enterprise Structure in SAP S/4HANA

In this chapter, we will explore how to:

- Define Company Code in Global Settings and assign Company to Company Code.

- Define Fiscal Year Variants and the assignment of Fiscal Year Variants to Company Code.

- Define Open and Close Periods, how to define Open and Close Periods Variants, and the assignment of the defined open and close to Company Code.

Enterprise Structure (ES) is the foundation upon which your entire organization is built in the SAP S4 HANA System. The advantage of ES is that it gives you the platform upon which various models in your Organization units are provided. The Financial (FI) Organizational Elements you create in this chapter will form the basis upon which other configurations in subsequent chapters will be built upon.

Note How your project is structured is determined by how your organization unit is defined. Hence definition of your organizational unit is very important. You should only create the new organization unit that is required by your existing data structures. Since you cannot easily change an organization unit once created, it is therefore important to have an understanding of what your organization may look like in the future.

© Andrew Okungbowa 2023
A. Okungbowa, *SAP S/4HANA Financial Accounting Configuration*,
https://doi.org/10.1007/978-1-4842-8957-0_1

Let's look at the steps involved in this Customizing

When you logon to SAP S4 HANA, the **SAP Easy Access** screen is displayed, as in Figure 1-1.

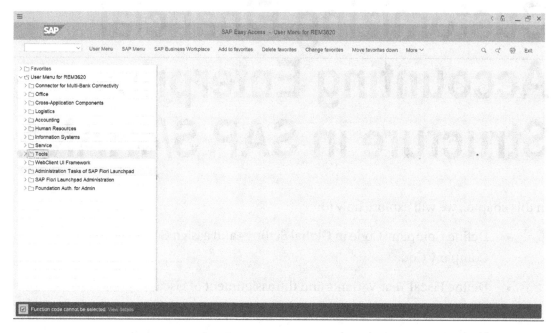

Figure 1-1. *Select Tools to start customizing*

The Easy Access screen contains a list of functions to choose from. It is the initial point of entry into SAP S4 HANA. To call up the Customizing: Execute Project screen where you will start your customization, follow the menu path: **SAP Easy Access ➤ Tools – Customizing ➤ IMG ➤ Execute Project (SPRO) ➤ SAP Reference IMG.**

A quicker way to access the Customizing: Execute Project screen is by using a transaction code (SPRO). Transaction codes are used to navigate tasks in a single step thereby bypassing the standard menu path that involves several time-consuming steps. You use a transaction code to access the task you want to execute by simply typing it into the Command Field at the top left hand corner of the Easy Access screen (Figure 1-1). Transaction codes are standard sets of alphabets and figures recognized by the SAP System that allow you to access specific tasks. The advantage of using transaction codes is that it is faster to access tasks or enter a customizing workspace that you want to execute in SAP quicker.

The SAP Project Reference Object (SPRO) is a standard transaction code to access the Customizing: Execute Project screen without having to use the menu path. SAP comes with a set of tables containing predefined transaction codes. This table can be accessed by typing SE38 into the command field to go to ABAP Editor: Initial Screen where you can see a list of transaction codes you may want to use. The ABAP Editor is beyond the scope of this book. However, you can also access transaction codes on the Easy Access Screen by choosing ***More ➤ Extra ➤ Settings*** on the menu bar at the top right hand of the screen or by simply pressing Shift+F9 on your keyboard. The Setting Screen will come up with what you can choose from. Select Display Technical Names, which is the fourth item on the displayed list of available options, by ensuring that the checkbox is activated and by pressing enter on your keyboard. This action will allow the system to display technical names with transaction codes before every function. We have also provided a list of useful technical codes in Appendix 1 which you can use as a reference.

To display the Customizing: Execute Project screen, type SPRO into the Command Field. The screen where you can start your customizing will be displayed, as in Figure 1-2.

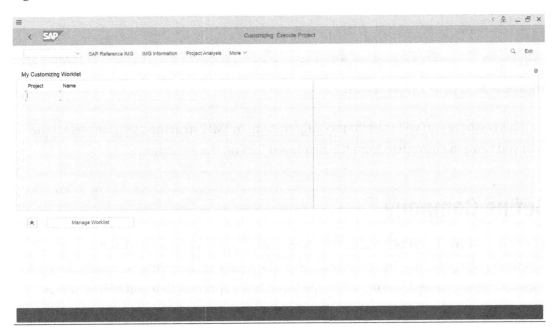

Figure 1-2. *SAP reference implementation guide*

At the top left hand of the screen, you will see the SAP Reference IMG button. IMG stands for Implementation Guide for customizing in SAP S4 HANA. When you click the SAP Reference IMG button, this action will take you to the **Display IMG** screen, as in Figure 1-3.

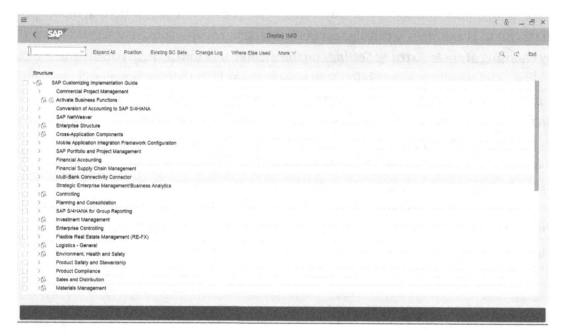

Figure 1-3. *Display IMG screen*

This is where you will start your configuration. In IMG structure, you can select the item you want to customize from the displayed lists on the structure.

Define Company

A company is an organizational unit for accounting purposes from which financial statements are generated in accordance with the legal requirements. Secondly, financial transactions are viewed at company code level. It is important that you define at least one company in the Enterprise Structure as part of the financial accounting component to which one or more company codes are assigned. You will define a company code at this initial stage and then later in this chapter you will also define company codes and assign the company codes you have defined to the company you have defined.

There are two ways to access the screen where you will define your company in SAP S4 HANA. You can either follow this menu path: ***Enterprise Structure ➤ Definition ➤ Financial Accounting ➤ Define Company***. This is a standard transaction code for creating a company in SAP S4 HANA. When you use either the menu path or the Transaction code, this will take you to the ***Change view "Internal trading partners":*** screen, as in Figure 1-4. This screen is where you will define the parameters for your Company.

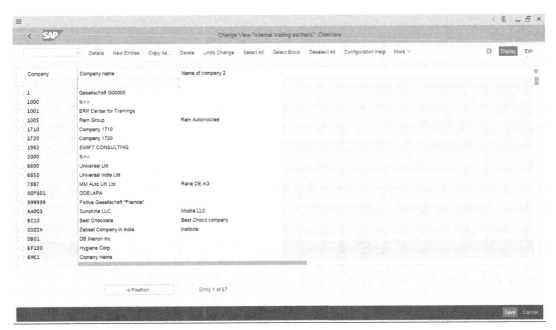

Figure 1-4. *Defining company*

Note   You will notice on the previous screen that a list of company codes are displayed on this screen. This is normal, as other Company codes may already exist in the system. All you need to do is to only create your own company code by hitting the New Entries button above.

Case study: As an SAP functional consultant working in a team of SAP consultant as part of your responsibility you are to customize the company code for your client – Spoxio Inc., a social media app company using C100 as the company code.

Click the New Entries button at the top left of the screen. This function will take you to the next screen ***New Entries: Details of Added Entries*** where you will define your company using up to a maximum of six characters and your company details, as in Figure 1-5.

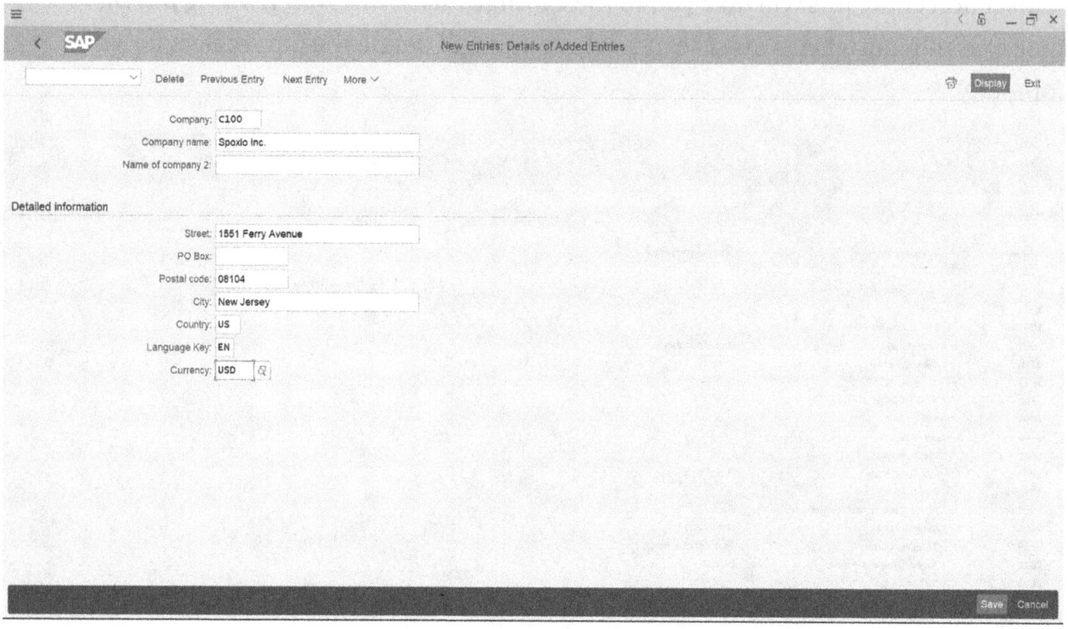

Figure 1-5. *New Entries screen to enter your company's details*

The New Entries: Details of Added Entries screen, Figure 1-5, is divided into two sections. The first section contains fields where you will enter your Company code and Company name. You have the option of entering a second company in the section if you have more than one company name. The second section is the detailed information section which contains fields that will enable you to enter the company's address, language key (your company language, for example, if you are in the USA, your company language key will be EN which stands for English) and your company currency (this is your company local currency in the USA, for example, the local currency key is USD which is United States Dollar). Update the following fields using the information below:

> **Company:** You can enter up to six characters as your company code in this field. You can use the details in Figure 1-6 as a guide. The code you enter here will serve as your company identifier, especially in an environment where other company codes are existing in the system. **Company name:** Enter your company

name in this field. For example, the company name we used in this activity is **Spoxio Inc**. This field allows you to use up to a maximum of 25 characters as your company name.

Detail information: This section will allow you to enter further detailed information about your company as part of your company definition. Details entered here will be used as your correspondence address and currency for generating company code financial statements. Enter your company's address, post code, city, country code, language key, and currency code in the appropriate fields.

Note   The SAP system comes with standard codes/keys for most countries:

- Country code/key: This key is represented in SAP S4 HANA as the country key where your company is operating. For example, the country code for Great Britain is GB, for the United States it is US, Germany it is DE, etc.

- Language code/key: This is your company language code. For example, Great Britain Language code is EN, USA is EN, and Germany is DE. Enter your company language key in this field. If you are not sure of your language key, you can search for it using the search function.

- Currency code/key: For example, for Great Britain the code is GBP, for the United States it is USD, and for Germany it is EUR. This is your company code local currency.

  After you have entered your company code and address, as in Figure 1-5, click the save button at the bottom right of the screen to save your work. Click the Exit button at the top right of the screen to exit the screen.

  The next step in this exercise is to define a company code for your company.

Define a Company Code

To meet a country-specific tax and legal reporting requirements, it is important to define at least one company code (you can define more than one company code depending on your requirements) that will be assigned to the company you defined above. All Company Codes are country specific. In SAP S4 HANA, the company code is an organizational unit used in FI (Financial Accounting) to structure a business process for financial reporting purposes.

In SAP S4 HANA you have the option to either define your company code from scratch or you can copy an existing company code supplied by SAP in the system. SAP recommends that you use the standard company code 0001 supplied by SAP in the system when copying an existing company code which you can modify to your own company code. The advantage of copying a company code supplied by SAP is that you are copying the existing company code-specific parameters you can modify to fit your requirements, and this will save you time in customizing.

To define your company code, follow this menu path: ***IMG ➤ Enterprise Structure ➤ Definition ➤ Financial Accounting ➤ Edit, Copy, Delete, Check Company Code.***

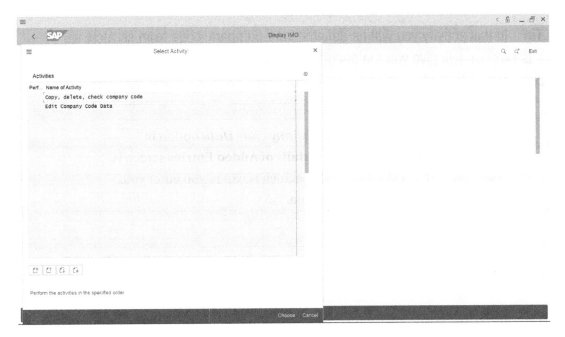

Figure 1-6. *Select Activity screen where you define company code*

The screen in Figure 1-6 gives you two activity options to choose from: (1) either to copy an existing company code supplied by SAP using the ***Copy, delete, check company code*** option or (2) to create your own company code from scratch using the ***Edit Company code Data*** option.

Note   If you choose to copy the company code supplied by SAP in the system instead of creating your own company code from scratch, use the activity option ***Copy, delete, check company code*** in Figure 1-6. This will allow you to copy the standard company code supplied by SAP with its parameters. The recommended sample of the standard company code supplied by SAP is 0001. When you copy a company code, the copied company code will retain most of its properties. If you decided to follow this option, note that not all the properties of a copied company code are retained, so make sure you go through each step involved in your customizing and modify all the inherited properties from the copied company code to your own company code.

Tip   In this activity you will be defining your company code from scratch, as this exercise will give you the opportunity to go through all the steps involved in company code configuration.

When you choose the *Edit Company code Data* option in Figure 1-6, the **New Entries: Details of Added Entries** screen is displayed, as in Figure 1-7. This screen is where you enter your company code and company data.

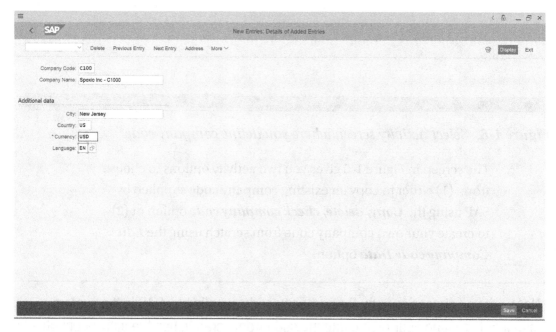

Figure 1-7. *The initial screen where you enter your company code details*

This screen is self-explanatory. Enter your company code details in the appropriate fields. The company code details you entered in this screen will be treated by the system as your company data. When you click the Save button at the bottom right corner of the screen, the Edit Address screen comes up (Figure 1-8).

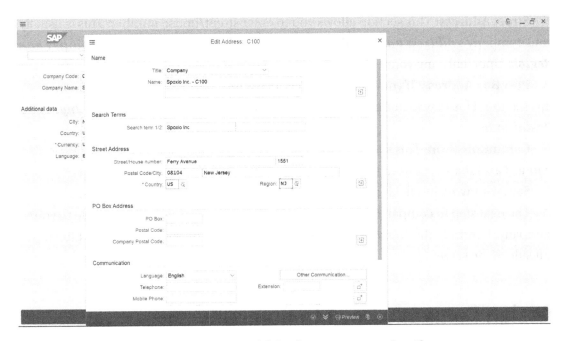

Figure 1-8. *Edit Address screen to add further company details*

This screen is divided into five sections: Name, Search Terms, Street Address, PO Box Address, and Communication. This screen will allow you to add further details to your company code in your customization. Update each section with your company code data.

Note   It is not mandatory that you must complete every field of this screen. Update only the fields that are relevant to you. You can use the screen in Figure 1-8 as a guide on how to complete your company code data.

Name: In this section, you can enter your company **title** and name in the appropriate fields. In our example above we used ***Spoxio Inc. – C100*** as our company name. The name you entered here will represent your company code name in the system.

Search terms: You have the choice of entering up to two search terms in this section, but this is optional. The search term you use here is optional, but we recommend that you use meaningful search terms. You can use up to 20 characters in the search terms field. The search term you use here is discretional, but it is important that you use a meaning search term you can remember. In our example, we used our company name – Spoxio Inc. The advantage of search terms is that they will allow you to search for a company code quicker in an environment where you have several company codes in the system.

11

Street Address: This section allows you to enter street/house number. This is usually your company's *address and number, your company Post Code and City, Country and Region*. Upon entering your Country and Region.

Post Box Address: If your company uses a Post Box address, you can enter it in this section. This may include a company's *Post Box, Postal Code, and Company Postal code.*

Communication: This section allows you to enter the language, Phone, Mobile Phone, Fax, Email, etc., used by your company for correspondence and contacts.

Save your work by clicking the Save button at the bottom right of the screen.

The next step in company code customizing is to assign your company code to your company. Return to the *Display IMG* screen by hitting the Back button twice at the top left side of the screen.

Assign Company Code to Company

Case Study: You have been asked by your team to assign the four-digit company code you created to the company you created.

To complete the customizing task involved in defining your company code, you have to assign the company code you have created to your company for your company code to work efficiently. This process is a simple logical sequence. You define your company code, set the values for your company code, and assign your company code to your company. The following diagram (Figure 1-9) depicts the basic steps involved in defining and assigning company code to a company.

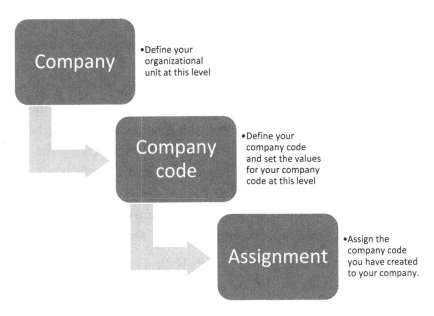

Figure 1-9. *Steps involved in defining and assigning company code to a company*

You assign your company code to your organizational unit from the ***Change View "Assign Company Code ➤ Company" Overview*** screen. To get to this screen use the menu path: ***Enterprise Structure ➤ Assignment ➤ Financial Accounting ➤ Assign Company Code to Company*** or you can use the Transaction code OX16.

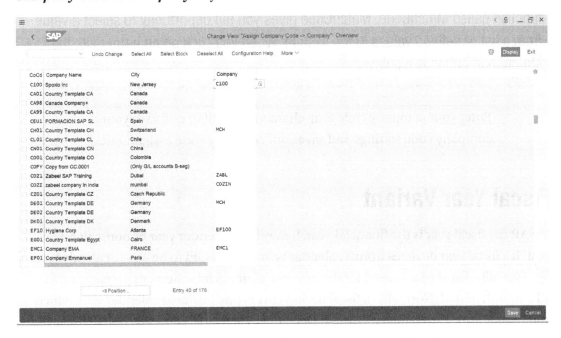

Figure 1-10. *Assignment of company code to organizational unit*

The ***Change View "Assign Company Code ➤ Company" Overview*** screen is displayed containing a list of company codes existing in the system. This is the screen where you will assign your company code to your company. Scroll up or down to look for your company. In an environment where you have a large list of several company codes in the system, it will be a lot easier to use the Position. You can use the Position button to locate your company code by clicking the Position button at the bottom of the ***Change View "Assign Company Code ➤ Company" Overview*** screen. The ***Another Entry*** dialog screen pops up. Enter your company code four identifier characters in the Company code field and hit continue at the bottom of the ***Another Entry*** screen below. Your company code will be automatically displayed on top of the company codes list on the ***Change View "Assign Company Code ➤ Company" Overview*** screen.

> You will notice that your company code is displayed on top of all the company code in the system. Your company code and city are displayed, and the company field is blank. Simply type your four-character company code in the company field.

Tip   In a situation where you cannot remember your company code, use the search function or MatchCode button by the company field to search for your company code, as depicted in Figure 1-9. For some fields, SAP provides a search function called MatchCode. MatchCode gives you the opportunity to select a value from a list of defined values in the system. When you click on an entry field, the MatchCode button is displayed.

> Enter your company code four-character identifier and save your company code settings and save your company code assignment.

Fiscal Year Variant

In SAP, the fiscal year is the financial year. It may be a calendar year or non-calendar year. If a fiscal year deviates from a calendar year then, is said to be a non-calendar year.

Typically, fiscal year is used for the purpose of financial statement preparation for a 12-month period. Normally, a fiscal period covers one business calendar year, which often starts from 1st of January to 31st of December each year. However, not all fiscal years starts from 1st January and end 31st of December. Some fiscal years start from 1st of April and end 31st March and so on. What is more important is that a fiscal year must cover a 12-month period. The normal rule is that business transactions are assigned to the period in which the transaction took place. This is often referred to as the principle of matching concept.

Matching concept is a principle that expenses relative to the income are recorded within the same accounting period, which is usually a 12-month period.

Technically, in SAP S4 HANA, business transactions are assigned to different periods. Fiscal year variant is customized to match your company's fiscal year. Interestingly, fiscal year does not necessarily have to be the same with the normal calendar year (i.e., January to December). What is more important is that SAP S4 HANA is quite dynamic to fit your company's fiscal year.

Fiscal year variant is defined with posting periods. Posting periods are technical terms used to refer to months in SAP S4 HANA. A Fiscal Year is made up of 12 posting periods. Besides the normal 12 posting periods, you can define up to a maximum of 4 special posting periods, which are used for posting yearend adjustments to a closed period. For example, if the normal fiscal period is closed, adjustments can still be posted in one of the four special periods.

Note   In SAP S4 HANA, you cannot exceed a maximum of 16 periods. The system cannot determine posting periods automatically, so you must specify your special posting periods manually in the document header posting field. We will see how this is done later when we look at posting periods.

In SAP S4 HANA, Posting Periods are identified by posting dates. Fiscal year Variant can be defined either as:

- Year independent or
- Year specific (dependent).

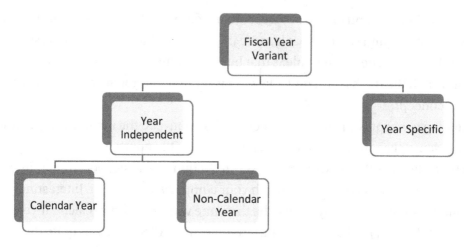

Figure 1-11. *Types of fiscal year variants*

Year independent: This is when the accounting periods of a company remains the same each year (i.e., the financial reporting year is the same each year). For example, an organization's fiscal year is January to December each year. We have two types of year independent fiscal year variants in SAP:

> *Calendar year:* Posting period is the same as the calendar year, usually 12 months. Posting period runs 12 months each year (for example, the USA financial year starts in January and ends in December).

> *None Calendar year:* Are those periods that starts and ends any month of the year, except January and December. Some countries' fiscal year starts any other month and not January. In the UK, for example, the fiscal year starts in April and ends in March. Since the non-calendar year did not start in January 1st, then use indicator −1 or +1 for the period of the year that belongs to the formal or latter fiscal year.

Note   February is counted as 29 days irrespective of actual number of days in February in order for the system to take leap year into consideration.

The SAP system comes with standard fiscal year variants. We recommend that you use the standard fiscal year variant supplied by the System. Example of Fiscal Year variant that comes with SAP S4 HANA system: Fiscal Year Variant for USA (January to December) is K4 and Fiscal Year Variant for UK (April to March) is V3.

Tip   Copy and modify the standard fiscal year variant supplied by SAP in the system.

If you decided to define your own fiscal year variant, use a two-digit alphanumeric identifier of your choice as your variant and maintain your fiscal year variant as appropriate.

Year-Specific or Year dependent

This is the case where the fiscal year/posting periods varies from year to year. This is uncommon in practice.

An example of a situation when this will arise is when posting periods are either greater than 12 months (extended fiscal year) or posting periods are less than 12 months (shortened fiscal year). The reason for shortened fiscal year could be as a result of a company winding-up or any other special reasons.

Maintain Fiscal Year Variant

Case Study

As SAP functional consultant for Spoxio Inc., your responsibility is to define your company fiscal year variant from January–December for your company code. You were told by a colleague to copy the fiscal year variant K4 supplied by SAP in the system and modify the copied fiscal year variant to meet your requirement, instead of going through the rigorous process of defining another fiscal year variant.

To maintain the fiscal Year Variant is simply to customize the fiscal year variant for your company code. To get to the screen where you will maintain your fiscal year variant, as in Figure 1-12, use the menu path: ***IMG ➤ Financial Accounting ➤ Financial Accounting Global Settings ➤ Ledgers ➤ Fiscal Year and Posting Periods ➤ Maintain Fiscal Year Variant (Maintain Shortened Fiscal. Year)***. The transaction code is ***OB29***.

> ***Change View "Fiscal year variants" Overview*** screen is displayed. This screen is split into two sections. The Dialog structure section and Fiscal year variants section in Figure 1-12, where you can customize your fiscal year. Since you want to copy fiscal year variant K4 supplied by SAP in the system. Use the Position button at the button of ***Change View "Fiscal year variants" Overview*** screen with a list of fiscal year already in the system. You can either search for the Fiscal year variant K4 you want to use by clicking the Position bottom at the bottom of the screen or by using the scroll bar. The advantage of using the Position button is that it saves you time scrolling to look for the variant you want to use.

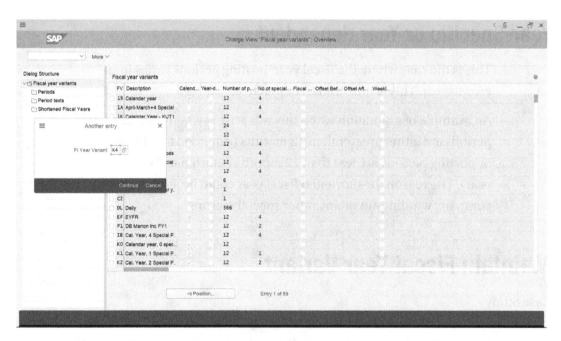

Figure 1-12. *The screen where you configure fiscal year variant*

In this exercise, we will be using the Position button. When you choose the position button a dialog box *Another entry* pops up, as in Figure 1-12. This dialog box will enable you to carry out a quick search for the fiscal year variant – K4 supplied by the system that you want to adapt to your fiscal year variant.

Tip   If you chose to define your own Fiscal Year Variant, choose the **New Entries** button at the top left corner of the screen and update the following fields:

FV: Enter two-digit characters as your fiscal year variant identifier key. It is recommended that you use alphanumeric as your fiscal year identifier. In the example above, the standard fiscal year variant supplied by SAP in the system – **K4** (calendar Year) was copied and modified to meet the desired requirement.

Description: This field allows you to describe or name your fiscal year variant. This could be the name of your company.

Year–Dependent: If the fiscal year/posting periods vary each year, activate the Year-Dependent checkbox by making sure that it is ticked. This is not very common in practice.

Calendar Yr: If the fiscal year is the same as the normal calendar year each year, activate Calendar year checkbox.

Number of posting periods: Here you specify the number of posting periods. This will normally be a 12-month period as your company's accounting period.

No. of special posting periods: SAP S4 HANA system allows up to 4 special periods for making postings outside the normal accounting periods.

Enter K4 in *FI. Year Variant* field to call up K4 from the list of variants in the system. Select K4 from the variant list and click Continue at the bottom of the dialog screen. The *Change View "fiscal Year Variants": Overview* screen is displayed. This screen will allow you to copy an existing Fiscal year supplied by SAP in the system. To copy a fiscal year variant, select K4 from the list of fiscal year variants and choose Copy As at the top left corner of the screen. If you are creating your own fiscal year variant, choose the New Entries button at the top right corner of the screen.

Since we are copying fiscal year variant K4 supplied by SAP in the system, select fiscal year K4 to select or highlight it. Choose Copy As at the top of the screen to copy Fiscal Year Variant – K4.

Note   When you copy fiscal year variant, you are also copying all its dependent properties or settings defined by SAP in the system.

Tip   This function will allow you to copy the standard fiscal year variant **C4** – January to December supplied by the system. When you copy a fiscal year variant, you must change the fiscal year variant key to your own key. Otherwise, you will not be able to save the fiscal year variant you have copied, as the system does not allow duplicate fiscal year keys. Once you have copied K4, change the fiscal year variant from K4 to any variant of your choice. For example, in this activity we used **C4** as the Fiscal year variant identifier key and enter **Fiscal year variant – C100** as the Fiscal year variant description.

Note   if possible, avoid using letters K or V as part of your fiscal year variant key because some of the standard fiscal year variant keys supplied by the system starts with either K or V. The system does not allow a duplicate fiscal year variant key.

When you update the screen by changing content of *FV* field to C4 and the Description field to **Fiscal Year Variant – C100,** your screen should look like the screen in Figure 1-13.

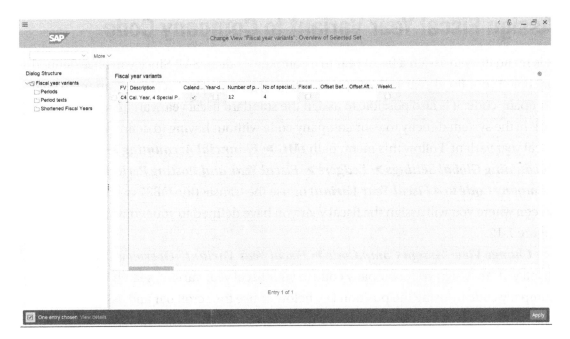

Figure 1-13. *Modification of the fiscal year variant*

Click Apply button at the bottom right corner of the screen
or press enter on your keyboard. ***Specify object to be copied
dialog*** screen pops up. This screen will allow you to copy just
the dependent entries or all the dependent entries of the fiscal
year variant you have selected to copy. Since you want to copy all
the dependent entries of Fiscal Year Variant K4, choose Copy All
command button.

Information dialog pops up telling you the number of dependent
entries you have copied from fiscal year variant K4. Choose
Continue at the bottom right corner of the information pop-up
screen or Press enter on your keyboard to confirm your entries.

Change View "Fiscal year variants" Overview screen is displayed
containing the fiscal year variant C4 that you have defined. Save
your variant. The system will notify you on the status bar below
that Number of copied entries (including transactions):1.

Assign Fiscal Year Variant to Company Code

It is mandatory to assign a fiscal year to a company code in SAP. Since you have defined or copied your fiscal year variant, the next step is to assign the fiscal year variant to your company code. It is also possible to assign the standard fiscal year variant supplied by SAP in the system directly to your company code without having to define your own fiscal year variant. Follow this menu path *IMG ➤ Financial Accounting ➤ Financial Accounting Global Settings ➤ Ledgers ➤ Fiscal Year and Posting Periods ➤ Assign Company Code to a Fiscal Year Variant* or use the transaction OB37 to get to the screen where you will assign the fiscal year you have defined to your company code in Figure 1-13.

Change View "Assign Comp.Code ➤ Fiscal Year Variant":Overview screen is displayed. To assign your company code to your fiscal year variant, search for your company code by using the position key below or use the scroll bar and assign your fiscal year variant – C4 to your company code (C100).

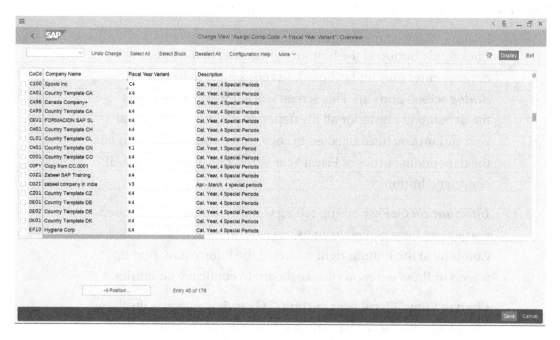

Figure 1-14. *Assigning Company Code to fiscal year variant*

To save your work, choose Save at the bottom right corner of the screen.

Note   The system may issue a warning message below that *"No postings are possible without fiscal year"* and the save button is suppressed. This normally happens when some Company Codes are not assigned with fiscal year variants. If this happens, hit the enter button or press the enter key on your keyboard several times until the Save button is activated. Then save your work. The system will notify on the status bar below that your Data was saved.

Defining Posting Periods

As mentioned above, accounting transactions are usually assigned to periods. Posting periods are defined in the fiscal year variant. The benefit of defining the variant for open periods is to avoid the problem of posting accounting transactions to the wrong accounting period. This is achieved by opening current periods and closing all other periods. At the end of the current period, the period is closed and the next period is opened. It is compulsory that at least two posting period intervals must be opened at any given time. On the other hand, you can open several posting periods at the same time.

Posting periods are independent of Fiscal Year, that is, they are not dependent on or controlled by Fiscal Year. Posting periods are defined at the global level in SAP S4 HANA. This makes it accessible to several company codes in the system.

In SAP S4 HANA, opening and closing periods are differentiated by account types. This will allow you to determine which accounts are posted to at a specific posting period. For example, posting can be permitted for accounts payable and not to accounts receivable. You can specify several account types simultaneously as part of your customizing in open periods: below we have listed the basic account types in SAP S4 HANA.

Account types in open period

+   Valid for all Account types

A   Assets

D   Debtors

K   Creditors

> M   Materials
>
> S   General Ledger (G/L) Accounts
>
> V   Contract Accounts

IN SAP S4 HANA, it is mandatory that you specify the minimum account type "+." This account types is valid for all account types for each open period in SAP S4 HANA. The benefit of applying account types to an open period is to enable the system to determine whether the posting period can be posted to using the posting date in the document header.

When customizing open periods, it is important that you define the following items:

- Define variants for open posting periods.

- Assign variants to company code.

- Specify open and close periods.

Let's look at the steps involved in customizing each in turn.

Define Variants for Open Posting Periods

Case study: Your task is to define the Variants for Posting Periods for your company code and assign the Variant you have define to your company code.

To define Variants for Open Posting Periods, follow the menu path: ***IMG: Financial Accounting ➤ Financial Accounting Global Settings ➤ Ledgers ➤ Fiscal Year and posting Periods ➤ Posting Periods ➤ Define Variants for Open Posting Periods***

The **Change View "Posting Periods: Define Variants". Overview** screen where you will define your variants for opening posting period appears. Click the **New Entries** at the top left corner of the screen.

The New Entries: Overview of Added Entries screen is displayed (Figure 1-15). This screen is where you define your variant key and variant name. In practice the variant key is usually defined using your company code and your company name as the variant name.

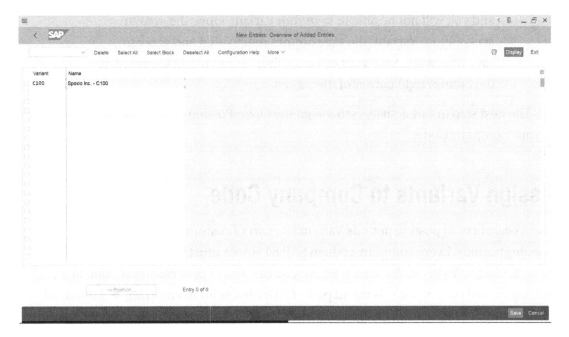

Figure 1-15. *Defining variant key and name*

Update the following fields:

> **Variant:** Enter four characters as the posting variant key in the variant field. Preferably your company code. The code you enter here will be used when assigning a posting variant later to your company code.

> **Name:** Enter the description or a variant name that best describes your variant in this filed. In our example, we used ***Open Period Variant – C100*** as our variant name.

> Hit the enter button to confirm the variant you entered into the system. If the variant already exists in the system, when you hit the enter button, the system will notify you on the status bar below that "An entry already exists with the same key"; SAP S4 HANA does not allow duplicate variant keys. All you have to do when faced with this problem is to use another variant key that the system will accept. Otherwise, the save icon will be suppressed

and you will not be able to save your variant. Once the system accepts your variant, the save bottom is activated and you can save your work. Save your open posting variant by clicking save at the bottom right corner of the screen.

The next step in this activity is to assign the Open Posting Period Variant you created to your Company Code.

Assign Variants to Company Code

The Assignment of posting periods Variant is a part of customizing variants for opening periods. Every company code in SAP S4 HANA must be assigned with posting periods variant. To get to the screen where you can assign your company code to a posting period variant use this menu path: *IMG: Financial Accounting ➤ Financial Accounting Global Settings ➤ Ledgers ➤ Fiscal Year and posting Periods ➤ Posting Periods ➤ Assign Variants to Company Code.*

Change View "Assign Comp.Code ➤ Posting Period Variants": Overview screen is displayed. This is the screen where the assignment of your variant to your company code is carried out. Using the Position button at the bottom of the screen, search for your company code and update the Variant fields by entering the variant for Open Posting Periods that you defined in Figure 1-16.

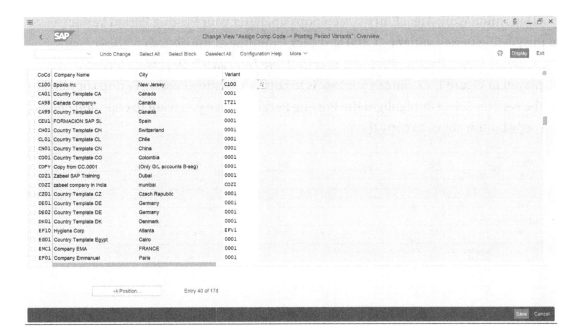

Figure 1-16. *Assign company code to posting period variant*

Enter your four-digit variant key – C100 identifier in the variant field, as in Figure 1-16, and save your work.

Open and Close Periods

Case Study

You can define your posting periods from scratch, or you can copy an existing posting period and modify them to meet your requirement. To simplify your configuration, your colleagues have asked you to copy the standard posting period from company code – 1000 supplied by SAP in the system and modify them to meet the requirements of your client.

As mentioned above, posting periods are opened in fiscal year variants. You can open and close several posting periods simultaneously in SAP S4 Hana. The advantage of opening and closing periods is that it helps prevent the mistake of posting transactions to the wrong period in the sense that only the valid period is open and the other periods not relevant for posting are closed. To go to the screen where you can Open and Close posting periods, follow this menu path: ***IMG: Financial Accounting ➤ Financial Accounting Global Settings ➤ Ledgers ➤ Fiscal Year and posting Periods ➤ Posting Periods ➤ Open and Close Posting Periods.***

Determine Work Area: Entry screen pops up. Enter your Posting Period Variant Key in the Posting period variant – C100 and click Continue at the bottom of the screen.

Change View "Posting Periods: Specify Time Intervals": Overview screen is displayed in Figure 1-17. Since your task is to copy an existing Posting Period supplied by the system. Select or highlight the Posting Periods range you want to copy and choose the copy button above to copy them.

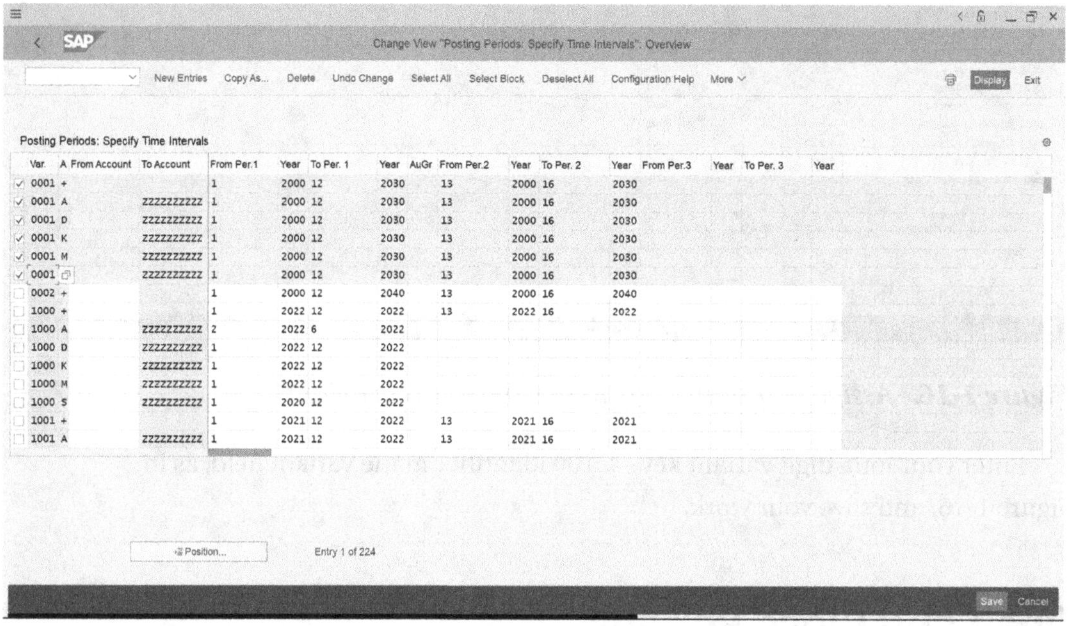

Figure 1-17. *Copy Posting Period intervals*

Select all the accounts (+ A D K M S) belonging to Company code 0001 that you want to copy from the list of displayed variants.

1. Choose Copy As… at the top of the screen from the menu bar above to copy the Posting Periods you have selected. The system will now copy the variants you copied from Company Code 0001 in Change View "Posting Periods: Specify Time Intervals": Overview screen. Modify the screen contents, as in Figure 1-18, by replacing the existing Variant 0001 with your own variant – C100.

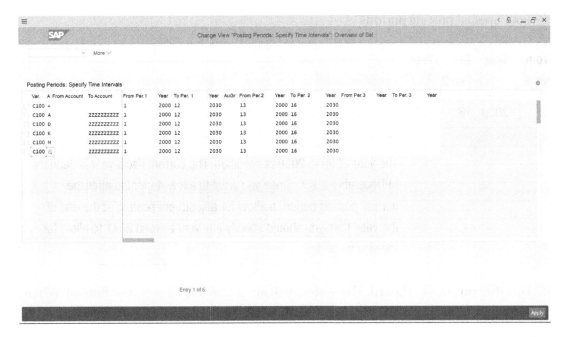

Figure 1-18. *Update Posting Period Intervals*

Tip   SAP has 12 normal posting periods and up to 4 special periods.

From Per. 1	Year	To Per. 1	Year	
1	2000	12	2030	Periods 1 to 12 represent an accounting period of 12 months.
				The year 2000 to 2030 is specified. Note that the year range you specify here must include your current fiscal year. Otherwise, the system will assume that the posting period is closed, and you will not be able to post any transactions in the system.

Four Special posting periods

From Per. 2	Year	To Per. 2	Year	
13	2000	16	2030	Period 13 to 16 represents the special periods of 4 months, for posting year-end adjustments to a closed fiscal year.
				The year 2000 to 2030 is specified. The current fiscal year is January to December 20XX. Since you want to allow 4 months after the normal posting period to allow for adjustment posting at the end of the year, then you should specify any year beyond 20XX to allow for the special period.

Hit enter on your keyboard. The system will automatically accept your entries. When you click save at the bottom right corner of the screen, the system will notify you that your variant is saved at the task bar below.

Note   If your entries are rejected, it is obvious that you are using variant keys already existing in the system. Make sure your variant keys are unique to your company code.

Summary

In this chapter, we looked at the basic financial accounting customization in enterprise structure, which is fundamental to the remaining customizing presented in subsequent chapters in this book. In this chapter, you learned how to define company and assign company to company code, define fiscal year variant, and assign the variant to define to your company. Finally, you also learned how to maintain open and close periods. In the next chapter, we will be looking at how to customize master date, chart of accounts, and retained earnings.

CHAPTER 2

Defining Chart of Accounts

In this chapter, you will learn how to define Chart of Accounts, Create General ledgers, and assign chart of accounts to company codes.

At the end of this activity you will be able to:

- Define Chart of Accounts.

- Create General Ledgers.

- Define the Chart of Accounts (using four characters ID).

- Define the properties of the Chart of Accounts.

- Assign Chart of Accounts to Company Code.

Master Data

Master Record contains vital data or information held in a business system database that remains relatively unchanged over a long period of time. This is the case in an environment where sets of data are commonly accessed, used, and shared by different individuals for different purposes across an organization in order to fulfill business processes in real time.

Information that aids efficient business processes, which tends not to change frequently relating to an object, are held in the system database. The idea behind this process is to avoid having to re-enter the same information twice by users, thereby saving input time, and avoiding unnecessary waste of system resources and redundancies by having to enter information in the system more than once.

© Andrew Okungbowa 2023
A. Okungbowa, *SAP S/4HANA Financial Accounting Configuration*,
https://doi.org/10.1007/978-1-4842-8957-0_2

Typical Examples of Master Data in a database in SAP S4 HANA are Customer Data, Vendor Data, Bank Data, GL Account, Material, etc.

Transaction Data: These are information triggered as a result of events arising from day to day business transactions. A typical transaction data is time driven with numerical value and often refers to one or more objects in the system.

Examples of transaction data in SAP S4 HANA are Invoice, Payment, Credit memo, Goods Receipt.

Table data: Contains information about objects, like Payment Terms, Tolerances, and Pricing Conditions.

Defining Chart of Accounts

Chart of Accounts consists of G/L accounts that a company or several company codes uses. In configuration at Account group, we define the length of account numbers. A workshop has to be conducted by the implementation team to complete this activity. Before defining chart of accounts, the implementation team must understand the following points:

> Determine the accounts classification.

> End users' requirements to ascertain which G/L accounts are needed.

> Identify the accounts which are no longer required.

> The G/L accounts that are used for automatic postings.

> The G/L accounts which are non-operating accounts under P&L group.

> The legal framework to define financial statement version.

> The fort of report.

> B/S and P&L formats.

> Internal reporting requirements.

In SAP S4 HANA, a chart of accounts is a fundamental tool that contains a listing of accounts in the general ledger used by a company or several company codes for posting transactions. Transactions are categorized by transaction type in the chart of accounts.

The Chart of Accounts contains basic information about the structure of general ledger accounts in SAP S4 HANA, such as account number, account name, and other control information relating to how the GL account is created and functions within SAP S4 HANA.

The benefits of chart of accounts:

- Define the basic structure for creating general ledger accounts.

- Gives one or more company codes the option to use the same chart of accounts.

In addition to the minimum operational chart of accounts, you can assign two more charts (country specific and/or group) to your operational chart of accounts. Country specific chart of accounts will allow you to generate reports to meet country specific reporting requirements, while group chart of accounts helps with consolidation reporting.

Three steps are involved in the customizing of Chart of Accounts in SAP S4 HANA (Figure 2-1.)

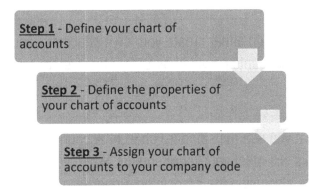

Figure 2-1. *Steps involved in Chart of Accounts customization*

It is mandatory that each company code in SAP S4 HANA be assigned an operational chart of accounts. One operational chart of accounts can be assigned to several company codes with the same general ledger structure.

Three charts of accounts are presented in SAP S4 HANA, namely:

- Operational Chart of Accounts.

- Group Chart of Accounts.

- Country Specific Chart of Accounts.

The functions of each of the chart of accounts are explained below:

Operational Chart of Accounts: this is often referred to as common chart of accounts. It is used to post, record, and report financial accounting and cost transactions on a daily basis. Each company code in SAP S4 HANA must be assigned an operational chart of accounts.

Group Chart of Accounts: this is applicable in an environment where each company code in the same company generates its own financial reports, and the company also prepares its own consolidated financial reports by bringing together the financial reporting of each company code in a single financial report. Consolidation financial reporting is possible in SAP S4 HANA via group chart of accounts.

Let's look at how to define chart of accounts in SAP S4 HANA.

Creating Chart of Accounts

Case study: Your task as SAP FI consultant is to create the Chart of Accounts and assign the chart of accounts you have created to your company code.

Note   You have a choice to either create your own chart of accounts or our use the standard chart of accounts provided by SAP in the system.

Tip   We advise that you use the standard chart of accounts INT supplied by SAP in the system as this will meet your requirements. When you use a standard chart of accounts, you are also using the associated properties with it.

The chart of accounts you create will contain a list of General Ledgers (G/L) that will be used by your company code for posting transactions and financial reporting. Chart of Accounts is created at the global level. This means that the chart of accounts you created will be available to all company codes in the client. The following menu path will take you to the screen where you can customize your chart of accounts: *IMG: Financial Accounting* ➤ *General Ledger Accounting* ➤ *Master Data* ➤ *G/L Accounts* ➤ *Preparations* ➤ *Edit Chart of Accounts List.*

The Change View **"List of All Chart of Accounts": Overview** screen will be displayed (Figure 2-2).

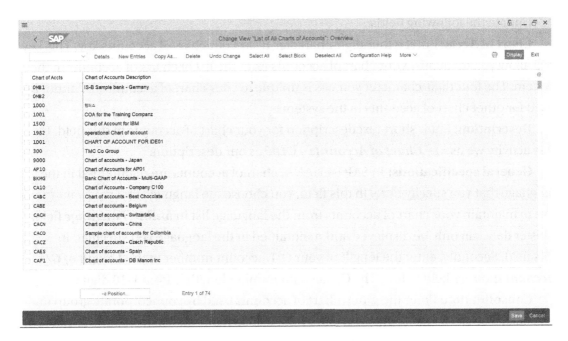

Figure 2-2. *The initial screen where you start creating chart of accounts.*

Click the New Entries at the top left of the screen, to go to the **New Entries: Details of Added Entries**.

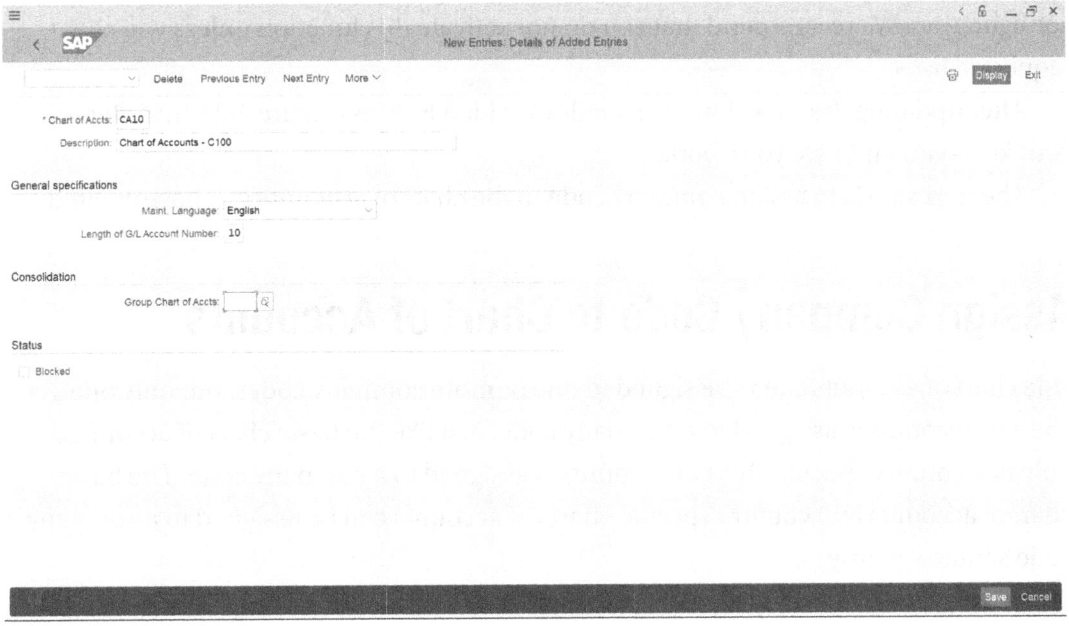

Figure 2-3. *The screen you define your chart of accounts*

Update the following fields:

Chart of Accts: Enter a four digit-character ID as your chart of accounts key. This key will allow you to identify your chart of accounts from the list of charts of accounts in the system. The four digit-character you use is unique to your chart of accounts. It cannot be used for other chart of accounts in the system.

Description: Enter short text description for your chart of accounts in this field. In this activity we used – *Chart of Accounts – C100* as our description.

General specifications: In SAP S4 HANA, chart of accounts are maintained in the language that you specify here. In this field, you choose the language that you want to use to maintain your chart of accounts from the language list in *Maint. Language* field. Master data can only be displayed and maintained in the language you specified in this field. Secondly, enter the length of your G/L account number in the *Length of G/L account number* field below. The GL account number length is from 1-10 digits.

Consolidation: Enter the group chart of accounts used by your corporate group in this field. The chart of accounts you enter here will be required when creating corporate General Ledger accounts that are used for consolidation financial statements for corporate groups.

Status: This field allows you to activate the block checkbox. This function will allow the system to block posting to the general ledger, unless deactivated. For example, you can activate block status during customizing until you have completed you configuration. We recommend that you do not activate this function unless you client requested it.

After updating the New Entries: Details of Added Entries (Figure 2-3), hit enter on your keyboard and save your work.

The next step is to assign company code to the chart of accounts you have created.

Assign Company Code to Chart of Accounts

One chart of accounts can be assigned to one or more company codes, but only one chart of accounts is assigned to a company code. Just like the basic chart of accounts, only one country specific chart of accounts is assigned to a company code. The basic chart of accounts and country specific charts of accounts can be assigned to a company code simultaneously.

Country Specific Chart of Accounts: This is optional. However, it may be mandatory in a situation where a company code in a corporate group is required to produce a financial report to meeting a country's reporting requirements.

To assign your chart of accounts to your company code follow this menu path: ***IMG: Financial Accounting ➤ General Ledger Accounting ➤ Master Data ➤ G/L Accounts ➤ Preparations ➤ Assign Company Code to Chart of Accounts***.

Change View "Assign Company Code ➤ Chart of Accounts Overview" screen is displayed. Using the position button below search for your company code. Your company code will be displayed on top of the list of company codes displayed, as in Figure 2-4.

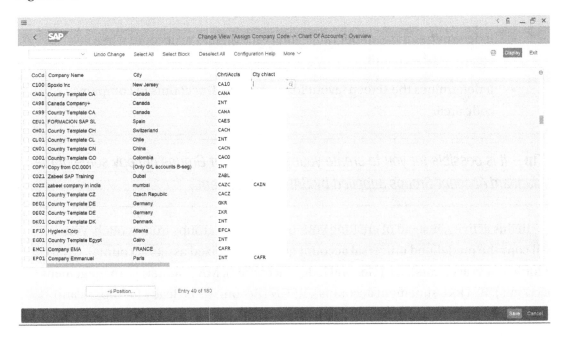

Figure 2-4. *The screen where chart of accounts are assigned to company codes*

Using the Match code search for your chart of accounts and enter your chart of accounts in the Chrt/Accts field. If your client is required to complete country specific financial reporting, then update the Cty ch/act field with your country specific chart of accounts.

After assigning your chart of accounts to your company code, press enter on your keyboard and save your work.

Define Account Group

The next step in our customizing is to define account groups. A chart of Accounts holds a large number of account types and they determine how G/L Accounts are created in SAP S4 HANA. For proper accounting management, account types are systematically classified into appropriate account groups by grouping similar accounts together within the same General Ledger. For example, all G/L accounts relating to revenue are grouped together and assigned to the same number range interval. GL Accounts belonging to the following account groups such as Liabilities Expenditure, Assets, etc., are grouped together in the appropriate group and number range.

Two main reasons why Account Groups are important to Account:

- It determines the number range interval assigned to account when creating G/L account.

- It determines the screen layout for creating G/L accounts in company code area.

Tip   *It is possible for you to create your own Account Groups or copy some of the standard Account Groups supplied by SAP in the system.*

In this activity, instead of creating your own account groups from scratch, you will copy the predefined universal account groups: AS (Fixed assets accounts), CASH (Liquid funds accounts), GL (General ledger accounts), MAT (Materials management accounts), PL (P&L statement accounts), RECN (Recon. Accts Ready for input), and SECC (Secondary costs/revenues) from Chart of Accounts – INT, supplied by SAP in the system and modify them to meet your requirements. Chart of accounts are not company specific; they can be used across company codes.

Note   You can create your own account groups using up to 10 digits. However, we advise you to copy the predefined account groups supplied by SAP in the system and modify to meet your requirements.

Case study: You are required to define Account Groups for your company code by copying INT account groups supplied by SAP in the system and modifying them to meet your requirements.

Tip *It is a lot easier to copy predefined chart of accounts supplied by SAP in the system and modify them to meet your requirements instead of creating fresh charts of accounts from scratch.*

Whether you are copying or creating your own account groups follow this menu path: *IMG – Financial Accounting* ➤ *General Ledger Accounting* ➤ *Master Data* ➤ *G/L Accounts* ➤ *Preparations* ➤ *Define Account Group*

Change View "G/L Account Groups": Overview screen is displayed. Since your goal is to copy chart of accounts INT, use the position key at the bottom of the screen to search for **INT** (International Chart of Account) from the supplied chart of account list. The *Another entry* dialog box pops up (Figure 2-5).

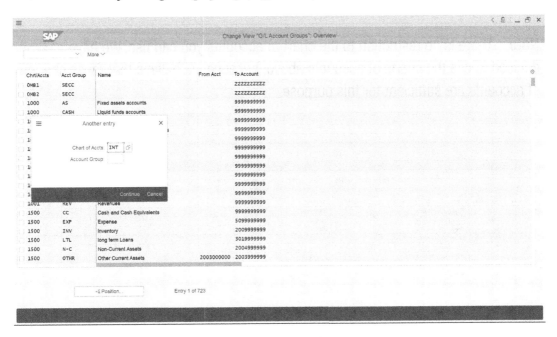

Figure 2-5. *Another entry dialog box*

Enter INT in the Chart of Accts field in the dialog box, choose Continue at the bottom right of the dialog box or press enter on your keyboard. The system will automatically display all the chart of accounts in INT. To copy the predefined account groups, select the following INT chart of accounts with the associated account groups and copy the following chart of accounts:

Table 2-1. *A List of Values You Can Use for Your Account Groups*

Chrt/Accts	Acct Group	Name	From Acct	To Acct
INT	AS	Fixed assets accounts		999999999
INT	CASH	Liquid funds accounts		999999999
INT	GL	General ledger G/L accounts		999999999
INT	MAT	Material management accounts		999999999
INT	PL	P&L accounts		999999999
INT	RECN	Recon. Account ready for input		999999999
INT	SECC	Secondary Costs/Revenues		ZZZZZZZZZZ

Note   There is no restriction to the chart of accounts you can use. We have decided to use the charts of accounts above, because we believe that these charts of accounts are sufficient for this purpose.

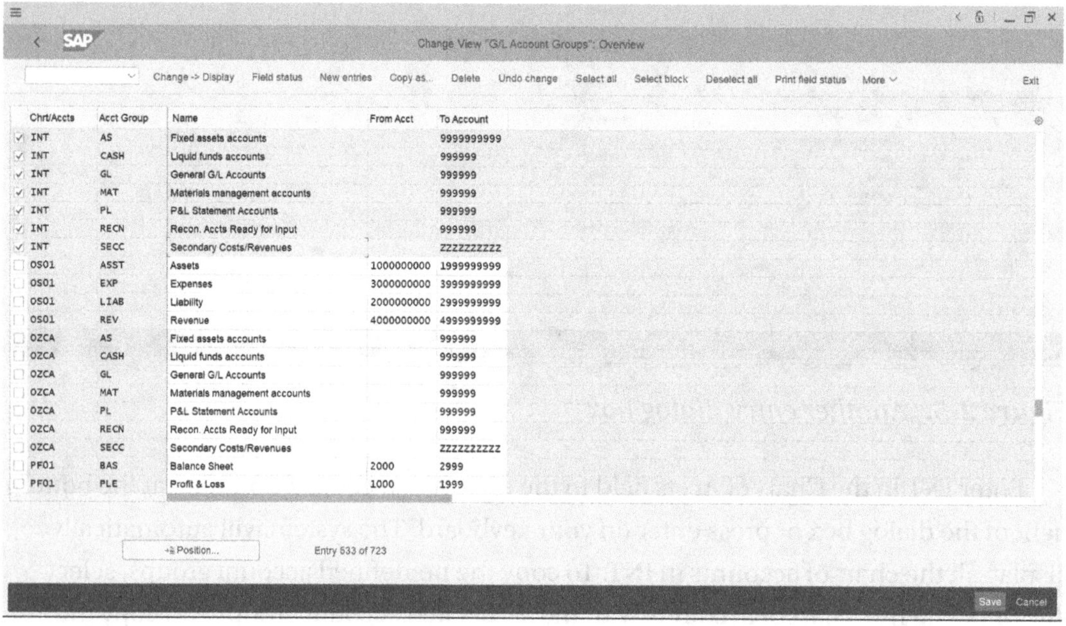

Figure 2-6. *List of Chart of Accounts*

To copy INT account groups, make sure you select the account groups from the list, by making sure that the checkboxes in front of the INT Chrt/Accts you want to copy are ticked, as in Figure 2-6. Click **Copy as...** This is the fourth item from the left from the list of items on the menu bar at the top of the screen. The Change View "G/L Account Groups": Overview of Selected Set screen is displayed (Figure 2-7).

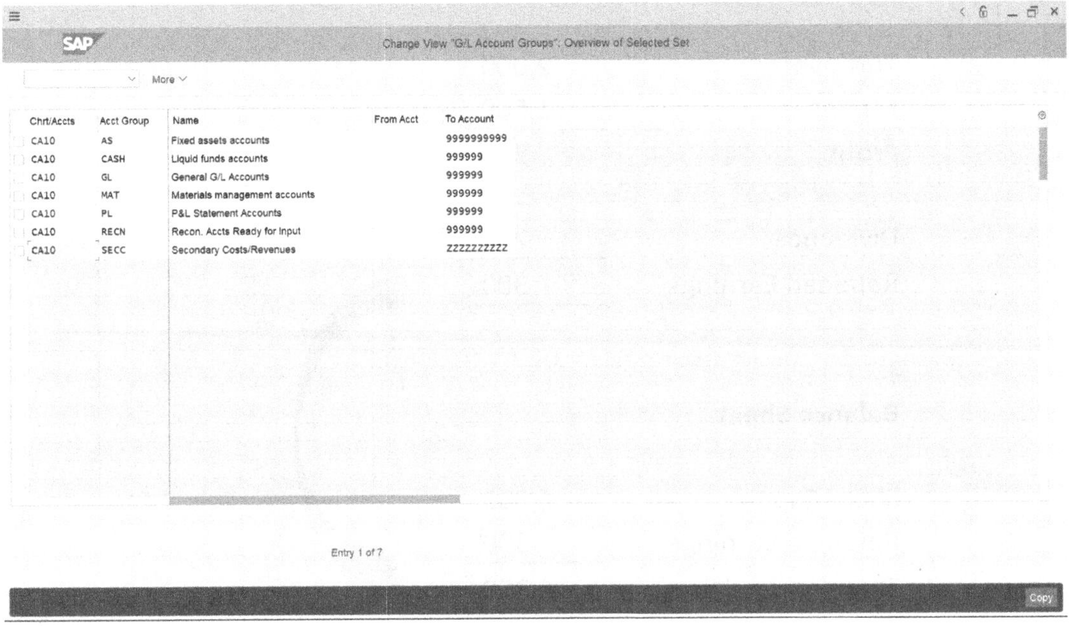

Figure 2-7. *Updated chart of accounts list*

The system will ask you to Specify target entries on the status bar at the bottom left of the screen. Change the Chart of Accounts INT to your chart of accounts (CA10) and Click the Copy button at the bottom right of the screen. The system will notify on the Status bar at the bottom of the screen that the **Number of copied entries (including transactions):7**. Save your account groups.

The final step in this activity is to define the Retained earnings account. This account will allow the system to transfer the net profit or loss in the P&L account to the balance sheet at the end of the year. Although P&L account Group is defined in the chart of accounts, it is also important to define retained earnings account separately as this will allow the system to carry forward profit and loss in the P&L account at the end of the year to the balance sheet as retained earnings.

Define Retained Earnings Account

In accounting, a portion of the profit made at the end of a fiscal year is held back as Retained Earnings (Net Profit) after distributing dividends to the shareholders in proportion to their investment in a corporation. Normally, the Net Profit or net loss figure at the end of a fiscal year is carried forward to Retained Earnings in the Balance Sheet.

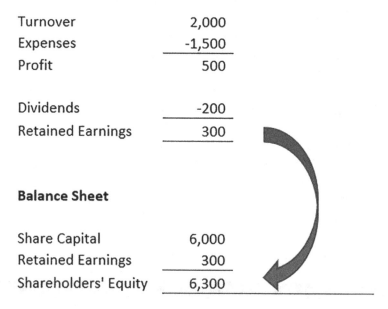

Turnover	2,000
Expenses	-1,500
Profit	500
Dividends	-200
Retained Earnings	300

Balance Sheet

Share Capital	6,000
Retained Earnings	300
Shareholders' Equity	6,300

Figure 2-8. *Illustration of Retained Earnings in Income statement and balance sheet*

The amount carried forward is either added to the shareholders' equity if profit is realized or deducted from the shareholders' equity if loss is incurred. This indicates the profit position of a corporation.

In customizing, retained earnings are assigned to Profit and Loss (P&L) Statement account type defined in the Chart of Accounts area of the P&L account. What happens is that at the end of the year, the system will automatically carry forward the balance of the P&L account to the Retained Earnings account.

To go to the screen where you will define Retained Earnings follow this menu path: *IMG: Financial Accounting ➤ General Ledger Accounting ➤ Master Data ➤ G/L Accounts ➤ Preparations ➤ Define Retained Earnings Account.* The Enter Chart of Accounts dialog box pops up. This dialog box will allow you to assign your chart of accounts to the retained earnings you defined.

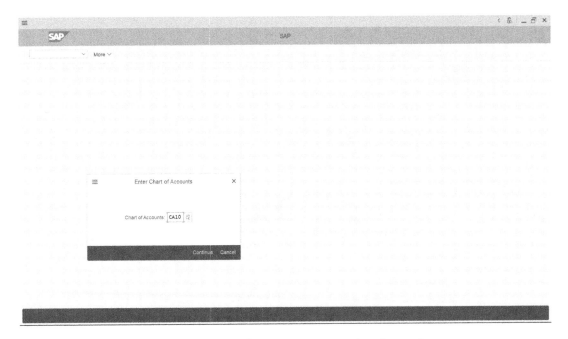

Figure 2-9. *Assigning your chart of accounts to retained earnings*

Enter your chart of accounts in the chart of accounts field (CA10) and click Continue at the bottom of right of the dialog box (Figure 2-9).

The Maintain FI Configuration: Automatic Posting – Accounts screen appears in Figure 2-10.

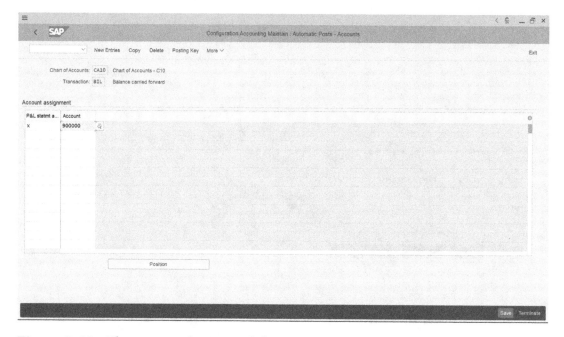

Figure 2-10. *The screen where you define your retained earnings account.*

Enter X as your account type in the P&L ststmt (Statement) column and your G/L account in the Account column. In this activity, we used X as our account type and 900000 as our G/L account. Click save at the bottom right of the screen. Since you have not created a G/L account for retained earnings, the system will issue a warning message on the message status bar at the bottom of the screen that Account 900000 was not created in the charts of accounts XXXX (CA10). Later in Chapter 5 you will learn how to create G/L accounts. Hit the enter button on your keyboard twice and the system will automatically save the retained earning you have defined. The system will notify you that your Changes have been made in the status bar at the bottom of the screen.

Note   X is the symbol used in SAP to represent an account type for retained earnings in the P&L statement. If you have more than one retained earnings, you will not be able to use account type X again since it has been used. You have to assign account type Y and the next one Z to another account types, respectively.

Summary

In this chapter, we looked at what a chart of accounts is and how to define chart of accounts. You learned how to create a chart of accounts, which will serve as the structure for G/L accounts that you will be creating in Chapter 5. You also learned how to assign the chart of accounts you created to a company code. In order to complete this activity, you copied account groups from INT (international chart of accounts), which you modified to meet your requirements. Finally, you learned how to define retained earnings account and an account type which you assigned to your P&L account. This enables the system to automatically transfer the net profit or loss to the balance sheet.

The next chapter looks at the importance of document control in SAP S4 HANA and explains how it affects the documents posted in the system.

CHAPTER 3

Document Control

In this chapter, you will be looking at the purpose of Document Control and the application of important Document types in SAP S4HANA. What are Posting Keys, and what is the importance of different Posting Keys?

At the end of this activity, you will be able to:

- Define number ranges.

- Define field status variants.

- Create variants for posting periods.

Document Control

Hundreds of documents are created by companies as a result of transactions arising from business operations. To be able to manage documents storage in the SAP system, it is important that documents posted in the system are categorized and stored sequentially for easy of retrieval. Once a transaction is posted, then the system generates a document, assigns a document number to the document, and saves the generated document in the system.

Every posting in the SAP system generates a document and the document remains open in the system until the document is cleared and archived. For example, when a transaction is posted in the system, the system generates a document and assigns it a number, and it remains open in the system until cleared.

As mentioned earlier, hundreds of transactions are posted in SAP S4 HANA. Identifying a single transaction in an environment where you have hundreds of transactions stored in the same system can be very daunting. To eliminate this problem, SAP uses a document-control technique that allows the system to structure documents storage in the system in a systematic way using document numbering, company code, and fiscal year.

© Andrew Okungbowa 2023
A. Okungbowa, *SAP S/4HANA Financial Accounting Configuration*,
https://doi.org/10.1007/978-1-4842-8957-0_3

The document number assigned to a document is obtained from the number range you will define in an activity later for your company code and your company's code fiscal year. Hence when defining document number range the following items are important:

- Document number: This is a unique number that is assigned to a document by the system automatically from the number range you have defined in the system. We will be looking at how to define number range in this chapter.

- Company code: This is your company's identification code. We looked at how to define company code in chapter 1.

- Fiscal year: This is your company's accounting year. Normally, the accounting year is a 12-month period.

When entering a document in SAP S4HANA, the user must specify a document type and a posting key. Every document in SAP is controlled by two items:

- Document types.

- Posting key.

Document types – Document types are defined at the client level. This makes document types available to all company codes within the client. Document types are used to control different business transactions in SAP R/3.

Document types controls the following items:

- The appropriate account type to be posted,

- Document header fields, and

- The number ranges for document numbers.

Document type

A document type is identified by two-character values and plays a very significant role in SAP S4 HANA. The purpose of document types is specifically to distinguish between different business transactions and the accounts the system will post a transaction to in the system for ease of identification and classification, such as Vendor invoice, customer invoice, Vendor invoice payment, and so on. We have provided a list of some of the important document types presented by SAP in the system in Table 3-1.

Table 3-1. *A List of Some of the Important Document Types in SAP S4 HANA*

Document Types	
KR	Vendor Invoice
KZ	Vendor Invoice Payment
KG	Vendor Credit Memo
DR	Customer Invoice
DZ	Customer Invoice Payment
DG	Customer Credit Memo
AB	Accounting Document
SA	G/L Account Document
AA	Asset Posting
AF	Asset Depreciation

The document type controls the following:

- The nature of business transactions and the account types where they are posted. The importance of this is that it is easier to display line items based on the type of business transactions involved.

- Posting to account types when you assign appropriate document types to business transactions. For example, the document type DR will post to a customer account, KR will post to a vendor account, and so on. During document posting, you enter the document types in the document header field. This enables the system to differentiate between accounts where transactions are posted.

- The number ranges for document numbers. The system assigns a number range to a document during posting, using the number range you created. The number range allows the system to store documents in the system based on similar number ranges. Number ranges therefore control document storage in the system.

Note   SAP S4 HANA comes with standard document types, which you can use as your document types. Some of the document types delivered by SAP are listed in Table 3-1. It is also possible to create your own document types, but we advise that you use the document types supplied by SAP, instead of creating your own from the scratch. The reason we recommend that you use the standard document types supplied by SAP is that they meet your requirements.

When defining document number range, two options are possible:

Up to a future fiscal year: This is the situation where a number range is used over one fiscal year. The system uses the available number range by choosing the current number from the number range that comes up next. This method has the drawback of running out of numbers when an entire number range is used up.

Each fiscal year: At the beginning of each year, the system starts all over again by choosing the first number in the number range defined for that fiscal year. The advantage of this method is that number range is always sufficient.

Document number can be assigned to a document either internally or externally. The internal number is assigned by the system, and the external number is assigned by the user. Follow this menu path to go to the screen where you can customize your document types if you feel like doing so: *IMG: Financial Accounting* ➤ *Financial Accounting Global Settings* ➤ *Document* ➤ *Document Types* ➤ *Define Document Types*

Posting Key

Posting Key – Used for line items.

Posting keys are defined at the client level and are available to all company codes within the client.

Importance of posting keys:

➤   Controls which account is to be post to.

➤   Controls whether the line item will be posted as a debit or credit.

➤   Determines field statuses.

SAP S4 HANA comes with predefined posting keys with the following default posting key values.

	Debit	Credit
GL Transaction	40	50
Customer Invoice	01	50
Vendor Invoice	40	31

Figure 3-1. *Important Posting keys*

We recommend that you use the predefined posting keys supplied by SAP in the system instead of creating your own posting keys, as the supplied posting keys in the system are sufficient for your requirements. To access the screen where posting keys are defined follow this menu path: ***IMG: Financial Accounting ➤ Financial Accounting Global Settings ➤ Document ➤ Define Posting Keys.***

Definition of Number Range Intervals

A document type in SAP S4 HANA must be assigned a number from a predefined number range you have defined. A document type is assigned to a number range. When a transaction is posted, the system will automatically assign a number to the document from the number range you have defined via the document type you assigned to the document. You can either define your own number ranges or you can copy the predefined number ranges provided by SAP in the system.

Note During your configuration you can define whether you want the system to assign a number from the number ranges you have defined automatically or whether you want the user to manually assign a number to a document during posting. This decision is based on your client requirements.

There are three steps to create number range intervals in SAP S4 HANA. We will be looking at each of these steps in turn in this activity.

In this activity, we will be looking at how to define your own number ranges by copying a subject from another company code.

Defining Document Number Ranges using Copy Subobject Function

The number ranges you defined in the activity will be automatically assigned by the system sequentially to documents during posting. To go to the screen where to define your own number ranges follow this menu path: ***Financial Accounting*** ➤ ***Financial Accounting Global Settings*** ➤ ***Document*** ➤ ***Document Number Ranges*** ➤ ***Define Document Number Ranges.***

The Edit Intervals: Accounting document. Object RF-BELEG screen is displayed, as in Figure 3-2.

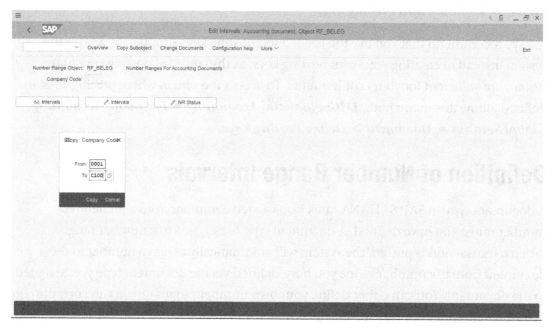

Figure 3-2. *Copying another company code number ranges using the Copy Subobject function*

The first Interval button from the right on the screen will allow you to look up existing number ranges in the system. The second Interval button will allow you to create your number interval. Since you want to copy another company code number ranges using Copy Subobject. Click Copy Subobject at the top of the screen. Copy Company Code dialog box appears. Enter the company code you want to copy in the **From** field

and enter your company code in the **To** field and click **Copy** at the bottom of the Copy
Company Code dialog box. The Number Range Interval Transport message screen will
be displayed with the message "The intervals are not included in automatic recording of
customizing change..." as in Figure 3-3.

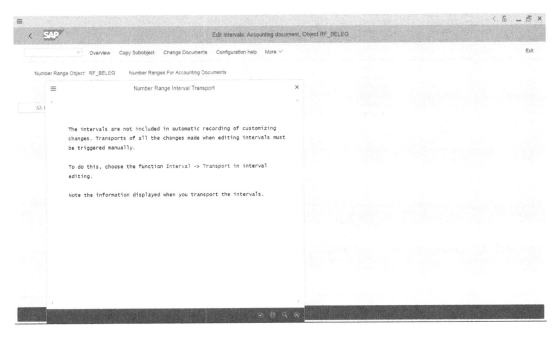

Figure 3-3. *Number range interval transport message*

Click Enter, which is the green tick at the bottom right of the screen. The Edit
Intervals: Accounting document, Object RF-BELEG screen has the message your source
company code was copied to your company code. To view the number ranges you have
copied, click the Display Intervals button (this is the intervals button with a goggle icon),
which is the first button from the left side of the screen. The Edit Intervals: Accounting
document, Object RF-BELEG, Subobject (your company code) screen is displayed
(Figure 3-4).

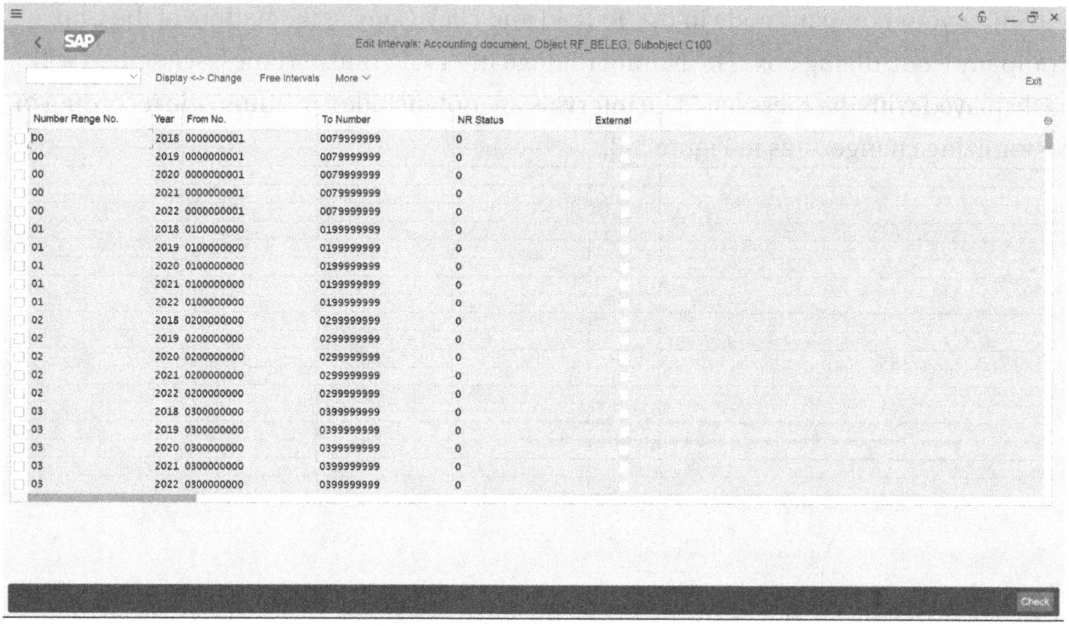

Number Range No.	Year	From No.	To Number	NR Status	External
00	2018	0000000001	0079999999	0	
00	2019	0000000001	0079999999	0	
00	2020	0000000001	0079999999	0	
00	2021	0000000001	0079999999	0	
00	2022	0000000001	0079999999	0	
01	2018	0100000000	0199999999	0	
01	2019	0100000000	0199999999	0	
01	2020	0100000000	0199999999	0	
01	2021	0100000000	0199999999	0	
01	2022	0100000000	0199999999	0	
02	2018	0200000000	0299999999	0	
02	2019	0200000000	0299999999	0	
02	2020	0200000000	0299999999	0	
02	2021	0200000000	0299999999	0	
02	2022	0200000000	0299999999	0	
03	2018	0300000000	0399999999	0	
03	2019	0300000000	0399999999	0	
03	2020	0300000000	0399999999	0	
03	2021	0300000000	0399999999	0	
03	2022	0300000000	0399999999	0	

Figure 3-4. *Number range intervals you copied to your company code*

Note Assigning years to your number ranges has a drawback. This means each year you have to define other number range intervals for the year that are missing from your number ranges. To ensure that you never run out of number ranges, you can enter 9999 in the year column. For example, instead of using years like 2018, 2019, 2020, and so on, you enter 9999 in all of the year column. This means your number ranges are valid infinitely. This will save the time of maintaining number range intervals each year.

How to Delete Number Range Intervals

To delete a number range interval, go back to the Edit Intervals: Accounting document, Object RF-BELEG using the back arrow at the top left of the screen. Click the Change Intervals with a pencil icon (this is the second button from the left on the screen). Select the number range intervals you want to delete and click the **Delete Line** at the top of the screen, as in Figure 3-5, and save your work.

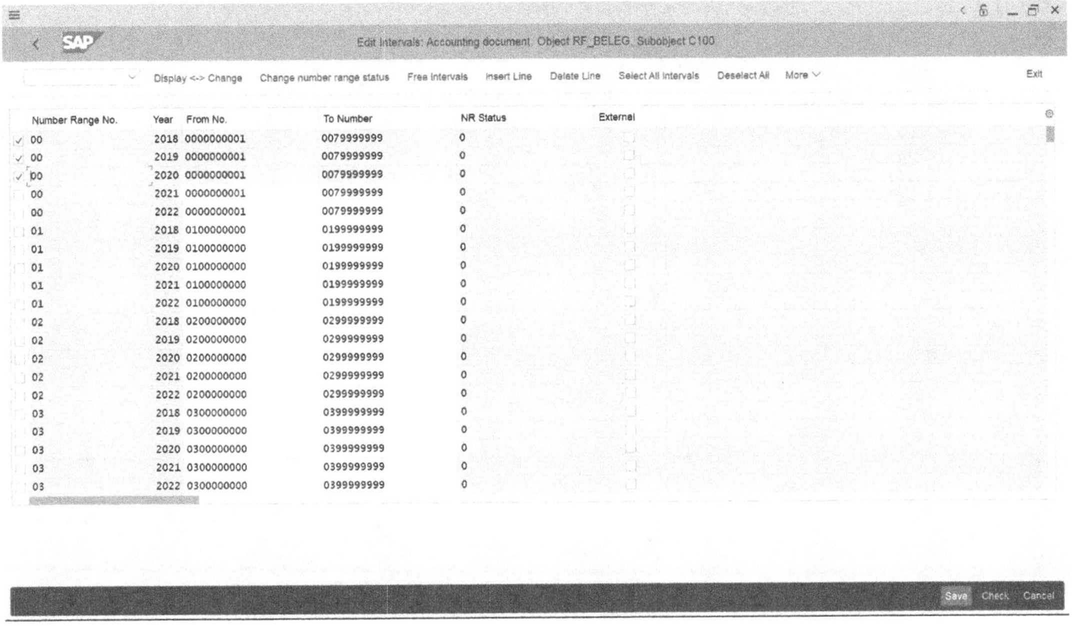

Figure 3-5. *How to delete number range intervals*

Creating your number range intervals from scratch

This is when you decide to create your own unique number range intervals.

The number ranges you defined in the activity will be automatically assigned by the system sequentially to documents during posting. To go to the screen where you can define your own number ranges follow this menu path: ***Financial Accounting ➤ Financial Accounting Global Settings ➤ Document ➤ Document Number Ranges➤ Define Document Number Ranges.*** The Edit Intervals: Accounting document, Object RF-BELEG screen is displayed (Figure 3-6). Enter your company code in the Company Code field.

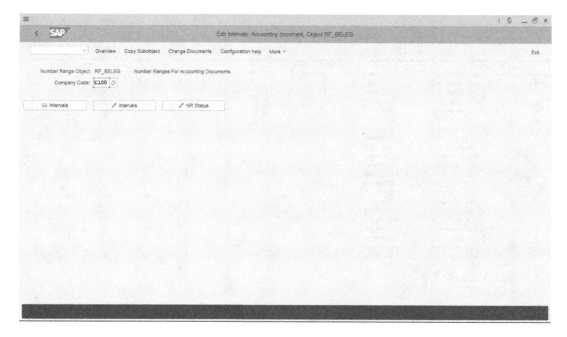

Figure 3-6. *The screen where you start defining your document number ranges*

To maintain number ranges for your company code, choose change Intervals button. That is the second button from the left with a pencil icon on the Edit Intervals: Accounting document, Object RF-BELEG screen.

The Edit Intervals: Accounting document, Object RF-BELEG screen subobject (your company code) screen is displayed, as in Figure 3-7.

Update the following fields:

No: This is the field where you will enter your number range identifier. For example – 01

Year: The years you enter here determine the validity of your number range. It is important that you include the current year in your number range.

From number: This is the lower limit for your number range intervals (i.e., the starting point of your number range).

To number: This is the upper limit for your number range intervals (i.e., where your number range ends).

Current number: No entry is needed here. This field shows the current number range that has been assigned by the system. During configuration this filed is always defaulted as 0.

Ext: When this check box indicator is selected, the system will allow the users to assign an external number to documents during posting. If the check box is left blank, the system will assign a number to documents automatically from the number range intervals that you have defined.

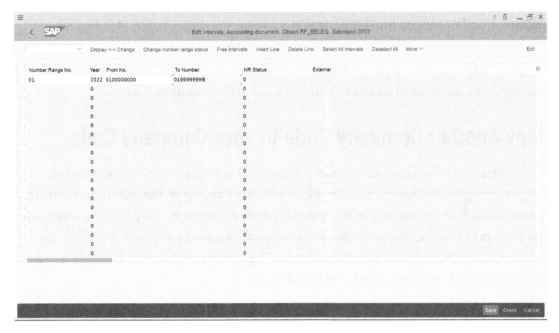

Figure 3-7. *The screen where you maintain your number range intervals*

Note   Enter two numeric character – 01 or alphanumeric character – A1 or alpha character – AB identifier for your number range intervals. The choice of what character to use is discretionary.

It is important to stress here that the characters used as above are only for illustration. There is no restriction to the digits you can use as your number range identifier. You can use any character as deemed fit, but it is advisable to use meaningful and sequential characters. In the following example, we used numeric characters.

Repeat the same process as above by clicking the change Intervals button and enter another number range interval for Fiscal year – 2023, 2024, and so on.

Once you have completed creating your number ranges for the desired years, save the number ranges you have defined. The ***Transport number range intervals*** screen pops up. Accept the warning by choosing the Enter button. The system will then notify you at the status bar below that your changes were saved.

Note   Number ranges must not overlap.

Let's look at the final step of how to define document number ranges by copying the number range intervals of another company code to your company code.

Copy Another Company Code to your Company Code

To copy the intervals of document number ranges of another company code to your company code follow this menu path: ***Financial Accounting ➤ Financial Accounting Global Settings ➤ Document ➤ Document Number Ranges➤ Copy to Company Code.*** The Transport Number Range Intervals screen is displayed, as in Figure 3-3. Click the Enter button at the bottom right of the screen. The Document Number Ranges Copying to Company Code screen is displayed (Figure 3-8).

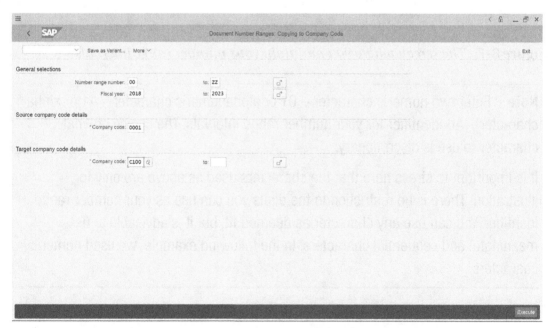

Figure 3-8. *Copying document number range intervals from a source company code to a target company code*

Update the following fields:

In the General selections section of the screen, enter the start number of the number range of the source company in the Number range number field and the end number range in the To field. Enter the year range you are copying in the Fiscal Year field. You can use our example, as in Figure 3-8. In the Source company code details section, enter the company code you are copying the number range intervals from in the Company code field. In the Target company code details section, enter your company code in the Company code section.

Note   Source company code is the company code you are copying the document number ranges from. In this activity, we copied company code 0001 and the target company is your company code you are copying company code 0001 document number ranges to. In this activity, our company code is C100.

This action will allow you to copy the entire number range for company code –0001.

Finally, let's look at how to copy document number ranges to fiscal year.

Copying Number Ranges to Fiscal Year

You can also copy document number ranges from an earlier fiscal year to a new fiscal year. To go to the screen where you can carry out this exercise use this menu path: *Financial Accounting* ➤ *Financial Accounting Global Settings* ➤ *Document* ➤ *Document Number Ranges* ➤ *Copy to Fiscal Year.* The **Transport Number Range Intervals** information screen pops up with the information that "The intervals are not included in automatic recording of customizing changes..." Press enter on your keyboard or click enter – the green tick at the right bottom of the Transport Number Ranges Intervals screen. The **Document Number Ranges: Copy to Fiscal Year** screen is displayed in Figure 3-9.

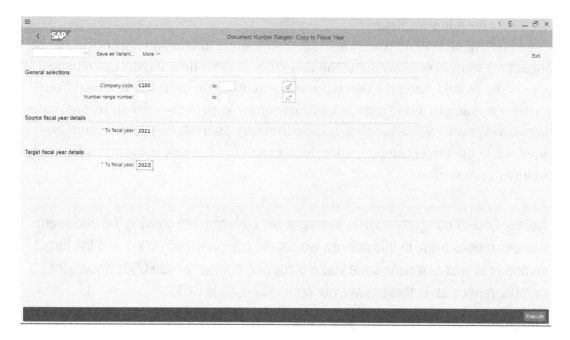

Figure 3-9. *Copying document number range intervals from one fiscal year to another fiscal year*

Update the following fields: In **General selections** section of the screen of the screen enter your company code in the **Company code** field. In the **Source fiscal year details** section enter the fiscal year you are copying in the **To fiscal year** field and in **Target fiscal year details** section, enter your new fiscal year in the **To fiscal year** field and click the Execute button at the bottom right of the screen. The Document Number Ranges: Copy to Fiscal Year screen appears displaying a list of all the intervals added to your new fiscal year.

Field Status Variants

Field Status variants are variants that comprise the Field Status group in SAP S4 HANA. A Field Status Group defines the screen layout for a general ledger account entry and also controls document creation within a company code. Based on your specification, the Field Status Group will determine which fields will accept input during documents entry, whether a field should be hidden, displayed or suppressed, required or optional.

In SAP S4 HANA, field statuses are defined at global settings and are assigned Field Status Groups. Field status variants are independent of company codes (that is they are available to all company codes in the client); hence they are created at client level. A Field Status Group is entered in the company code section of the G/L accounts master record during the creation of a G/L account.

A field status group allows you to determine which fields require entry, which fields are optional or suppressed during document entry.

Note   We recommend that you copy the standard field status variants supplied by SAP. Defining your own field status variants will require you to update the associated tables as well, and this can be cumbersome in practice.

Define Field Status Variants

Problem: You are to copy the Company code 0001 Field Status Variants supplied by Sap in the system and modify them to meet your requirements. As part of this customizing exercise, you are to specify field status variants and assign your company code to the field status variant you have defined.

To access the screen where you will define your field status variants follow this menu path: *Financial Accounting* ➤ *Financial Accounting Global Settings* ➤ *Ledgers* ➤ *Fields* ➤ *Define Field Status Variants.* Change View "Field Status": Overview screen is displayed (Figure 3-10). This is the screen where you define your field status variants and assign field status groups to it.

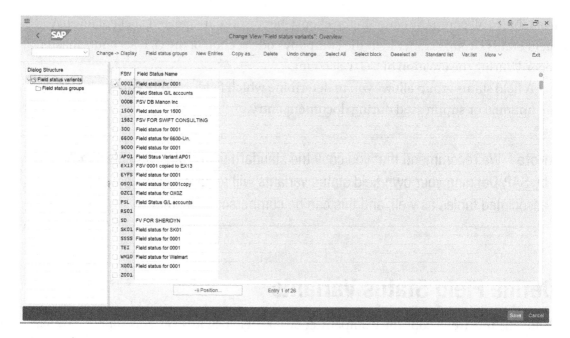

Figure 3-10.   *The screen where you define and maintain field status variants*

Since you are going to copy an existing field status variants supplied by SAP in the system, use the Position button at the button of the screen search for the company code whose field status variants you want to copy. You can copy the field status variants of any of the sample company supplied by SAP in the system for your country.

Note   In this activity, we will be copying the field status variants for Company code – 0001. SAP have supplied a list of field status variants you can copy from. For example, you can copy field status variants from 0001 or 1000, 2000, etc. You will get the same result.

Select the field status variant you want to copy from the list of field status variants provided by SAP in the system (see Figure 3-10 as an example), click **Copy as...** at the top of the screen. **Change View "Field Status Variants": Overview of Selected Set** screen is displayed with details of the field status variant you have copied.

Modify the copied field status to meet your requirements by changing the exiting field status variant in the **FStV** (Field Status Variant) field to your company code identifier and enter a description you will remember in the **Field Status Name** field.

Note   We advise that you use your company code as your field status variant and use a description you will remember for your field status variant as we did in Figure 3-11. This will make it easy for you to identify your field status variant from the list of field status variants in the system.

Once you have maintained your field status variant click the Copy button at the bottom right of the screen. **Specify object to copy** screen pops up with three options to choose from: **copy all**, **only copy entry,** or **cancel**.

When you choose the **copy all** button, this will allow you to copy the entries of the field status variant you copied and its dependent entries. Similarly, when you choose the **only copy entry** button, only the entries associated with the field status variant will be copied.

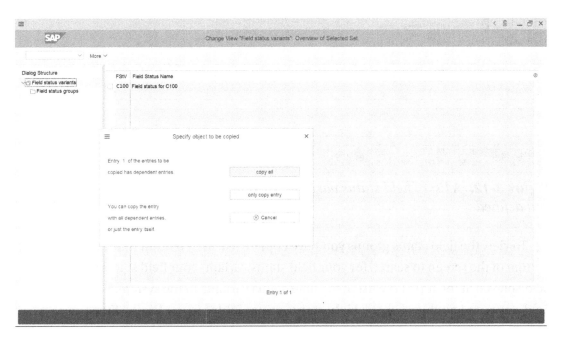

Figure 3-11. *Copying Field Status Variant*

Choose the **copy all** button in order to copy the entry with all dependent entries associated with the field variant you have copied. The Information screen pops up telling you the Number of dependent entries copied. When you click the Continue button at the bottom right of the Information screen, the field status you have defined will appear at the top of the list of field status variants in the **Change View "Field status": Overview** screen (Figure 3-12).

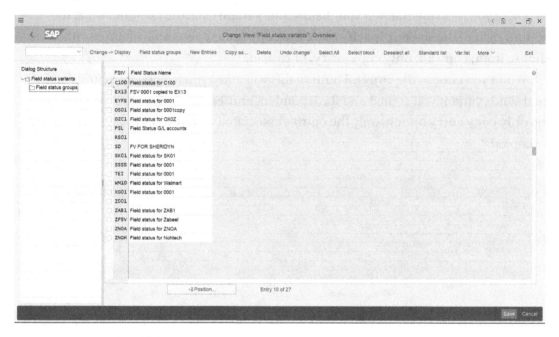

Figure 3-12. *A list of field status variants, including the field status variant you defined*

To view the field status groups you have copied, use the **Position** button at the bottom of the screen to search for your field status variant; your field status variant will be displayed at the top of the list of the field status variants in the system. Select your field status and double click the **Field status group folder** in the **Dialog Structure** on the left side of the screen, a list of field status groups depending on entries for your field status variant will be displayed, as in Figure 3-12.

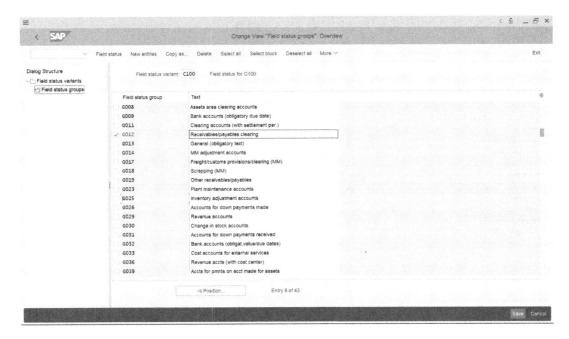

Figure 3-13. *A view of the field status group you copied*

As we mentioned earlier, the Field Status group controls the appearance of certain data entry fields in the data screen for G/L accounts. For example, you can decide which field in the G/L account should be suppressed, required entry, or optional entry. For example, let's assume that your client wants you to make **Due Date** and **Payment terms** field a required entry fields during Receivables/Payable clearing.

To go to the screen where you will maintain your field status group for receivables/payables clearing, search for G012 – Receivables/payables clearing in the list of field status groups displayed in the **Change View "Field status": Overview** screen (Figure 3-13). Double click the **G012 – Receivables/payables**, **Maintain Field Status Group: Overview** screen is displayed. Since you want to make due date and payment terms compulsory entry field, double click Payment transactions from the Select Group section (Figure 3-14).

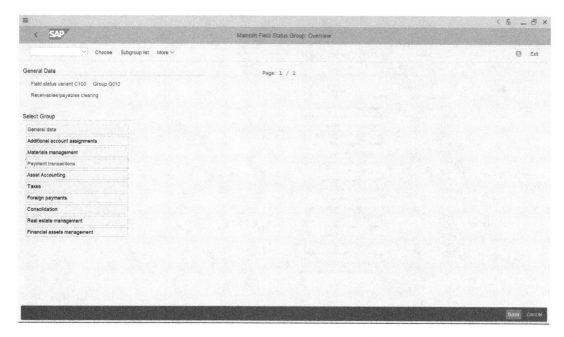

Figure 3-14. *The screen where you select the field status group you want to maintain*

The Maintain Field Status Group: Payment transactions screen is displayed in
Figure 3-15.

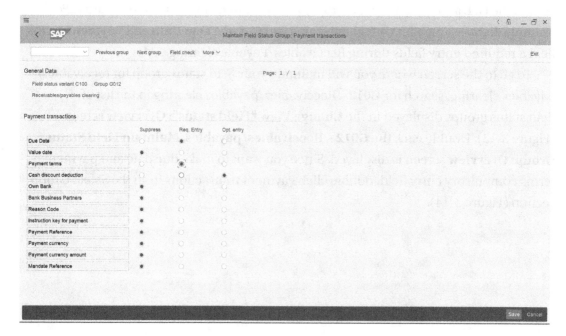

Figure 3-15. *The screen where you specify document entry fields*

Select Due Date and Payment terms under Req. Entry radio buttons, as in Figure 3-15, and save your customizing by clicking the Save button at the bottom right of the screen.

Assign Company Code to Field Status Variants

The final step in this activity is to assign the field status variant you have defined to your company code. The field status variant you assigned to your company code will control the appearance of the data entry field in the data screen. To go to the screen where you will assign your company code to the field status variant you have defined follow this menu path: *Financial Accounting* ➤ *Financial Accounting Global Settings* ➤ *Ledgers* ➤ *Fields* ➤ *Assign Company Code to Field Status Variants.* **Change View "Assign Company Code _> Field Status": Variant"** Overview screen is displayed (Figure 3-16).

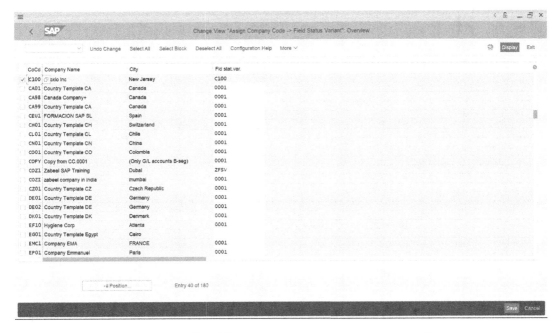

Figure 3-16. *Assignment of Field status variant to company code*

Using the Position button at the bottom of the screen, search for your company code and use the Match code function for your field status variant and assign it to your company code and save your work.

Summary

This chapter explained document control by looking at document types and posting keys and their functions in SAP S4 HANA. As part of the customizing exercise, you learned how to copy document number ranges from predefined number ranges supplied by SAP in the system, how to display the number ranges you defined, and how to delete number range lines. You learned about what field status variants are and the importance of field status variants. Finally, you learned how to create your own field status variants by copying predefined field status variants and field status variant groups and their dependent entries and how to assign a field status variant to your company code.

In the next chapter, we will be looking at how to customize tolerance groups and how to assign a user to a tolerance group.

CHAPTER 4

Defining Tolerance Groups for G/L Accounts and Employees

In this activity, we will be looking at the purpose of Tolerance Groups and how to define Tolerance Groups in SAP S4 HANA.

At the end of this activity you will be able to:

- Define tolerance groups for G/L accounts.

- Define tolerance groups for employees.

- Define tolerance groups for employees with a group.

- Assign users to tolerance groups.

Tolerance Groups

Tolerance groups determine limits upon which acceptable payment differences are based. During document posting, the system will check for differences and match them against the defined limits to determine if the difference is within the specified limits and automatically post the differences to a predefined account. If the difference is outside the set limit, the system will automatically reject the posting.

It is a normal business practice for payment differences to occur in a business transaction. The bottom line here is, what is the business willing to accept as an acceptable payment difference for a given business transaction? This occurs when an invoice amount entered in the system is different from the actual amount received to clear the outstanding invoice. For example, an outstanding invoice amount of $1,000 and

© Andrew Okungbowa 2023
A. Okungbowa, *SAP S/4HANA Financial Accounting Configuration*,
https://doi.org/10.1007/978-1-4842-8957-0_4

the amount paid to clear the outstanding invoice of $950, leaving you with a difference if $50. If the acceptable limit for your tolerance groups is $45, the system will reject your posting because the difference is above the acceptable limit. On the other hand, if the payment difference is $45 or less, the system will accept your posting and post the difference to a specified predefined account, because the difference is within the defined acceptable limit.

There are several reasons why differences occur. A typical example is as a result of goods damaged on transit that reduce the value of the goods delivered. This brings up the concept of materiality, which is what a business considers a material or significant difference that cannot be overlooked or ignored. To enable the system to perform limit checks, you must define an acceptable payment difference in SAP S4 HANA.

Tolerances are necessary mainly for control purposes. In SAP S4 HANA, maximum amounts deemed acceptable by your company are defined in the company code and assigned to a tolerance group. Tolerance dictates payment difference authorization.

Note   Tolerances are company code specific and determine the maximum amount accounting clerks are permitted to post in the system per transaction for invoice clearing.

Tolerance also allows you to specify settings that control the discounts that accounting clerks can grant per invoice and any tolerance over-payment.

The advantage of imposing restrictions by setting tolerances is to avoid major posting errors by clerks or users. During posting, the system will automatically determine if a payment difference is within the acceptable limits you defined. If the payment difference is within the payment difference limit, the system will accept the posting. On the other hand, if the payment difference exceeds the specified limit, the system will reject the posting.

There are three Tolerances represented in SAP R/3:

- Tolerance Groups for G/L Accounts.

- Tolerance Groups for Employees.

- Tolerances for Customers/Vendors.

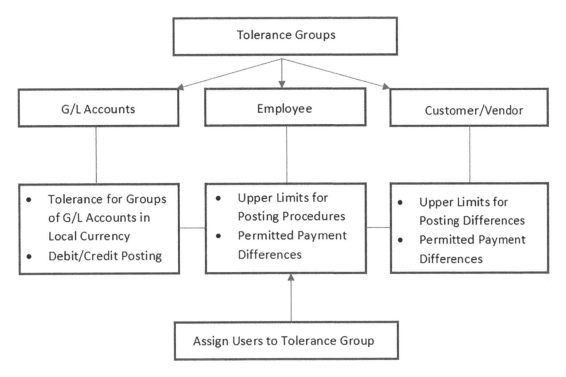

Figure 4-1. *The three levels of Tolerance Groups*

Tolerance Groups is divided into two sections:

1. Upper limits for posting procedure and

2. Permitted payment differences.

In the ***Upper limits for posting procedures*** section you enter the maximum amount an employee can post in the system in the following fields:

- The maximum amount per document the employee is authorized to post in the system.

- The maximum amount per open item account item the employee can enter in the line item in vendor/customer account.

- The maximum cash percentage cash discount per line item the employee can grant.

In the ***Permitted payment differences*** section you specify the allowed payment differences an employee is permitted in terms of ***Revenue*** and ***Expense***:

Note   The system gives you the flexibility to create as many tolerance groups as you may desire. Each employee or user should be assigned to a tolerance group.

In a tolerance group, the local Currency of the company code is valid. Tolerance group is part of the global settings in SAP S4 HANA.

Note   You will be looking at Vendor/Customer Tolerance Groups in Chapter 14 in Outgoing Manual Payments.

Define Tolerance Groups for G/L Accounts

Tolerance group for G/L accounts define the limits within which credit and debit differences in local currencies are considered acceptable. The accounts' differences are posted automatically during G/L account clearing. The tolerance groups you define for your G/L accounts in this activity will eventually be assigned to the G/L accounts' master record later in this chapter. During the account-clearing process, the system checks the tolerance groups to ascertain if the differences are within acceptable limits, as you specify in your settings, and automatically posts the difference, if any, to the predefined accounts.

The tolerance groups defined for GL accounts are assigned in the general ledger account master record in the system.

During account clearing, the system will check the tolerance groups to ascertain if differences are within acceptable limits that you defined here and automatically post the difference to predefined accounts.

Case Study

Company C100 accounts team have asked you to define acceptable payment differences that are posted automatically to different accounts during document posting.

In this activity, we will be looking at the two steps involved in customizing tolerance groups for G/L accounts. You will learn the steps involved in customizing default tolerance groups for G/L accounts and how to assign a group to the tolerance group you will define in this activity of your G/L accounts.

The two tolerance groups you will define under tolerance for G/L accounts are:

Default Tolerance Group:

This is a G/L tolerance without tolerance group. This is defined by leaving the tolerance group field blank (this is the default tolerance group, and it is valid for all G/L tolerance groups in the system).

Tolerance Group:

As opposed to default tolerance groups, this is a G/L tolerance with a tolerance group. Here, you will assign a specific tolerance group to the G/L tolerance. Unlike the G/L tolerance without a tolerance group, this tolerance group is valid only for the specified G/L tolerances groups. For example, if accounting clerks in group A are assigned to certain G/L tolerances, the system will not allow accounting clerks in group B to post to these G/L accounts during document entry.

To proceed to the screen where you will define the default tolerance group follow this menu path: ***IMG: Financial Accounting ➤ General Ledger Accounting ➤ Business Transactions ➤ Open Item Clearing ➤ Clearing Differences ➤ Define Tolerance Groups for G/L Accounts.***

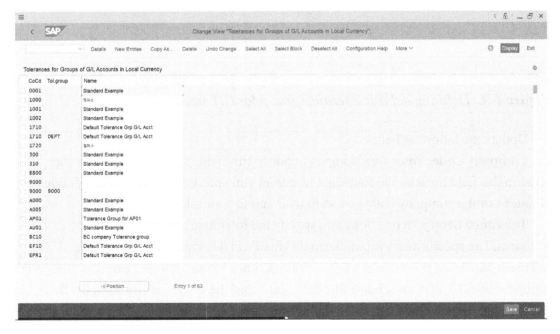

Figure 4-2. *The screen where to define tolerance groups for G/L accounts*

The **Change View "Tolerance for Groups of G/L Accounts in Local Currency"** screen displays a list of existing tolerance groups (Figure 4-2). Click New Entry, which is the second item from the left side at the top of the screen. The **New Entries: Details of Added Entries** screen is displayed (Figure 4-3). This is the screen where you specify tolerances for groups in G/L accounts.

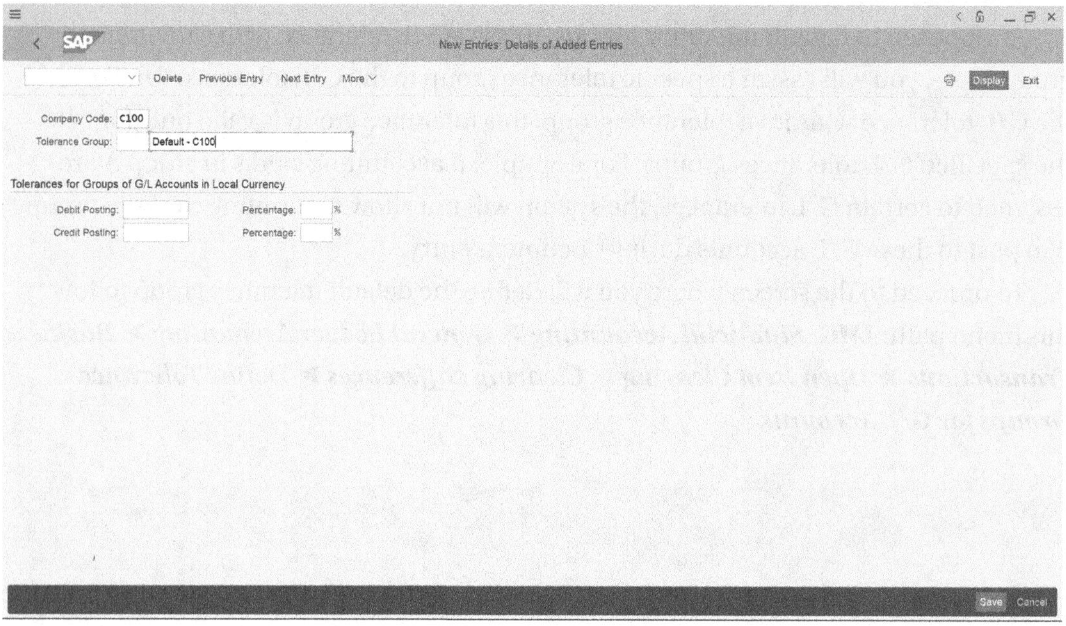

Figure 4-3. *Defining default tolerance group for G/L accounts*

Update the following fields:

Company Code: Enter your company code in this field. The company code you enter in this field must be the four-digit identifier you entered as your company code in chapter 1 or the company code you want to assign to your tolerance group.

Tolerance Group: In this field, you specify the tolerance group for your G/L accounts. The specification you make in this field will determine the acceptable payment difference posted to the G/L accounts. Since we are defining a default tolerance group for our G/L accounts, leave this field blank and the system will automatically assume that the tolerance group is a default tolerance group and is therefore valid for all G/L tolerance groups. Since a blank tolerance group is a default tolerance group, it is advisable to describe your tolerance group as "Default" in the Tolerance Group description field shown in Figure 4-3.

In the Tolerance for Groups of G/L Accounts in Local Currency section on the screen, you can specify debit/credit posting differences as absolute amount or percentage. During document posting, the system will check the amount and the percentage you specify and automatically use whichever is lower.

Save your customizing by clicking the Save button at the bottom right of the screen.

The second step in this activity is to define the G/L tolerances with a tolerance group. This is where you assign a group to the G/L tolerance. Only the assigned group can post differences within the acceptance limit in the system. To go to the screen where you will carry out this customizing exercise, use this menu path: **IMG: Financial Accounting ➤ General Ledger Accounting ➤ Business Transactions ➤ Open Item Clearing ➤ Clearing Differences ➤ Define Tolerance Groups for G/L Accounts.** The **Change View "Tolerance for Groups of G/L Accounts in Local Currency"** screen displays a list of existing tolerance groups (Figure 4-2). Click the **New Entries** at the top left of the screen to go to the **New Entries: Details of Added Entries** screen where you will define your tolerance group.

Update the following fields:

Company Code: Enter your company code in this field.

Tolerance Group: Enter a four-digit character that best describes your tolerance group in this field, as in Figure 4-4, and a description of your tolerance group. Save your work.

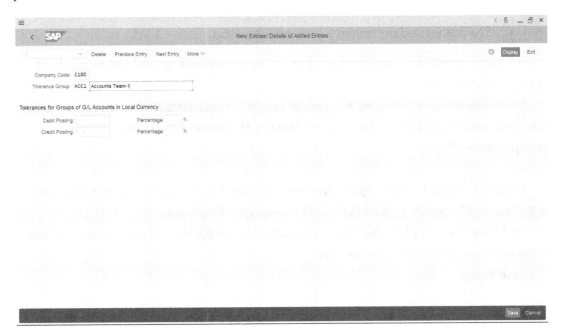

Figure 4-4. *Defining tolerance groups for G/L accounts with tolerance group*

Note   The relationship of the user ID and the tolerance group is a many-to-one relationship. That means that several user IDs can be assigned to the same tolerance group, but a user logon ID can be assigned to only one tolerance group.

Define Tolerance Groups for Employees

Tolerance groups set for employees define what an employee is permitted to post to the system. In order for the system to automatically determine the amount an employee can post to the system per document and put open items, you need to specify the following settings:

- The maximum amount per document an employee is permitted to post.

- The maximum amount the employee can enter in the system per open item in customer/vendor account item.

- The maximum cash discount per line item that an employee is permitted to grant to a customer or vendor.

- The authorized permitted payment difference.

Tolerance groups for employees are part of the global settings and can be accessed by either of the menu paths:

IMG: Financial Accounting ➤ *General Ledger Accounting* ➤ *Business Transactions* ➤ *Open Item Clearing* ➤ *Clearing Differences* ➤ *Define Tolerance Groups for Employees*

or

IMG: Financial Accounting ➤ *Financial Accounting Global Settings* ➤ *Document* ➤ *Tolerance Groups* ➤ *Define Tolerance Groups for Employees*

Problem: Your task is to define the tolerance groups for employees and assign users to the tolerance group you have defined.

Case Study

The accounting team wants you to Define Tolerance Groups for Employees that will determine:

1) The maximum document an employee is authorized to post.

2) The maximum amount per open item the employee can enter in the line item in vendor/customer account.

3) The maximum cash percentage cash discount per line item the employee can grant.

4) The maximum tolerance differences an employee can post at a given time.

As part of this task, it is also your responsibility to assign users to a tolerance group.

Note To complete this activity, you must define two tolerance groups: one is a default tolerance group (without a tolerance group key) and the second is a tolerance group with a group key.

Define Default Tolerance Groups for Employees

The default tolerance groups for employees setting is a minimum requirement for clearing differences that is valid for all employee groups. To go to the screen where you will define your tolerance groups for employees use any of the menu paths previously mentioned.

The *Change View "FI Tolerance Groups For Users": Overview* screen is displayed. Choose the New Entries button at the top left of the screen. You will then go to the **New Entries: Details of added Entries** screen. In the **New Entries: Details of Added Entries** screen update the following fields:

Group: Leave this field blank. The system will treat a blank tolerance group as a default tolerance group. A default tolerance group is a minimum requirement for all employee groups in the system. This is applicable when employees are not assigned to any specific tolerance group.

Company Code: Enter your Company Code in the **Company Code** field. The company code will serve as the company code for your tolerance groups for employees.

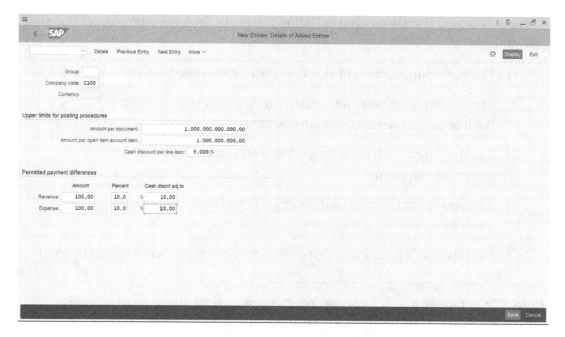

Figure 4-5. *Default tolerance groups for employees*

In the ***Upper limits for posting procedures*** section enter the maximum amount an employee can post in the system in the following fields:

- **Amount per document**: This is the maximum amount per document an employee is authorized to post. It is important to note that an employee will not be able to exceed the amount defined here during document posting.

- **Amount per open item account item**: This is the maximum amount per open item that an employee can enter in the line item in a vendor/customer account. An employee can post only an amount up to the specified amount defined here per open item. Any amount exceeding this amount will be rejected by the system during posting.

- **Cash discount per line item**: The maximum cash percentage cash discount per line item the employee can grant. When an employee grants a discount during document posting, the system will check to make sure that the discount granted is within the acceptable levels per line item you define here.

In the ***Permitted payment differences*** section of this screen, specify the Amount, Percentage, and Cash Discount adjustment in **Revenue/Expense** fields as permitted difference. During payment difference posting, the system will automatically check the amount posted against the percentage specified and use whichever is lower.

When you have updated the **New Entries: Details of Added Entries** screen (Figure 4-5), save you work by clicking the Save button at the bottom right of the screen. The system will notify you that your data was saved at the Status bar at the bottom of the screen.

Note   dot (.) is used to separate thousands and comma (,) is used to separate pence/cents. For example 190,222.22 is represented in SAP as 190.222,22

The next step is to create another Tolerance Groups for Employees.

Define Tolerance Groups for Employees

The group key you define in this activity will be assigned to one or more username(s) (i.e., log on IDs). Log on ID is the User ID the user uses to gain access to the system. This will be discussed further in a later chapter. The employees you assign to the tolerance group you have defined in the activity will be restricted to the payment differences you specified in the tolerance group. In other words, during document posting, the employees you assigned to this tolerance group will not be able to exceed the permitted payment differences you have specified.

Use this menu path: ***IMG: Financial Accounting*** ➤ ***Financial Accounting Global Settings*** ➤ ***Document*** ➤ ***Tolerance Groups*** ➤ ***Define Tolerance Groups for Employees*** to go to the

Change View "FI Tolerance Groups For Users": Overview screen, where you will define your tolerance group for employees. Click the **New Entries** button at the top left of the screen to go to the New ***Entries: Details of Added Entries*** screen create Tolerance Groups for Employees.

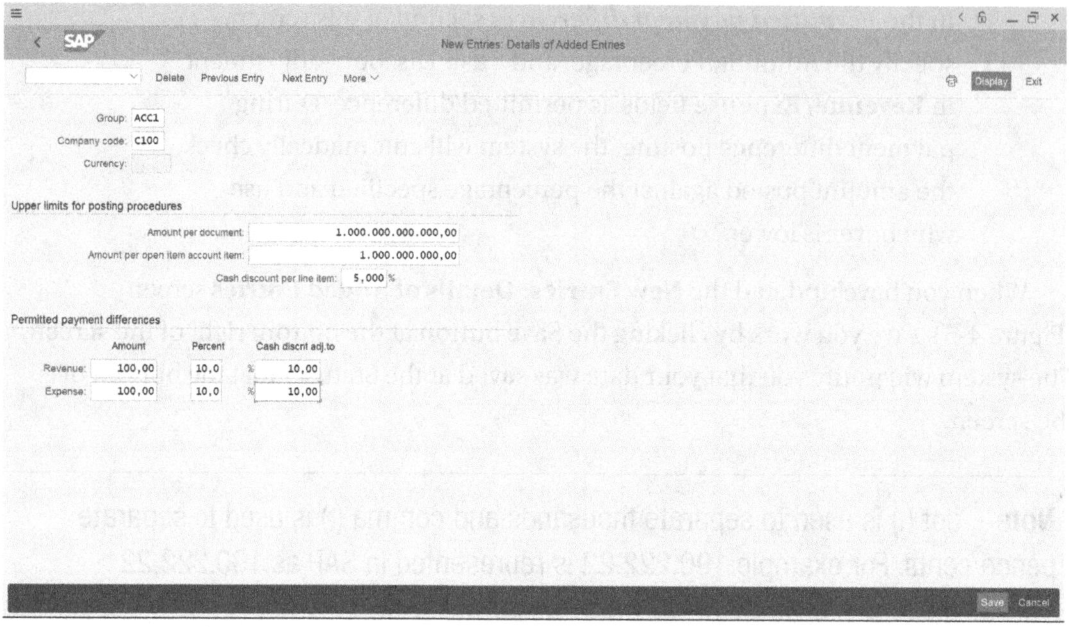

Figure 4-6. *Tolerance group for employees with a group key*

Update the following fields, as in Figure 4-6:

Group: Enter your tolerance group identifier you defined in Figure 4-4 – **ACC1 (Accounts Team-1)**. This is a four-digit character. You can create as many tolerance groups as you desire. The tolerance group identifier you will create in this activity will be assigned to a User logon ID in the next activity.

Company Code: Enter your Company Code in this field.

In the ***Upper limits for posting procedures*** section of the screen, enter the maximum amount an employee can post in the system in the following fields:

- Amount per document,

- Amount per open item account item,

- Cash discount per line item, and

- Permitted payment differences.

In the ***Permitted payment differences*** section on the screen, in the **Revenue/ Expense** fields specify the Amount, Percentage, and Cash Discount adjustment. The system will automatically use whichever is lower between Amount and Percentage you specify here during posting.

When you save your work, the system will notify you that your data was saved at the status bar below on the screen.

The final step in this activity is to assign users to the tolerance group you have created.

Assign Users to Tolerance Groups

After defining your employee tolerance group, it is important to assign users to the tolerance group you have defined.

Note   In this activity, you will only be assigning one user to the tolerance group you have defined for illustration purpose only. But in practice you may have to assign more than one user to your tolerance group.

To go to the screen where you will be assigning users to your employee tolerance group follow this menu path: ***IMG: Financial Accounting ➤ General Ledger Accounting ➤ Business Transactions ➤ Open Item Clearing ➤ Clearing Differences ➤ Assign Users to Tolerance Groups.***

The ***Change View "Assign Users ➤ Tolerance Group": Overview*** screen is displayed. Click the New Entries button at the top right of the screen to go to the next screen, the **New Entries: Overview of Added Entries** screen (Figure 4-7), where you will assign users to your employee tolerance group.

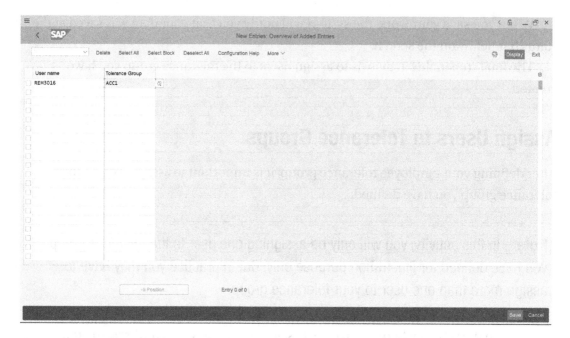

Figure 4-7. *The screen where you assign users to employee tolerance groups*

Update the following fields:

User name: Enter the user ID you want to assign to the tolerance group in this field. The username you enter here is the user's logon ID. This will allow the user to post an amount in the system up to the defined tolerance limit specified in the tolerance group you have assigned to the user.

Tolerance group: Enter the tolerance group key you defined, as in Figure 4-4. This will allow the user assigned to the tolerance group to post an amount within the tolerance limit defined in the tolerance group.

Note   The User Name is your logon user ID. For example, Student1 or Student2 or student3 or student4 or user1, and so on.

After assigning your user to your tolerance group, as in Figure 4-7, save your customizing.

Summary

In this chapter, we explained in detail what tolerance groups are and how tolerance groups serve as a control mechanism in SAP S4 HANA. We also looked at the steps involved in defining tolerances by exploring customizing processes in creating tolerance groups for G/L accounts. This included defining limits within which credit and debit differences in local currencies are considered by the system during posting. Secondly, we also looked at how to customize settings for tolerances for employees by looking at how to define default tolerance groups for employees without a group key and the tolerance with a group key.

Finally, as part of this activity, we also took you through the process involved in assigning a user to tolerance groups for employees.

In the next chapter, we will be looking at how to create General Ledger (G/L) accounts in SAP S4 HANA.

CHAPTER 5

Creating a General Ledger (G/L)

In this chapter, we will be looking at how to create G/L Accounts, use Line items, and open item management in G/L Account.

At the end of this chapter, you will be able to:

- Explain what a general ledger is.

- Describe what a master record is.

- Create a G/L account master record.

- Use a template to copy a G/L account.

General Ledger

General Ledger Accounts comprises the Chart of Accounts section and Company Code section. G/L Account is created in the chart of accounts and further configurations are carried out to meet company codes requirements.

Business transactions are sorted and stored in GL accounts that apply the double entry principle – dual control (debit and credit). Transactions posted to GL accounts are classified into assets, liabilities, income, and expenditures from which financial statement are drawn.

All transactions with business partners in SAP are posted to sub-ledgers in SAP S4 HANA. These transactions could be either debit or credit transactions. Several sub-ledgers are created to handle transactions in the system. The summary of all transactions in sub-ledgers are automatically posted to the reconciliation (general ledger) accounts by the system in real-time. For example, in Figure 1-5, the amounts of $1,500 and $2,000

85

© Andrew Okungbowa 2023
A. Okungbowa, *SAP S/4HANA Financial Accounting Configuration*,
https://doi.org/10.1007/978-1-4842-8957-0_5

were posted to Machinery and $5,000 posted to Buildings sub-ledgers. The system will automatically post the balance of both items in the sub-ledgers to a reconciliation (General ledger account) – Asset.

GL Reconciliation

Reconciliation accounts are GL accounts that hold sub-ledger balances. Reconciliation accounts could be referred to as GL accounts containing sub-ledger totals. All postings to sub-ledgers are automatically posted to GL reconciliation accounts by the system. Therefore, reconciliation accounts are GL Accounts summaries of sub-ledgers in SAP R/3.

Reconciliation accounts are assigned to business partners in the business partners' master record. A business partner could be an organization or a subsidiary that your organization does business with.

Sub-ledgers are subsets of the general ledger used in recording individual items and transactions in accounting. Sub-ledgers include individual accounts payable, accounts receivable, assets and bank accounts information. They hold accounts payable details such as vendor's name, number of transactions, dates, discounts, and payment terms. Transactions are posted in the system as they arise in the sub-ledger. The balance of the sub-ledger are posted to reconciliation accounts. Simply put, the balances in sub-ledger accounts are posted to reconciliation accounts. The advantage of a reconciliation account is that it gives you a snapshot of the sub-ledger.

Note   Reconciliation accounts are G/L accounts that hold sub-ledger balances. Reconciliation accounts could be referred to as G/L accounts containing sub-ledger totals. Therefore, reconciliation accounts are G/L account summaries of sub-ledgers in SAP HANA. Reconciliation accounts are assigned to business partners in the business partners' master records.

No postings are made to reconciliation account by users. All postings to reconciliation accounts are carried out by the system automatically in real-time.

Next, you need to know what a general ledger master record is and how it controls accounting transactions in the general ledger accounts.

What is a Master Record?

A master record contains vital information held in a business system database that remains relatively unchanged over a long period of time. This is the case when sets of data are commonly accessed, used and shared by different individuals for different purposes across an organization in order to fulfill business processes in real-time. For example, a vendor's details held in the system may be used by various departments. The sales team needs the vendors' details in order to send them sales offers; the marketing department needs this information to send out marketing promotions; the finance department needs the information for invoices and other accounting purposes; and so on.

Information that aids efficient business processes and tends to relatively remain unchanged (such as customer/vendor names and addresses) are held in the system's database. The idea behind maintaining a master record is to avoid having to re-enter the same information multiple times, thereby saving input time and avoiding unnecessary waste of system resources and redundancies (to free stage space and improve system speed). It is better to not have to enter or store the same data in the system database several times.

The function of the G/L account master is that it controls accounting transactions postings in SAP S4 HANA.

Some typical examples of master data in SAP S4 HAN include customer data, vendor data, bank data, G/L accounts, material data, and so on.

Transaction Data: Data triggered as a result of events arising from day-to-day nosiness transactions. A typical transaction data is time-driven with a numerical value and often refers to one or more objects in the system. Examples of transaction data in SAP S4 HANA include invoices, payments, credit memos, and goods receipts.

Table Data: Sets of tables containing data about objects, such as payment terms, tolerances, pricing conditions. and so on.

Now that you know what a master record is, let's look at how to create G/L account master records in SAP S4 HANA. A G/L master record contains data relating to a G/L account that remains in the system for a while. The data held in the G/L master record controls the general ledger accounts behavior. The G/L master record also governs the treatment and posting of accounting transactions to the G/L accounts in the system.

Creating G/L Account Master Records

Various options are available when creating G/L master records in SAP S4 HANA:

Creating G/L accounts with reference: This allows you to copy existing G/L accounts from another company code to yours. The company code you are copying the G/L accounts from is referred to as the "source" company code and your company code is the "target" company code. SAP comes with a standard chart of accounts and model company codes in the system, along with sets of G/L account master records. The benefits of copying existing G/L accounts master records is that your G/L account master records will inherit properties of the source G/L accounts you copied, which saves time.

Data transfer workbench: This is when you transfer G/L account master records from a legacy system. This function is ideal when you want to transfer G/L accounts from another system in SAP.

By copying: The system allows you to copy G/L account master records already in the system. This is possible only when you have an existing chart of accounts that meets your requirements. For example, a chart of accounts that has a structure that matches your G/L account master record could be copied.

By creating manually: This is when you have to physically create G/L account master records individually. The drawback to this method is that it is time consuming, especially when you have to create large numbers of G/L accounts.

Changes in SAP S4 HANA

- Mergeing of General Ledger and Cost Element.

- Secondary cost element, which is used in cost accounting, is now part of GL and can now be created in GL.

- General ledger extension to incorporate all changes in SAP S4 HANA.

- Removal of transaction codes such as KA01, KA02, and so on, have been removed from the GL.

- New field that allows for G/L Account Type specification of how the G/L account can function in Financial Accounting (FI) and Controlling (CO).

- Fiori App applicable for managing G/L Account Master Data.

- GL master data account type classifications such as:

X-Balance Sheet Account (Balance Sheet Accounts).

N-Non-operating Expenses or Income (Profit & Loss accounts used only in FI).

P-Primary Costs or Revenue (this forms part of Profit and Loss accounts applicable in both FI and CO).

S-Secondary Costs (this forms part of Profit and Loss accounts applicable in both FI and CO).

S-Secondary Costs (Profit and Loss accounts used only in CO for internal reporting).

Let's look at how to create G/L accounts in SAP S4 HANA. In this activity, we will create G/L accounts manually. This will give us the fundamental understanding of how to create G/L accounts step-by-step. We will also look at how to copy G/L accounts using existing accounts as a template.

Note   All transactions in SAP FI work with GL Accounts.

Case Study: You are to create a G/L account for Office stationery supplies.

Creating a G/L Account – Office stationery supplies

Let's start by creating a G/L account for Office supplies. Use this menu path to go to the screen where you will create your G/L account: *IMG: Financial Accounting ➤ General Ledger ➤ Master Data ➤ GL Accounts ➤ G/L Account Creation and Processing ➤ Edit G/L Account Centrally.*

You can also get to the screen on the user side of the system by following this menu path: *SAP Easy Access: Accounting ➤ Financial Accounting ➤ General Ledger ➤ Master Records ➤ GL Accounts ➤ Individual Processing ➤ Centrally.*

The **Edit G/L Account Centrally** screen is displayed in Figure 5-1.

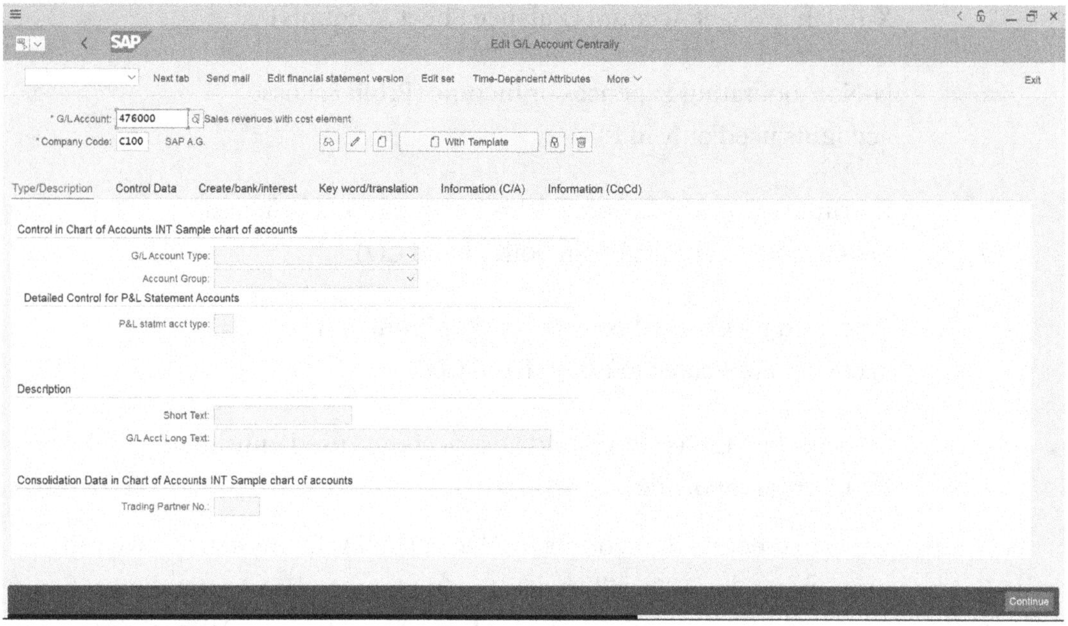

Figure 5-1. *The screen where you create your G/L account*

The **Edit G/L Accounts Centrally** has four important buttons that will help you create and navigate your G/L account:

Display ⌗ This button is used to display a G/L account already existing in the system. By clicking this button, the system will automatically display a list of all the G/L accounts in the system.

Change ✎ This button is used to change or edit G/L account details of existing G/L accounts. When you need to edit your G/L account click this button and the system will allow to edit your G/L account accordingly.

Create ▯ Tis button is used to create a new G/L account of your own from scratch.

Create with Template ▯ With Template This button allows you to copy an existing G/L account in the system using a template. This can be very handy if you want to copy similar G/L accounts because it allows the system to classify similar G/L accounts into the same account group and number range intervals.

Since we are creating our own G/L account, click the **Create** button and update the following fields:

G/L Account: Every G/L account in SAP S4 HANA must be assigned a number, which serves as the G/L account number. Enter your G/L account number in the G/L account field. The G/L account number you enter here is restricted to the length of the G/L account number you specified when customizing the "Create Chart of Accounts" section in Chapter 2. The G/L account number is used to reference the G/L account.

Company Code: Every company represented in SAP S4 HANA must be assigned a company code. Company codes are assigned to G/L accounts in the system. Enter your company code in the company code field. The company code you enter in this filed will allow you to assign a G/L account to your company code

---

Note   The number you enter in the G/L Account field must be within the number range intervals you defined for your account groups in Chapter 2.

The next step in this activity is to update the Description section of the screen. Click the **Create** button to activate the description section of the screen in Type/Description section of the screen.

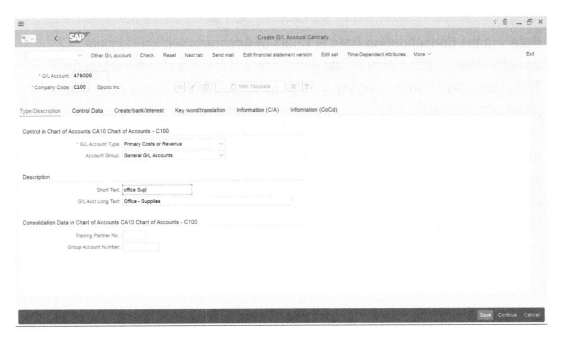

Figure 5-2. *Creating G/L account centrally in Chart of Accounts section*

Update the following fields:

Control in Chart of Accounts section of the screen

G/L Account type: When you click the dropdown arrow by the field, a list of account types is displayed. Select the appropriate account type from the list. In this activity, since we are creating a G/L account for Office supplies, we selected Primary Costs or Revenue as this best fit our requirements.

Account Group: Click the dropdown arrow at the right side of the screen and select the account group that fits your G/L accounts from the displayed account group list – General G/L Accounts.

In the Description section, enter a short text and a long text in each of the fields, respectively, as in Figure 5-2.

Description section of the screen

Short Text: When creating a G/L account, you need to give a short descriptive name to your G/L account. This will allow you to identify individual G/L accounts in your company code.

G/L Acct Long Text: Likewise, the G/L account long test account field will allow you to use a more detailed description for your G/L account.

Note   In the **Consolidation Data in Chart of Accounts** section in Figure 5-2, you can enter a trading partner and group account number for your G/L account. This is important if your company belongs to a group and prepares consolidated financial statements for its corporate group. In that case, you should enter the company code responsible for the preparation of the consolidated account for the corporate group in the **Trading Partner No**. field and enter the consolidated G/L account number in the **Group Account Number** field. The consolidated G/L accounts allows your organization to prepare consolidated financial statements for the corporate group in SAP S4 Hana.

The next step in this activity is to update the fields in the Control Data section of the screen.

Click the **Control Data** tab in the middle of the screen to go to the control section of the screen.

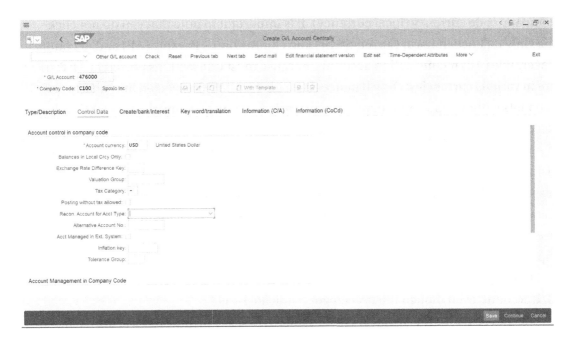

Figure 5-3. *Data control screen section of G/L Account*

Update the following fields in the Control Data screen:

Account control in company code Section

Account Currency: This is the company code section of the G/L account master record data where you specify the currency for your G/L accounts. It is important to use your company code local currency for your G/L account for each company code. The advantage of using local currency is that it allows postings to be made to the G/L account in any currency and then converted. Postings made in foreign currency are translated into local currency. However, you can also choose to specify foreign currency as your G/L account currency. The drawback to this approach is that posting to the G/L account can only be made in the foreign currency you have specified. The system automatically defaults to the local currency of your company code when creating a G/L account. In this activity we examined a US-based company, so the company code currency is USD (US Dollar).

Balances in Local Crcy Only: Select the Only Balances in Local Currency checkbox, if the transactions posted to this account must be maintained in local currency only. When you select this function, the system will display and manage all currencies in the G/L master record in local currency (i.e., the company code local currency). This is important if you do not want the system to post any exchange rate difference that may occur, but you want to clear several currencies arising from transactions with your company code currency (local currency). It is important to note that you do not click the Only Balance In Local Currency checkbox for Accounts Payable (AP) and Accounts Receivable (AR) reconciliation accounts, because most transactions posted in AP & AR are in various currencies. Only Balances In Local Currency is selected for Balance sheet accounts without open item management, cash discount account clearing, or Goods Received (GR)/ Invoice Receipts (IR) clearing accounts.

Tax Category: This function allows you to specify if the G/L account is tax relevant. Using the search function button next to the Tax Category field, select the appropriate tax symbol that you want to use in your G/L account from the displayed tax list. The Tax Category could either be input tax or output tax. For example, if input tax is selected, every posting to this G/L account must contain input tax. In this activity, we used in input tax "-" as the tax category.

Posting Without Tax Allowed: This allows postings without tax to be posted in the G/L account, even though the tax category indicate is set.

Recon. Account for Account type: In the G/L master record, you use the Reconciliation Account for Account Type dropdown menu to specify that the G/L account is a reconciliation account. This function allows you to select from a list of reconciliation account types, for example, Assets, Customers, Vendor, and so on. Once this option is set, the G/L account will be considered a reconciliation account by the system. It is advisable that you maintain at least one reconciliation in the general ledger. Every posting in the sub-ledger in SAP S4 HANA is automatically posted to a corresponding reconciliation account. The reconciliation accounts are updated with sub-ledger balances as soon as transactions are posted in the bus-ledger. This procedure allows you to generate financial statements at any time from the general ledger.

Open Item Management: By activating this checkbox in the G/L master record, when you display line items in an account, the system will display all line items in the account marked as open or cleared. This option is ideal if you want to see items not cleared, or outstanding balances at any given point in time in an account. This makes it possible for you to determine if a posting exists in the G/L account that needs offsetting against a particular business transaction (i.e., clearing an open item with payment).

Use open item management for the following accounts:

- Bank account.

- GR/IR Accounts.

- Salary accounts.

Sort key: When you enter a sort key in this field in the G/L account master record, it allows you to set the sort key according to the sort key number you assigned. In this activity, we used 001 as our sort key. SAP S4 HANA comes with a list of standard sort key you can choose from. The most commonly used sort keys are the first nine we listed below:

Sort Key	Description
001	Posting date
002	Doc. No, fiscal year
003	Document date
004	Branch account
005	Loc.currency amount
006	Doc.currency amount
007	Bill/exch.due date
008	Cost center
009	External doc.number

Note   You can access a detailed list of sort keys provided by SAP in the system by using the search function on the sort key field.

The system automatically fills the assigned field in the line item based on the sort key you assigned to your general ledger master (This is done in the company code segment of your company code). When you assign a posting date as your sort key, as we did in this activity, the system will automatically sort your line items based on your defined criteria according to posting date. Likewise, when you define a document date, the system will use the posting date to display your line items, and so on.

The final step in this activity is to assign a Field status group to the G/L account in the Control of document creation in the company code section. To go to the screen where you can do this, click **Create/bank interest** tab.

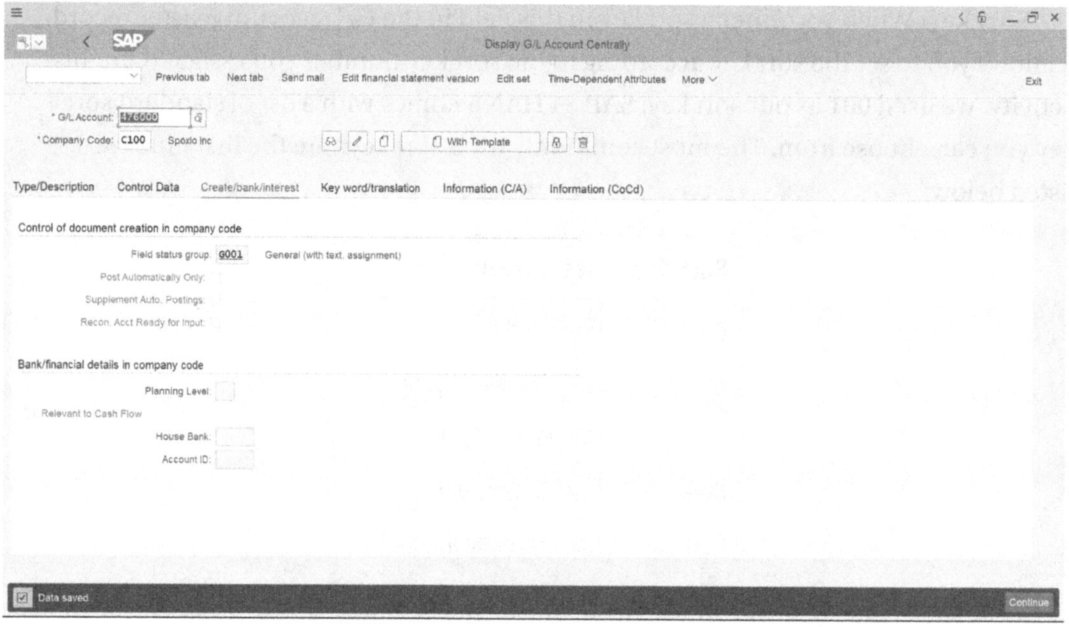

Figure 5-4. *Create/bank interest section of G/L account*

The field status group field determines whether a field should be suppressed, required, or optional during document entry. If a field is set to suppressed, users will not be able to enter data into it during document entry. If a field is set to required entry, users are required to enter data into the field during document entry. If optional entry is set for a field, users have the discretion to either enter data or not to enter data into the field. The field status groups are entered in the field status field of the general ledger master record in the company code-specific area of each G/L account.

A field status variant contains a field status group, and a field status group is assigned to a company code in SAP S4 HANA. SAP comes with predefined field status groups, which you can use as your field status variant. It is also possible to create your own field status group(s). However, we advise that you use the predefined field status group provided by SAP in the system. By creating your won field status group, you also have to define the associated tables, and this can be time consuming.

Figure 5-5 shows some predefined field status groups in SAP S4 HANA. You can also access this list by using the search function by the filed status group field.

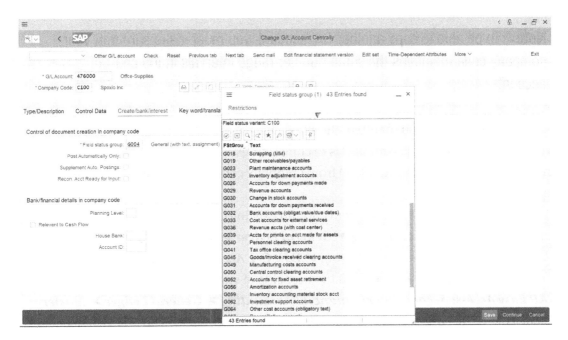

Figure 5-5. *A list of some of the standard SAP S4 HANA supplied field status groups*

Enter the field status group that meets your requirement in the **Field status group** field. In this activity, we used G004 – Cost accounts as our field status group. The reason we used G004 as the field status group is because office supplies is an expense, and when you post entries in the G/L account, the system will automatically ask for the cost center, which you have to enter in the cost center field of the document entry screen before you can post the document.

Once you have updated your screen, save your work by clicking the save button at the bottom right of the screen

Finally, in the next activity, we will be looking at how to create a G/L account with a template.

Creating G/L Account With Template

Creating a G/L account with a template allows you to copy an existing G/L account in the system from another company code using the With Template function. This can be very handy and make it easier for you to create G/L accounts by copying an existing G/L account and modifying it to meet your requirements.

Note   To be able to copy another G/L account, you must make sure that your company code maintains the same number range intervals in the chart of accounts.

Case study: Since you maintain the same chart of account number range interval with Company code 1000, your task is to copy Domestic Travels Expenses (flat Rate Input Tax) with G/L Account 474100 from company code 1000 and adapt it to meet your requirements.

To go to the screen where you will copy an existing G/L account follow this menu path: ***IMG: Financial Accounting ➤ General Ledger ➤ Master Data ➤ GL Accounts ➤ G/L Account Creation and Processing ➤ Edit G/L Account Centrally.***

You can also get to the screen on the user side of system by following this menu path: ***SAP Easy Access: Accounting ➤ Financial Accounting ➤ General Ledger ➤ Master Records ➤ GL Accounts ➤ Individual Processing ➤ Centrally.*** The Edit G/L Account Centrally is displayed in Figure 5-6.

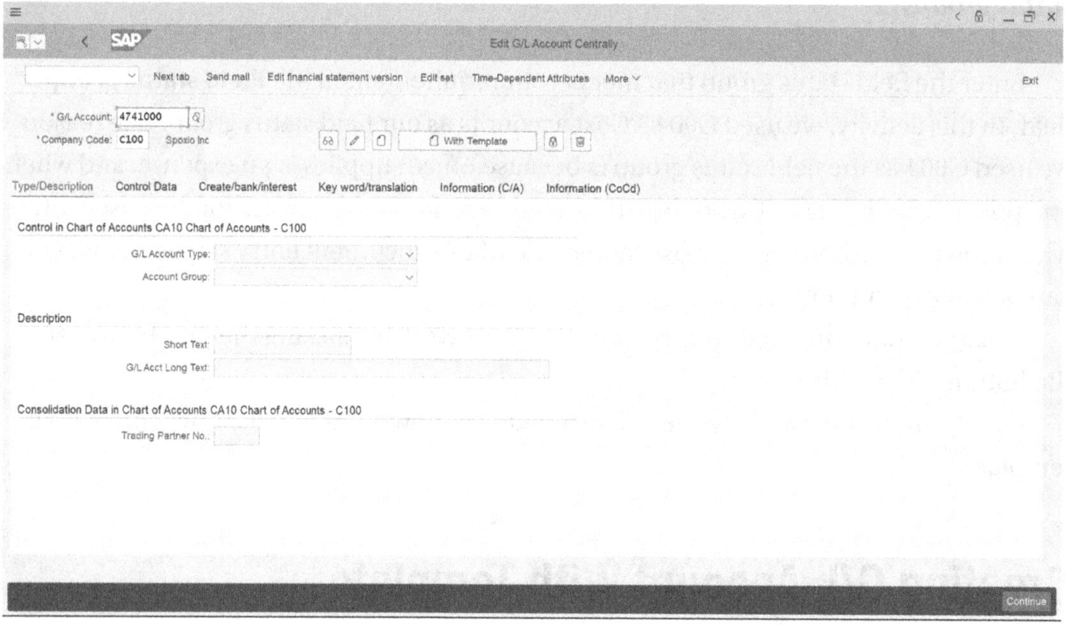

Figure 5-6. *Copying an existing G/L account*

Enter the G/L account you want to copy in the **G/L Account** field (474100) and enter your company code (C100) in the Company code field and Click the **With Template** button. The reference Account screen pops up (Figure 5-7).

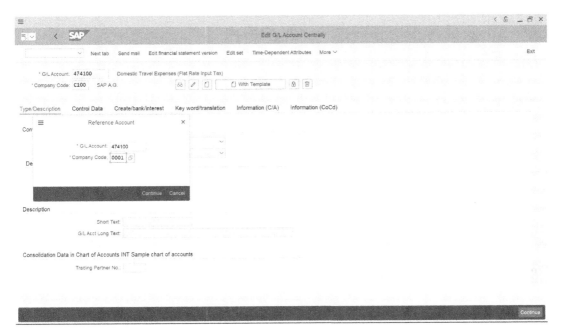

Figure 5-7. *Reference account screen*

Update the following fields:

G/L Account: Enter the G/L account you want to copy from the reference company you are copying in this field.

Company Code: Enter the reference company code of the company whose G/L account you want to copy in this field.

Click the continue button at the bottom of the screen. The G/L account you copied will be displayed in Figure 5-8.

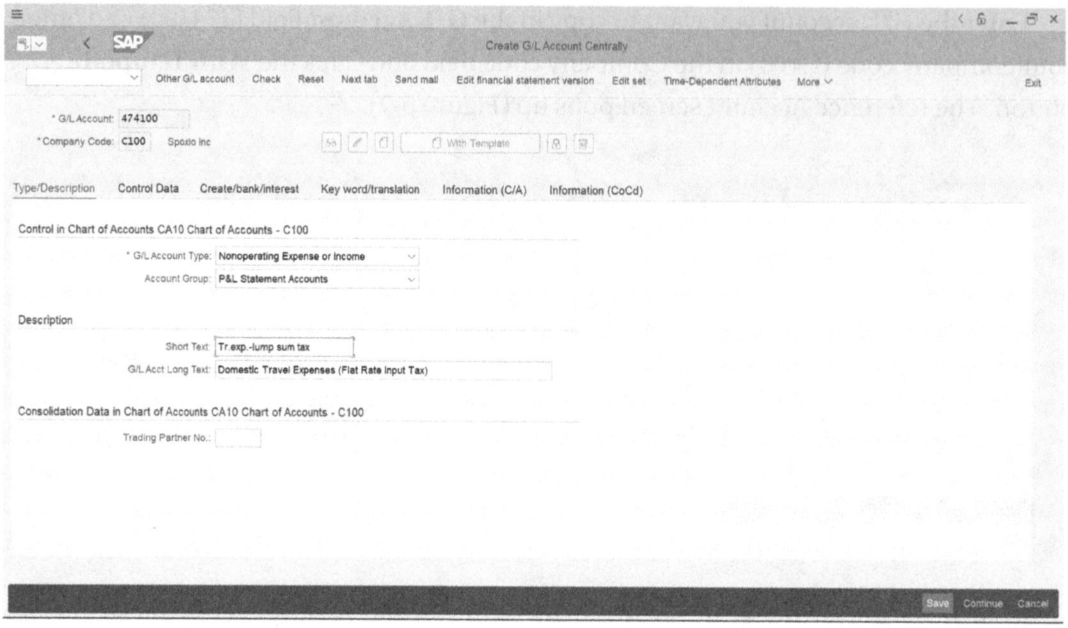

Figure 5-8. *Copied G/L account*

Save your work.

Summary

This chapter explained what a general ledger is and also described what a master record is. You went through the customization steps involved in creating a G/L account master record and learned to copy a G/L account using an existing G/L account as a template. You also looked at the relationship among G/L accounts, sub-ledger, and reconciliation accounts.

In the next chapter, you will learn how to set automatic open item clearing and how to define the exchange rate and foreign exchange rate valuations.

CHAPTER 6

Clearing Open Items

Objective

In this chapter, we will be looking at how to prepare automatic clearing for Open Items, define maximum exchange rate difference, and perform foreign currency valuation.

At the end of this chapter, you will be able to:

- Prepare Automatic Clearing.

- Create accounts for clearing differences.

- Define Maximum Exchange Rate.

- Specify settings for Currency Valuations.

Clearing Open Items

Transactions with business partners are said to be open or partially completed until full payments are made and related accounts are cleared. For example, a business partner sends in an invoice; the invoice is posted in the system. At this point, the transaction remains an open item in the account until payment of an equivalent amount of the invoice is made and the account is cleared.

Once payment is made and cleared with the associated open item, the system generates a document number. Only then is the transaction complete.

Account clearing can be carried out in SAP S4 HANA for an individual item or collective items in the system. Document clearing can be carried out manually or automatically using automatic clearing programs. Clearing open items manually means that the user performs the clearing process, whereas in automatic clearing, the system

101

© Andrew Okungbowa 2023
A. Okungbowa, *SAP S/4HANA Financial Accounting Configuration*,
https://doi.org/10.1007/978-1-4842-8957-0_6

performs the clearing automatically. For the system to carry out clearing automatically, you need to specify certain settings during customizing.

In this activity, we will be looking at how to customize automatic clearing and we will also look at the two options available in SAP S4 HANA on clearing open items in the system.

Types of open item clearing in the SAP ERP System:

- **Posting with clearing:** This is when an open item on an account is matched against payment and cleared to bring the account balance to nil. It is also possible to group open items, match them with payment, and clear them simultaneously. The system will mark these items as cleared items and assign a clearing document number and enter the date they are cleared in the system.

  Posting with clearing: In SAP S4 HANA, posting with clearing can be performed on an individual or on a group of items at the same time by assigning payment to open items. The net effect should be a nil balance (i.e., open items in the system are cleared with a payment simultaneously). Posting with clearing can be performed on an account type and several currencies at the same time by assigning payment to open items. When you use the posting with clearing option, the net effect should be that the business transactions end up with a zero balance. Open items and payment included in the clearing must be equal. For example, the balance on the account of 1,000USD must be equal to a payment receipt of 1,000USD.

  On the contrary, if the open item(s) and a payment is not equal, it is still possible to post the difference in the system. The system will treat the posting as a payment on the account and not as a cleared item. Payment on account is when the item remains in the system as an open item.

- **Account Clearing:** This functions with GL accounts and sub-ledgers managed in open item using an open item procedure. You don't need to post an item when performing account clearing. All you need to do is to select the items that balance out to zero. When you post them, the system flags the selected items as cleared and enters a clearing document number and clearing date for the cleared items.

Automatic Clearing Customizing

Problem: Your client's accounting staff want to be able to clear open items in SAP S4 HANA using the automatic clearing function. Your task is to customize the settings that will allow users to clear open items using the automatic function.

In this activity, you will define account types for customers, vendors, and general ledger account, and set the criteria for assignment number (used in relation to sort key, which enables the automatic clearing process in FI), business area and trading partners (used to control vendor/customer payment/transaction) for grouping an account with open items for automatic clearing. Once these settings are made, the system clearing program will look for open items in local currency that equal a zero balance, group them together, and clear them simultaneously. The system will generate a clearing number and clearing date and enter them in the cleared document.

For automatic clearing to be carried out, you have to define the following criteria:

- Account type.

- Account number.

You also have the option of defining up to five additional criteria in the field table.

You have the choice of creating your own automatic clearing or to copy existing ones supplied by SAP and modify them to meet your requirement.

To customize the automatic clearing program, follow this menu path: ***IMG: Financial Accounting ➤ General Ledger Accounting ➤ Business Transactions ➤ Open Item Clearing ➤ Prepare Automatic Clearing***

The ***Change View "Additional Rules For Automatic Clearing": Overview*** Screen is displayed, Choose New Entries at the top left side of the screen (Figure 6-1).

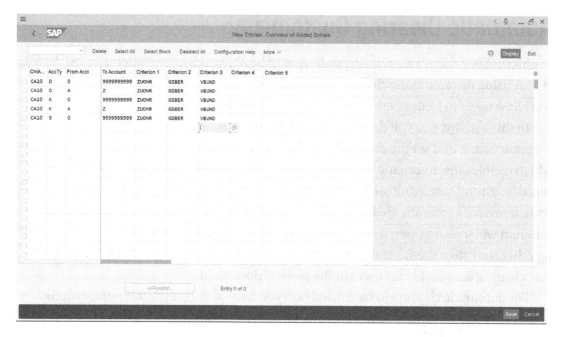

Figure 6-1. *Defining additional rules for automatic clearing*

Update the following fields:

Chart of Accounts: Enter your chart of accounts in this field. This is the four-digit character you defined in Chapter 2

Account Type: Enter the account type in this field. In SAP S4 HANA, account types are represented by letters such as: – **D (customer), V (Vendor), and S (General Ledger),** respectively.

From account /to account: Specify account range for each activity type for internal and external number range assignments. For Internal number Assignment use number range: **From account - 0 to account - 99999999999** and for External Number range assignment use number range: **From account - A to Account - Z**

Criterion 1-3: *Define the criteria for open item clearing for the information in the table below:*

Criterion 1 – ZUONR	Criterion 2 – GSBER	Criterion 3 – VBUND

Click the Save button at the bottom right of the screen to save your work. When your work is saved, the system will notify you that customizing was saved on the status bar at the bottom of the screen.

> **Note**   Account Type D – Debtors
>
> Account Type K – Vendor and
>
> Account Type S – General Ledger
>
> Criterion ZUONR – Assignment
>
> GSBER – Business Area
>
> VBUND – Trading Partner

In the next activity in this chapter, we will look at how to assign a G/L account for automatic clearing. This is an important aspect of the customizing process, as it gives you the opportunity to see how the G/L accounts are assigned to automatic clearing.

Create Accounts for Clearing differences

Chapter 4 looked at the three levels of tolerances represented in SAP S4 HANA, namely:

- Tolerance groups for G/L accounts.

- Tolerance groups for employees.

- Tolerance for customers/vendors.

You have also defined limits for acceptable payment differences during posting by setting the maximum amount per document that is permitted for posting, the maximum amount employees are authorized to post per open item in customer/vendor account item, and the maximum cash discount an employee is permitted to grant to business partners. During account clearing, the system will check the tolerance groups to ascertain if the differences are within acceptable limits and automatically post the difference to predefined accounts.

In this activity, you will assign a G/L account to a G/L account for posting payment differences. To begin the customizing process, follow this menu path: ***IMG: Financial Accounting ➤ General Ledger Accounting ➤ Business Transactions ➤ Open Item Clearing ➤ Clearing Differences ➤ Create Accounts for Clearing Differences.***

The **Enter Chart of Accounts** dialog box comes up. Enter your chart of accounts key in the **Chart of Accounts** field and click the Continue button at the right of the screen. The **Configuration Accounting Maintain: Automatic Posts – Rules** screen appears

(Figure 6-2). This is where you will activate the automatic posting rules to determine if accounts are posted as debit or credit and also where you include a tax code with your account assignment.

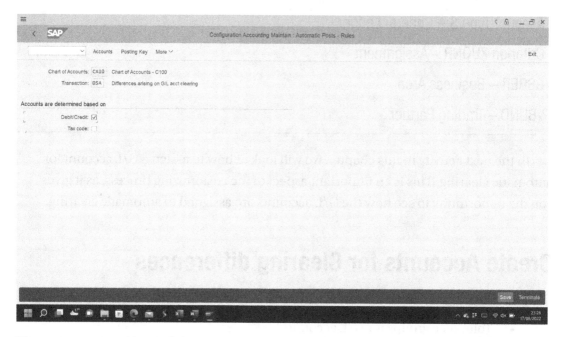

Figure 6-2. *Specifying debit/credit for account determination*

Click the Debit/Credit check box in the **Accounts are determined based on** section of the screen (Figure 6-2). This function allows you to assign G/L accounts for both debit and credit to automatic posting. If you activate the **Tax code** field, you will also need to specify your tax code. The Tax code you specify will be applied to the G/L account. If you leave your tax code blank, this means that all tax codes can be posted in the G/L account you assign for payment differences. Click the button at the bottom right of the screen to save your work.

The Configuration Accounting Maintain: Autom: Automatic Posts – Accounts screen comes up. This screen will allow you to specify the G/L account for posting payment differences for automatic postings.

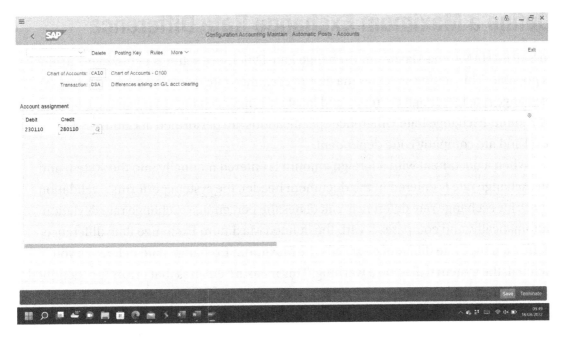

Figure 6-3. *Assigning G/L account to for automatic posting*

Enter the G/L account you created for G/L account clearing differences for debit transactions (in this activity we used 230110 as our G/L account debit clearing differences) in the Debit field in the account assignment section of the screen. Likewise, enter the G/L account you created for G/L account clearing differences for credit transactions (in this activity we used 280110 as our G/L account credit clearing differences) in the Credit field in the account assignment section of the screen and save your work.

Note   To be able to assign a G/L account, you must first create the G/L accounts for your account assignment for automatic postings for both debit and credit for posting clearing differences. If you have not done this yet, the system will not accept your G/L account. However, to overcome this bottleneck in the interim, press enter on your keyboard several time to force the system to accept the G/L accounts you have entered for your Debit and Credit clearing differences in the interim and save your work.

Define a Maximum Exchange Rate Difference

In SAP S4 HANA, the Maximum Exchange Rate Difference settings per foreign currency is possible. This setting specifies maximum exchange rate deviation allowed between exchange rate for foreign currency and local currency exchange in percentage terms. Maximum Exchange Rate Difference specifications are performed at Company Code level and are company code dependent.

When a document with a foreign amount is entered manually into the system and an exchange rate is entered in the document header, the system performs a validation check for exchange rate deference, calculates the percentage exchange rate deviation automatically, and compares it with the defined Maximum Exchange Rate difference. If the exchange rate difference exceeds the Maximum Exchange Rate deference you defined, the system will issue a warning. This measure ensures that errors are identified and rectified during posting.

For example, if 10% is specified as the maximum exchange rate difference, when the exchange rate exceeds the specified rate, the system will automatically identify this and issue a warning message.

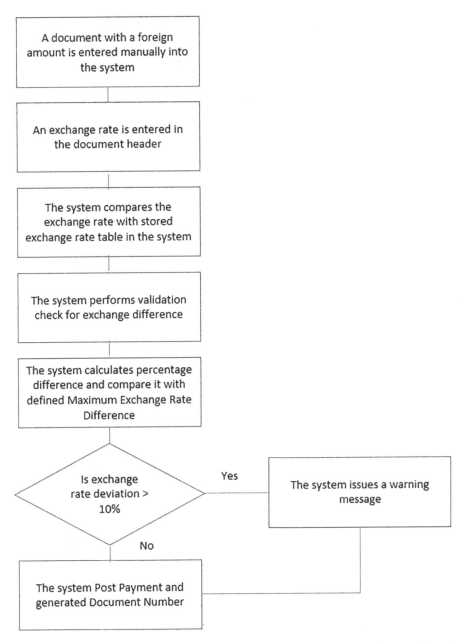

Figure 6-4. *A flowchart diagram depicting how Maximum Exchange Rate is processed in SAP S4 HANA*

Now let's explore how this maximum exchange rate difference customizing is carried out in SAP S4 HANA. To define maximum exchange rate difference follow this menu path: ***IMG: Financial Accounting ➤ Financial Accounting Global Settings ➤ Global Parameters for Company Code ➤ Currencies ➤ Maximum Exchange Rate Difference ➤ Define Maximum Exchange Rate Difference per Company Code.***

The **Change View "Maximum Difference Between Exchange Rates" Overview** screen is displayed (Figure 6-5).

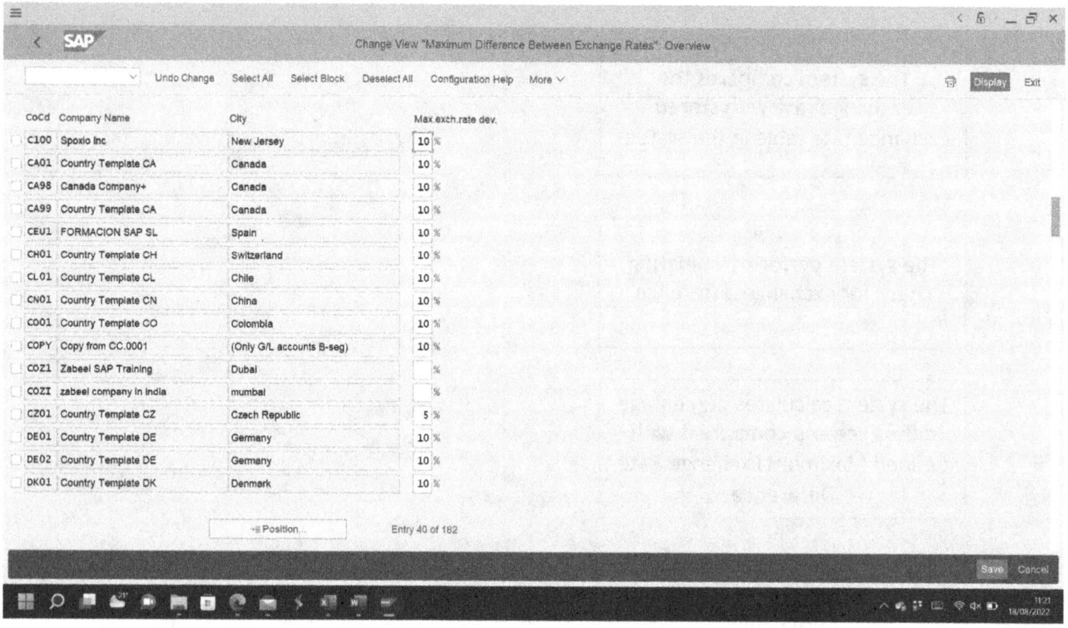

Figure 6-5. *Specification of maximum exchange rate difference*

Search for your company code using the position button at the bottom of the screen, your company code will be displayed on top of the displayed list of all the company codes in the system (you could use the scroll bar on the left side of the screen to look for your company code if you chose to do so instead of using the position button). Enter the maximum exchange rate agreed with your client in the **Max.exch.rate dev**. (maximum exchange rate deviation) field. In this activity, we used 10%. The model companies used by SAP in the system suggest 10% as the ideal maximum exchange rate deviation.

Save your customizing of Maximum exchange rate deviation by clicking the Save button at the bottom right of the screen.

Check Company Code Setting

Note   We advise that you should check your company code setting at this point. Although this is not a part of your customizing exercise, it will be interesting to see the customizing of your company code so far. This will also give you the opportunity to see the items you missed in your customizing and correct them and to also activate some functions considered important.

To see your company code settings, follow this menu path: ***IMG: Financial Accounting ➤ Financial Accounting Global Settings ➤ Global Parameters Company Code ➤ Enter Global Parameters***. The Change View "Company Code Global Data": Overview screen is displayed with the list of company codes in the system. Search for your company code using the position button at the bottom of your screen.

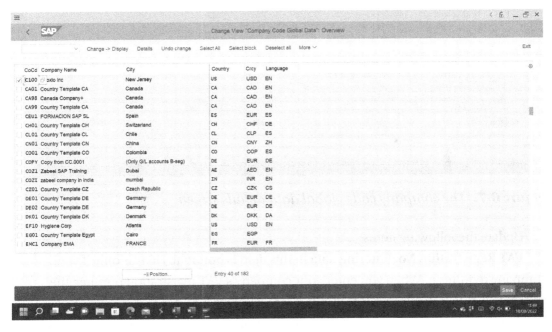

Figure 6-6. *Company code global data overview screen*

Your company code will be displayed at the top of the list of company codes in the system. Select your company code by clicking the checkbox in front of your company code and click the **Details** button at the top of the screen to go to the **Change View "Company Code Global Data": Overview** screen where you will view your company code settings (Figure 6-7).

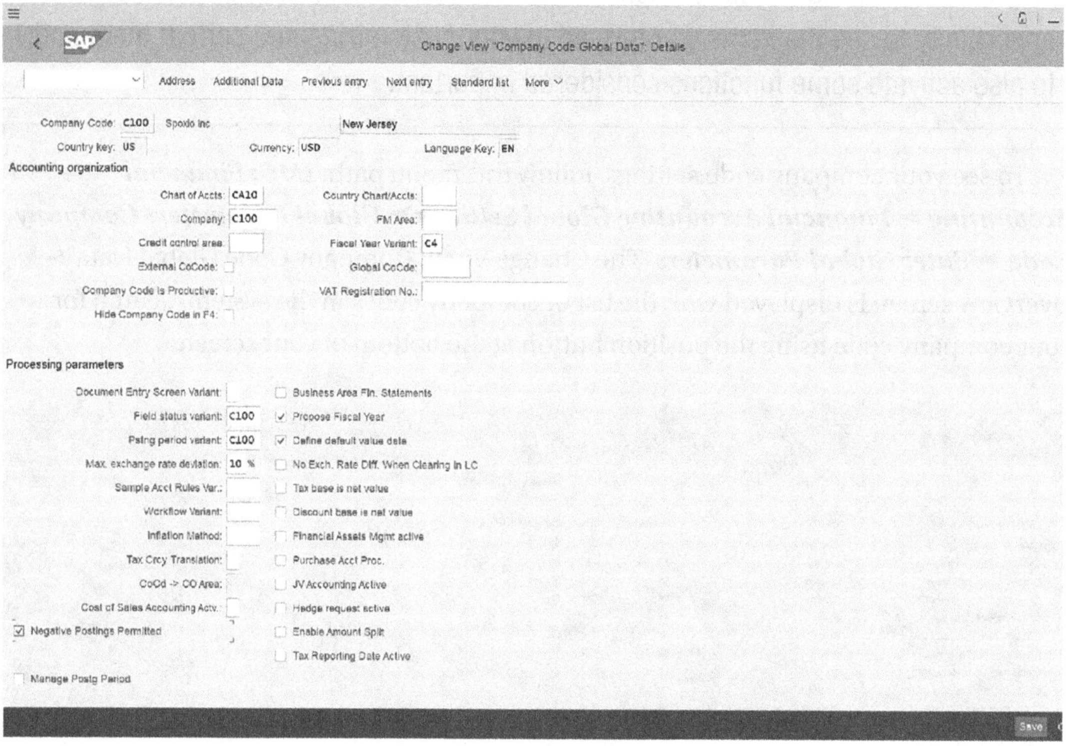

Figure 6-7. *The company code global data details screen*

Update the following items:

VAT Registration No: Entering data in this field is optional. Do this only if your company requires it. When you enter your company's VAT registration number, the system will automatically use this number for VAT correspondence.

Propose Fiscal Year: This field is optional. When you click this checkbox, the system will automatically propose a fiscal year during document entry.

Define Default Value Date: This is setting is also optional. When you select it during document entry, the system will automatically propose a current date when entering a document into the system.

Negative Postings Permitted: When this checkbox is clicked, this will allow you to reserve transactions in the system without posting the reversed document and the associated reversal document. In other words, the original transaction figures in the system will stay the same as above.

Save your company code setting.

Foreign Currency Valuation

Problem: The accounting staff wants to be able to maintain foreign currency and valuate open items in foreign currencies. Your task is to explain to the accounting staff what the exchange rate type is, to define the valuation methods, and to perform other settings that will allow the accounting staff to achieve their objectives.

In SAP S4 HANA to create a financial statement, you need to define Foreign Currency Valuation. The importance of defining Foreign Currency Valuation is that foreign currency balance sheets and open items in foreign currency are valuated as part of foreign currency valuation.

Once you have defined your foreign currency valuation and specified the appropriate accounts, the system will take the following accounts and items into consideration:

- G/L accounts in foreign currency relating to foreign currency balance sheet accounts.

- Open items posted in foreign currency.

You also have the option of either performing currency valuation in Group Currency (i.e., parallel currency) or in Company Code Currency.

It is recommended that you use average exchange rate type – *M* in your valuation method.

In this activity, you will define the valuation method for open item and group together with the specifications needed for balance and individual valuation. Before running your valuation procedure, the required valuation method must be specified.

Exchange Rate Types

The different exchange rates for each currency pair are defined in the system and are differentiated by exchange rate type. The following exchange rate types are represented in SAP S4 HANA using the following symbols:

- Bank selling rate – B (bank selling rate between currency pair).

- Bank buying rate – G (bank buying rate between currency pair).

- Average rate – M (average between selling rate and buying rate). You can obtain selling rate or buying rate using average rate as the spread. This is done by adding or deducting the spread from the average rate.

Exchange rate types will be discussed further in the next chapter.

Define Valuation Methods

Valuation methods determine the method used to perform foreign currency valuation, which constitutes part of the closing procedures in SAP S4 HANA.

In this activity you will create foreign currency valuation for.

1) Valuation Method for Customer & Vendor.

2) Valuation Method for Bank Balance.

In SAP S4 HANA, you have a list of valuation procedures to choose from. For example, the lowest value principle, the strict lowest value, and so on.

Now let's create foreign currency valuation methods for open items for customers/vendors maintained in foreign currency. To go to the screen where you do this, follow this menu path: *IMG: Financial Accounting* ➤ *General Ledger Accounting* ➤ *Periodic Processing* ➤ *Valuate* ➤ *Define valuation methods.*

The *Change View "Foreign Currency Valuation Methods": Overview* Screen is displayed (Figure 6-8).

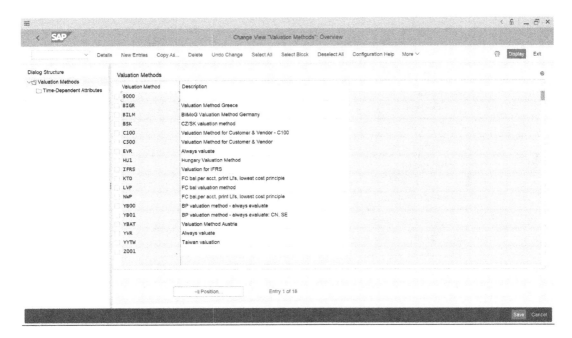

Figure 6-8. *The initial screen for foreign currency valuation methods*

Click the New Entries button at the top of the screen to go to the **New Entries: Details of Added Entries** screen, where you will specify your currency valuation method.

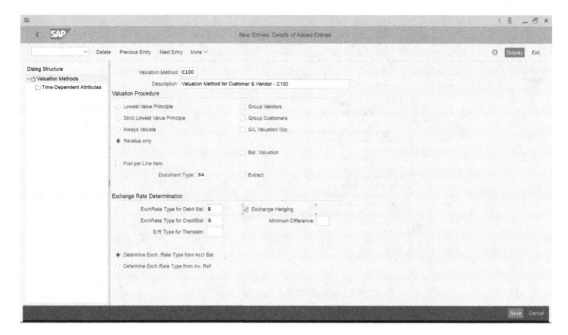

Figure 6-9. *Foreign currency valuation methods for customer/vendor*

As part of the customizing valuation method, you need to update the following fields on the screen.

Valuation Method: Enter a four-digit code as the key for your valuation method. This identifies your valuation method.

Description: Enter a short text description that best describes your valuation method.

Lowest Value Principle: The valuation calculation is carried out per item total. When this valuation procedure is set, the valuation is displayed only if exchange loss occurs (when the difference between local currency amount and the valued amount is negative).

Strict Lowest Value Principle: Valuation calculation is carried out per item total. The valuation is displayed only if the new valuation has a greater devaluation and/or revaluation for credit entries than the previous valuation.

Always Valuate: Allows revaluation to be taken into consideration.

Revalue Only: With this procedure, revaluation is considered when there is exchange loss.

Document Type: Enter an appropriate document type in this field. This is the key that distinguishes business transactions in SAP ERP. For example, SA is the G/L document type.

Exchange Type for Debit Bal: Enter B (the standard transaction at bank selling rate) in this field. This exchange rate type takes into consideration the valuation of foreign currency items having a positive balance.

Exch.Rate Type for Credit Bal: Enter G (the standard transaction at bank buying rate) in this field. Unlike the standard transaction at bank selling rate, this exchange rate type takes into consideration the valuation of foreign currency items having a negative balance.

Exchange Hedging: By clicking this checkbox, it means that you want the system to value your foreign exchange items at a hedged exchange rate. Hedging is a procedure employed to eliminating risk that may arise from business transactions in foreign currencies.

Determine Exch.Rate Type from Acct Bal: When this radio button is activated currency valuations are carried out based on account balances.

Determine Exch.Rate Type from Inv. Ref: When you click this radio button currency valuations are conducted based on currency valuation based on balance with reference to invoice reference.

Hit enter on your keyboard and save your customization using the Save button at the bottom right of the screen.

The next step in the foreign currency valuation method customization is to create a foreign currency valuation for bank balance. Use this menu path: ***IMG: Financial Accounting ➤ General Ledger Accounting ➤ Periodic Processing➤ Valuate ➤ Define valuation methods.*** The ***Change View "Foreign Currency Valuation Methods": Overview*** Screen is displayed. Click the New Entries button at the top of the screen to go to the **New Entries: Details of Added Entries** screen.

Use Figure 6-10 to update the screen.

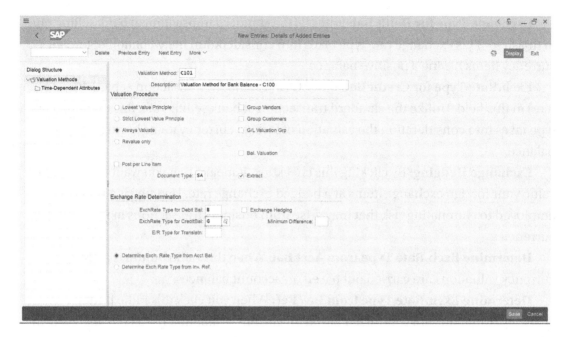

Figure 6-10. *Foreign currency valuation method for bank balance*

Note   Valuation method is unique. You cannot use the same valuation key twice. Hence we used a different valuation method identification key for our valuation method for bank balance as opposed to the one we used for the valuation method for customer/vendor.

Prepare Automatic Postings for Foreign Currency Valuation

Exchange rate differences normally arise when valuating open items in foreign currency. The settings here will allow the system to automatically Post Exchange rate differences arising from open items valuation and foreign currency balance to the accounts you specify. This exercise is simply assigning G/L accounts to where you want the system to post exchange rate differences.

To go to the screen where you will customize automatic postings for foreign currency valuation, follow this menu path: ***IMG: Financial Accounting ➤ General Ledger Accounting ➤ Periodic Processing➤ Valuate ➤ Foreign Currency Valuation ➤ Prepare Automatic Postings for Foreign Currency Valuation.*** The ***Configuration Accounting Maintain Automatic Posts – Procedure*** screen is displayed (Figure 6-11). The screen contains a list of exchange rate procedures and transaction key that you can choose from that you assign to accounts.

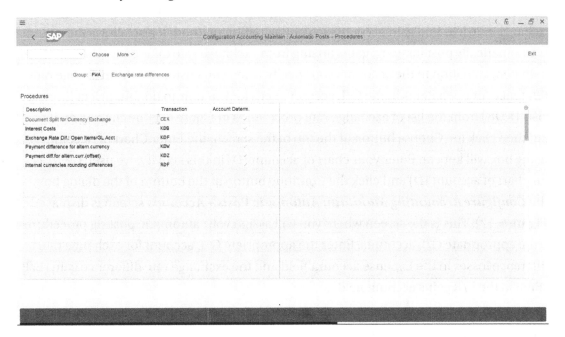

Figure 6-11. *A list of exchange procedures for exchange differences*

In this activity, we will be looking at two exchange rate procedures and transaction keys, namely:

- Interest costs (KDB).

- Exchange rate difference for open items (accounts receivable/ Payable)/GL account.

Interest Costs Using Exchange Rate key (KDB)

When valuating open items, such as business transactions, foreign exchange rate differences can be losses or gains. Exchange rate difference loss is an expense and is posted to the Foreign Exchange Loss account. Likewise, foreign exchange differences realized are posted to the Foreign Exchange Gain account and to a Balance Sheet Adjustment account.

The Interest Costs Using Exchange Rate Key (KDB) process allows you to assign exchange rate loss and gain accounts to your valuation method. It also allows the system to automatically post losses or gains arising from exchange rate differences during open item valuation to the accounts you specify when you customize the exchange rate difference for open items in the G/L account. Let's look at how to do this. Select Interest costs (KDB) from the list of exchange rate procedures in Figure 6-11 by clicking on it and then click the Choose button at the top of the screen; the Enter Chart of Accounts dialog box will appear. Enter your chart of account ID (in this activity, we used CA10 as our chart of account ID) and click the Continue button at the bottom of the dialog box. The ***Configure Accounting Maintain: Automatic Posts – Accounts*** screen is displayed (Figure 6-12). This is the screen where you will assign your automatic posting procedures to the appropriate G/L accounts. Enter the appropriate G/L account for exchange rate difference losses in the Expense account field and the exchange rate difference gain (E/R gains) in the E/R gains account field.

Note   If you have not created the G/L accounts for Exchange rate difference (Expense account and E/R gain account). When you enter a G/L account in any of the fields, the system will tell you that "No matches found." We advise that you should create the appropriate G/L accounts before attempting this exercise. However, you can bypass this by pressing Enter on your keyboard several times to force the system to accept the G/L accounts numbers you have entered in each of the fields and then you can create the G/L accounts later.

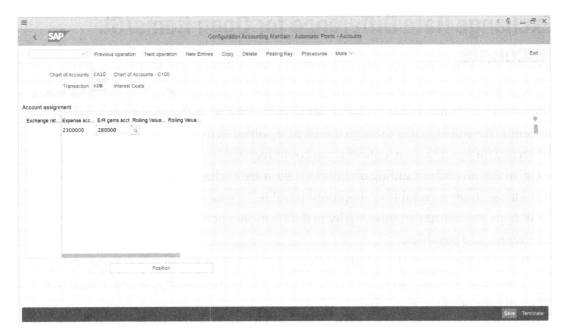

Figure 6-12. *Assigning G/L accounts for automatic posting of exchange rate difference*

Note   Leave the first column (the Exchange Rate Difference Key) blank. If you enter a key here, you will have to specify it in the related G/L account master record; otherwise, your foreign currency valuation account will not work.

Enter your GL Account for exchange expense – 230000 in Expense Account column and also enter your GL Account for exchange rate gain – 280000 in E/R gains acct column as above.

Let's look at how to assign Exchange rate difference for Open items – Account receivable and payable.

Exchange Rate Difference for Open Items/GL Accounts

In the next activity, we will explore how to maintain exchange rate differences for open items for account receivable and account payable for automatic posting to the G/L accounts. We will be going through the steps involved in maintaining exchange rate difference for open items accounts for account receivable and account payable. This will give you an understanding on how to customize exchange rate difference for open items for account receivable and account payable. In your spare time, you can follow the same steps you learned in this activity to define more open items for all your account receivables and payables.

First, let's look at how to maintain exchange rate difference for open items and the appropriate G/L accounts where the system will automatically post exchange rate difference for account receivable.

The settings you carried out in this activity will allow the system to automatically Post Exchange rate differences to the assigned GL accounts when valuating open items and foreign currency balance for accounts receivable.

You define the exchange rate difference for open items for account receivable using a foreign business partner as an example. Click on **Exchange rate Dif: Open Items/G/L Acc – KDF** from the list of exchange rate procedures, as in Figure 6-11, to select it and click the Choose button at the top of the screen to proceed to the screen where you will carry out your customization. The Enter Chart of Accounts dialog box appears. Enter your chart of account ID (in this activity we used CA10 as our chart of account ID) and click the Continue button at the bottom of the screen). The **Change View "Acct Determination for OI Exch. Rate Differences" Overview** appears. Click the New Entries button at the top left of the screen to go to **New Entries: Details of Added Entries** screen (Figure 6-13) where you will assign your G/L accounts to exchange rate difference for open items.

Update the following fields:

Chart of Accounts: The chart of accounts you enter in this field will allow you to assign the G/L accounts created in this chart of accounts to the appropriate fields (G/L account, Loss, Gain Val.loss 1, Val.gainl and Bal.sheet adj. l) and allow the system to carry out automatic postings to the specified GIL accounts.

G/L Account: Enter a G/L account for account receivable. This is the GIL account to be updated. In this activity, we used a GIL account for Trade Debtor (Foreign).

Loss: Assign the G/L account where losses arising from exchange rate differences are realized and posted.

Gain: Assign the G/L account where gains arising from exchange rate differences are realized and posted.

Val.loss 1: Assign the G/L account where you want losses arising from foreign currency valuation to be posted.

Val.gain 1: Assign the G/L account where you want gains arising from foreign currency valuation to be posted.

BS Adjustment Gain 1: Open items valuation of foreign currency adjustments of receivables and payables are posted in the G/L account you enter in this field.

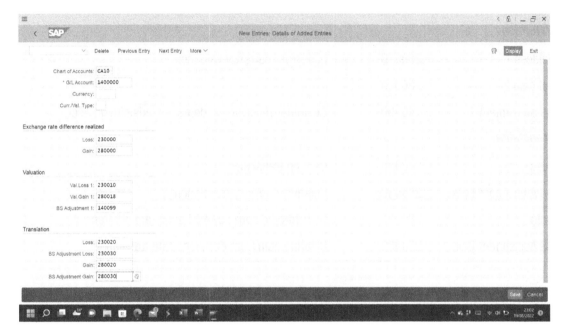

Figure 6-13. *Specifications for automatic posting procedures for G/L accounts*

Table 6-1 lists the G/L accounts used in this activity.

Table 6-1. *List of G/L accounts for automatic posting procedures – Account Receivables*

Fields	Values	Description
Chart of Accounts	CA10	This is defaulted, otherwise, enter it manually from your chart of account
G/L Account	141000	Customer – foreign receivables
Exchange rate difference realized		
Loss	230000	Loss from exchange rate differences
Gain	280000	Gain from currency exchange rate differences
Valuation		
Val.loss 1	230010	Loss from currency valuation
Val.gain 2	280010	
BS adjustment 1	140099	Customer receivables, domestic (adjustment acct)
Translation		
Loss	230020	Loss on translation
BS Adjustment Loss	230030	Clearing-currency translation
Gain	280020	Gain-foreign currency exchange rate differences
BS Adjustment Gain	280030	Clearing gain from exchange rate translation

After updating the **New Entries: Details of Added Entries** screen (Figure 6-13), Save your customization.

Note   If you have not created the G/L accounts for posting **Exchange Rate Difference for Open Items to GL Accounts,** when you enter a G/L account in any of the fields, the system will tell you that "No matches found." We advise that you should create the appropriate G/L accounts before attempting this exercise. However, you can bypass this by pressing enter on your keyboard several times to force the system to accept the G/L accounts numbers you have entered in each of the fields and then you can create the G/L accounts later. Please refer to Chapter 5 on how to create G/L accounts.

Finally, let's use the customize exchange rate differences for open items for account payable.

Exchange Rate Differences for Open Items – Account Payable

The setting you make here will allow the system to automatically post exchange rate differences to the assigned G/L accounts when valuating open items and foreign currency balances for accounts payable.

On the Configuration Accounting Maintain: Automatic Posts – Procedure shown earlier in Figure 6-11, Click on **Exchange rate Dif: Open Items/G/L Acc – KDF** from the list of exchange rate procedures, select it and click the Choose button at the top of the screen to proceed to the screen where you will carry out your customization. The Enter Chart of Accounts dialog box appears. Enter your chart of account ID (in this activity, we used CA10 as our chart of account ID) and click the Continue button at the bottom of the screen. The **Change View "Acct Determination for OI Exch. Rate Differences" Overview** screen appears. Click the New Entries button at the top left of the screen to go to the **New Entries: Details of Added Entries** screen (Figure 6-13) where you will assign your G/L accounts to exchange rate difference for open items.

Note   If you have not created the G/L accounts for posting **Exchange Rate Difference for Open Items to GL Accounts**, when you enter a G/L account in any of the fields, the system will tell you that "No matches found." We advised that you should create the appropriate G/L accounts before attempting this exercise. However, you can bypass this by pressing Enter on your keyboard several times to force the system to accept the G/L accounts numbers you have entered in each of the fields and then you can create the G/L accounts later. Please refer to Chapter 5 on how to create G/L accounts.

Using the data in Table 6-2 update the screen.

Table 6-2. *List of G/L accounts for automatic posting procedures – Account Payables*

Fields	Values	Description
Chart of Accounts	CA10	This is defaulted, otherwise, enter it manually from your chart of account
G/L Account	160000	Accounts payable-domestic
Exchange rate difference realized		
Loss	230000	Loss from exchange rate differences
Gain	280000	Gain from currency exchange rate differences
Valuation		
Val.loss 1	230010	Loss from currency valuation
Val.gain 2	280010	
BS adjustment 1	160099	Accounts payable-domestic, adjustments
Translation		
Loss	230020	Loss on translation
BS Adjustment Loss	280030	Clearing-currency translation
Gain	280020	Gain-foreign currency exchange rate differences
BS Adjustment Gain	280030	Clearing gain from exchange rate translation

Summary

This chapter explained how to clear open items in SAP ERP. As part of the discussion, you learned how business transactions are generated and posted in the system as open items, and how open items are cleared with payments. You learned about various ways of clearing open items in SAP ERP.

These included posting with clearing (when payments are matched with open items in the system to achieve a nil balance) and account clearing (by selecting a group of items and matching them against a payment results in nil balance). We went on to show you how to customize settings for automatic clearing. As part of the automatic clearing configuration, you learned how to define account types for customers, vendors, and G/L accounts and set criteria for assignment, business areas, and trading partners for grouping an account with open items for automatic clearing. You also looked at maximum exchange rate difference settings per foreign currency in a company code. You saw how the maximum exchange rate differences you specify are executed in the system.

You also learned how to check your company code settings in the global parameters to ensure that you did not omit important settings. The process you used was the Negative Posting Permitted checkbox.

It allows you to reverse transactions in the system without altering the original transaction figures.

Before creating a financial statement, it is important that you define foreign currency valuation, so that the foreign currency balance sheet and open items in foreign currencies are valuated as part of foreign currency valuation. You also learned how to define foreign currency valuation and specify the appropriate accounts the system will use during that valuation.

Finally, you looked at how to prepare automatic postings for foreign exchange valuation that will allow the system to post exchange rate differences to appropriate G/L accounts automatically.

The next chapter looks at how to maintain an exchange rate in SAP ERP that will allow you to translate amounts into the appropriate currency. In the process, you will maintain the relationship between currency pair using appropriate ratios.

CHAPTER 7

Maintaining Currency Types and Currency Pairs

In this chapter, you will be looking at how to customize local and foreign currencies for company codes. At the end of this chapter, you will be able to:

- Maintain exchange rate types.

- Define a standard quotation for exchange rates.

- Enter prefixes for direct/indirect quotation exchange rates.

- Define translation ratios for currency translation.

Currencies

Generally, accounting transactions are measured in monetary terms. SAP S4 HANA also adopted this principle. As a result, it is important that you specify a currency for each transaction you enter in the system. In order for the system to manage the currency ledgers, during document entry users (accounting clerks responsible for data entry in the system) must specify a standard currency code during data entry. The International Organization Standardization (ISO) sets these currency codes, such as USD for United States of America Dollar, GBP for British Pound sterling, and so on. The company code currency is usually referred to in SAP S4 HANA as the local currency; other currencies are termed foreign currencies.

SAP S4 HANA is dynamic in the sense that it allows you to simultaneously maintain ledgers in parallel currencies in conjunction with the company code currency (local currency), for example, either in group currency or hard currency.

© Andrew Okungbowa 2023
A. Okungbowa, *SAP S/4HANA Financial Accounting Configuration*,
https://doi.org/10.1007/978-1-4842-8957-0_7

You need to maintain exchange rates in order for the system to translate amounts into appropriate currencies. It is important to maintain the relationship between currencies per currency types and currency pair applying appropriate ratios. Inflation can affect the relationship between currencies; hence it is ideal to perform the translation ratio periodically.

As part of your customizing exercise, you will define the following items:

- Standard quotation for exchange rates.

- Prefixes for direct/indirect quotation exchange rates.

- Translation ratios for currency translation.

SAP S4 HANA uses two major currency quotations for currency translation: direct and indirect quotations. In addition to translating amounts into appropriate currencies, exchange rates can also be used for valuation, conversion, transactions, and planning.

Exchange Rate types:

In SAP S4 HANA, several exchange rates are defined and stored for each currency pair. Several exchange rates are held in the system. Hence the differentiation between exchange rates in the system is very important. An exchange rate type serves as the mechanism by which exchange rate are differentiated (Figure 7-1).

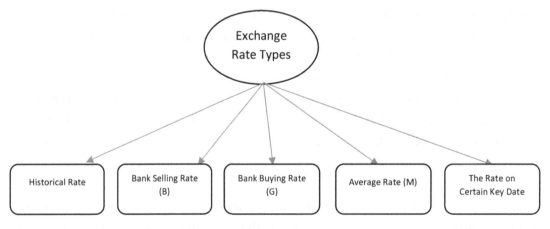

Figure 7-1. *Available exchange types*

When you are maintaining exchange rate for exchange rate type you can use one of the following tools:

- **Inversion:** Use to calculate an opposite rate from a given exchange rate. The drawback with this inversion is that the calculation based on an opposite rate is inadequate; therefore, it is recommended that you do not use for average rate (M)

- **Base currency:** The currency type (for example, USD) that you use in currency pair for foreign currency translation for a given exchange rate type. This is ideal when you have to translate between several currencies. By using a base currency, you can simplify the problem involved in maintaining several exchange rates.

- **Exchange rate spread:** The constant difference between exchange rate types. For example, the difference between the average rate and bank selling or bank buying rate.

SAP gives you the flexibility to either use direct or indirect quotations as standard quotations for exchange rates. A standard quotation is the universal quotation used for managing exchange rates in foreign currency. You have the choice of defining direct or indirect quotations for each currency pair in an exchange rate. We will be looking at this in detail in the following section.

Define Standard Quotation for exchange Rates

Problem: Your client wants to be able to maintain exchange rates in SAP R/3 system. To meet this requirement, you have been asked to define both direct and indirect quotations for each USD/GBP currency pair.

In SAP S4 HANA, currency exchange rates are quoted as direct or indirect. In this activity we will be taking you through how to maintain direct and indirect quotation for each currency pair that we will be using for the standard quotation for our exchange rate:

- Direct quotation: When one unit of foreign currency is expressed as one unit of your company code currency. For example, one unit of the foreign currency USD 1.00 is displayed in the local currency as GBP 0.85.

- Indirect quotation: When one unit of local currency (your company code) is quoted for one unit of foreign currency. For example, one unit of the local currency GBP 1.00 is quoted as the foreign currency USD 1.18.

You can define a direct or indirect quotation in the exchange rate table, which becomes available to the users during data input. The exchange rate table contains a list of all exchange rates between various currencies for a range of dates in the system. To display the exchange table, use this menu path: ***Accounting ➤ Financial Accounting➤ Accounts Payable➤ Environment➤ Current Settings➤ Enter Exchange Rate***.

Let's look at how to define standard quotation for exchange rates. To go to the screen where you will do this, follow this menu path: ***IMG: SAP NetWeaver ➤ General Settings ➤ Currencies ➤ Define Standard Quotation for exchange Rates***. The ***Change View "Maintenance View TCURN": Overview*** screen is displayed to begin customizing your currency quotation, click New Entries at the top left of the screen. The New Entries: Overview of Added Entries screen is displayed (Figure 7-2). This is where you define the settings for your currency quotations.

On the ***New Entries: Overview of Added Entries*** screen, Specify the following items:

Your currency pair: In this exercise, we used USD (US dollar)/GBP (Great Britain Pound) as our currency pair.

Validity date: Enter the date you want your exchange rate quotation to start. The system will consider the date you entered in this field as the start date for your exchange rate quotation (this is the date you want your exchange rate quotation to be valid from).

Quotation: Enter the quotation type your company is using as an exchange rate quotation (whether you want your currency pair to be direct quotation or indirect quotation).

Note   The currency pair we used in this activity is for illustration purposes only. You can use any currency pair of your choice. The choice of the currency pair you ultimately use will depend on your client's requirements.

Tip   Use today's date in the valid from field as the start date of your exchange rate quotation.

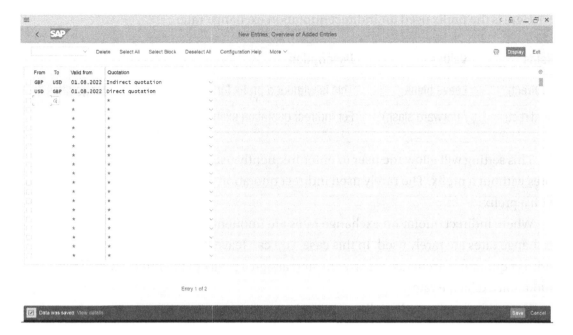

Figure 7-2. *Exchange rates quotation specification*

Click the Save button at the bottom right of the screen to save you exchange rate quotation customizing.

Enter Prefixes for Direct/Indirect Quotation Exchange Rates

In SAP S4 HANA, exchange rates are either entered as direct or indirect quotation to differentiate between direct and indirect quotation by maintaining prefixes for exchange rates that can used during document entry and display. If no prefix is entered, the SAP standard setting applies. To demonstrate how to affix prefixes to exchange rate quotations, we will first look at three setting scenarios and then assign a prefix to the direct/indirect quotation exchange rates.

Scenario 1

In a situation where direct quotation exchange rate is frequently used, you should leave the exchange rate setting for direct exchange rates field blank and append a prefix to indirect exchange rate so that users are compelled to enter a prefix when entering indirect quotation exchange rates.

Here is the prefix used for indirect quotation exchange rate:

Fields	Values	Description
D (Direct)	Leave blank	This is without a prefix for direct quotation exchange rates
I (Indirect)	/ (forward slash)	For indirect quotation exchange rates

This setting will allow the user to enter frequently used direct quotation exchange rates without a prefix. The rarely used indirect quotation exchange rates must be entered with a prefix.

Where indirect quotation exchange rates are frequently used, and direct quotation exchange rates are rarely used. In this case, you can leave the exchange rate setting for indirect quotation exchange rates blank and assign a prefix to the rarely used direct quotation exchange rates.

Here is the prefix used for direct quotation exchange rates

Fields	Values	Description
I (Indirect)	Leave blank	This is without a prefix for indirect quotation exchange rates
D (Direct)	*Sign	For direct quotation exchange rates

This setting will allow the user to enter frequently used indirect quotation exchange rates without a prefix. The rarely used direct quotation exchange rates must be entered with a prefix.

Scenario 3

In a situation where both indirect and direct quotation exchange rates have equal use, then you should append a prefix to both of them individually. Here are the prefixes you can use for direct and indirect quotation exchange rates:

Fields	Values	Description
D (Direct)	*Sign	For direct quotation exchange rates
I (indirect)	/ (Forward slash)	For indirect quotation exchange rates

This means that anytime quotation for exchange rates is entered either for direct or indirect quotation exchange rates, the user must assign a prefix. This will allow the system to recognize whether the exchange rate is a direct or indirect quotation exchange rate.

Problem: Your client uses direct quotation exchange rate frequently and seldom uses indirect quotation exchange rate.

You have been asked by your team to define indirect quotation exchange rate, which is less frequently used with a prefix. This will help users enter the correct quotation rate.

This activity assumes that indirect quotations are rarely used and that direct quotation exchange rates are frequently used. To assign a prefix to direct/indirect quotation exchange rate follow this menu path: ***IMG: SAP NetWeaver* ➤ *General Settings* ➤ *Currencies* ➤ *Enter Prefixes for Direct/Indirect Quotation Exchange Rate*.** The Change View "Direct/Indirect Quotation Prefixes foe Exchange Rate" Overview screen appears. Click New Entries at the top left side of the screen to go to the screen where you can append a prefix to indirect/direct quotation exchange rate. The New Entries: Overview of Adding Entries screen comes up (Figure 7-3).

Figure 7-3. *The screen where you assign prefix to exchange rates quotations*

Enter prefix / (forward slash) in I (indirect) field as in Figure 7-3 and save your customizing by clicking the Save button at the bottom right of the screen.

Define Translation Ratios for Currency Translation

In this activity, we will specify the ratios for each currency pair and for each exchange rate type. For example, we specify 01/08/2022 the exchange rate for USD is calculated as a 1:1 ration. This translation ratio will apply during currency translation and will be displayed during exchange rate translation. To go to the screen to define your currency translation ratio use this menu path: *IMG: SAP NetWeaver* ➤ *General Settings* ➤ *Currencies* ➤ *Define Translation Ratios for Currency Transaction*.

A warning screen is displayed with a message that changes to the table of translation factor may cause unwanted inconsistencies in the system (Figure 7-4).

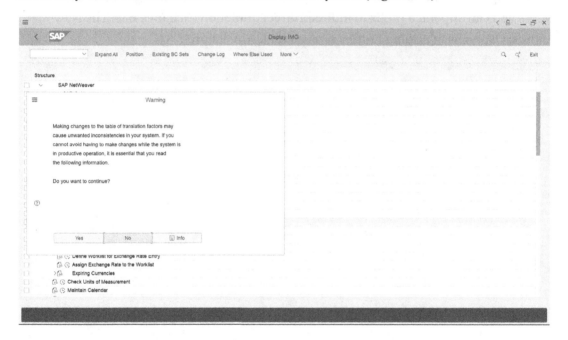

Figure 7-4. *Warning of possible inconsistencies because of changes to the table of translation factor*

Click the Yes button at the bottom left of the Warning screen to confirm your action. The **Change View "Currencies: Translation Ratios": Overview** screen is displayed. This is the screen where you maintain the translation ratio for your currency translation. Click the New Entries at the top left of the screen to go to the **New Entries: Overview of Added Entries** screen where you will define your translation ratio.

Update the following fields

ExRt: This field allows you to specify an exchange rate for your currency pair. For example, M is the standard translation at average rate. Enter the exchange rate that you want to use in this field. In this activity, we used M (average rate). When you use exchange rate type M, you can easily determine the bank selling or bank buying exchange rate by adding or subtracting the exchange rate from the average rate.

There is no hard rule about the exchange rate type you use here. You can use any of the three exchange rate types, (G-bank buying rate, B-bank selling rate, and M-average rate), but we advise that you stick to your company's standard exchange rate type.

From/To: Enter your currency pair. In this activity, we used USD/GBP as our currency pair.

Valid From: This is the date you want your exchange rate translation to be valid from. It is recommended that you use the current date.

Ratio (From): Enter the ratio you want to use for your currency translation in this field. In this activity, we used a ratio of 1:1.

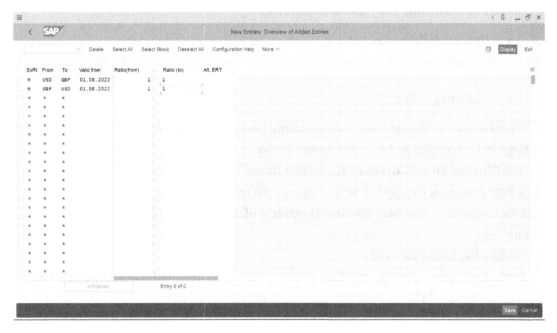

Figure 7-5. *Definition of translation ratio for currency pair*

Save your translation ration by clicking the Save button at the bottom right of the screen.

Enter Exchange Rates

Exchange rates are used to translate one currency to another and are defined on a period basis (valid from) and this plays an important role:

- During posting and clearing, because they are used to translate foreign amounts posted and cleared to company code code's currency (local currency).

- Determine the gain or loss arising from exchange rate differences.

- Valuate open item and balance sheet accounts in foreign currency during closing process.

Exchange rate setting is applicable to all company codes. Exchange rate type *M* is supplied by SAP. It is advisable to use it for foreign currency translation during documents posting or clearing in Exchange rate – *ExRt*. It is compulsory that exchange rate type must exist in the system, and this exchange rate is applicable to all company codes.

Specify the following conversion objects for:

- Exchange Rate type.

- Valid from.

- Currency codes.

To enter your exchange rate, use this menu path: *IMG: SAP NetWeaver ➤ General Settings ➤ Currencies ➤ Enter Exchange Rates*.

The **Change View "Currency Exchange Rates": Overview** screen is displayed. Click New Entries at the top left side of the screen to go the screen where you will specify your exchange rate. The **New Entries: Overview of added Entries** screen is displayed (Figure 7-6).

Update the following fields:

ExRt: Enter the exchange rate that you want to use in this field. We recommend that you use M (average) rate as your exchange rate type.

Valid from: This is the date you want the system to recognize as the date your exchange rate will be valid from. We recommend that you use the current date (today's date).

From/To: Enter your currency pair in this field. In this activity, we used USD/GBP as our currency pair.

Dir.quot.: Since we are using direct quotation for our exchange rate, enter the exchange rate for USD and GBP in this field.

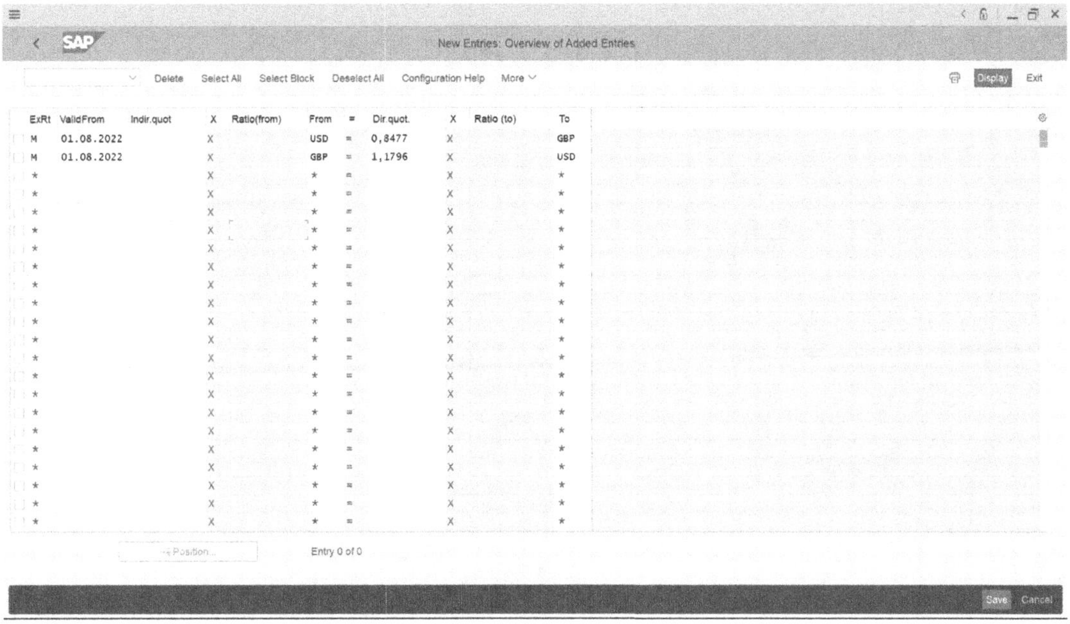

Figure 7-6. *General settings for exchange rate*

Save your exchange rate customizing.

Summary

This chapter explained how to maintain currency types and currency pairs in SAP ERP. We looked at why it is necessary to specify a currency for each transaction entered in the system. This must be done so that the system can manage the currency ledgers properly. We also looked at various exchange rate types represented by SAP and learned the various steps involved in maintaining exchange rate for each exchange rate type.

We explore how to maintain direct and indirect quotations and how to append prefixes to exchange rate quotations. We also walked through the steps involved in setting prefixes in SAP ERP using three scenarios. We learned how to define translation ratios for currency translation and how to specify translation ratios necessary for currency translations.

Finally, we explained the importance of the exchange rate and the role exchange rate plays when posting or clearing transactions in foreign currencies. We also went through the steps involved in customizing exchange rates and exchange rate ratios.

Chapter 8 looks at how to maintain goods receipt/invoice receipt (GR/IR) clearing and looks at how to maintain accounts for automatic postings during GR/IR clearing.

GR/IR Clearing

Objective

In this chapter, we will explore Goods Receipt/Invoice Receipt (GR/IR) and look at how to define adjustment accounts for GR/IR.

At the end of this chapter, you will be able to:

- Understand how GR/IR clearing accounts are posted in the system using a double entry principle.

- Customize GR/IR settings for goods that have been invoiced but not yet delivered.

- Customize GR/IR settings for goods that have been delivered but not yet invoiced.

- Customize GR/IR settings for posting offsets to a GR/IR clearing.

GR/IR Clearing

It is a normal business practice for goods to be delivered before the associated invoice arrives. This type of transaction is referred to in SAP R/3 as "***Delivered but not yet invoiced***." It is also possible for an invoice to arrive earlier and the goods be delivered later. This is referred to in SAP R/3 as "***Invoiced but goods not yet delivered***."

To account for movement of invoice and goods in the system, Provisional Accounts (clearing accounts) are defined for off-setting postings when goods are delivered but invoice not yet received and vice versa to account for timing differences between invoice receipt and goods delivery.

141

© Andrew Okungbowa 2023
A. Okungbowa, *SAP S/4HANA Financial Accounting Configuration*,
https://doi.org/10.1007/978-1-4842-8957-0_8

For example, when an invoice is received and the goods have not yet been delivered or vice versa, you define adjustment accounts and targets accounts for automatic posting of Goods Receipt/Invoice Receipt (GR/IR) for off-setting postings.

For the system to reflect invoice receipt of which goods are not yet delivered or goods delivered and invoice not yet received, transfer postings are made at the balance sheet date. The system analyzes the transactions in the GR/IR clearing accounts and posts outstanding balances to adjustment accounts and subsequently posts differences to offsetting accounts for goods receipt with pending invoices and vice versa.

Quantity differences between goods delivered and invoice receipt results in a debit balance in the GR/IR clearing account. When you receive an invoice for part of a delivery, the invoice amount is posted to the inventory account and the GR/clearing account based on your settings on the balance sheet key date. Transfer postings are performed to identify the part of goods delivered but not yet invoiced to the relevant adjustment account. The program then posts the offsetting entry to the goods delivered but not yet invoiced adjustment account (i.e., target account).

After the financial statement has been generated at a given key date, these postings are reversed.

We have illustrated this transaction with account postings in Figure 8-1. For example, goods worth 1500 are delivered, but a part invoice of 1000 was received.

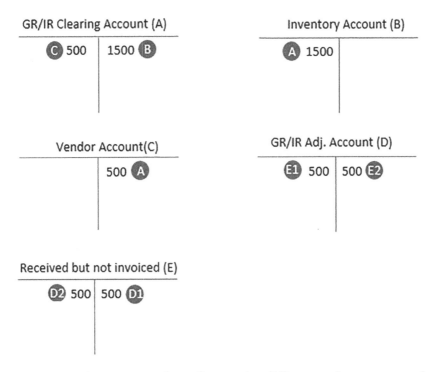

Figure 8-1. *Accounting transaction of quantity differences between goods delivered and invoice receipt*

The 1500 of goods receipt is posted as a debit item in the inventory account and the corresponding credit posting is carried out by the system to the GR/IR clearing account.

The balance of 500 (i.e., the goods delivered of 1500 less the part delivery invoice of 500) arising from the goods delivery and the part delivery invoice is posted to the credit side of the vendor's account and a corresponding debit balance is posted to the GR/IR account.

The system will then post the 500 quantity differences between goods delivered and invoice receipt to GR/IR Adjustment Account and post an Offsetting entry to Receive but not invoice account. Upon the creation of financial statements, these postings are reversed at a balance sheet key date.

Let's take a further look at some double entry examples of how GR/IR transactions are posted in the system.

Note   Before you proceed with this activity, it is important that you create the G/L accounts for Reconciliation account, Adjustment account, and Target account. Please refer to Tables 8-1 and 8-2 to see the G/L accounts we used in this activity.

The next section presents the steps involved in customizing the GR/IR clearing accounts when an invoice is received but goods have not yet been delivered.

Invoiced But Not Yet Delivered

When an invoice is received and goods not yet delivered, the inventory account is credited, and the GR/IR Clearing Account is debited.

You will define the following clearing accounts for off-setting posting in this activity for this to happen:

- Reconciliation accounts,

- Adjustment accounts, and

- Target accounts.

Problem: You have been asked to define clearing accounts for offsetting goods that have been invoiced but not yet delivered. This is when an invoice has been received but the goods have not been delivered. When the invoice is posted in the system, the inventory account is credited and the GR/IR clearing account is debited.

To define the clearing account for offsetting a posting in the system, use this menu path to go to the screen where you will perform the setting for the GR/IR clearing account in the system: *IMG: Financial Accounting* ➤ *General Ledger Accounting* ➤ *Periodic Processing* ➤ *Reclassify* ➤ *Define Adjustment Accounts for GR/IR Clearing.* The Configuration Accounting Maintain: Automatic Posts – Procedures screen is displayed (Figure 8-2).

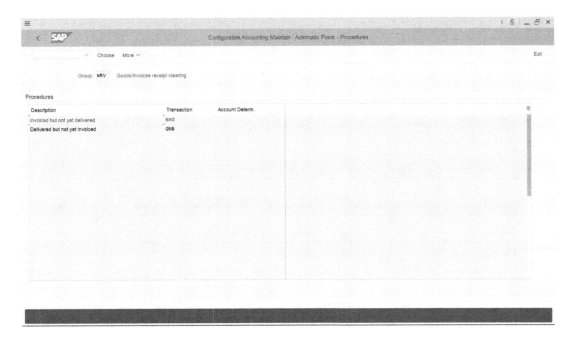

Figure 8-2. *Defining automatic postings for GR/IR clearing*

Since we are maintaining settings for goods invoiced but not yet delivered, select Invoiced but not yet delivered from the list of procedures on the screen by double clicking it. The Enter Chart of Accounts screen pops up. Enter your chart of accounts in the Chart of Accounts field. In this activity we used CA10 as our chart of account. Click Continue at the bottom right of the screen to go to the Continue Accounting Maintain: Automatic Posts – Accounts screen (Figure 8-3). Define reconciliation accounts, adjustment accounts, and targets accounts for automatic posting of Goods Receipt/Invoice Receipt (GR/IR) for off-setting posting by assigning the GL accounts in Table 8-1.

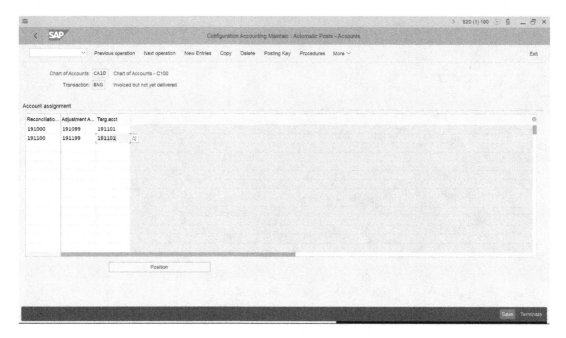

Figure 8-3. *Accounts determination for automatic posting of goods invoiced but not yet delivered*

You will assign the reconciliation accounts, adjustment accounts, and target accounts for automatic posting of GR/IR in the Account assignment section of the screen by using the G/L accounts in Table 8-1.

Table 8-1. *List of G/L Accounts for GR/IR Clearing for Goods Invoiced But Not Yet Delivered*

	GL accounts
Reconciliation	191000 – GR/IR clearing – own production
	191100 – GR/IR clearing – external procurement
Adjustment	191099 – GR/IR clearing – own production (adjustments)
	191199 – GR/IR clearing – own production (adjustments)
Target	191101 – GR/IR – Goods/services not yet delivered
	191101 – GR/IR – Goods/services not yet delivered

After updating the screen save your work

Note   If you have not created the appropriate G/L accounts yet, the system will notify you in the status bar at the bottom of the screen that the account is not created in chart of accounts. You can force the system to accept your G/L accounts temporarily, until you create your G/L accounts, by hitting the enter button on your keyboard.

Delivered but not yet invoiced

When goods are received but not yet invoiced, the inventory account is debited, and the GR/IR Clearing Account is credited.

You define the following clearing accounts for off-setting posting for this to happen:

- Reconciliation accounts,

- Adjustment accounts, and

- Target accounts.

Problem: Define clearing accounts for off-setting posting for Goods Delivered but not yet Invoiced.

In order for the system to carry out automatic postings to various accounts that are affected by this transaction, you must assign appropriate accounts to your GR/IR clearing. You need to go to the screen where you will carry out accounts assignment for GR/IR clearing for offsetting postings. Follow this menu path: ***IMG: Financial Accounting ➤ General Ledger Accounting ➤ Periodic Processing ➤ Reclassify ➤ Define Adjustment Accounts for GR/IR Clearing.*** The Configuration Accounting Maintain: Automatic Posts – Procedures screen is displayed (Figure 8-2).

Since we are maintaining settings for goods delivered but not yet invoiced, select Delivered but not yet invoiced from the list of procedures on the screen by double clicking it. The Enter Chart of Accounts screen pops up. Enter your chart of accounts in the Chart of Accounts field. In this activity we used CA10 as our chart of account. Click Continue at the bottom right of the screen to go to the Continue Accounting Maintain: Automatic Posts – Accounts screen (Figure 8-4). Define reconciliation accounts, adjustment accounts, and targets accounts for automatic posting of Goods Receipt/ Invoice Receipt (GR/IR) for off-setting posting by assigning the GL accounts in Table 8-2.

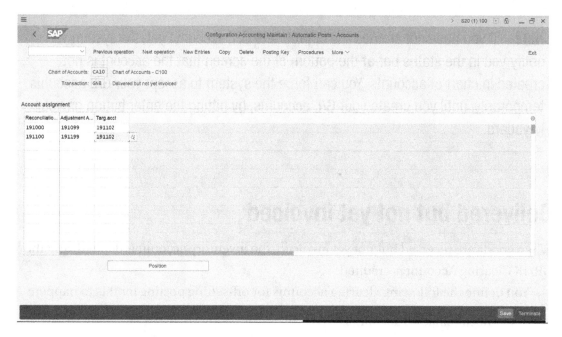

Figure 8-4. *Continue Accounting Maintain: Automatic Posts – Accounts screen*

You will assign the reconciliation accounts, adjustment accounts, and target accounts for automatic posting of GR/IR in the Account assignment section of the screen by using the G/L accounts in Table 8-2.

Table 8-2. *List of G/L Accounts for GR/IR Clearing for Goods Delivered But Not Yet Invoiced*

	GL accounts
Reconciliation	191000 – GR/IR clearing – own production
	191100 – GR/IR clearing – external procurement
Adjustment	191099 – GR/IR clearing – own production (adjustments)
	191199 – GR/IR clearing – own production (adjustments)
Target	191102 – Goods and services not yet invoiced
	191102 – Goods and services not yet invoiced

After updating the screen save your work

Note   If you have not created the appropriate G/L accounts yet, the system will notify you in the status bar at the bottom of the screen that the account is not created in chart of accounts. You can force the system to accept your G/L accounts temporarily, until you create your G/L accounts, by hitting the enter button on your keyboard.

Summary

When accounting for invoices and movement of goods in the system, you must define provisional accounts (clearing accounts) that offset postings when goods and invoices are not simultaneously delivered and paid. This chapter illustrated how GR/IR clearings are posted in the system using the double entry principle. We then learned how to define adjustment accounts, reconciliation accounts, and target accounts for automatic posting for GR/IR clearing in SAP S4 HANA.

We also explored how to assign G/L accounts to GR/IR clearing and learned how this works in SAP S4 HANA during posting of transactions whereby goods are received, and the invoice is not yet delivered, and whereby the invoice is received, and goods are not yet delivered.

Chapter 9 defines House Bank and explains how it is configured in SAP S4 HANA. We will also be looking at how SAP S$ HANA supports bank statements. As part of this chapter, we will also explore how to define posting keys and posting rules for bank statements and check deposits, respectively.

CHAPTER 9

Bank

In this chapter, we explore how to customize the house bank in FI.

At the end of this chapter, you will have a thorough understanding of:

- What a house bank is.
- Identify the components of a master record in a house bank.
- Define a house bank.
- Use a house bank ID and an account ID.
- Identify bank statements supported by SAP S4 HANA.
- Assign global settings for an electronic bank statement.
- Configure a manual bank statement.
- Define posting keys and posting rules for check deposit.
- Define variants for check deposits.

Introduction

The banks that hold your company code bank account are referred to as house bank in SAP ERP (for example, City Bank. Bank of America, etc.). A company code can have more than one house bank assigned to it.

Each Bank Account has its own Master Record stored centrally in the Bank Directory. Bank master data in the bank directory is made up of:

- Bank Account Data (Bank Account Number, Currency, Bank Key, GL Account...).
- House Bank Data (Bank Country and Bank Key, Bank Name).

© Andrew Okungbowa 2023
A. Okungbowa, *SAP S/4HANA Financial Accounting Configuration*,
https://doi.org/10.1007/978-1-4842-8957-0_9

- Communication Data (Telephone, Contact Person, Address, EDI Partner Profile and Data Medium Exchange).

- Control (SWIFT Code, Bank Number...).

The SWIFT code is used for identifying banks in international payment transactions.

- The first 4 characters contains the bank code (alphabets only).

- The next 2 characters contain the ISO (this is numeric digit) and 2 alpha digits as the country code.

Bank details are required for printing payment forms.

A combination of House Bank ID & Account ID makes up the bank account in the SAP R/3 system. You enter the Hose Bank ID and Account ID in the GL account so that the system can recognize the appropriate GL account during bank transactions.

The bank group is used for classifying banks. The key is freely assignable. The aim of the classification is to group banks together in such a way that payment transactions within a group can be carried out as fast as possible (this is referred to as payment optimization).

Note   When customer/vendor has more than one bank account, the bank type in the customer master record is used to distinguish between different banks. During invoice processing, the user can decide which bank to use by using the match-code in the partner bank field.

Likewise, the House Bank ID and the Account ID is used by the payment program to determine the banks to use during invoice payment.

Now, configure House Banks for Barclays bank and HSBC Bank.

Defining House Bank

Banks used by company codes in SAP_ERP system are called House Banks. A combination of both House Bank ID & Account ID makes up the bank account in the SAP R/3 system.

The House Bank ID and the Account ID are used by the payment program to determine the banks to use during invoice payment.

Note   The SAP system comes with examples of standard House Banks. It is advisable to take a look at them as a guide if you are not confident with House Bank configuration.

Problem: Company C900 plc has two bank accounts (Barclays Bank and HSBC Bank). You are to define the House Banks for both Bank Accounts.

To define house bank, follow this menu path: ***IMG: Financial Accounting ➤ Financial Accounting Global IMG: Financial Accounting ➤ Bank Accounting ➤ Bank Accounts ➤ Define House Bank.***

The Display View "Company Codes": Overview screen is displayed with a list of company codes in the system, search for your company code using either the Position button at the bottom of the screen or use the scroll bar at the right side of the screen. Select your Company code (C100) by ticking the checkbox attached your company code, as in Figure 9-1.

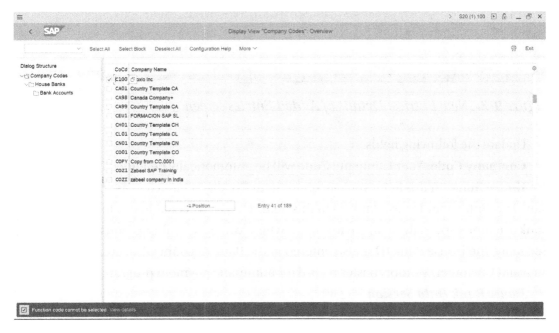

Figure 9-1. *The Display View "Company Codes": Overview screen*

Double click the House Bank folder in the Dialog Structure at the left side of the screen. The Display View "Company Codes": Overview screen is displayed. Click the New Entries button at the top left of the screen, the New Entries: Details of Added Entries screen (Figure 9-2) comes up.

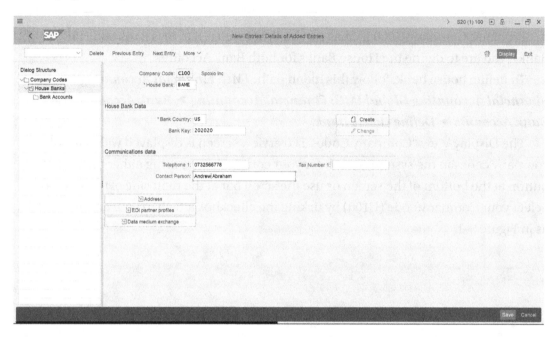

Figure 9-2. *New Entries: Details of Added Entries screen*

Update the following fields

Company Code: Your Company Code will be automatically defaulted by the system.

House Bank: In this field, you can enter up to five digit characters as your house bank key. Enter your House Bank ID in this field. This ID will enable you to identify this bank account, especially in an environment where you have multiple House Banks. Secondly, the House Bank ID is also entered in the Bank Account GL account master data and Customer/Vendor master record for automatic payment program.

House Bank Data Section

Bank Country: Enter your country ID (for example, for the United States of America enter – **US)** in this field. This will allow you to identify your House bank country. Another important factor of Country ID is that it forms part of IBAN and SWIFT for international payments.

Bank Key: Enter your Bank Sort Code. This helps identify your bank and the branch. This key is very important as it forms part of IBAN & SWIFT used for international payments.

Communications Data Section

Telephone: This is usually your bank telephone number.

Contact person: This is your account manager or someone that is designated by the bank to your account.

After updating the screen in Figure 9-2, click the Create button at the right side of the screen. This will call up the Bank Data form, where you can enter further bank information about your house bank. For example, you can enter your bank name, address, region, and so on. Once you have added your entries, click Continue at the bottom of the screen to confirm your entries and save your house bank by clicking the Save button at the bottom right of the screen.

The next step is to define Bank Account for your house bank.

Define Bank Account for your House Bank

To define bank accounts for your house bank, follow this menu path: ***IMG: Financial Accounting ➤ Financial Accounting Global IMG: Financial Accounting ➤ Bank Accounting ➤ Bank Accounts ➤ Define House Bank.***

Unfortunately, bank accounts and accounts assignments can no longer be maintained in SAP S4 HANA as earlier SAP versions. Bank statements now have to be maintained in SAP NetWeaver Business Client, and this is outside the scope of this book.

Save your house bank customization. Follow the steps in defining house bank above and using the information in Table 9-1, define another house bank, for example, HSBC.

Table 9-1. *Data to Define a House Bank for HSBC Bank Account*

Field Name	Bank Data
Company Code	Enter your company code in this field
House Bank	Enter a house bank data in this field, such as HSBC
Bank Country	Enter your country code in this field such US or GB or DE and so on
Bank Key	Enter your bank unique sort code in this field
Address	Enter your company address in this field
Account ID	Enter a unique account Id in this field – such as HSBC
Description	Enter a short text that best describes your House Bank, Such as HSBC Bank

The next step in this activity is to look at how to maintain a bank statement in SAP S4 HANA.

Bank Statement

A bank statement is a summary of financial transactions, such as incoming and outgoing payments that took place during a given period on an account. This is the state of your cash position. SAP ERP supports two types of bank statements: electronic bank statements and manual bank statements.

Before you create your electronic and manual bank statements, it is recommended that you first create the following clearing accounts (refer to Chapter 9 on how to create G/L accounts), which your bank transactions will be posted to:

Main Balnc Account: As the name suggests, this is the general bank account entered in the house bank master data. This account serves as a reconciliation account that holds the bank account balance.

Checks Received: The checks you received for invoice amounts from your customers or business partners for supplying them goods or for providing services are posted to this account.

Other Interim Posting: Reconciliation items are posted to this account.

Check Issued out: Check payments made by your company to its creditors or business partners for goods/services received are posted to this account.

Outgoing Wire Transfer: This is an electronic method of funds transfer from your company to a business partner to mitigate due invoice(s). This is a very fast way of transferring money from one person to another or from one company to another.

Incoming Cash: Cash received by your company from business partners for a business transaction are posted to this account.

Outgoing Cash: Cash payments made by your company relating to business transactions to business partners are posted to this account.

Note   We have provided information in "Appendix A, Chapter 9 Bank Statement" that will enable you to create the Gil account that you will need to customize your bank statement. We recommend that you first create the necessary Gil account before creating your bank statement.

The next section defines an electronic bank statement and explains how to set up an electronic bank statement (EBS) framework. Later in this chapter, you will define manual bank statements.

SAP R/3 supports two types of bank statements, namely Electronic Bank Statement and Manual Bank Statements.

Before we go further to look at how to create Electric Bank Statements and manual Bank Statements. You will need to create the following Accounts to support your customization:

- Check Received.

- Other Interim Posting.

- Check Issued Out.

- Outgoing Wire Transfer.

- Incoming Cash.

- Outgoing Cash.

Note   Go to **Appendix 1– Chapter 9** Bank Statement below to create the necessary G/L Account for your configuration.

Electronic Bank Statement

An electronic bank statement is simply a bank statement generated by your bank in an electronic format. It provides detailed information about the movement of funds in your bank account created at the house bank during any given period. With SAP R/3, it is possible to retrieve bank statements electronically using bank communication management. Bank communication management manages multiple bank communication interfaces that allow you to connect to your bank using a defined standard protocol. When a bank statement is uploaded to SAP ERP, it can serve the following purposes:

- Clears all bank clearing accounts in the system to the bank main account (this is the general bank account entered in the house bank master data).

- Uses the bank statement to perform automatic bank reconciliations in the system.

SAP R/3 supports various electronic bank statement formats, including Multicash, SWIFT, BAI, BAI2, and others:

- Multicash: Invented by Omikron a German Company, Multicash is an electronic bank statement format that allows the SAP ERP system to communicate with the bank system. The format is split into two file formats. AUSZUG.TXT holds the bank statement header information and UMSATZ.TXT contains the bank account transactions information.

- SWIFT (Society for World-Wide Interbank Financial Telecommunication): This is a computer-based switching system used by banks for making payments related to international transactions.

- BAI (Bank Administration Institute): This is a standardized electronic file format used for cash management between the bank and the account holder. The bank transmits BAI file formats to the account holder who in turns downloads or inputs the file into the system, generates a bank statement, and performs bank reconciliation.

- BAI2: This is the latest release of a cash management balance report. It is very similar to BAI in functionality. The only difference is that BAI2 contains more detailed information.

Now let's define Electronic Bank Statement and setup Electronic Bank Statement (EBS) framework.

Electronic Bank Statement

With SAP S4 HANA it is possible to retrieve bank statements electronically using the defined bank communication standard. When a bank statement is uploaded to SAP system, it can serve the following functions:

- Clears various bank clearing accounts to the main account and

- Perform automatic bank reconciliations.

SAP S4 supports various electronic bank statement formats like Multicash, BAI, BAI2, SWIFT, etc.

Defining Global Settings for Electronic Bank Statement

In this activity, you will need to make seven global settings. These seven global settings are listed on the Dialog structure on the left pane of the *Account symbols overview* screen.

The following four settings that you will be carrying out in this activity are also applicable to manual bank statement, so you don't need to create or define them again during manual bank statement configuration:

- **Create Account Symbols:** The accounts symbols you created as part of your electronic bank customizing will specify the G/L accounts and subledgers that the bank statement transaction are posted to.

- **Assign Accounts to Account Symbol:** This will allow you to assign or map account symbols to appropriate GL accounts and subledgers.

- **Create Keys for Posting Rules:** Posting key decides the posting rules applicable to general ledger and subledger.

- **Define Posting Rules:** Posting rules represents business transactions in the bank statement by using appropriate posting keys, document types, and posting. For example incoming check, check out, Bank Transfer, Bank Charges, etc.

Note   To ensure that your configuration is complete, we advise that you work from top to bottom. Using this technique will ensure that all the required aspects of the required configurations are covered.

Problem:

Spoxio Inc.'s accounting team wants to be able to upload their bank statement electronically using defined bank communication standards. SAP supports various electronic bank statement formats like Multicash, BAI, BAI2, SWIFT, etc.

As a part of your task, it is your responsibility to define appropriate settings needed to allow the accounting team to be able to upload bank statements electronically to the SAP system from the bank to be able to clear several bank clearing accounts and also be able to carry out automatic bank reconciliation.

To define global settings for electronic bank statement, follow this menu path: ***IMG: Financial Accounting ➤ Bank Accounting ➤ Business Transactions ➤ Payment Transactions ➤ Electronic Bank Statement ➤ Make Global Settings for Electronic Bank Statement.***

The Determine Work Area: Entry dialog box pops up, enter your company chart of accounts key in the Chart of Accounts field and click Enter at the bottom of the dialog box. A Warning screen comes up saying that *"All fields which define the area have initial values."* Ignore the warning and click the Continue button.

Change View "Create Account Symbols": Overview screen is displayed (Figure 9-3).

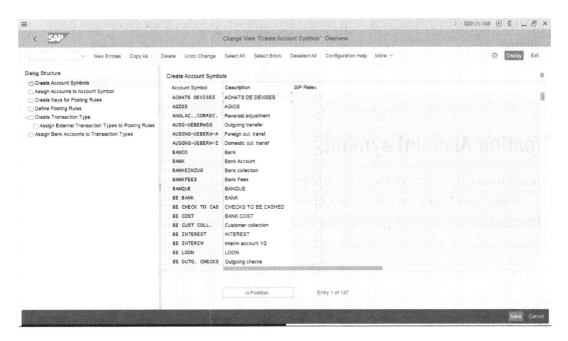

Figure 9-3. *Global Setting for Electronic Bank Statement – Specify Account Symbols*

On this screen you will define the following items:

- Create Account Symbols.

- Assign Accounts to Account Symbol.

- Create Keys for Posting Rules.

- Define Posting Rules.

- Create Transaction Type.

- Assign External Transaction Types to Posting Rules.

- Assign Bank Accounts to Transaction Types.

Tip   *To ensure that your configuration is complete work through the folders on the Dialog Structure on the left-hand side of the screen systematically in steps from top down.*

The first step in this activity is to create account symbols for your electronic bank statement.

Step 1

Creating Account symbols

You will notice that the ***Create Account Symbol*** folder on the ***Dialog Structure*** is open.

Choose New Entries at the top left of the screen. The ***New Entries: Overview of Added Entries*** screen is displayed. This screen will allow you to create your own account symbols.

Update the ***New entries*** screen with your account symbol. For this activity use the data in the following table as your account symbol to update the screen for account symbols:

Account	Text
C900-BANK	Main Bank Account
C900-BANKCHGS	Bank Charges
C900-CHECK-IN	Incoming Checks
C900-CHECK-OUT	Outgoing Checks
C900-BANKTRANS	Bank Transfers
C900-INTERPOST	Reconciliation Items

Note   There is no hard rule to creating Account Symbols. You don't necessarily have to use the account symbols used in this activity; it is only for illustration. You can formulate your own account symbols.

Once an account symbol has been used by someone else, the system will not allow you to use the same account symbol again. So, use your own initiative when creating your account symbols by trying other symbols – be creative.

Once you have specified your account symbols (as in Figure 9-4), hit the enter key on your keyboard and save your Account Symbols.

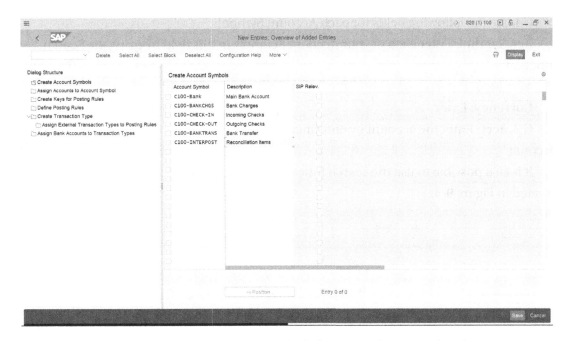

Figure 9-4. *Specification of account symbols for your electronic bank statement*

The second step in this activity is to assign accounts to the account symbols you have created for your electronic bank statement.

Step 2

Assigning Accounts to account symbols

By assigning accounts to accounts symbol during configuration, the system automatically specifies the G/L accounts that transactions are posted when users retrieve bank statements electronically. For example, Checks received are posted to Incoming Checks account, charges are posted to Bank Charges account, and so on.

In Figure 9-4, double click the Assign Accounts to Account Symbol folder on the **Dialog structure** on the top left hand corner. The ***Change View "Assign Accounts to Account Symbol": Overview*** screen is displayed. To Assign Accounts to Account Symbol, choose New Entries at the top left of the screen. This will display the ***New Entries: Overview of Added Entries*** screen, where you will assign the symbols you have created above to your account.

Update the following fields for each Account Symbol:

Act. Symbol: Enter each of your Account Symbols in this field by using the Search function.

Acct Mod: Enter account modifier "+."

Currency: Enter "+."

G/L acct: Enter the account by entering series of "+" signs as part of your GL account.

It is also possible to use the search function to look for the Account Symbols that you created in Figure 9-4.

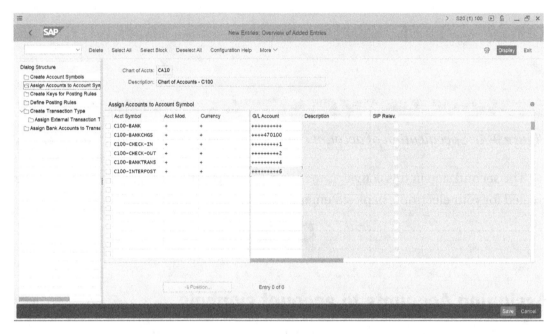

Figure 9-5. *Assignment of accounts to account symbols*

Account symbols can be assigned in two ways: either by entering the full GL account number or replacing your GL account or most of the first parts of your GL account with series of "+" signs.

For example, your Bank Account could be replaced with "++++++++++" (this is up to 10 symbols). What happens is that the system will automatically replace these signs with the GL account assigned to House Bank during house bank configuration.

On the other hand, for example, when part of your Check Received GL account is replaced with "+++++++++1," the system will automatically replace the GL account you created for Incoming Checks.

Note   Always use the last G/L account number. The system automatically recognizes the other ten characters.

Hit Enter on your keyboard and save your work.

Note   By appending "+" signs to your GL account you don't have to keep defining a symbol for every house bank when a new GL is maintained. Instead use symbol "+++++++++++." The system will automatically recognize the GL account for your house bank. Likewise, to avoid input error when maintaining GL accounts for other items, use "++++++++n" and enter the last GL account number at the end for each signs (item). For example, the GL Account for Check Received with Account Symbol CHECKOUT is 111412, then our GL Account should look like this +++++++++2. Hence your symbol for CHECKOUT GL Account is +++++++++2 as above.

Note   Only your Main Bank Account should be masked without a number at the end. The bank charges should contain all the GL code.

The next step in this activity is to create keys for posting rules for each of the account symbols you created in step 1.

Step 3

Creating Keys for Posting Rules

To create keys for posting rules, double click the Create Keys for Posting Rules folder in the **Dialog structure** on the top left hand pane of the screen to create the keys for posting rules. The Change View "Define Posting Rules": Overview screen is displayed. Choose New Entries at the top left of the screen to go to the New Entries: Details of Added Entries screen where your will create the posting rules for your electronic bank statement.

Update the following items by creating posting rules for each of your account symbols. In this activity, you should create six keys for posting rules and we describe the keys for posting rules in the next section.

Note   You can use the Posting Keys supplied by SAP or you can create your own posting keys from scratch. In this activity, we recommend that you create your own posting keys.

Tip   *The system allows a maximum of four characters for a posting rule key.*

Update the *New Entries: Overview of Added Entries* screen, as in Figure 9-6.

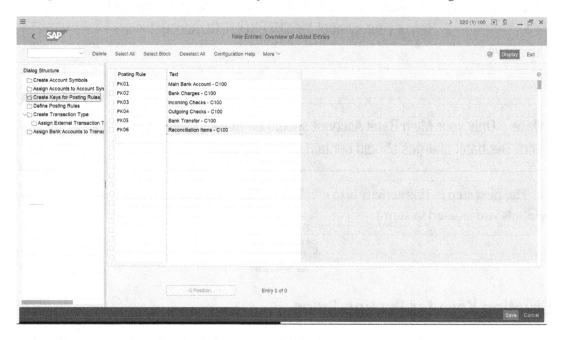

Figure 9-6.   *Customizing keys for posting rules*

Save the keys for your posting rules.

Note   The posting keys we used in this activity are only for illustration. You can use any posting key and description of your choice in this activity.

In step 4, you will define posting rules that are assigned to your account symbols.

Step 4

Defining Posting Rules

To define posting rules, Double click the Define Posting Rules folder on the **Dialog structure** on the top left hand pane in order to create posting rules. The Change View "Define Posting Rules": Overview screen is displayed. Choose the New Entries at the top left of the screen to proceed to the New Entries: Details of Added Entries screen (Figure 9-7) where you will define your posting rules.

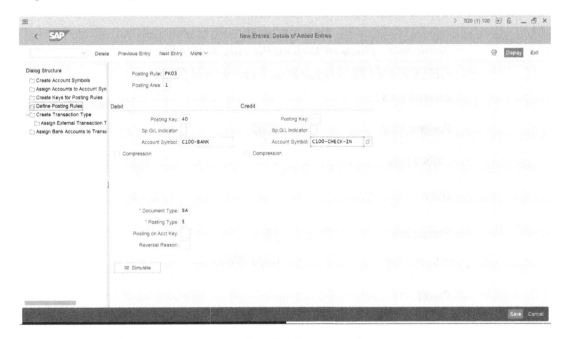

Figure 9-7. *Defining posting rules for check received*

Update the following fields:

Posting Rule: Enter the Keys for Posting Rules that you defined above in the Posting Rule fields. Posting Rules are used by the system to determine which GL accounts and subledgers to post transactions to.

Posting Area: The SAP ERP System comes with two standard values for posting area (1 – Bank Accounting and 2 – Subledger Accounting). Posting Area will allow the system to post to either of the specified areas**.**

Posting Key: Enter the appropriate posting key in this field. Posting key allows the system to determine whether a line item should be treated as debit or credit and the account type to post a transaction to. It also controls the field status for document entry.

Acct Symbol: You have already defined a number of account symbols above. Enter the appropriate account symbol in this field. The account symbol you entered here will allow the system to determine to which account the related transaction is posted when users retrieve bank statements electronically.

Document Type: Allows you to differentiate between transactions and also allows the system to determine which business transactions to post.

Posting Type: It is mandatory that you enter one posting type in the Posting Type field during customizing. The importance of posting type is for account clearing. For example, Posting Type 5-clears credit G/L Account.

Table 9-2.   Data to Define Posting Rules for CHECK-IN (This is for checks received from customers)

Posting Rule	S003
Posting Area	1
Debit	
Posting Key	40
Acct Symbol	C900-BANK
Credit	
Acct Symbol	C900-CHECK-IN
Document Type	SA
Posting Type	5

Note   This configuration is for incoming checks. The accounting entries for check receipt is to debit your bank account using debit posting key – 40, since money is coming in. Likewise, credited a corresponding Incoming Check clearing account.

Similarly, the configuration for outgoing checks is the reverse. Credit your Bank Account using Posting Key – 50 and Debit the corresponding Outgoing Check Clearing account.

Save your posting rules for check received.

To complete the customizing of your posting rules you have to also create posting rules for the remaining account symbols you created in step 1 using the data in Tables 9-2 to 9-6 to complete the posting rules for each activity.

Table 9-3. Data to Define Posting Rules for CHECK-OUT (This is for checks paid out to vendors)

Posting Rule	PK04
Posting Area	1
Debit	
Acct Symbol	C100-CHECK-OUT
Credit	
Posting Key	50
Acct Symbol	C100-BANK
Document Type	SA
Posting Type	4

Table 9-4. *Data to Define Posting Rules for BANKTRANS (This is for bank transfers from the bank)*

Posting Rule	PK05
Posting Area	1
Debit	
Acct Symbol	C100-BANKTRANS
Credit	
Posting Key	50
Acct Symbol	C100-BANK
Document Type	SA
Posting Type	4

Table 9-5. *INTERPOST (this is for other Interim Posts)*

Posting Rule	PK06
Posting Area	1
Debit	
Posting Key	40
Acct Symbol	C100-INTERPOST
Credit	
Posting Key	50
Acct Symbol	C100-BANK
Document Type	SA
Posting Type	1

Table 9-6. *Data to Define Posting Rules for BANKCHGS (This is for bank charges)*

Posting Rule	PK02
Posting Area	1
Debit	
Posting Key	40
Acct Symbol	C100-BANKCHGS
Credit	
Posting Key	50
Acct Symbol	C100-BANK
Document Type	SA
Posting Type	1

Once you have completed your posting rules customizing using the data in Tables 9-2 to 9-6, save your posting rules.

The next step is to create transaction types under electronic bank statement.

Create Transaction Type

Transaction type allows you to assign the appropriate external transactions to posting rules.

Before you assign external transaction type to posting rules, first you have to define transaction type.

To Create transaction type, Double click The Create Transaction Type folder on the **Dialog structure** on the top left hand pane in order to create posting rules. The Change View "Create Transaction Type": Overview screen is displayed. Choose the New Entries at the top left of the screen to proceed to the New Entries: Details of Added Entries screen (Figure 9-8) where you will Create Transaction Type.

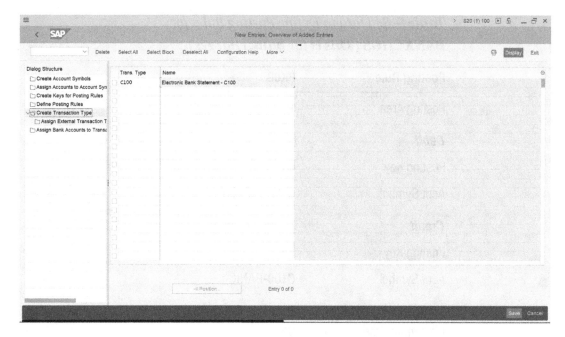

Figure 9-8. *The screen where you create transaction type for your electronic bank statement*

Update the following fields:

Trans. Type: Enter your transaction type in this field. Transaction type can be up to a maximum of eight characters (in this activity, we used C100 as our transaction type).

Name: The name-field will allow you to describe your Transaction type – ***Electronic Bank Statement – C100.***

Press Enter on your keyboard and Save your transaction type.

The next step in your electronic bank customizing is to assign external transaction types.

Assign External Transaction Types to Posting Rules

You assign external business transaction codes to internal posting rules, so you can use the same specifications you configured for different business transactions codes in your house banks. To proceed to the screen where you will assign external transaction types to posting rules, first select the transaction type you created in step 5, by making sure that the checkbox is ticked, then double click **Assign External Transaction Types to Posting**

Rules folder from the ***Dialog Structure.*** The Change View "Assign External Transaction Types to Posting Rules": Overview screen is displayed (Figure 9-9). Click the New Entries at the top left of the screen. This will take you to the "New Entries: Overview of Added Entries" screen where you will assign external transaction types to posting rules.

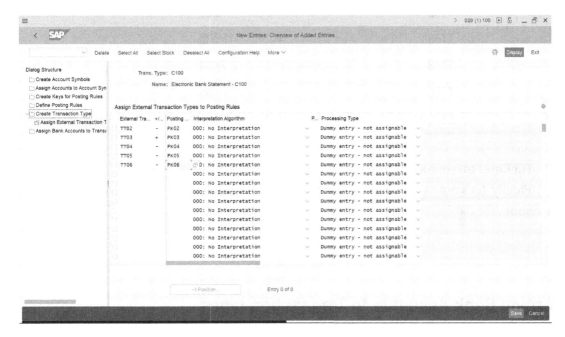

Figure 9-9. *Assignment of External Transaction Types to Posting Rules*

Update the following fields:

External Transaction: Enter your external transaction codes which could be up to a maximum of four characters for each transaction type for the system posting rule.

+/− Sign: this field allows you to specify further transaction differentiation for external transaction. The '+' sign in the front of external transaction code indicates receipt and '−' sign indicates payment.

Posting Rule: Enter posting rules already defined above.

Assign External Transaction Types to Posting Rules with the information in Table 9-7 and save your work.

Table 9-7. *The data to update the assignment of external transaction types to posting rules*

External Trans	+/-	Posting
TT02	-	PK02
TT03	+	PK03
TT03	-	PK04
TT05	-	PK05
TT06	-	PK06

Hit Enter on your keyboard and Save your transaction types.

Finally, let's now assign the transaction type you have just created to your Bank Account.

Step 7

Assign Bank Accounts to Transaction types

It is not uncommon in an environment where there is more than one bank account for each bank to use its own individual transaction type to differentiate business types. If this is the case, each bank must be assigned its own transaction type. In this activity only one transaction type is created. You can define more than one transaction type. It all depends on your requirement.

On the Dialog Structure pane, double click the *Assign Bank Account to Transaction Types* folder to call-up the *Assign Bank Account to Transaction Types Overview* screen. When you select the *New Entries* button, this will allow you to assign transaction types to your bank account.

To go to the screen where you will assign bank account to transaction types, double click the Assign Bank Accounts to Transaction Types folder in the dialog structure on the left pane of the screen. The Change View "Assign Bank Account to Transaction Types": Overview screen is displayed. Click the New Entries at the top left of the screen, the New Entries: Overview of Added Entries screen comes up (Figure 9-10).

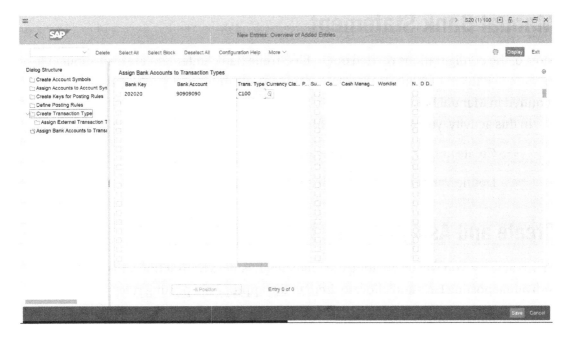

Figure 9-10. *Assignment of your bank account to transaction types*

Update the following fields:

Bank Key: This is your bank key or sort code that you created during House Bank customization.

Bank Account: Your House Bank Account number. This is normally your company's bank account number.

Transaction Type: Enter the transaction type you created in step 5.

Note Although you created two house banks, in this activity, you will only be assigning one house bank (Barclays Bank) to your transaction type, this is only for illustration purposes. There is no restriction to the number of banks you can assign to transaction type.

The Bank Key and the Bank Account used here are obtained from the House Bank you created above.

Save your work.

Manual Bank Statement

Most of the configurations carried out in Electronic Bank Statement are also applicable to Manual Bank Statement configuration. Hence only minimum configuration is required in Manual Bank Statement.

In this activity, you will only be performing the following customizing:

- Create and Assign Bank Transaction.
- Define Variants for Manual Bank Statement.

Create and Assign Business Transactions

In this activity, you will be creating the following business transactions, assign them to individual posting keys and allocate them to the appropriate posting rules:

- Bank Charges.
- Bank Transfer.
- Incoming Check.
- Outgoing Check.
- Reconciliation Items.

Note   You don't need to create new posting rules, you can use the posting rules you created for electronic bank statement for your manual bank statement.

Follow this menu path to the screen where you will create and assign business transactions for your manual bank statement customizing: *IMG: Financial Accounting* ➤ *Bank Accounting* ➤ *Business Transaction* ➤ *Payment Transactions* ➤ *Manual Bank Statement* ➤ *Create and Assign Business Transaction*.

The "*Change View: Manual Bank Statement Transactions*": *Overview* screen is displayed, click the New Entries button at the top left of the screen. *New Entries: Overview of Added Entries* screen is displayed (Figure 9-11). This is the screen where you will create new business transactions and assign them to the posting rules you defined previously in Electronic Bank Statement.

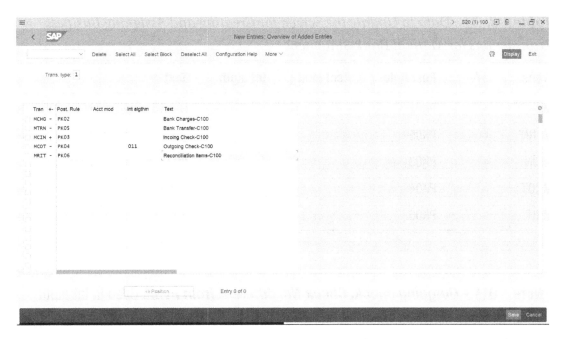

Figure 9-11. *The screen where you create and assign business transactions for your manual bank statement*

Update the following items:

Transaction: Enter your transaction codes in this field. This could be up to a maximum of four characters for each transaction type for the system posting rule.

+/− Sign: This field will allow you to specify further transaction differentiation for your business transaction. The "+" sign in the front of business transaction code indicates receipt and "−" sign indicates payment.

Posting Rule: Enter posting rules that you defined during automatic bank statement configuration.

Update your Manual Bank Statement Transactions Overview Screen with the information in Table 9-8

Table 9-8. *The Data to Update the Screen for Creating and Assigning Business Transactions for Manual Bank Statement*

Trans	+/−	Post Rule	Acct mod	Int algth	Text
MCHG	−	PK02			Bank Charges-C100
MTRN	−	PK05			Bank Transfer-C100
MCIN	+	PK03			Incoming Check-C100
MCOT	−	PK04		011	Outgoing Checks-C100
MRIT	−	PK06			Reconciliation Items-C100

Note   011 - *Outgoing check. Check No. different from Pymt.* Used in Int algth field will allow outgoing check to be referenced.

Save your work.

Tip   *You don't need to define other posting keys and rules for manual bank statements; you can use the posting keys you defined for electronic bank statement*

Finally, you will now have to define Variants for Manual Bank Statement.

Define Variants for Manual Bank Statement

SAP supplied a standard variant – SAP01 as a default. Only minimum modification is allowed for this standard variant. You can use this standard variant for your manual bank statement. It is advisable to copy the standard variant – SAP01 and modify it to meet your company's specific requirements.

Note   If you choose not to use the standard variant – SAP01 supplied by the system, instead you decide to create your own your variant. First you have to deactivate the standard variant SAP01 and then activate your variant.

To go the screen where you define variants for manual bank statement, follow this menu path: ***Financial Accounting ➤ Bank Accounting ➤ Business Transaction ➤ Payment Transactions ➤ Manual Bank Statement ➤ Define Variants for Manual Bank Statement.***

The Maintain Screen Variant: List screen is displayed.

In this activity, you will be copying the standard variant – SAP01 supplied by SAP in the system and modify it to meet your requirement. On the ***Maintain Screen Variant: List*** screen click on SAP01 – Standard (this is the last item in the displayed list) and click Copy... at the top right of the screen. The ***Copy variant*** screen pops-up (Figure 9-12). Enter the variant you want to copy – SAP01 in the ***From Variant*** field and enter your own variant identification key in the ***To Variant*** field (in this activity, we used C100) and choose the Enter button below to confirm your request. This action will allow you to copy the properties of standard variant – SAP01 to your variant (C100).

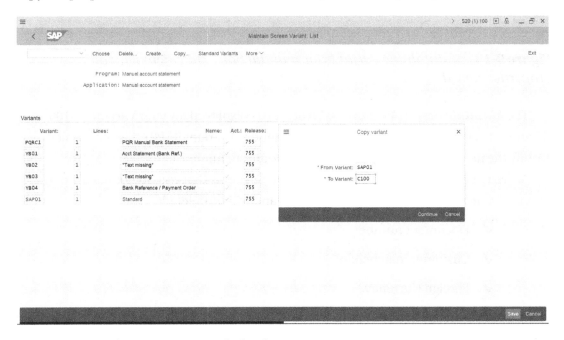

Figure 9-12. *The copy variant dialog box*

Click Continue at the bottom left of the screen for the Variant SAP01 you are copying to be copied to your variant (C100). An Information screen with warning that ***"Field FEBMKA-MEHRW is missing on reference screen"*** pops up. Ignore the warning and click Continue at the bottom right of the screen. Once copy is confirmed, the system will automatically copy the standard variant – SAP01 to your variant.

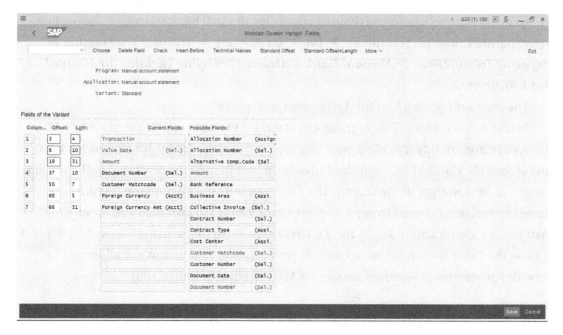

Figure 9-13. *Maintaining variants for manual bank statement with all properties copied*

The ***Maintain Screen Variant Fields*** screen is displayed for your Variant – C100 (Figure 9-13) inheriting the properties of the standard variant SAP01 that you copied. Modify the item on this screen to meet your requirement.

As part of your modification process, delete the items that you do not need. For this activity delete the following items not needed and will be deleted:

- ✓ Document number.

- ✓ Customer matchcode.

- ✓ Foreign Currency.

- ✓ Foreign Currency amt.

To delete an item, click on the item to select it and click Delete Field (this is the second item from the left at the top of the screen in Figure 13-14). For instance, we are deleting Document Number (circled), click on it and choose the Delete Field at the top of the screen. This action will delete Document Number from the displayed field list of your variant.

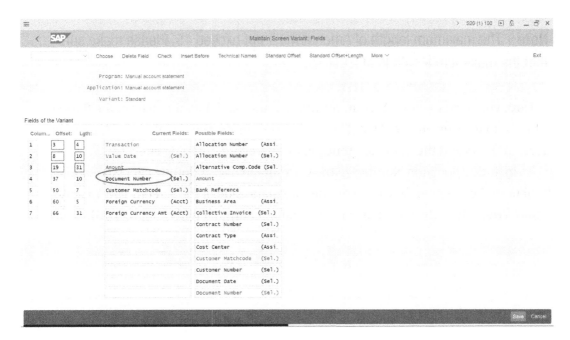

Figure 9-14. *Deleting a field from your variant for manual bank statement*

As part of your customizing exercise in this activity, delete the remaining items we listed above for deletion. After deleting the items, your screen will now look alike the one in Figure 9-15.

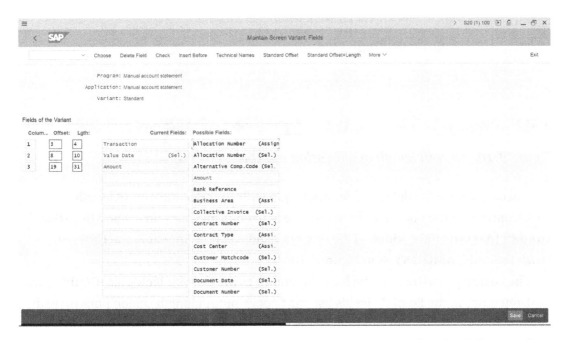

Figure 9-15. *Maintain variant for manual bank statement after the deletion of unwanted items*

Note   The maximum length of Amount must not exceed 15. Please make sure that the maximum length is at least 15.

Next, you need to move Allocation Number and Bank Reference from the Possible Fields list to the Current Field list. The Allocation Number field will record incoming check numbers and the Bank Reference field will record outgoing checks.

To include Allocation Number in the Current Fields list, double click Allocation Number in the Possible Fields List on the right hand side of the screen. The **Specify output length** dialogbox pops up with a defaulted output length (Figure 9-16).

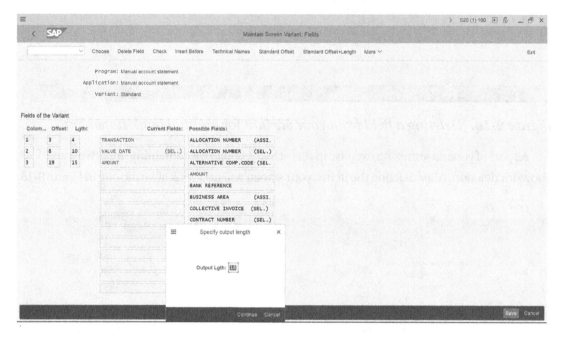

Figure 9-16. Output length of allocation number

You can replace the defaulted output length with your desired output length. Click Continue at the bottom right of the screen to confirm your entry. The **Allocation Number (Ass)** you have added to the Current Field will now appear in the *Current Fields* list under **AMOUNT** as in Figure 9-16.

The next step is to include the Bank Reference to the Current Fields list. Double click Bank reference in the Possible Fields list, the Specify output length screen pops up with a default output length. You can replace the defaulted output length with your desired output length. Click Continue at the bottom right of the screen to confirm your entry.

The **Bank reference** you have added to the Current Field will now appear in the *Current Fields* List under **Allocation number**.

Save your variant.

The next step is to change the variant name to your own. Click the Back button at the top left of the screen to return to the previous screen, the Maintain Screen variant: List. Search for your variant (C100) among the variant list and change the copied variant name (Standard) to your own. In this activity, we used Manual Bank Statement – C100 as our variant name, and Save your modification.

Finally, select your variant from the variant list by clicking on it and click Activate at the top of the screen. The system will notify you on the status bar at the bottom of the screen that your variant was activated.

Note   You must activate the variant for your manual bank statement for the manual bank statement settings to work effectively.

Save your variant.

Check Deposit

Check deposit customization is useful in an environment where large volumes of checks are processed simultaneously in the system. The settings carried out here will allow checks received to be entered into the system.

Customizing check deposit involves the following steps:

1.   Create and Assign Business Transactions.

2.   Define Posting Keys and Posting Rules for Check Deposit.

3.   Define Variants for Check Deposit

Note   We recommend that you Define Posting Keys and Posting Rules for Check Deposit first before you Create and Assign Business Transactions to Posting Rules. The reason for this is that the Accounting Symbols needed for Business Transactions during customizing are first defined during customizing of Posting Keys and Posting Rules for check deposit.

Define Posting Keys and Posting Rules for Check Deposit

In this activity, you will define the following items:

- Create Account Symbols.

- Assign Accounts to Account Symbol.

- Create Keys for Posting Rules.

- Define Posting Rules.

To Define Check Deposit, follow this menu path: **IMG: Financial Accounting ➤ Bank Accounting ➤ Business Transactions ➤ Check Deposit ➤ Define Posting Keys and Posting Rules for Check Deposit**.

The Determine Work Area: Entry dialog box pops up, enter your company chart of accounts key in the Chart of Accounts field and click Enter at the bottom of the dialog box.

The **Change View "Create Account Symbols": Overview** screen is displayed (Figure 9-17).

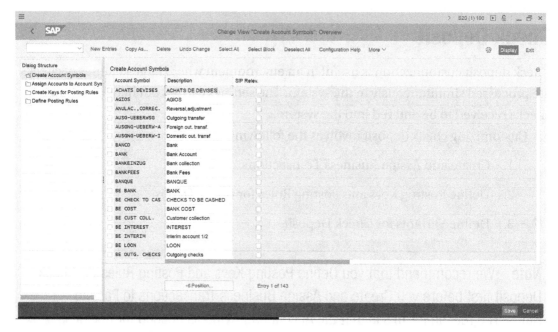

Figure 9-17. *Creating Account Symbols for check deposit*

On this screen, you will define the following items:

- Create Account Symbols,

- Assign Accounts to Account Symbol,

- Create Keys for Posting Rules,

- Define Posting Rules,

Tip   *To ensure that your configuration is complete, work through the folders on the Dialog Structure on the left-hand side of the screen systematically in steps from top down.*

The first step in this activity is to create account symbols for your check deposit.

Step 1

Creating Account symbols for Check Deposit

You will notice that the ***Create Account Symbol*** folder on the ***Dialog Structure*** is open.

Choose New Entries at the top left of the screen. The ***New Entries: Overview of Added Entries*** screen is displayed. This screen will allow you to create your own account symbols

Update the following fields:

Account Symbol: Enter a symbol of your choice in this field. In this activity, we used CHKDEPOSIT as our account symbol.

Description: Enter a short description in this field, such as Check Deposit.

Note   There is no hard rule to creating Account Symbols. You don't necessarily have to use the account symbols used in this activity; it is only for illustration. You can formulate your own account symbols.

Once an account symbol has been used by someone else, the system will not allow you to use the same account symbol again. So, use your own initiative when creating your account symbols by trying other symbols – be creative.

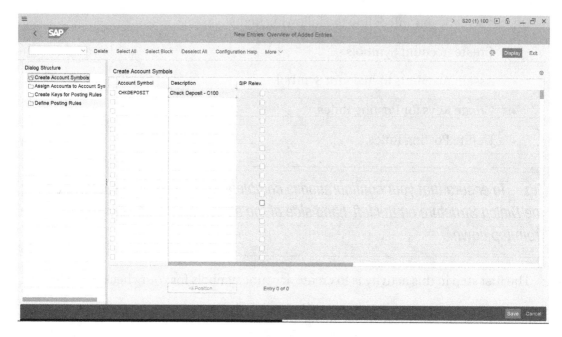

Figure 9-18. *Specification of account symbols for your check deposit*

Once you have specified your account symbol (as in Figure 9-18), hit the Enter key on your keyboard and save your Account Symbols.

The second step in this activity is to assign accounts to the account symbols you have created for your check deposit. Save your account symbol.

Step 2

Assigning Accounts to account symbols

By assigning accounts to accounts symbol during configuration, the system automatically specifies the G/L accounts that transactions are posted to when check deposit transactions are carried out.

In Figure 9-18 double click the Assign Accounts to Account Symbol folder on the **Dialog structure** on the top left hand corner. The *Change View "Assign Accounts to Account Symbol": Overview* screen comes up, displaying the accounts you assigned to account symbol in Electronic Bank Statement earlier during your customizing (Figure 9-19). So you don't need to create another account symbol.

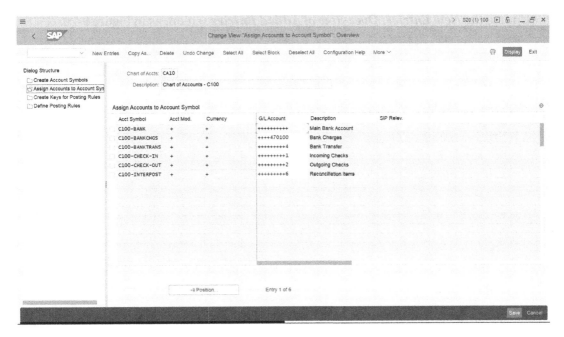

Figure 9-19. *Previously assigned accounts to an account symbol*

Step 3

Creating Keys for Posting Rules

To create keys for posting rules, double click the Create Keys for Posting Rules folder in the **Dialog structure** on the top left hand pane of the screen to create the keys for posting rules. The Change View "Define Posting Rules": Overview screen is displayed. Choose New Entries at the top left of the screen to go to the New Entries: Details of Added Entries screen where your will create the posting rules for your check deposit.

Note   You can use the Posting Keys supplied by SAP or you can create your own posting keys from scratch. In this activity, we recommend that you create your own posting key.

Tip   *The system allows a maximum of four characters as a posting rule key.*

Update the *New Entries: Overview of Added Entries* screen, as in Figure 9-20.

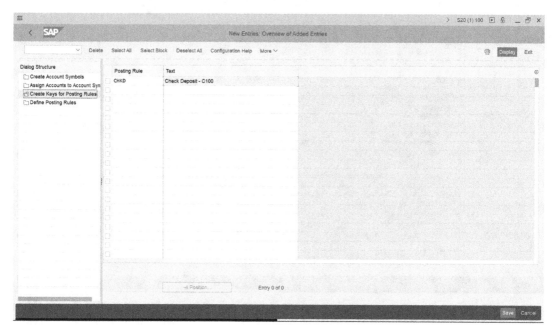

Figure 9-20. *Customizing keys for posting rules for check deposit*

Save the keys for your posting rules.

Note   The posting keys we used in this activity are only for illustration. You can use any posting key and description of your choice in this activity.

The final step in this activity is to define posting rules that are assigned to your account symbols.

Step 4

Defining Posting Rules

To define posting rules, Double click The Define Posting Rules folder on the **Dialog structure** on the top left hand pane in order to create posting rules. The Change View "Define Posting Rules": Overview screen is displayed. Choose the New Entries at the top left of the screen to proceed to the New Entries: Details of Added Entries screen (Figure 9-21) where you will define your posting rules.

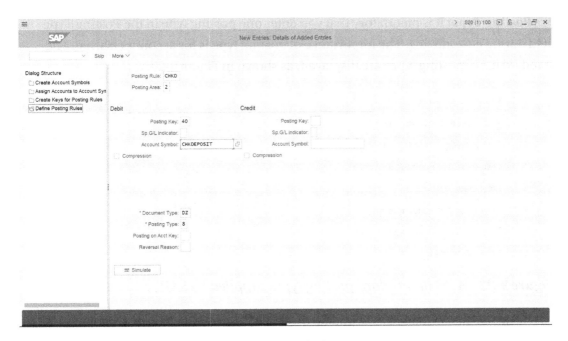

Figure 9-21. *Defining posting rules for check deposit*

Update the following fields:

Posting Rule: Enter the Keys for Posting Rules that you defined above in the Posting Rule fields. Posting Rules are used by the system to determine which GL accounts and subledgers to post transactions to.

Posting Area: The SAP ERP System comes with two standard values for posting area (1 – Bank Accounting and 2 – Subledger Accounting). Posting Area will allow the system to post to either of the specified areas.

Posting Key: Enter the appropriate posting key in this field. Posting key allows the system to determine whether a line item should be treated as debit or credit and the account type to post transaction to. It also controls the field status for document entry.

Acct Symbol: You have already defined a number of accounts symbols above. Enter the appropriate account symbol in this field. The Account symbol you entered here will allow the system to determine which account the related transaction is posted to when users retrieve bank statement electronically.

Document Type: Allows you to differentiate between transactions and also allows the system to determine which business transactions to post.

Posting Type: It is mandatory that you enter one posting type in the Posting Type field during customizing. The importance of posting type is for account clearing. The standard list of posting types are displayed, as shown in Figure 9-22.

1	Posting to g/L accounts
2	Post Subledger Account - Debit
3	Post Subledger Account - Credit
4	Creditors Clear bebit G/L account
5	Clear credit G/L account
7	Clear debit subledger account
8	Clear credit G/L subledger account
9	Reset & rev, clear

Figure 9-22. *A list of standard posting types supplied by SAP*

Using the data in Table 9-9 to update the screen for defining posting rules for check deposit:

Table 9-9. *Data to Define Posting Rules for Check Deposit*

Posting Rule	CHKD
Posting Area	2
Dedit	
Posting Key	40
Acct Symbol	CHKDEPOSIT
Document Type	DZ
Posting Type	8

Note   SAP supplied standard Posting Rules. You can copy the standard posting rules supplied by SAP and modify them to meet your requirements or you can create your own Posting Rules.

1. Hit the Enter ✅ button to confirm your entries.

2. Save 💾 your Posting Rules.

Note   It is easier for you to search for the Posting Rule and the Account Symbol you created above and use them.

Step 5

Create and Assign Business Transactions

In this activity, you will create and assign business transactions by specifying indicators for your check deposit and allocate the indicators to defined posting rules. To create and assign business transactions for your check deposit, follow this menu path: ***IMG: Financial Accounting – Bank Accounting – Business Transactions – Check Deposit – Create and Assign Business Transactions.***

1. The ***Change View "Check Deposit Transactions": Overview*** screen is displayed. Choose New Entries at the top left of the screen and the New Entries: Overview of Added Entries comes up.

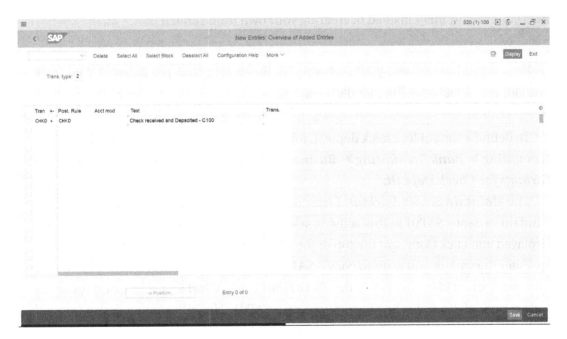

Figure 9-23. *Creating and assigning business transactions for check deposit transaction*

Update the following fields:

- Define your transaction indicator. This is a maximum of four characters.

- Assign your predefined posting rule to your transaction indicator.

- Specify which business transaction is a positive value or negative value using sign +/−.

Using the information below update the ***New Entries: Overview of Added Entries*** screen:

Trans	+ −	Post. rule	Acct mod	
CHKD	+	CHKD		Check Received & deposited − C100

The final step in Banking is to define the Variant for Check Deposit.

Define Variants for Check Deposit

In this activity, you will define variants for check deposit by copying the standard variant supplied by SAP, simply because it is a lot easier to copy standard variants and modify to meet your requirement instead of creating your own from scratch.

Note   if you are defining your own variant, make sure that you activate your own variant and deactivate the standard variant.

To define a variant for check deposit, follow this menu path: ***IMG: Financial Accounting*** ➤ ***Bank Accounting*** ➤ ***Business Transactions*** ➤ ***Check Deposit*** ➤ ***Define Variants for Check Deposit.***

The ***Maintain Screen Variant: List*** screen is displayed. Since you are copying the standard variant – SAP01 in this activity, select SAP01-Standard from the list of variants displayed and click Copy... at the top of the screen. The ***Copy variant*** dialog box pops up. Enter the variant you want to copy – **SAP01** in the ***From Variant*** field and also enter your own variant identifier key in the ***To Variant*** field – **C100** and click Continue at the bottom right of the dialog box to copy variant – SAP01. The Information dialog box with a warning that *"Field FEBMKA-MEHRW is missing on reference screen"* will pop up.

Ignore the information and click Continue at the bottom right of the screen. Once copy is confirmed, the system will automatically copy the standard variant – SAP01 to your variant – C100.

The *Maintain Screen Variant Fields* screen for your Variant – C100 is displayed. Modify the content of this screen to meet your company's requirement.

1. As part of your modification process, delete the items you do not need. In this activity, delete the following items not needed in the **Current fields** section of the screen:

    ✓ 3-digit check number.

    ✓ 8-digit bank key.

    ✓ Document number.

To do this, click the item you want to delete to mark it for deletion and click Delete Field at the top left of the screen.

Once you have deleted the items above, your screen will now look like the one in Figure 9-24.

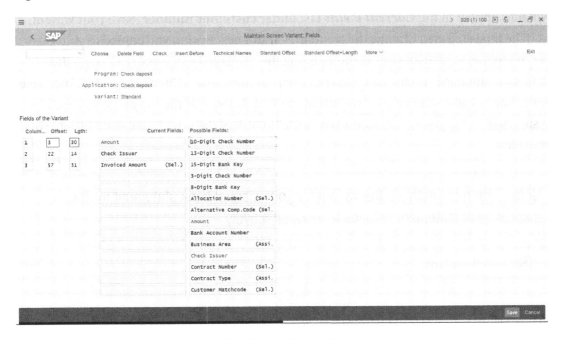

Figure 9-24. *Maintain Variant for Check Deposit*

The next step is to include some items in the **Possible Fields** section to the **Current Fields**. These items will appear as input fields when entering documents into the system.

As part of your customizing exercise, you will need to include the Check Number field in **Possible Fields** list to your **Current Fields** list.

Note   Make sure that the Maximum Length for Amount did not exceed 14. Otherwise, you will not be able to carry on with your customizing. Check the defaulted output length and change it from 30 to 14.

Make sure that the Maximum Length for Invoice Amount did not exceed 15. Otherwise, you will not be able to carry on with your customizing. Check the defaulted output length and change it from 31 to 15.

To add an item to your **Current Fields** list, double click the item **10-Digit Check number** in the **Possible Fields** list. The **Specify output length** dialog box pops up with a defaulted output length. Enter your desired field length in the **Output length** field and click the Continue at the button at the right of the screen. The 10-**digit check number** will now appear in the **Current Fields** List under **customer number**. Save your variant.

The final step is to Change the standard variant description you copied to your own variant name. Search for your variant among the displayed variants list. Change the defaulted Standard variant name to your own variant name – **Check Deposit-C100.** Save your changes and activate your variant by clicking Activate at the top of the screen. The system will notify you on the status bar at the bottom of the screen that your variant was activated.

Note   You must activate the variant for your manual bank statement for the manual bank statement settings to work effectively.

Save your variant.

Summary

This chapter explained what a house bank is and demonstrated how house banks are maintained in SAP ERP. You learned about each specification when configuring your house bank and learned what each does. As part of customizing the house bank, you defined a bank ID and an account ID, which are the key aspects of your house bank configuration and learned how to apply them to the G/L account where your bank account transactions are posted.

You went on to learn about various house banks represented in SAP S4 HANA. You defined the accounts that bank statement transactions are posted to and learned how to customize electronic and manual bank statements. You went through the stages involved in customizing global settings for electronic and manual bank statements. In doing so, you created account symbols that the system uses to determine the G/L accounts and created subledgers, where the bank statement transactions are posted. You then looked at how to assign accounts to account symbols and how to create keys for posting rules. You learned how to define posting rules that are assigned to appropriated transactions (for example, for checks in, checks out, bank transfers, and bank charges). You then learned how to define variants to meet your company code-specific account requirements.

You learned how to customize settings for check deposits. You also learned how to create account symbols, create keys for posting rules for check deposits, and assign accounts to the account symbols you created.

Chapter 10 looks at how to define taxes on sales and purchases in SAP ERP. As part of those exercises, you will look at the basic settings, learn the calculation procedures, and define tax codes for sales and purchases.

Tax on Sales / Purchases

In this chapter, we will learn how tax on sales and purchases are represented in SAP S4 HANA and explore how to define VAT on sales and purchases.

At the end of this chapter, you will be able to:

- Demonstrate an understanding of what a tax on sale/purchase is.

- Create a sales/purchase tax code.

- Specify Tax Category in the GL accounts to which tax will be posted.

- Identify basic tax codes for sales and purchases.

- Specify the accounts to which different tax types are posted.

- Assign tax code to non-taxable transactions.

Sales and Purchases Tax

SAP supports various tax codes for different countries. This chapter covers only sales purchases taxes. Sales/Purchases Taxes are often referred to as VAT (Value Added Tax) in most countries. These are taxes levied on invoiced goods and services payable by the consumer and are held on behalf of the Tax Authority. There are two major VATs. Namely, Input Tax and Output Tax. Input Taxes are levied on purchases of goods and services received from vendors. While on the other hand, Output Taxes are charged on sales of goods and services provided to customers. For example, company A buys goods from company B and is charged 10% on the invoice price of the goods. Company A sells and charges customer Y a 10% VAT. Company A reconciles its VAT account, and the difference is sent to the tax authority. In the case of the United States, the VAT is sent to the United States government revenue department and in the UK VAT is sent to HMRC (Her Majesty Revenue and Custom). Figure 10-1 illustrates this scenario.

© Andrew Okungbowa 2023
A. Okungbowa, *SAP S/4HANA Financial Accounting Configuration*,
https://doi.org/10.1007/978-1-4842-8957-0_10

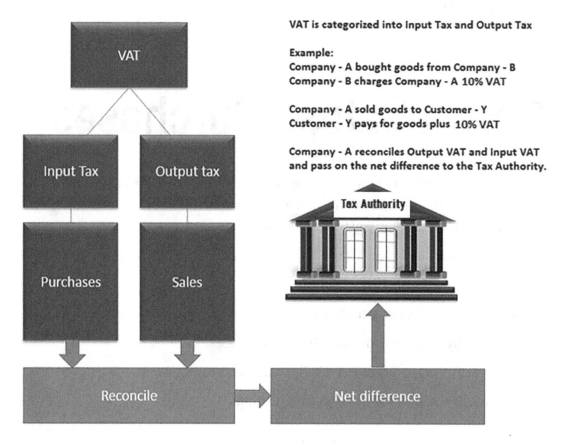

Figure 10-1. *How Tax on Sales/ Purchases (VAT) works*

VAT is split into Input tax and Output tax. A Tax Category is specified in the GL accounts in order for the system to determine and post the right tax to the appropriate account. SAP S4 HANA comes with the following tax categories:

- < is for input tax.

- > is for output tax.

The specification of tax category is very important, because it allows the system to determine whether tax posted is an input tax or output tax and make posting to the appropriate accounts in the system.

If you do not want to post tax manually (i.e., you want the system to automatically post tax during document posting), then you must select **Post Automatically Only** in the appropriate General ledger.

All other G/L accounts may have one of the following entries in the Tax Category field:

Table 10-1. *A list of Tax categories in SAP S4 HANA*

Value	Description
Blank	Non-tax relevant postings (e.g., bank postings)
-	Postings that require an input tax code (for example, reconciliation account for payables from goods and services
+	Postings that require an output tax code (for example, reconciliation account for receivables from goods and services
*	Postings that require any tax code
XX	Posting with the predefined tax code

Basic Settings

SAP S4 HANA comes with standard calculation procedures settings for most countries. It is recommended that you stick with the standard settings in the system, because they are up to date and typically adequate for most tax requirements. The only time you should define calculation procedure for your country is only when your country settings are not included in the standard setting system. However, we recommend that you check the standard calculation procedure to make sure that your country setting is included in the list of calculation procedures provided by SAP in the system.

The standard calculation procedure setting comes with the basic specifications for sales/purchases taxes and contains the calculation and account posting for various countries.

To check the condition types and procedures for every tax group and application rules, follow this menu path: ***IMG: Financial Accounting ➤ Financial Accounting Global Settings ➤ Tax on Sales/Purchases ➤ Basic Settings ➤ Check Calculation Procedure.***

Note   SAP S4 HANA comes with most standard calculation procedures settings for most countries; you do not need to do anything here. The standard calculation procedures setting provided by SAP in the system is sufficient for this activity.

The next step in this activity is to also check if your country is assigned to the calculation procedure provided in the system by SAP. Otherwise, you have to assign your country to an appropriate tax calculation procedure or else your tax calculation will not work.

Check Calculation Procedure

As mentioned above, it is advisable that you use the standard calculation procedure supplied by SAP in the system.

The standard calculation procedures provided by SAP in the system come with the basic specifications for sales/purchases taxes containing the calculation and account postings for various countries. Here you will check the Condition types and Procedures for every tax procedure groups and the applicable calculation rules.

To assign your country to your calculation procedure, follow this menu path:
IMG: Financial Accounting ➤ Financial Accounting Global Settings ➤ Tax on Sales/ Purchases ➤ Basic Settings ➤ Assign Country to Calculation Procedure.

The Change View "Assign Country _> Calculate Procedure": Overview screen is displayed (Figure 10-2).

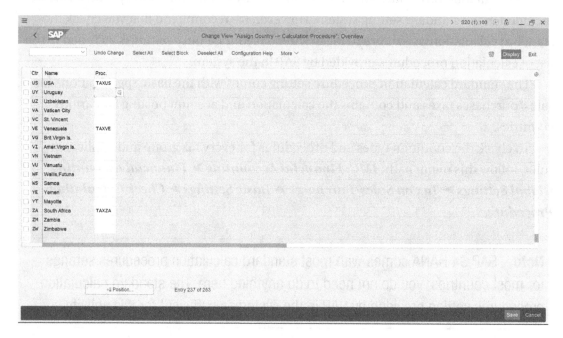

Figure 10-2. Assigning country to calculation procedure

Using the position button at the bottom of the screen search for your country code. For example, the country code for the United States of America is US, for Great Britain is UK, for Canada is CA, and so on.

Assign your country calculation procedure to your country (Figure 10-2). In our activity, our country is USA, and the calculation procedure is TAXUS. Upon the assignment of your tax calculation to your country, save your work by clicking the save button at the bottom right of the screen.

For any other country other than the USA, you have to search for the appropriate country's tax procedure using the search function button and assign it adequately.

The next step in this activity is to define tax codes for sales and purchases. The tax code you will define for sales will be specific to your company based on your country's requirements.

Define Tax Codes for Sales

A tax code contains one or more tax rates that are applicable to different tax types represented in SAP S4 HANA. It is recommended that you define different tax codes for different tax types and rates. If your company has operations in more than one country, you should define separate sales/purchase tax codes for each country. Secondly, in some countries, you must report tax-exempt or non-taxable items to the tax authority. Hence, we advised that you should define 0 (zero) value tax code to report tax-exempt or non-table sales.

Problem: Let's assume in the US, the output sale tax (VAT) is 10%. Spoxio Inc. – C100 want you to define 10% sales tax codes that users will apply to sales during document entry and specify the G/L account output sales tax are posted to.

To define your tax code for sales and purchases, follow this menu path: ***IMG: Financial Accounting ➤ Financial Accounting Global Settings ➤ Tax on Sales/ Purchases ➤ Calculation ➤ Define Tax Codes for Sales and Purchases.*** The Country dialog box pops up. Enter your country code in the Country field and click the continue bottom at the bottom right of the dialog box. The **Maintain Tax code: Initial Screen** is displayed (Figure 10-3).

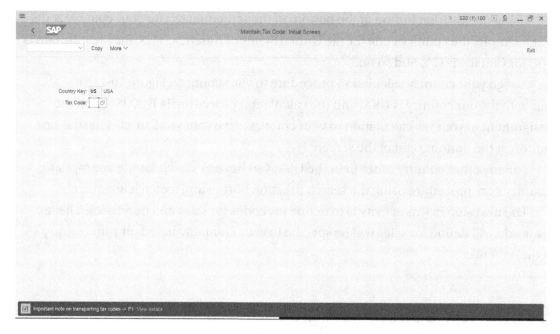

Figure 10-3. *Maintain a tax code for output/sales tax*

Update the following fields:

Country Key: Enter your company code country tax code in this filed. This is your country identification key. This is usually the first two characters of your company code country. For example, the country code for the United States of America is US, for France is FR, Italy IT, and so on. In this activity, we used US as our country code since our company code country is the United States of America.

Tax Code: Enter a tax code in this field. This is a two-digit character. SAP S4 HANA comes with a predefined tax code in the system. To access the predefined tax code provided by SAP in the system, use the search function by the tax code field. A list of tax codes is displayed. Select the appropriate tax code that best fit the item you are creating a tax code for, better still, you can create your own tax code to meet your requirements. In this activity, we are creating our tax code as the list of tax codes provided in the system did not meet our requirements. The tax code we are creating is I2(i2).

Hit enter on your keyboard for the system to accept your tax code. The Properties screen pops up, as in Figure 10-4.

Note   Tax codes are unique; you cannot use the same tax code twice, when defining another tax code with a different tax type. For example for a tax rate of 5%, use I1, as your tax code, I2 for 10%, and so on.

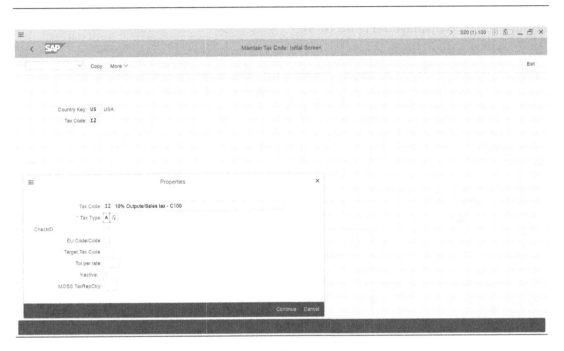

Figure 10-4.   *The screen where you describe your tax code and assign a tax type to your tax code*

Tip   You can define more than one tax code for 5%, 10%, 20%, and so on. The percentage you define for your tax code is based on your country tax requirements. There is no restriction to the number of tax codes you can create.

Update the following fields:

Tax code I2: Enter a description that best describes your tax code in the description field. In our example for tax code I2, we used "10% Output/Sales tax" as our tax code description.

Tax Type: This field is mandatory. SAP S4 HANA comes with a predefined tax type in the system. Using the search function, select the tax type A- Output tax

Tip   A is for output tax and V is for input tax. Since we are defining the tax code for an output tax, enter tax type A in this field.

Click the Continue button at the bottom right of the screen. The Maintain Tax Code: Tax Rate screen is displayed (Figure 10-5).

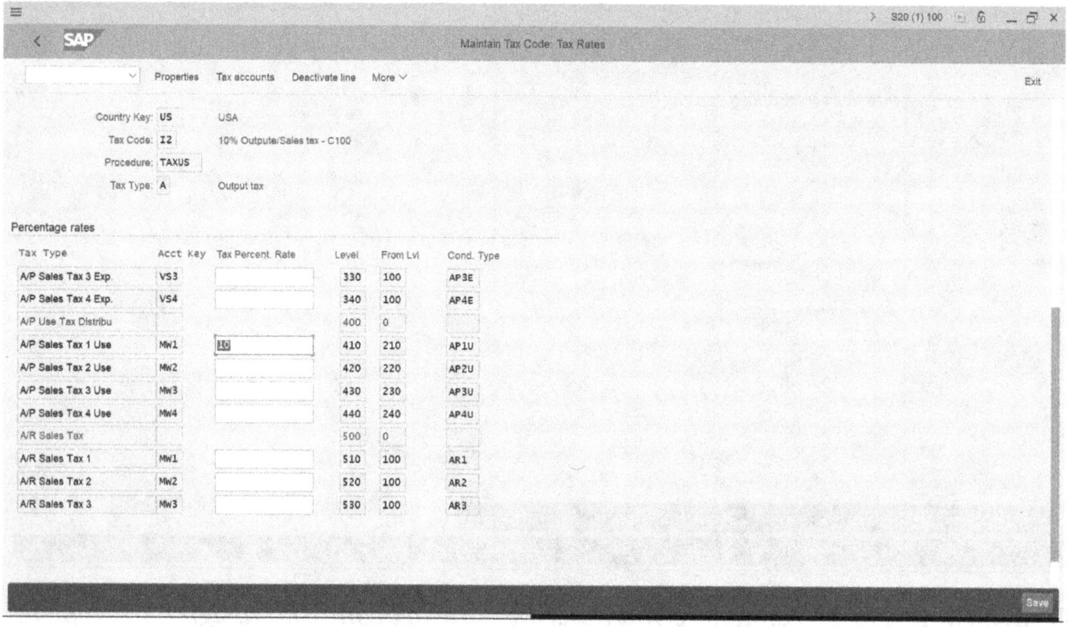

Tax Type	Acct key	Tax Percent. Rate	Level	From Lvl	Cond. Type
A/P Sales Tax 3 Exp.	VS3		330	100	AP3E
A/P Sales Tax 4 Exp.	VS4		340	100	AP4E
A/P Use Tax Distribu			400	0	
A/P Sales Tax 1 Use	MW1	10	410	210	AP1U
A/P Sales Tax 2 Use	Mw2		420	220	AP2U
A/P Sales Tax 3 Use	Mw3		430	230	AP3U
A/P Sales Tax 4 Use	Mw4		440	240	AP4U
A/R Sales Tax			500	0	
A/R Sales Tax 1	MW1		510	100	AR1
A/R Sales Tax 2	Mw2		520	100	AR2
A/R Sales Tax 3	Mw3		530	100	AR3

Figure 10-5. *Maintain Tax code for tax rates screen*

Using the scroll bar at the right side of the screen, search for the Acct key (Account key) from the account keys list supplied by SAP in the system that meets your requirement. This activity assumes that 10% is the tax rate for our tax code. Since we are creating an output tax for our tax code, we are using A/R Sales Tax 1 Inv – MW1. Enter your percentage rate in the A/R Sales Tax 1 Inv – MW1 field. In this activity, we used 10% as the percentage rate for our tax code (Figure 10-5).

The next step is to define the tax account for our tax code. This setting determines the G/L accounts where the tax amounts arising from tax calculations are posted. The system will apply 10% tax assigned to our tax code to the invoice amount and calculate the tax amount for the output tax. The calculated tax will then be posted to the G/L account you have assigned in the next activity.

Define Tax Account for Output/Sales

In this step, we will specify the G/L account for tax type that output taxes are posted to. The system will automatically determine the G/L account that tax type is posted based on our specifications. The system will calculate the tax amount based on the percentage entered in our tax code and apply the specified tax type and automatically post the tax amount to the account you assigned to your tax code.

Note   Before proceeding with this exercise, we advise that you should create a G/L you are assigning to your tax code. Please refer to Appendix 1 - Chapter 10 for details on how to create a G/L account for output and input taxes.

To go to the screen where account assignment is customized, follow this menu path: ***IMG: Financial Accounting*** ➤ ***Financial Accounting Global Settings*** ➤ ***Tax on Sales/Purchases*** ➤ ***Posting*** ➤ ***Define Tax Accounts*** or you could use the Transaction code (TC): OB40.

Note   Because of the complexity involved in using the menu path, we recommend that you use the TC: OB40 instead of using the menu path.

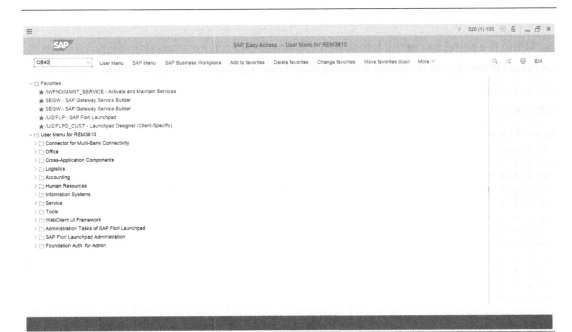

Figure 10-6. *SAP Easy Access – User Menu screen*

On the SAP Easy Access screen (Figure 10-6), enter OB40 in the command field at the top left of the screen. When you press the enter key on your keyboard, the Configuration Accounting Maintain: Automatic Posts – Procedures screen is displayed (Figure 10-7).

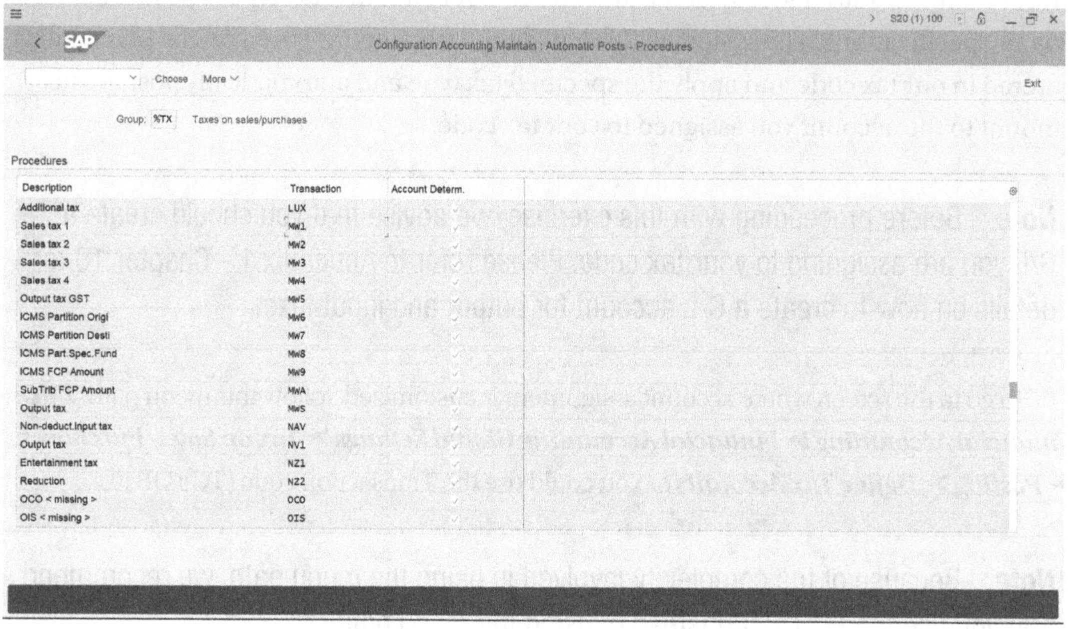

Figure 10-7. *Maintaining automatic posting procedure for tax codes*

Using the scroll bar at the left side of the screen search for transaction key Sales tax 1 – MW1. When you double click transaction key Sales tax 1 – MW1, the Enter charts of accounts dialog box pops up. Enter your chart of account ID in the Chart of Accounts field. In this activity, we used CA10 as our chart of account ID. Click continue at the bottom right of the screen, the Configuration Accounting Maintain: Automatic Posts – Procedure screen is displayed. Click the save button at the bottom right of the screen. The Configuration Accounting Maintain: Automatic Posts – Accounts screen comes up. This is the screen where you will assign a G/L account where output tax will be posted.

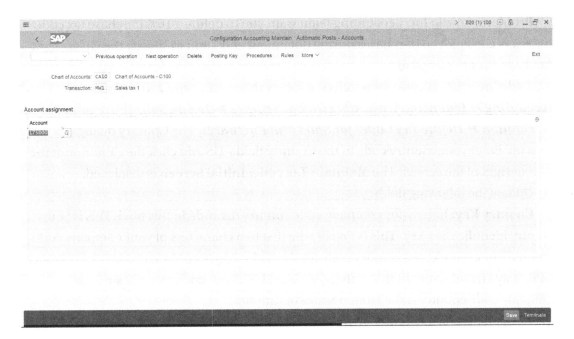

Figure 10-8. *Assign G/L account for Automatic of output/sales tax*

Enter the G/L account for output tax in the account field and save your work.

Note   if you have not created the appropriate G/L accounts yet, the system will notify you that "No matches found," as in Figure 10-8. If you click the save at the bottom right of the screen, the system will notify you in the status bar at the bottom of the screen that the account is not created in chart of accounts. You can force the system to accept your G/L accounts temporarily, until you create your G/L accounts by hitting the enter button on your keyboard.

Define Tax Codes for Input/Purchases

The same steps are followed when customizing the tax code for input/purchases. The only difference is using a different tax code, tax type, and G/L account. It is important to create different tax code for purchases for different countries (if your company operates in more than one country), because each country tax requirements and specifications are different. Now let's define the tax code for input/purchases.

Problem: Spoxio Inc. accounting team want you to define a 10% Purchase tax code that users can apply to purchases during document entry and to specify the GL account Purchase Tax are posted to.

To define your tax code for purchases, follow this menu path: ***IMG: Financial Accounting ➤ Financial Accounting Global Settings ➤ Tax on Sales/Purchases ➤ Calculation ➤ Define Tax Codes for Sales and Purchases.*** The Country dialog box pops up. Enter your country code in the Country field – US and click the Continue at the bottom right of the screen. The **Maintain Tax code: Initial Screen** is displayed.

Update the following fields:

Country Key: Enter your company code country tax code in this filed. This is your country identification key. This is usually the first two characters of your company code country. For example, the country code for the United States of America is US, for France is FR, Italy IT, and so on. In this activity, we used US as our country code since our company code country is the United States of America.

Tax Code: Enter a tax code in this field. This is a two-digit character. SAP S4 HANA comes with predefined tax codes in the system. To access the predefined tax code provided by SAP in the system, use the search function by the tax code field. A list of tax codes is displayed. Select the appropriate tax code that best fits the item you are creating a tax code for; better still, you can create your own tax code to meet your requirements. In this activity, we are creating our tax code, as the list of tax codes provided in the system did not meet our requirements. The tax code we are creating is U2.

Hit enter on your keyboard for the system to accept your tax code. The Properties screen pops up, as in Figure 10-9.

Note   Tax codes are unique; you cannot use the same tax code twice, when defining another tax code with a different tax type. For example, for a tax rate of 5%, use I1, as your tax code, I2 for 10%, and so on.

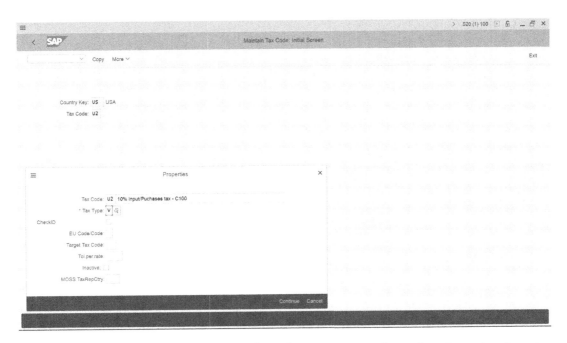

Figure 10-9. *The screen where you describe your tax code and assign a tax type to your tax code*

Update the following fields:

Tax code U2: Enter a description that best describes your tax code in the description field. In our example for tax code U2 we used "10% Input/Purchases tax" as our tax code description.

Tax Type: This field is mandatory. SAP S4 HANA comes with predefined tax type in the system. Using the search function, select the tax type V– Input tax

Click the Continue button at the bottom right of the screen. The Maintain Tax Code: Tax Rate screen is displayed (Figure 10-10).

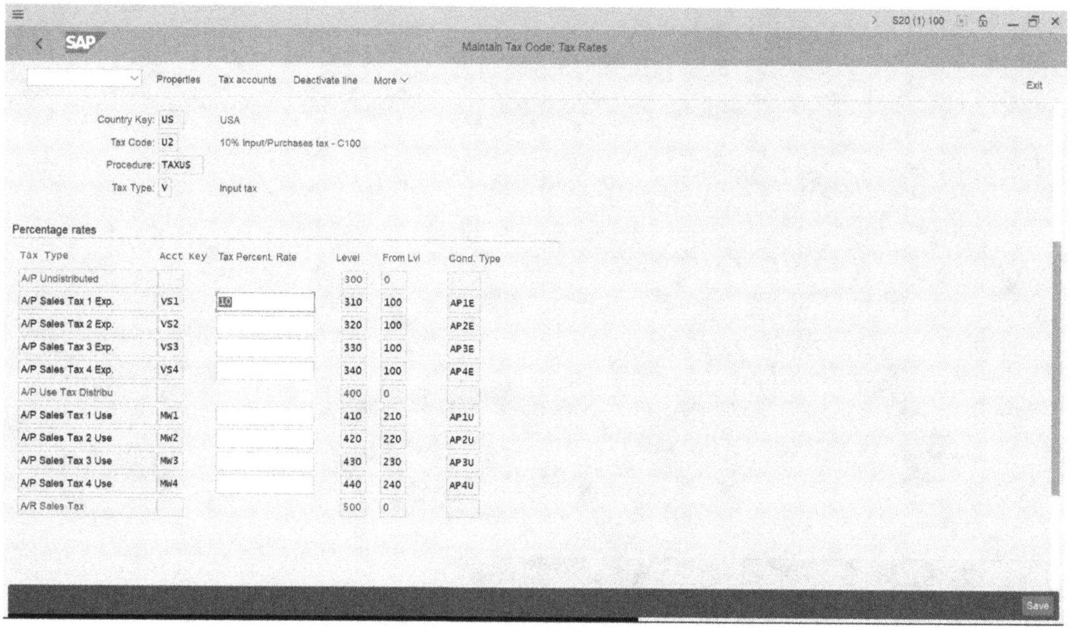

Figure 10-10. *Maintain Tax code for tax rates screen*

This activity assumes that 10% is the tax rate for our tax code. Since we are creating an output tax for our tax code, enter a percentage rate in the A/P Sales Tax 1 Exp. – VS1 Field. In this activity, we used 10% as the percentage rate for our tax code (Figure 10-5).

The next step is to define the tax account for our tax code. This setting determines the G/L accounts where the tax amounts arising from tax calculations are posted. The system will apply 10% tax assigned to our tax code to the invoice amount and calculate the tax amount for the output tax. The calculated tax will then be posted to the G/L account you have assigned in the next activity.

Define Tax Account for Output/Sales

Note   Before proceeding with this exercise, we advise that you should create a G/L you are assigning to your tax code.

In this activity, you specify the G/L account for posting taxes. The system will automatically determine the G/L account where the tax type is posted. To go to the screen were account assignment is customized, follow this menu path: ***IMG: Financial***

Accounting ➤ *Financial Accounting Global Settings* ➤ *Tax on Sales/Purchases* ➤
Posting ➤ *Define Tax Accounts* or you could use the Transaction code (TC): **OB40.**

Note   Because of the complexity involved in using the menu path, we recommend
that you use the TC: OB40 instead of using the menu path.

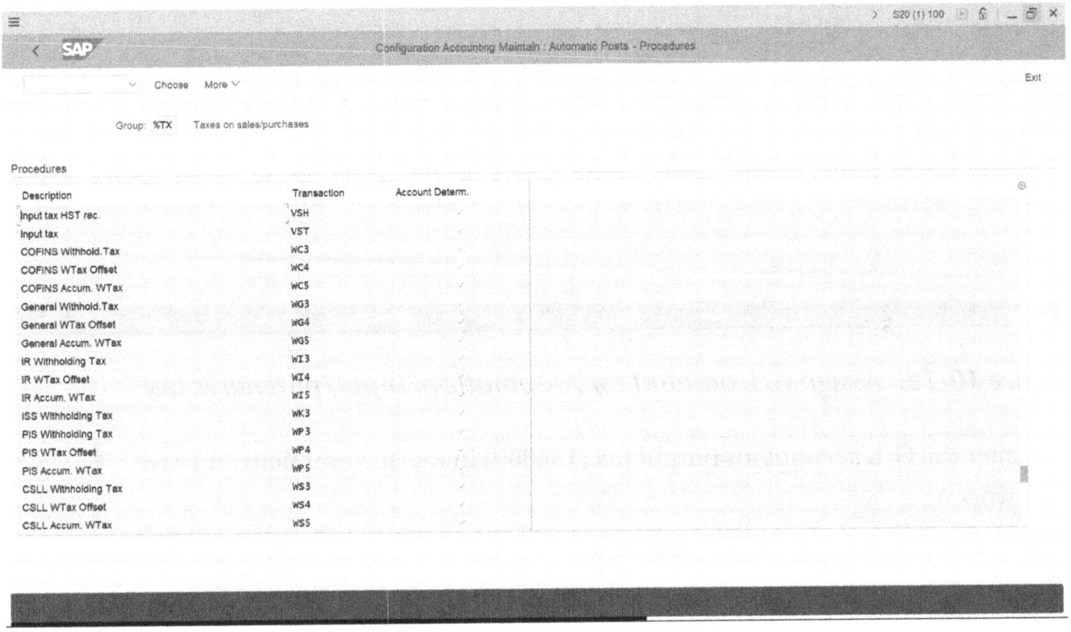

Figure 10-11. *Maintaining automatic posting procedure for tax codes*

In the SAP Easy Access screen (Figure 10-6), enter OB40 in the command field at the
top left of the screen. When you press the enter key on your keyboard, the Configuration
Accounting Maintain: Automatic Posts – Procedures screen is displayed.

Using the scroll bar at the left side of the screen search for transaction key Input tax –
VST from the list of procedures listed on the screen. When you double click transaction
key Input tax – VST, the Enter charts of accounts dialog box pops up. Enter your chart
of account ID in the Chart of Accounts field. In this activity, we used CA10 as our chart
of account ID. Click continue at the bottom right of the screen, the Configuration
Accounting Maintain: Automatic Posts – Procedure screen is displayed. Click the save
button at the bottom right of the screen. The Configuration Accounting Maintain:
Automatic Posts – Accounts screen comes up. This is the screen where you will assign
the G/L account where the input tax will be posted.

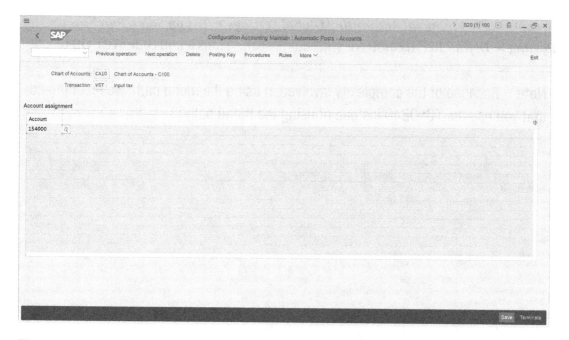

Figure 10-12. *Assign G/L account for Automatic of input/purchases tax*

Enter the G/L account for output tax (154000) in the account field and save your work.

Note   As we said earlier, if you have not created your G/L for this activity, when you try to save your customization, the system will tell you that your G/L is created. You can either stop and create your G/L for input/purchase tax that you will be assigning here or you force the system to accept the G/L account you have assigned temporarily. However, refer to Appendix 1 – Chapter 10 for a sample of the G/L account for this activity.

The next step in this activity, which rounds up this exercise, is to explain how to assign taxable codes for non-taxable transactions in SAP S4 HANA. In some countries, it is mandatory to report tax-exempt or non-taxable items to the tax authority. SAP S4 HANA allows you to report tax-exempt or non-Taxable items by assigning a tax code to non-taxable transactions.

Assign Taxable Codes for Non-Taxable Transactions

When you report tax-exempt or non-taxable sales/purchases to a tax authority, it is best to define a 0 (zero) value tax code to track these types of transactions.

In this activity, you specify tax codes for input tax and output tax for your company code, which is used to post non-taxable transactions to the relevant GL accounts.

Tip   SAP S4 HANA provided standard non-taxable tax codes for input and output for most countries. Although standard non-taxable codes are provided in the system, the system also gives you the flexibility to create your own non-taxable tax code if you chose to do so. However, we recommend that you use the standard non-taxable codes supplied by SAP instead of creating your own codes.

To assign tax code to tax-exempt or non-taxable transactions, follow this menu path: *IMG: Financial Accounting➤ Financial Accounting Global Settings ➤ Tax on Sales/ Purchases ➤ Posting ➤ Assign Tax Codes for Non-Taxable Transactions*. The *Change View "Allocate Co. Cd. ➤ Non-Taxable Transactions" Overview* screen comes up (Figure 10-13).

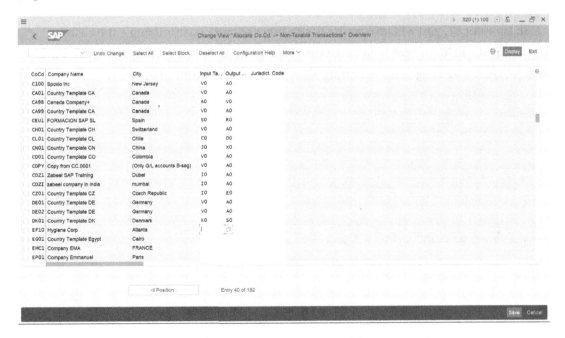

Figure 10-13. *Assignment of tax codes to non-taxable transactions*

Search for your Company Code using the position button at the bottom of the screen. Assign V0 (exempt from input tax) to input tax and A0 (exempt from output tax) to output tax for your company code. Then save your work by hitting the save botton at the bottom right of the screen.

Summary

This chapter explained sales and purchase taxes and gave examples of sales and purchase taxes in practice. You looked at how sales and purchase taxes are reconciled and how the differences are passed on to the tax authority. You also looked at the various tax categories in SAP and learned how they are applied in the system. Thereafter, you looked at the basic settings involved in customizing taxes and learned about their relationship to country-specific settings. You learned how to assign a country to the calculation procedures.

You created two tax codes for sales and purchases taxes using two-digit codes. You went on to look at how to define tax accounts so that the system will automatically post them where you specify.

Finally, you learned how to assign taxable codes to non-taxable transactions using the standard non-taxable codes.

In Chapter 11, you will look at the final aspect of bank customizing – the cash journal. You will learn how to set up a new cash journal, define a company code for the cash journal, and assign G/L accounts where cash transactions are posted.

CHAPTER 11

Cash Journal

Objective

In this chapter, we look at what a cash journal is in SAP S4 HANA and go through the steps involved in customizing a cash journal.

At the end of the chapter, you will be able to:

- Set up a cash journal.

- Create G/L accounts for your cash journal.

- Specify the amount limit for your cash journal.

- Define number range intervals for our cash journal.

- Create, change, and delete business transactions.

- Set up Print Parameters for Cash Journal.

Introduction

Cash Receipts and cash Payments transactions are managed in SAP R/3 using Cash Journals. A cash Journal is a sub-module in Bank Accounting that serves as a cash management tool in SAP R/3. You can maintain separate Cash Journals for each company code in the system for each currency and make postings to appropriate accounts in FI.

© Andrew Okungbowa 2023
A. Okungbowa, *SAP S/4HANA Financial Accounting Configuration*,
https://doi.org/10.1007/978-1-4842-8957-0_11

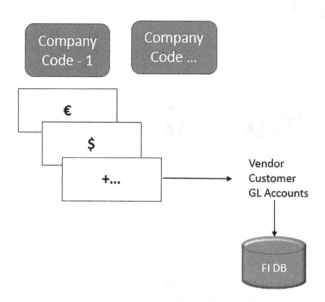

Figure 11-1. *Setting up a cash journal in SAP S4 HANA*

In SAP S4 HANA, you can create a separate cash journal for each currency maintained by your company code, post to customer, vendor and general ledger accounts in FI, and maintain more than one cash journal per company code.

The advantage of using the SAP cash journal tool is that it displays opening and closing balances, calculates total cash receipts and total cash payments, and reconciles the cash balance at any given time.

When setting up a new cash journal, the following items are defined as part of your Cash Journal configuration:

- The company code that will use the cash journal.

- Identification key (usually a four-digit code). This will allow you to identify your Cash Journal.

- The name of the cash journal (a short text describing your Cash Journal)

- The General Ledger Accounts in which Cash Transactions are posted.

- The currency for your cash journal.

- The document type for the following items:

  ✓ General Ledger postings.

  ✓ Outgoing payments to vendors.

✓ Incoming payments from vendors.

✓ Outgoing payments to customers.

✓ Incoming payments from customers.

Tip   *We recommend that you create different cash journals for each currency and each company code you use.*

Create G/L Account for Cash Journal

Cash transactions are posted to the G/L accounts assigned to the cash journal. We will take you through how to assign G/L accounts to a cash journal when looking at how to customize "Set Up Cash Journal" and "Create, Change, and Delete Business Transactions" later in this activity.

Problem: Company C900 plc operates large cash transactions and they want you to set up a Cash Journal for cash transaction that will make postings to the following accounts in FI:

- Petty Cash.

- Cash Transfer from Bank.

- Cash Transfer to Bank.

- Cash Purchase.

- Cash Sale.

Note   You will need to create G/L accounts for the following that you will be assigning to your cash journal during your customization:

- Petty Cash.

- Cash Transfer from Bank.

- Cash Transfer to Bank.

- Cash Purchase – Office Materials.

- Cash Sales.

Please refer to Chapter 5 on how to create a G/L account. In addition, you will be provided more details in Appendix A – Chapter 10, where you will find more useful information on how to create G/L accounts for a cash journal.

Specify the Amount Limit for a Cash Journal

The function of Amount Limit is to set a cash limit for Cash Journal in FI. The limit you set for your cash journal serves as a control mechanism, because it allows the system to determine the maximum amount that can be posted per transaction to the cash journal. In this customizing, you will define the Company Code, Currency, and the Amount Limit. The currency posted will be automatically adjusted to the Company Code Currency. Where limits are exceeded, the user will get an error message. To go to the screen where you will set the amount limit for your cash journal follow this menu path: ***IMG: Financial Accounting*** ➤ ***Banking – Business Transactions*** ➤ ***Cash Journal*** ➤ ***Define Amount Limit.***

Tip   *You may not need to specify Amount Limit or Define Document Types for Cash Journal Documents for this activity.*

The Change View "Cash Journal: Amount Limit": Overview screen is displayed. Click New Entries at the top left of the screen to go to the screen where you will specify the amount limit for your cash journal. The New Entries: Overview of Added Entries screen comes up (Figure 11-2).

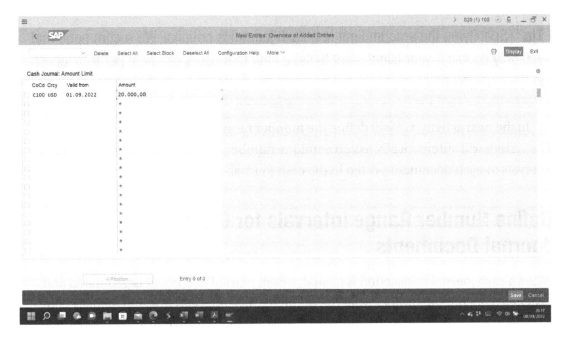

Figure 11-2. *Cash journal – Amount limit specification screen*

Update the following fields:

CoCd: Enter the company code you are using for the cash journal in this filed. In this activity, we used our company code – C100.

Crcy: Enter the currency key you want to use in your cash journal in this field.

Valid From: This is the date you want your cash journal amount limit you specified to be valid from.

Note: We recommend that you use today's date. However, nothing stops you from using an earlier or future date.

Amount: The amount you enter in this field defines the maximum amount that users can post per transaction in the cash journal.

Note   If no amount limit is specified, there will be no restriction to the amount the user can post in the cash journal.

After you update the screen, as in Figure 11-2, click the save button at the bottom right of the screen to save your cash journal amount limit settings.

Tip   Specifying the amount limit in a cash journal is optional. We recommend that you only do this if your client want to set a limit that users can post per transaction in the cash journal.

In the next activity, we will define the number range intervals for our cash journal. The system will automatically assign a unique number from the defined number range intervals to each document posted in the cash journal.

Define Number Range Intervals for Cash Journal Documents

When a cash journal transaction is posted, a cash journal document is generated and assigned a document number from the number range intervals that you defined. The document number assigned to the posted cash journal transaction coupled with your company code will allow you to identify a given document within a fiscal year.

Note   We recommend that you copy the number range of a company supplied by SAP in the system instead of creating your own to save time and to ensure that the number range you copied is accurate. We suggest that you copy any of the number range of company code, 0001 or 1000 or 2000.

Problem: To save time and to ensure that number range intervals for the cash journal are accurate, you have been asked to define a cash journal number range by copying the number range intervals of company code 0001 supplied by SAP S4 HANA and modify them to meet your requirements.

To define the number range number intervals for your cash journal, follow this menu path: *IMG: Financial Accounting ➤ Banking – Business Transactions ➤ Cash Journal ➤ Define Number Range Intervals for Cash Journal Documents*. The Edit Interval: Cash Jour.Doc. Numbs. Object CAJO_DOC2 screen is displayed.

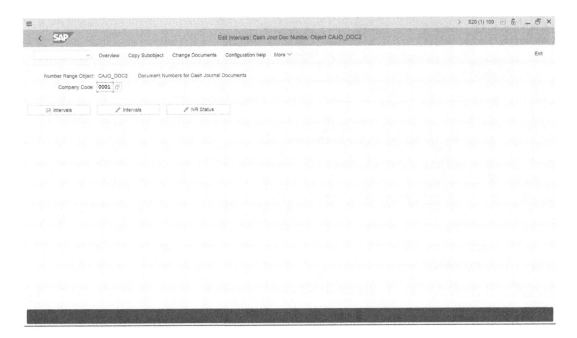

Figure 11-3. *The initial screen where you will copy the source company code number range intervals to your company code*

Since you are copying the number range interval of company code 0001, enter the company code – 0001 in the Company code field and click Copy Subobject at the top of the screen. When the Copy Company Code dialog box pops up, update the following fields:

From: The system will automatically default the company code you are copying its number range intervals. Otherwise, you should enter it manually. Since we want to copy the number range intervals of company code – 0001, enter this company code in this field.

To: Enter the company code you are copying to (this is often referred to as the target company) in this field. In this activity, we used company code – C100.

Click copy at the bottom of the dialog box. The Number Range Interval Transport screen will be displayed with information, as in Figure 11-4.

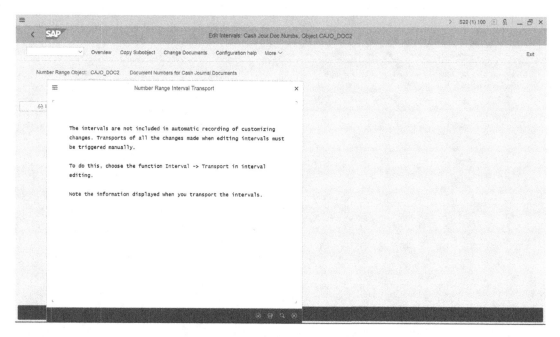

Figure 11-4. Number range interval transport information screen

When you click the enter button (this is the circled green button at the bottom right of the screen), this will take you back to the Edit Interval: Cash Jour.Doc. Numbs. Object CAJO_DOC2 screen again, but this time the system will notify you in the status bar at the bottom of the screen that the source company code (0001) was copied to the target company code (0001).

To display the number intervals copied, follow this menu path: ***IMG: Financial Accounting ➤ Banking – Business Transactions ➤ Cash Journal ➤ Define Number Range Intervals for Cash Journal Documents.***

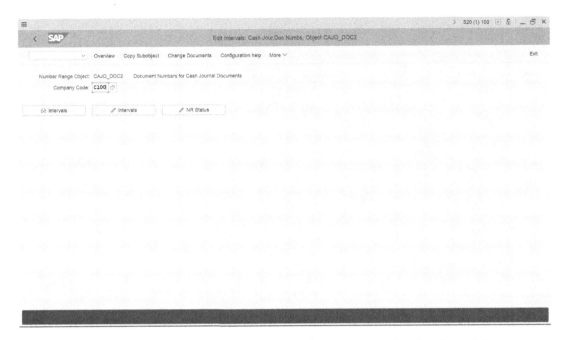

Figure 11-5. *The intial screen where you will commence the display of the company code number range intervals you have copied*

Enter your company code in the Company code field and click the first Intervals button (with a google) in the middle of the screen. The Edit Intervals: Cash Jour, Doc. Numbs. Object CAJO_DOC2. Subject screen appears displaying the number intervals you have copied, as in Figure 11-6.

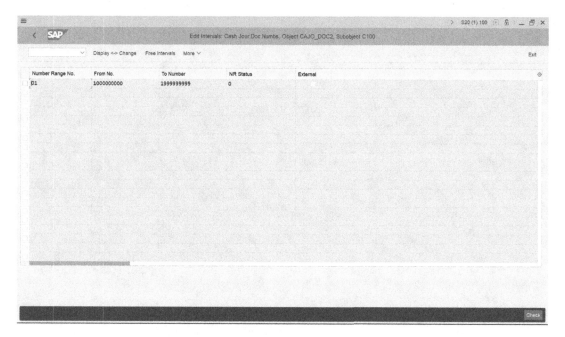

Figure 11-6. *The display of your copied company code number range intervals*

The next step in this activity is the setting up of the cash journal.

Set Up Cash Journal

In this section, you will specify the settings for your cash journal. This includes the company name that you want to use for your cash journal, the number that will identify the cash journal, the G/L account where the cash journal transactions are posted. To set up cash journal, follow this menu path: *IMG: Financial Accounting* ➤ *Banking* ➤ *Business Transactions* ➤ *Cash Journal* ➤ *Set Up Cash Journal.*

The *Change View "Maintain View for Cash Journals": Overview* screen is displayed. Click New Entries at the top left side of the screen. This will take you to the New Entries: Overview of Added Entries screen. This is the screen where you will define the setting for your cash journal.

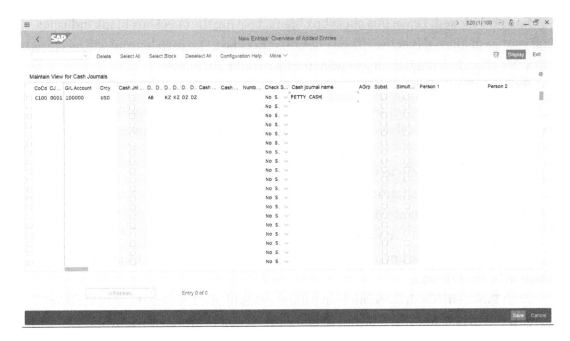

Figure 11-7. *Cash journal settings*

Update the following fields:

CoCd: Enter your company code in this field. This is the company code that you want to use for the cash journal you defined in this activity. It is important to define individual cash journals for each company code. You can define a cash journal per transaction or per currency.

CJ Number: You can enter a maximum of four digits of your choice in this field. If you are creating more than one cash journal, make sure that the numbers you use are logical and sequential (for example, 0001, 0002, 0003, and so on). This number will identify your cash journal. This is important when you have more than one cash journal in the system.

G/L Account: Enter the G/L account number 100000 (for petty cash) you created earlier. When cash journal transactions are entered in the system, they are automatically posed to the G/L account you assign for your cash journal.

Crcy: Enter the currency you want to use in your cash journal. This is usually the company code's currency. On the contrary, if you choose to run your cash journal in a different currency, you must make sure that the option Only Balances in Local Crcy in your cash journal G/L account master data is not checked.

Cash Jnl Closed: Leave this checkbox blank. Leaving the checkbox blank indicates that your cash journal is active. If you click this checkbox, the cash journal will be closed. Click this checkbox only when you want to close your cash journal.

DT: Specify the document types for cash journal postings. Document type determines the business transaction and account to post your cash journal transaction to. SAP comes with several document types to choose from, for example:

AB-G/L Account

KZ-Outgoing payment to vendor

KZ Incoming payment from vendor

DZ-Incoming payment from customer

DZ-Outing payment to customer

You can access these document types by using the matchcode or using the search function by the DT field.

Cash Payment/Cash Receipt: Leave these fields blank. Leaving these fields blank enables you to post both cash payment and cash receipts to your cash journal.

Check Split: The specification you make here will determine whether the line items of the total posting are split when processing check deposits. You have three options:

- Offsetting Item of Total Document Split: When you specify this item, only the offsetting item of the total posting is split.

- All Items of Total Document Split: When this item is specified, the checks posted to the cash journal and the offsetting totals are split.

- No Split of Line Items of Totals Document: No splitting is performed.

For this activity, Select No Spit of Line Items of Totals Document. This allows the user to carry out the split manually.

Cash journal name: Enter the description of your cash journal in this field. For instance, Petty Cash.

Save your cash journal settings by click the save button at the bottom right of the screen.

In the next activity, you will specify the company code, the transaction number, the business truncation, the G/L accounts, the tax code, and the cash journal business transactions for your cash journal.

Maintain Business Transactions

The maintain business transaction function will enable you to Maintain View for Cash Journal Transaction Names. It is possible to copy the standard *maintain business transactions* predefined by SAP in the system and modify them to meet your requirement or you can create your own afresh. It is a matter of choice. You will get the same result.

In this activity, you will be maintaining your own View for Cash Journal transaction from scratch instead of copying the predefined one supplied by SAP as this will give the opportunity to have a feel of how to create your own function from scratch. To go the screen where the business transactions is customized, follow this menu path: *IMG: Financial Accounting (New)* ➤ *Banking* ➤ *Business Transactions* ➤ *Cash Journal* ➤ *Maintain Business Transactions.*

The *Change View "Maintain View for Cash Journal Transaction Names": Overview* screen is displayed. Choose the New Entries button at the top left of the screen. The *New Entries: Overview of Added Entries* screen comes up (Figure 11-8).

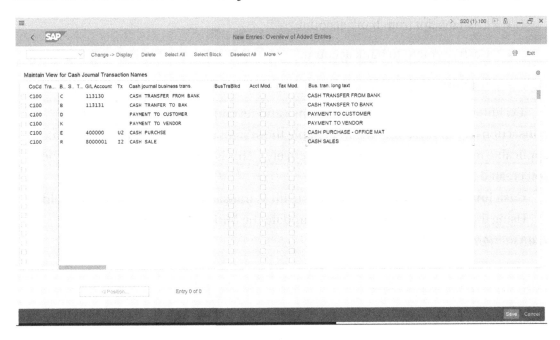

Figure 11-8. *The maintain view for journal business transactions*

Update the following fields:

CoCd: Enter the company for which you want the Cash Journal Transaction to be created. For this activity, enter your company code. Our company code in this activity is C100.

Tran.no: Enter a four-digit identifier number that will uniquely identify your cash journal transaction.

Bus.tran.type: Choose the appropriate business transaction from the list of six Business Transaction Type supplied by SAP in the system.

C-Receipt from bank account

B-Payment to bank account

R-Revenue

E-Expenses

D-Customer posting

K-Vendor posting

G/L account: Enter the GL accounts where you want the transactions relating to the following items to be posted:

- Cash receipt from bank account.

- Cash payment to bank account.

- Expense.

Tx: Enter the right tax codes for expense and revenue in this field for business transactions for the system. This will enable the system to determine the appropriate applicable tax (input or output tax, respectively). This is the input and output tax codes you created in Chapter 10.

Cash journal business trans: Enter business transaction description in this field.

Using the information in Table 11-1, update the **_Maintain Business Transactions_** screen:

Table 11-1. *Details for the Maintaining Business Transaction Screen*

Co. Code	Trans. no	Bus. Trans	Trans Classification	G/L Account	Tax Code	Cash Journal business trans
C100		C		113130		CASH TRANSFER FROM BANK
C100		B		113131		CASH TRANSFER TO BANK
C100		D				PAYMENT TO CUSTOMER
C100		K				PAYMENT TO VENDOR
C900		E		460000	B2	CASH PURCHASE – OFFICE MAT
C00		R		800001	A2	CASH SALES

Note   The GL Accounts entered here will allow cash transactions to be posted to the appropriate GL accounts during document posting. Secondly, the tax code you entered here will allow the system to calculate Input/Output tax, respectively, during cash transactions and also post to the appropriate accounts in FI.

Save your work.

Note   Make sure you use the tax codes you created earlier in Chapter 10 for Input/Output tax, respectively. Otherwise, the system will not accept your tax code. In your configuration above, U2 – Input tax and I2 – Output tax were created.

The final step in this activity is to set up print parameters for a cash journal.

Set up Print Parameters for Cash Journal.

To be able to print the cash journal transactions, you need to set up Pint Parameters for your Cash Journal for each Company Code represented in the system. In this activity, you will copy the standard print parameter of company code 0001 supplied by SAP in the system. To do this, follow this menu path: ***IMG: Financial Accounting (New)*** ➤ ***Banking*** ➤ ***Business Transactions*** ➤ ***Cash Journal*** ➤ ***Set Up Print*** ➤ ***Parameters for Cash Journal.*** The Change View: "Maintain Print Parameter View for Cash Journal" Overview screen is displayed (Figure 11-9).

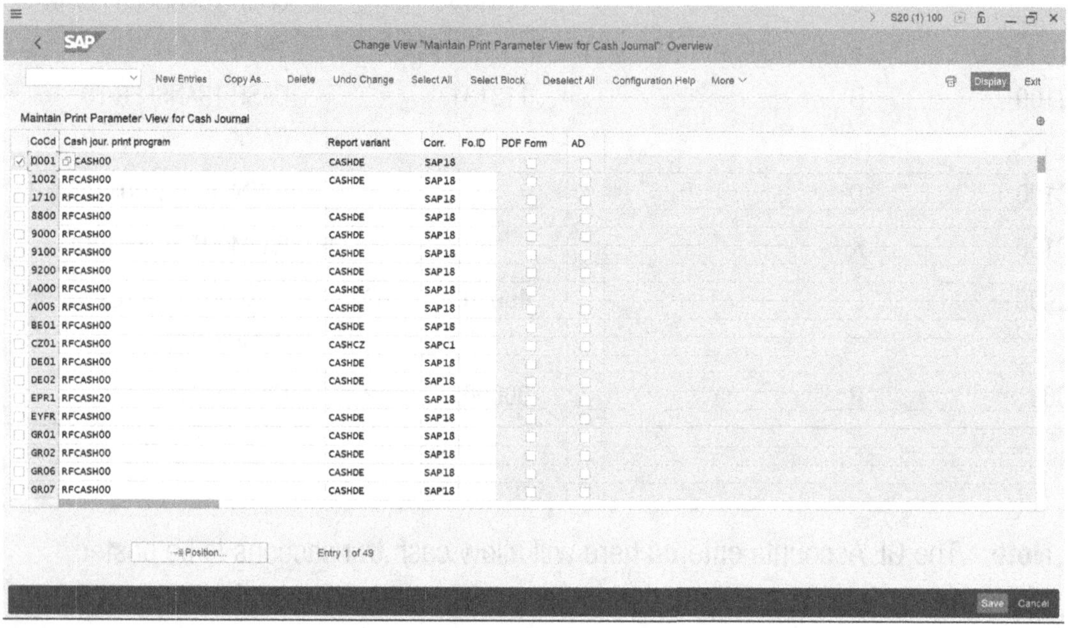

Figure 11-9. *The screen where you may copy predefined or maintain print parameter*

Note SAP comes with predefined Print Parameters. It is advisable to copy a standard Print Parameter and modify it to meet your requirement.

Select the company code whose print parameter you want to copy (in this activity, we copied company code – 0001 supplied by Sap in the system) by making sure the checkbox in front of the company code you are copying is ticked or activated and click the Copy As… function at the top left of the screen. The Change View "Maintain Print Parameter View for Cash Journal": Overview screen is displayed (Figure 11-10).

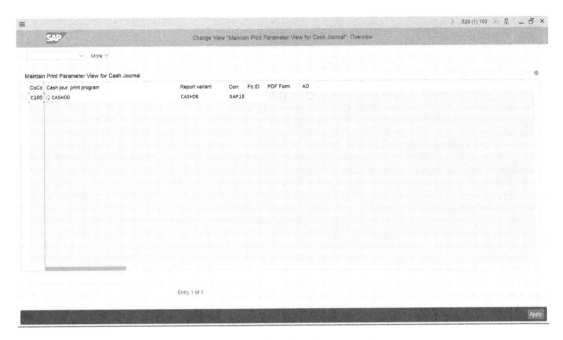

Figure 11-10. *Copy Print Parameters for Cash Journal*

Save your print parameter.

Summary

This chapter explained how cash receipts and payments transactions are managed using the cash journal and discussed the importance of using cash journals as cash-management tools. You went on to look at various settings that allow you to customize your cash journals.

As part of customizing the cash journal, you specified the menu path for creating G/L cash accounts.

You then learned how to set an amount limit, which determines the maximum amount that can be posted per transaction to the cash journal. You also learned how to define number range intervals for the cash journal by copying and modifying standard number range intervals in the system. You learned how to set up a cash journal and how to create, change, and delete business transactions. You also learned how to assign documents to your cash journal that will determine how transactions are posted. Finally, you set up the print parameters for your cash journals.

The next chapter explains what a financial statement is and describes the steps involved in defining financial statement versions. You'll learn how to map financial statement versions and assign appropriate G/L accounts from which financial statements are drawn.

CHAPTER 12

Financial Statement Versions (FSV)

Objective

In this chapter, we will explain what a financial statement version (FSV) is and work through the basic settings involved in defining financial statement versions.

At the end of this chapter, you will be able to:

- Explain and define Financial Statement Version (FSV)

- Define an FSV using appropriate specifications

- Assign FSV hierarchy nodes to appropriate GL Accounts

Financial Statement Versions

In SAP R/3, hundreds of business transactions are posted to the general ledger. To be able to know how well a business is performing from the GL accounts is not possible. Hence, the need for FSV, which form the basis for drawing up financial statements. FSV customization allows users to generate summarized financial reports that show the performance of the business over a given period.

FSV is part of the closing procedure in SAP ERP. It is a tool designed specifically for generating financial statements (such as profit and loss statements and balance sheets) to meet specific legal disclosure requirements related to certain items (such as assets, liabilities, income, expenses, and so on) in financial reports.

© Andrew Okungbowa 2023
A. Okungbowa, *SAP S/4HANA Financial Accounting Configuration*,
https://doi.org/10.1007/978-1-4842-8957-0_12

SAP ERP comes with standard, predefined FSV that you can use as a template and adjust to meet your requirements. You can also define your own FSV afresh if you choose not to use the standard FSV supplied by SAP. Interestingly, you can define more than one FSV if you need to meet individual financial statement reporting needs of various stakeholders, such as the tax authority, investors, and internal management reporting.

To define FSV in SAP ERP, you must specify the following items:

- The items to be included in your FSV, the order and the hierarchical structure of each item.

- The text describing each item.

- The Chart of Accounts.

- Totals to be displayed in your report.

FSV is a combination of G/L accounts structured in hierarchical levels that are defined in the financial statement version's directory and assigned to appropriate accounts. You can define more than one FSV to a specific chart of account or to a group of chart of accounts. Basically, FSV allows you to assign groups of accounts to items in the hierarchy.

Note   To create or change FSVs, we can also consider using Fiori App "Manage Global Hierarchies."

To create or edit FSVs in Manage Global Hierarchies, a business role that contains the business catalog, a General Ledger – Master Data for Chart of Accounts (SAP_SFIN_BC_MD_COA) is to be assigned to user ID first. The business role template General Ledger Accountant (SAP_BR_GL_ACCOUNTANT) is delivered by SAP.

Let's take a look at the basic steps involved in creating an FSV using Global Hierarchies to create a new FSV.

Define Financial Statement Versions

In this activity, you will go through the various steps involved in customizing an FSV. You can define your FSV from scratch or copy a predefined FSV supplied by SAP and modify it to meet your requirements.

Problem: The accounting team is not sure of the benefits and function of an FSV. You have been asked by Spoxio Inc., to advise the accounting team on the benefits of using an FSV and then to create an FSV in SAP S4 HANA.

To define an FSV, follow one of these menu paths:

IMG: Financial Accounting ➤ General Ledger Accounting ➤ Periodic Processing ➤ Document ➤ Define Financial Statement Versions.

_Or_

IMG: Financial Accounting ➤ General Ledger Accounting ➤ Master Data ➤ G/L Accounts ➤ Define Financial Statement Versions.

The **_Change View Financial Statement Version Overview_** screen is displayed. Click New Entries at the top left of the screen to call up the **_New Entries: Details of Added Entries_** screen where you will specify the key for your financial statement version and describe the FSV's general specifications (Figure 12-1).

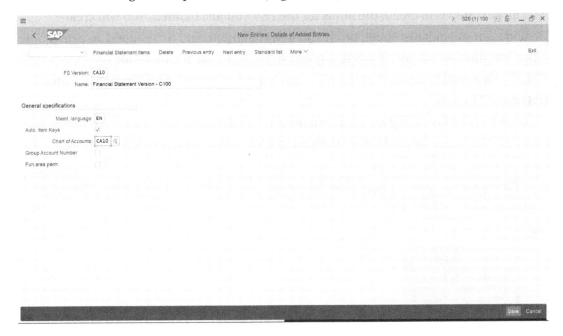

Figure 12-1. _Initial entry screen where you start your FSV customizing_

1. Update the following fields:

   Fin.Stmt.Version: Enter your proposed FSV in this field. You can enter up to four digits in this field. This will serve as an identification key for your FSV. We recommend that you use your chart of accounts key here. This is ideal for FSV identification for your company code, especially when you have several FSV and company codes in the system.

   Name: Enter the text that best describes your FSV.

General Specifications: Specify the following items:

Maint.language: The language code is the language you want the system to use when maintaining FSV. For example, in this exercise we used EN (English).

Chart of Accounts: In this field, you enter your company code's chart of account that you defined in Chapter 2.

Upon the completion of your specification (Figure 12-1), click the Save button at the bottom right of the screen. The system will notify you in the status bar at the bottom of the screen that your data was saved.

The next step is to create the items for the FSV you just defined. You will create the nodes for the balance sheet, profit and loss statement, and unassigned accounts, which will then be enhanced in subsequent steps. To create the items for your FSV, click the Financial Statement Items at the top left of the screen. **The Change Financial Statement Version**

screen is displayed (Figure 12-2), where you will define the FSV hierarchy nodes for your FSV. The items for the FSV are defined in SAP ERP in a hierarchical structure.

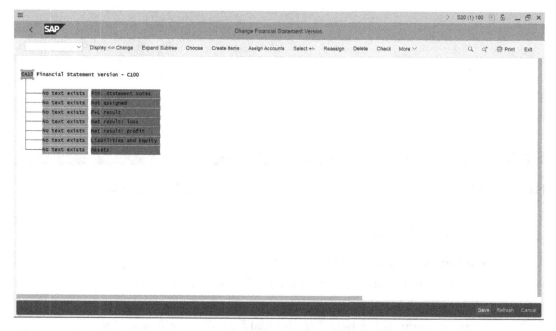

Figure 12-2. *The standard hierarchical structure where you start creating your FSV*

To simplify the customization process, we will break it into four steps:

1. Create items.

2. Reassign items as subordinates.

3. Assign FSV nodes to G/L accounts.

4. Define the credit/debit shift.

Note   In practice, before you start creating the hierarchical structure of an FSV, it is advisable that you draw up a paper sketch of your FSV structure. This will serve as a guide when you are defining your FSV.

Let's start going through the steps involved in creating an FSV.

Step 1: Create Items

You will notice in Figure 12-2 that the FSV you defined earlier is displayed as the heading in the FSV hierarchy structure and a list of the basic list of items in the FSV that you will be working on in your customizing. In the activity, we used C100 as our FSV.

Click Create Items. This is the fourth item from the left on top of the Change Financial Statement Version screen (Figure 12-2).

The Create Items screen pops up. Click each line in the structure and update the *Create Items* screen with the following items headings:

✓ Balance Sheet.

✓ Profit and Loss Statement.

✓ Unassigned Accounts.

As shown in Figure 12-3.

Figure 12-3. *The screen where you create your FSV items*

When you have updated your FSV with your headings, click Continue at the bottom right of the Create Items for the system to accept your modifications. You will notice that the items you have entered will be copied into your FSV. Your FSV will look like the one in Figure 12-4.

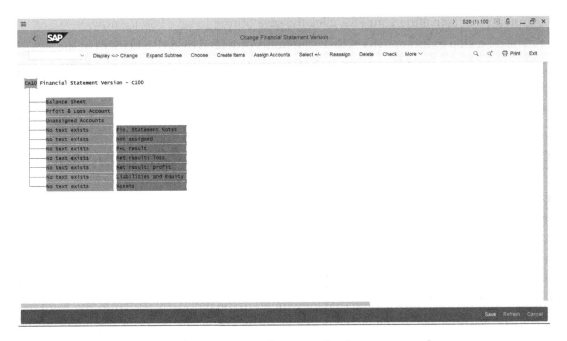

Figure 12-4. *FSV hierarchy structure showing the items created*

Save your FSV. When you click the save bottom at the bottom right of the screen, the Financial Statement version Save and Activate screen pops up (Figure 12-5).

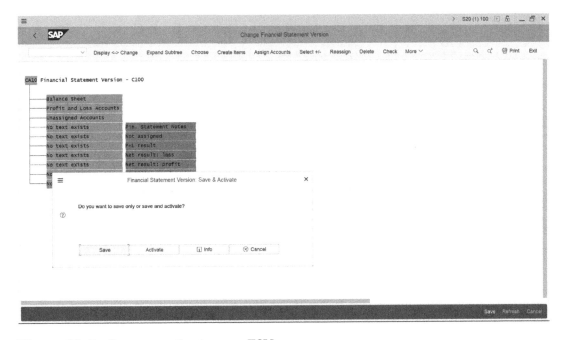

Figure 12-5. *Save or activate your FSV screen*

You are not activating your FSV, click the save button to save FSV for now.

The next step in this activity is to assign items provided by SAP S4 HANA in the system, as in Figure 12-4 (for example, P+L result, Net result loss, Net result profit, Liabilities and equity, Assets, and so on) to our FSV as subordinates to the heading you created in the FSV hierarchy (Figure 12-4).

Step 2: Assign Items to your FSV as Subordinates

First, let's start by assigning the Liabilities and Equity items (this is the second to the last item on the displayed list in your FSV hierarchy structure) as a subordinate to the balance sheet in your FSV hierarchy to the item. To do this, click on the item you are reassigning (Liabilities and Equity), then click the Select +/− (this is the sixth item from the top left side of the screen) to activate it. The item (Liabilities and Equity) you selected will turn yellow. Click on the item (balance sheet) in the hierarchy structure you want to assign a subordinate (Liabilities and Equity) and click Reassign (the seventh item from the left) at the top of the screen. The Reassign Node screen pops up, you will notice on the screen that the **From nodes** field: − "No text exists" and the **To nodes** field: Balance sheet are displayed. Under the Reassign Node section, select the Subordinate radio button on the screen (Figure 12-6).

Figure 12-6. *Reassigning subordinate as a node to an item*

Note   Choose the Same Level option on the Reassign Node screen if you want the item you are reassigning to be in the same level as the item you are assigning it to.

Click the Continue button at the bottom right of the screen in Figure 12-6. The Reassign Node screen disappears and the subordinate you assigned is copied to the balance sheet item.

Following the steps above, reassign Assets node as a subordinate to balance sheet and your FSV will be like the one in Figure 12-7.

Figure 12-7. *Reassigned subordinates displayed*

The next step is to add text to the items you have reassigned and determine which totals to output. During FSV review, the texts and totals will be displayed in the balance sheets and profit and loss statements.

Change Nodes Texts

You will notice in Figure 12-7 that the node for Assets, and Liabilities and Equity displayed under balance sheet item states that No text exists; you need to add text to your nodes.

To add texts to an item in the financial statement (for example, balance sheet – asset). Click on the Assets you have reassigned to the balance sheet to select it and click on Choose at the top of the screen (this is the third item from the left at the top of the screen). The Item: Change Texts screen is displayed (Figure 12-8).

Figure 12-8. *Text Item change screen*

Note   When you are defining items in FSVs, special codes are assigned to maintain the classification of similar items under the same code and heading. These codes are designated in a systematic manner to form a local sequence, often referred to as code classifications. For example, the code for Asset is 1000000, and the next subordinate under Asset will 1000100, 1000200, and so on. We will not be covering code classifications as this is outside the scope of this book.

Update the following fields:

Item: Enter the item code and required text and select the totals to be output. We used 1000000 (see Figure 12-8).

Start of Group: Enter the heading name for the specific group of items. The name you enter in this field will be displayed as the heading for the group in the report. If a G/L account is posted, this text is displayed before the item's sub-items during the period.

End of Group: The text you enter here will end the group. For example, Total Assets will be displayed as the last item in the group. If you enter text and select the Display Total option in this section, the total balance for assigned G/L accounts is output during the selected period.

The system should default to the Display Total checkbox being selected; if not, you have to activate it by making sure that it is ticked. This will display the total amount for the group in the report.

Click the Enter button (this is the green circle button at the bottom right of the screen).

Repeat the same process above for *Liabilities and Equity* using the information below:

1. Enter **2000000** in the Item field.

2. Enter **Liabilities** in the Start of Group field.

3. Select the Display Total check box.

Your FSV will look like the FSV in Figure 12-9.

Figure 12-9. *Reassigned additional subordinates displayed*

Save your FSV.

Creating Subordinates for Liabilities and Equity

Next, you need to create more items as subordinates for 2000000 Liabilities and Equity using the Create Items button on the top-left side of the screen. To do this, select 2000000 –Liabilities and Equity by clicking it, and click the Create button at the top of the screen. The Create Items screen is displayed (Figure 12-10). In the Balance Sheet section of your FSV, update the fields under 2000000 with the appropriate items.

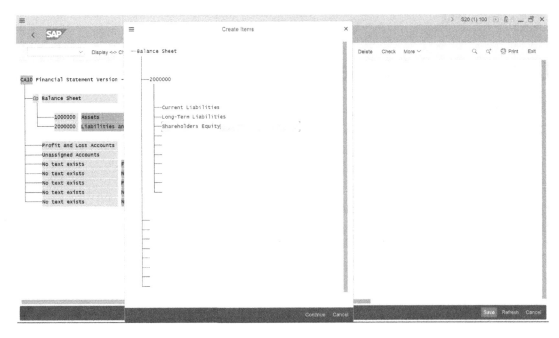

Figure 12-10. *Creating more items in an FSV*

Click Continue at the bottom right of the Create Items screen.

Your screen should now look like the one in Figure 12-11.

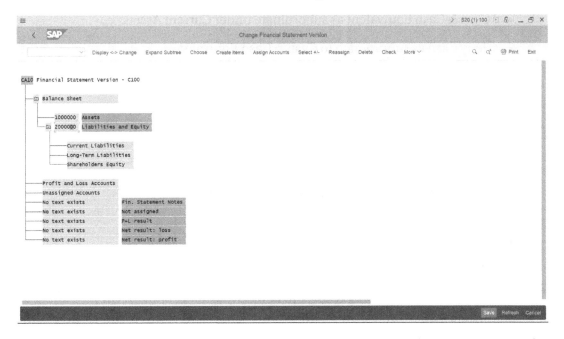

Figure 12-11. *FSV hierarchy structure showing the additional items you created*

Save your FSV.

Completing the Nodes for your FSV

Following steps 1 and 2, create more items and reassign them as subordinates to your FSV for the following items:

1. Create Intangible Assets, Fixed Assets, and Current Assets as subordinates to Assets.

2. Reassign the P+L Results node as subordinate to Profit and Loss Accounts

3. Reassign Net Result: Loss to Shareholders Equity as a subordinate.

4. Reassign Net Result: Profit to Shareholders Equity as a subordinate.

5. Change the name of Net result: loss to Retained Earnings.

6. Change the name of Net result: profit to Retained Earnings.

7. Reassign the node not assigned to Unassigned Accounts.

Create the following nodes:

-   Cash & Cash Equivalent as subordinate under Current Assets.

-   Petty Cash as subordinate to Cash & Cash Equivalent.

-   Current Bank Account as subordinate to Cash & Cash Equivalent.

-   Short-Term Borrowings as subordinate to Current Liabilities.

-   Bank Short-Term Loans as subordinate to Current Liabilities.

-   Bank Overdraft as subordinate to Short-Term Borrowings.

-   Bank Short-Term Borrowings as subordinate to Short-Term Borrowings.

-   Bank of America as subordinate to Current Bank Account.

-   HSBC as subordinate to Current Bank Account.

-   Bank of America as subordinate to Bank Overdraft in Short-Term borrowings.

-   HSBC as subordinate to Bank Overdraft in Short-Term borrowings.

Using the details above, complete your FSV. Your FSV will look like the one in Figure 12-12.

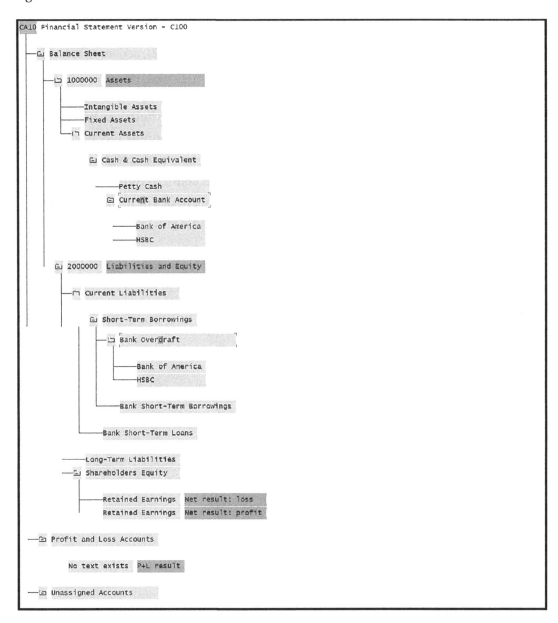

Figure 12-12. *An extended FSV Hierarchy structure showing the items created*

After you have reassigned nodes and created the nodes, as we asked you to above, then save your FSV by clicking the Save button at the bottom right of the screen.

The next step in this activity is to assign FSV nodes to G/L accounts.

Step 3: Assign FSV Nodes to G/L Accounts

FSV is designated specifically for creating the financial statements that serve as measures of financial performance of an organization. It is important to assign G/L accounts to FSV so that the summary of business transactions posted to the G/L accounts for a given period can be generated as financial statements.

To assign G/L accounts to FSV, you will need to select the appropriate items or nodes in your FSV hierarchy structure and use the Assign G/L accounts' function. We will not be able to take you through the complete process involved in assigning FSV nodes to G/L accounts in this activity. However, we will only be showing how to this with assigning G/L accounts to a Bank account. If you can assign a G/L account to your bank account, you should be able to assign G/L accounts to the remaining nodes or items in your FSV, because the principle is pretty much the same. We advise that you try assigning more G/L accounts to the nodes in your FSV.

To assign your bank account node to a G/L account, select the Bank of America node under Current Assets by clicking on it and then click on Assign Accounts at the top of the screen (this is the fifth item from the left at the top of the screen). The Change Accounts screen pops up as in Figure 12-13. This screen will allow you to assign your FSV node (Bank of America) to the appropriate G/L accounts designated for your bank account.

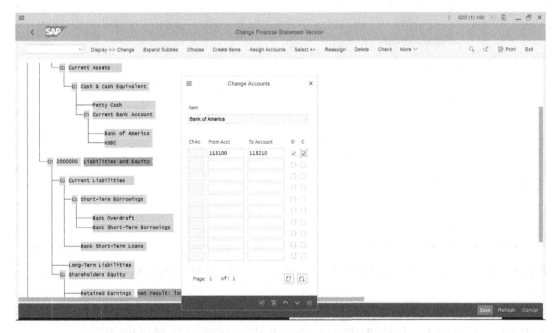

Figure 12-13. *Assigning G/L Accounts to an FSV node*

Update the following fields by entering the G/L account range you want to assign to your FSV node. You also must specify whether your G/L accounts are debit or credit.

From Acct: Enter the starting G/L account number range of the G/L account you want to enter. In this activity, we used 113100 as the starting point of our G/L accounts.

To Account: Enter the ending G/L account number range in the field. In this activity, we used 113210 as the ending point of our G/L accounts.

Note   The benefits of using a number range is that when you have multiple G/L account numbers, you only need to enter the start and end G/L accounts, and the system will assign the entire range.

D: Stands for debit. When this field is activated, the system will include all the debit G/L accounts in your bank account in the FSV. Select this checkbox.

C: Stands for credit. When this field is activated or selected, the system will include all the credit G/L accounts in your bank account in the FSV. Select this checkbox.

Then click the Enter button (this is the green circle button at the bottom right of the screen). This action will then assign your chart of accounts and G/L account number range to your FSV and indicate if the assigned G/L accounts are debit and/or credit by marking them X. You will notice that the range of G/L accounts that you have assigned will appear under the Bank of America account node in the FSV hierarchy structure (Figure 12-14).

Figure 12-14. *How the G/L accounts assigned to an item are displayed in FSV*

Step 4: Define the Credit/Debit Shift

When your bank has a debit balance, it is considered an asset. This means that you have surplus cash in your bank account. On the other hand, if your bank has a credit balance, it is considered a liability. This means that you owe the bank; it is referred to as overdraft (short-term borrowings). Cash balance surplus and deficit are disclosed separately in financial statements under different headings. For example, a debit bank balance is treated as an asset and a credit bank balance is treated as overdraft under liabilities. So that the system can identify these transactions and disclose them separately in the financial statements (to meet accounting disclosure requirements), you have to specify these in your FSV.

Let's look at how this is done using your bank account (Bank of America) node in your FSV hierarchy structure as an example.

Select your Bank Account (Bank of America) under the current Assets by clicking on it. Then click Select +/− at the top right of the screen. (This is the sixth item from the left.) The item you have selected will turn yellow. Then select your bank account (Bank of America) in Short-Term Borrowings – Bank Overdraft in your FSV (Figure 12-15).

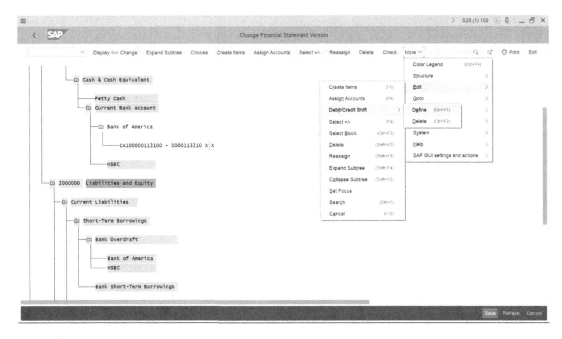

Figure 12-15. *Defining the debit/credit shift*

Click More at the top right of the screen, a pull-down menu comes up, select
Edit ➤ Debit/Credit shift ➤ Define. The Define Debit/Credit Shift screen comes up
(Figure 12-16). The system will automatically default to the first ratio button on the
screen. Click Continue at the bottom right of the Define Debit/Credit Shift screen.

Figure 12-16. *The screen where you confirm the Debit/Credit for your bank account*

Your FSV should look like the one in Figure 12-17.

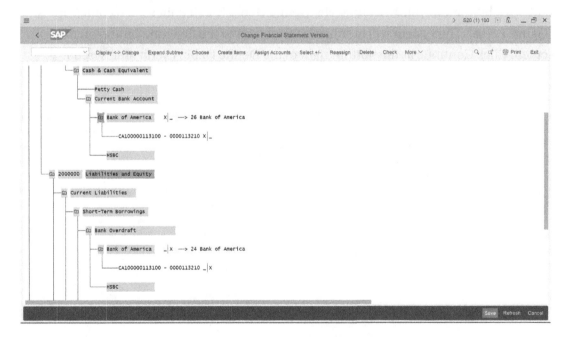

Figure 12-17. *FSV hierarchy structure depicting the nodes assignment to G/L accounts*

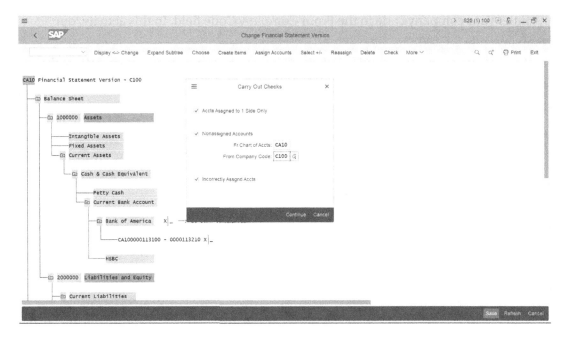

Figure 12-18. *Activating the items you want displayed in your check result*

The final step in this activity is to check the assigned G/L accounts to your FSV.

Check Assigned G/L Accounts to FSV

After assigning G/L accounts to your FSV nodes, it is important to carry out a check to find out if any of the items (G/L accounts) are not allocated to your FSV in your company code.

To check whether G/L accounts are assigned to FSV nodes, click Check at the top right of The Change Financial Statement Version screen. The Carry out Checks screen pops up. The following items on the screen are automatically activated as defaults by the system:

- Accts Assigned to 1 side only.

- Nonassigned Accounts.

- From Chart of Accts.

- Incorrect Assigned Accts.

You can deactivate or activate the items you want displayed in your check result.

Enter your company code in the From Company Code field. In this activity, our company code is C100.

To generate your check result, click the Continue button at the bottom right of the screen and The Check financial statement version screen is displayed (Figure 12-19) showing your check result.

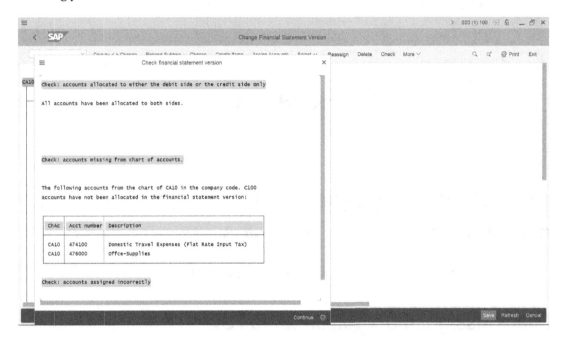

Figure 12-19. *Financial statement version check result*

The result in Figure 12-19 shows that some items have been allocated in the FSV. Go back and allocate the displayed G/L not allocated in the report to the appropriate FSV nodes (Refer to Step 3 above to see how G/L accounts are assigned to FSV nodes).

When you click Continue at the bottom right of the screen, the Check financial version pop up screen disappears. Save your FSV customization. When you click Save at the bottom right of the Change Financial Version screen, the Financial Statement Version: Save & Activate screen pops up. If you are convinced that you have completed your FVS customizing, you can choose the activate button on the Financial Statement Version: Save & Activate screen (Figure 12-20).

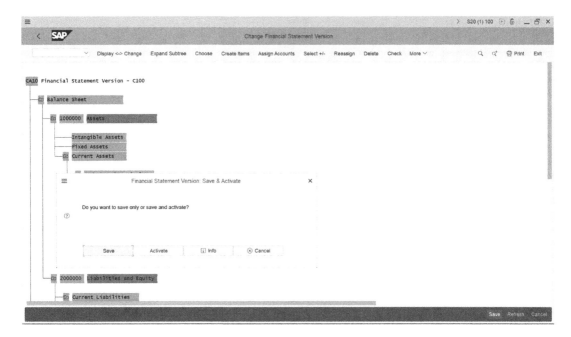

Figure 12-20. *Financial Statement Version: Save & Activate screen*

Summary

This chapter shows you how to customize a Financial Statement Version (FSV). In doing this, you learned how to define your own FSV from scratch. This included how to create FSV items using the create function.

As part of this activity, you created the following items in your FSV hierarchy structure:

- Balance sheet.

- Profit and loss account.

- Unassigned accounts.

You went on to create other nodes and items as subordinates for your FSV. You assigned codes to the items you created and assigned G/L accounts to items in the FSV. Finally, you learned how to check the items assigned to the FSV.

In the next chapter, we will look at how to integrate FI into other modules, such as Material Management (MM) and Sales and Distribution (SD). In Material Management, we will look at the various steps that allow the system to carry out automatic posting from MM to FI.

Finally, we will look at how to assign G/L accounts to SD. In doing this, we will determine the sequence to be used to achieve this objective.

CHAPTER 13

Integration of FI with other SAP S4 HANA modules

In this chapter, we will explore how to integrate FI with other SAP S4 HANA modules as well as how to customize and integrate Material Management (MM) and Sales & Distribution (SD) modules.

At the end of this chapter, you will be able to:

- Integrate the FI module with other SAP modules.

- Explain the Material Management (MM) module.

- Configure automatic postings.

- Explain the Sales & Distribution (SD) module.

- Prepare revenue account determination.

Integrate FI with Other SAP Modules

Most, if not all, transactions in the SAP system in other modules have financial implications and trigger postings in the FI module. As a result, some form of assignment of other modules to GL accounts in FI is mandatory. The following modules are available for integration with FI in the system. (Figure 13-1 depicts the integration of FI with other modules).

© Andrew Okungbowa 2023
A. Okungbowa, *SAP S/4HANA Financial Accounting Configuration*,
https://doi.org/10.1007/978-1-4842-8957-0_13

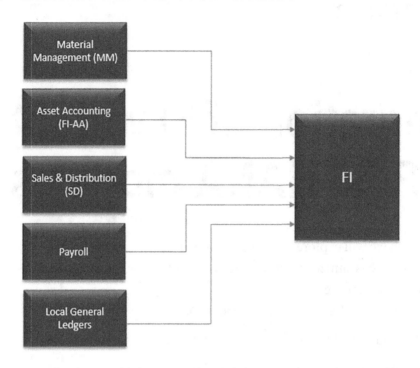

Figure 13-1. *Integration of other SAP Modules to FI*

The concept of assigning other modules to FI module is to allow the system to automatically post transactions posted in other modules to FI. As a result, you need to perform some assignments between these modules and FI in order to allow the system to form automatic posting between them. For example, when you integrate the payroll module to the FI module, postings made in the payroll module will automatically post to G/L accounts in FI in real time based on defined criteria.

In Figure 13-1, the Material Management (MM), Asset Accounting (FI-AA), Sales & Distribution (SD), Payroll, and Local General Ledgers are integrated into FI. Therefore, postings of these modules are automatically posted to FI based on the integration procedures defined.

In this chapter, we will be looking at how to integrate Material Management (MM) and Sales & Distribution (SD) only. We will not be covering Payroll and Asset Accounting (FI-AA) as these are outside the scope of this book. For more details on how to integrate Asst Accounting (FI-AA) to FI, please refer to our book "Asset Accounting Configuration in SAP ERP: A Step-by-Step Guide" by the same author.

Note   Before you commence with the integration of other modules to FI, it is advisable to create the appropriate G/L Accounts that will be needed in your configurations. Go to **Appendix 1** – under **Chapter 13** to first create the appropriate G/L accounts for this customization exercise.

Material Management (MM)

Movements of material from one stage to another takes place in MM which need to be posted in FI, for example, Goods Issues and Goods receipts. To represent the movement of these items in FI, they have to be assigned to GL accounts in valuation class.

In order for the system to automatically post Transactions posted in MM module with financial Implication to the FI module, some specifications need to be conducted in valuation class in the system that will allow the integration of one module to another.

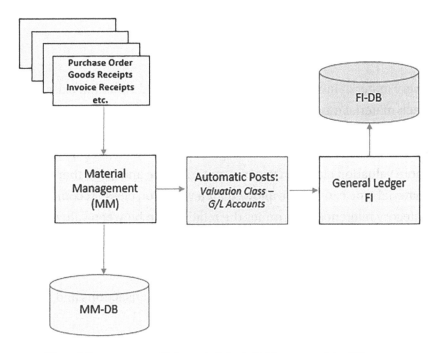

Figure 13-2. *How Movement of Material in MM is posted in FI*

Because of various movement of material within the SAP system, there is a need for valuation class in the SAP system. For proper classification of materials, you have to define the valuation class for every material in the valuation class field. SAP supplied standard valuation classes in the system that you can use.

There are three settings you have to carry out in your customization for the system to perform automatic postings from MM to FI:

1. **Valuation Class**

    The Valuation class of material is an important key which determines the GL account group of materials with the same account determination posted at different stages during material movement. For example, it allows posting of goods receipt of Raw Materials to a different GL account as opposed to when it is Finished Goods. This is achieved by assigning a different valuation class to materials at different stages:

    - Raw Material – 3000.

    - Semi-Finished products – 7900.

    - Finished Products – 7920, etc.

    Every material in SAP R/3 has a master data and valuation class. Each material must be entered in the accounting data view of material master data for a valuated-material. The valuation classes for a material must be assigned to material type. One or more valuation class can use one material type and more than one material type can also be allowed for a valuation class. Account category reference determines the relationship between valuation classes and material type.

2. **Transaction key or code:**

    The Transaction codes differentiate between transactions and determine the GL account to be posted.

    SAP supplied standard Transaction Keys. See Material Management Postings.

3. **Account:**

   This is where the GL accounts are assigned. By assigning GL
   Accounts to posting transactions for every valuation class,
   postings in MM will generate a posting in FI.

Configuring Automatic Postings

Automatic postings customization makes automatic postings to GL accounts for every
material movement possible in the SAP R/3 system. Therefore, having to manually input
material movement in FI will not be necessary because the system will do the postings
automatically.

Let's use an example to illustrate how the customization of MM integration with G/L
accounts in FI works in principle.

Assume Goods receipt (GR) of £200K posting is made to Purchase Order.

In accounting, the double entry for this transaction will be:

1. Debit Inventory Account and

2. Credit GR/IR Clearing Account:

Figure 13-3 shows Accounting Double Entry of Goods Receipt (GR).

Figure 13-3. *Double entry accounting for goods receipt (GR)*

To make this work in SAP, you assign BSX Transaction Key – Inventory Posting to GL
Account for Inventory Account.

Two Menu Paths are available for this function in the SAP ERP system:

1) ***IMG – Financial Accounting*** ➤ ***General Ledger Accounting*** ➤
   Periodic Processing ➤ ***Integration*** ➤ ***Material Management*** ➤
   Define Accounts for Material Management

2) ***IMG*** ➤ ***Material Management*** ➤ ***Valuation and Account***
   Assignment ➤ ***Account*** ➤ ***Determination*** ➤ ***Account***
   Determination without wizard ➤ ***Configure Automatic Postings***

The ***Configuration Accounting Maintain: Automatic Posts – Procedures*** screen is displayed. This screen contains a list of procedures you can choose from. Choose inventory Posting-BSX from the procedures list by clicking on it, and click choose at the top left of the screen.

The ***Enter Chart of Accounts*** dialog box pops up. Enter your chart of accounts key in the ***Chart of Accounts*** field. In this activity, we used CA10, which is our chat of accounts key. Click Continue at the bottom right of the screen. The ***Configuration Accounting Maintain: Automatic Posts – Rules*** screen is displayed. You will notice that the system has automatically defaulted your chart of accounts – CA10 and the transaction code – BSX for inventory posting. This is the screen where you determine the valuation class for your accounts assignment.

In the **Accounts are determined based on** section of the screen, specify the basis on which you want your material valuation accounts to be determined. Since you want to customize Valuation Modification, valuation class and G/L accounts. Activate **Valuation modif** and **Valuation class** checkboxes by ticking them, as in Figure 13-4.

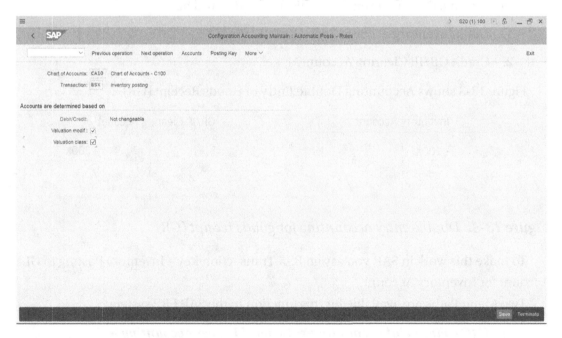

Figure 13-4. *Specifying Valuation modification and Valuation class for automatic posting account assignment*

Click the Save button at the bottom right of the screen. The ***Configuration Accounting Maintain: Automatic Posts – Accounts*** screen is displayed (Figure 13-5). This is where you will maintain the settings for automatic postings of MM transaction to FI.

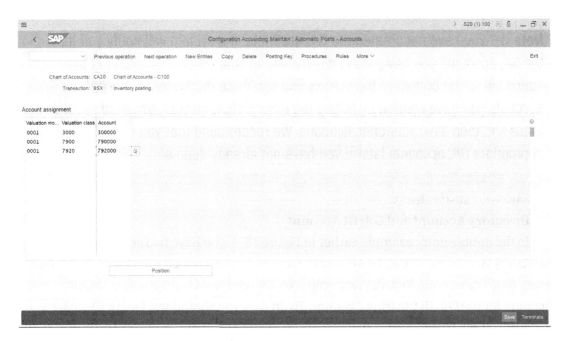

Figure 13-5. *Maintaining the automatic posting of G/L accounts for automatic posting*

Update the following fields:

> **Valuation modification:** Enter **0001** in this field for each material (Raw Material, Semi Finished Goods, and Finished Goods). This determines accounts posting based on valuation area or plant (if your valuation area is based on plants)

> **Valuation Class:** Select the appropriate valuation class from the ones supplied by SAP in the system by using the search function button. In this instance, select the **validation class** for **Raw Material -3000**, **Semi Finished Products -7900**, and **Finished Products -7920**.

> **Account:** Enter **GL Account** for **Raw Material -300000, Semi Finished Products -790000** and **Finished Products -792000** n this **field.**

> **Note**   If you have not created the G/L accounts, the system will notify you that the G/L accounts you assigned is not created in your chart of accounts at the status bar at the bottom of the screen. You can force the system to accept the G/L accounts you have created by hitting the enter button on your keyboard several times and then save your specifications. We recommend that you should create the appropriate G/L accounts later if you have not already done so.

Save your customizing.

Inventory Account and **GR/IR Account**

In the double entry example earlier in Figure 13-3, you have two accounts (i.e., *Inventory Account* and *GR/IR Account*). Since you have created the Inventory Account using **BSX** Transaction Key, the next step is to also create a corresponding Credit Account for the GR/IR Clearing Account. To do this, you should use GR/IR Clearing Account – **WRX** Transaction Key.

Hit back at the top left of the screen button to return to the previous page or follow this menu path: *IMG – Financial Accounting* ➤ *General Ledger Accounting* ➤ *Periodic Processing* ➤ *Integration* ➤ *Material Management* ➤ *Define Accounts for Material Management* to return to the *Configuration Accounting Maintain: Automatic Posts – Procedure*. From the list of procedures displayed on the screen using the scroll bar at the right side of the screen, search for GR/IR clearing account – WRX. Click on it to select it and click Choose at the right side of the screen. The *Enter Chart of Accounts* dialog box pops up. Enter your chart of accounts key in the *Chart of Accounts* field, click Continue at the bottom right of the screen. The *Configuration Accounting Maintain: Automatic Posts – Rules* screen is displayed. You will notice that the system has automatically defaulted your chart of accounts – CA10 and the transaction code – WRX-GR/IR clearing account. You do not need any specifications on this screen. Click the Save button at the bottom right of the screen. The *Configuration Accounting Maintain: Automatic Posts – Accounts* is displayed (Figure 13-6).

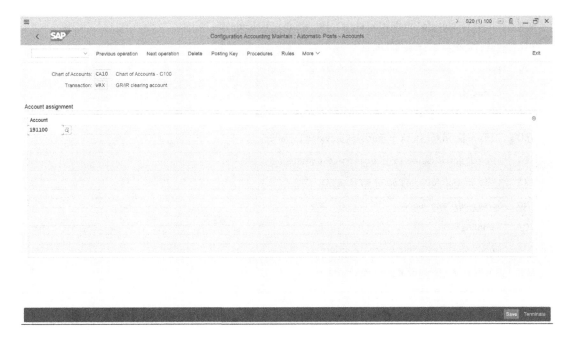

Figure 13-6. *Maintain Automatic Posting for GR/IR Clearing Account*

Enter the GR/IR clearing account G/L account 191100 in the Account field and save your account assignment.

In automatic posting procedure, there are several transactions and transaction keys that you may want to explore on your own. The following transaction keys are important:

GBB	Offsetting entry for inventory posting
PRD	Cost (price) differences
KON	Consignment payables

In this activity, you will only be looking at Offsetting entry for inventory posting (GBB). Basically, the procedure for assigning other transaction keys are the same.

GBB has several account groupings that you can choose from based on the relevant movement types. The following accounting groupings can be assigned to the relevant movement types in GBB:

AUF	Goods receipts for production orders with account assignment
BSA	Initial entries of stock balances
INV	Expenses/revenue for inventory differences
VAX	Goods issues for sales orders without account assignment
VAY	Goods issues for sales orders with account assignment
VBO	Consumption for stock of material provided to vendor
VBR	Internal goods issues to production/cost centre
VKA	Consumption for sales order without SD
VNG	Scrapping/Destruction
VQP	Sampling
ZOB	Goods receipts without purchase orders
ZOP	Goods receipts without production orders

Let's look at when Goods or materials are issued to production or Cost Center

Offsetting Entry for Inventory Posting

In this activity, you will be updating the general modification VBR (a predefined transaction key supplied by SAP in the system for internal inventory posting to G/L accounts) with Material Consumption. After you configure the GBB-offsetting entry for inventory posting, the system will automatically post materials or goods issued to production or cost center to offsetting accounts in FI by debiting the Material Consumption account and crediting the inventory account for materials.

Inventory Account for Material is credited and Material Consumption is debited.

Ok let's see how this is done. Follow this menu path: *IMG: Financial Accounting➤ General Ledger Accounting ➤ Periodic Processing ➤ Integration ➤ Material Management ➤ Define Accounts for Material Management.*

The *Configuration Accounting Maintain: Automatic Posts - Procedures* screen is displayed. Using the scroll bar at the right side of the screen search for **Offsetting entry for inventory – GBB** in the procedure list. Select it and click Choose at the top left of the screen. The *Enter Chart of Accounts* dialog pops up. Enter your Chart of Accounts in the *Chart of Accounts* field and click Continue at the bottom right of the screen. The *Configuration Accounting Maintain: Automatic Posts – Rules* screen is displayed (Figure 13-7).

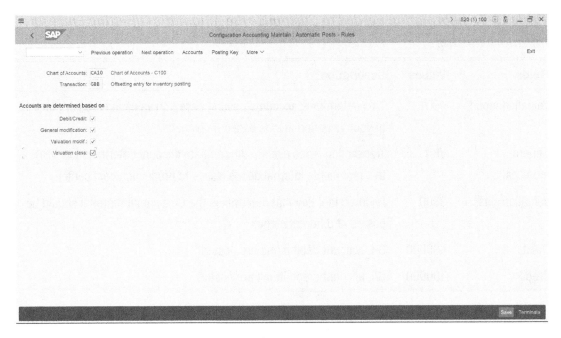

Figure 13-7. *Maintain Posting Rules for Automatic Posting*

In the **Accounts are determined based on** section of the screen, activate the following checkboxes by selecting them:

- ✓ Debit/Credit,

- ✓ General modification,

- ✓ Valuation modification, and

- ✓ Valuation class.

These items are made available for input on the next screen. Click Save at the bottom right of the screen. The ***Configuration Accounting Maintain: Automatic Posts –***
Accounts screen is displayed (Figure 13-8). Update the screen using the information in Table 13-1.

Table 13-1. *Information needed to Customize the Automatic Offsetting Entry for Inventory Posting*

Fields	Values	Description
Valuation modif.	0001	This determines accounts posting based on valuation area or plant (if your valuation area is based on plants).
General modification	VBR	Transaction types used to differentiate account determination. VBR – this represents Internal goods issues to production/cost center.
Valuation class	3000	An important key that determines the GL account material should be posted at different stages.
Debit	400000	G/L account debit items are posted.
Credit	400000	G/L account credit items are posted.

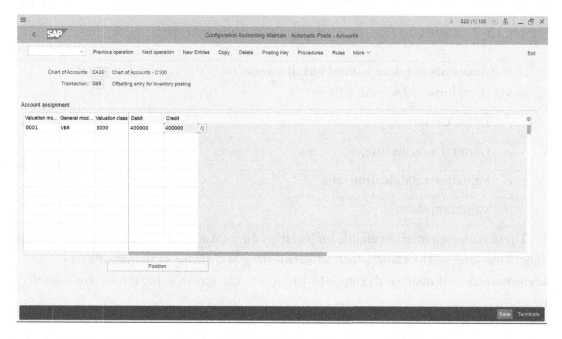

Figure 13-8. *Maintain Automatic Posting for Offsetting entry for inventory posting*

Save your work.

The final step in this activity is to customize the integration of Sales & Distribution (SD) with FI to allow the system to automatically post transactions in SD to FI.

Integration with Sales & Distribution (SD).

Sales and Distribution (SAP) is a part of SAP modules. Business processes from Sales order to delivery are executed in SD. This module handles activities ranging from Customer Sales Order, Shipping, Billing of Products, Services, Risk Management, etc.

Billing is a part of SD function and all billing transactions that took place in SD module also form part of FI transactions, which results in FI – General Ledger posting.

Let's look at an example of SD billing transaction in accounting. Assume that a bill is raised in SD for £200k, the accounting transaction will look like the double entry accounting transaction below:

Figure 13-9. *Accounting Double Entry when SD document is posted to FI*

Prepare Revenue Account Determination

Account determination is an important integration process in SAP R/3 that enables the system to post transactions in SD (e.g., sales, sales deductions, and freights) to appropriate G/L accounts in FI via Account Keys.

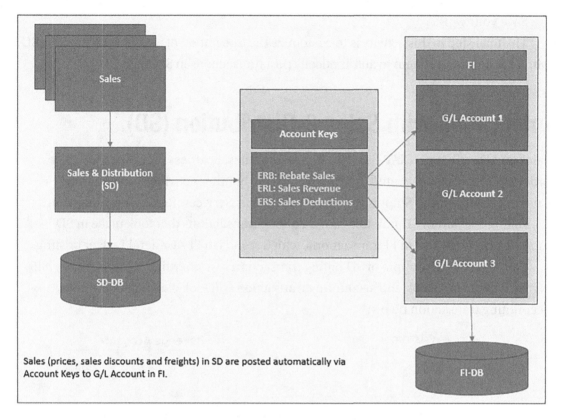

Figure 13-10. *How SD Transactions are posted to FI*

Available Account keys in SAP ERP system that you can use

In this configuration, you will specify the following items for your G/L Accounts:

Table 13-2. *Items needing specifications when integrating SD to G/L Accounts in FI*

Field	Description
Application	This is where you specify the key for Sales and Distribution application. The standard application key for SD is V. You can access this key using the search function or the match code next to the application field.
Condition Type for Account Determination	SAP comes with standard condition types: KOFI and KOFK. If your company code is making Sales & Distribution (SD) post to FI and not to Controlling (CO), use the condition type KOFI for your account determination. On the other hand, if you want the system to post Sales & Distribution (SD) to FI and CO use the condition type KOFK.
Chart of Accounts	Here you specify Chart of Accounts for your G/L Account structure. In this activity, we used the chart of account key – CA10
Sales Organization	Here you specify the Sales Organization you want to apply to your account determination. For example, sales organization 0001, 0002, and so on. Sales organizations are distinguished with an identification number in SAP S4 HANA.
Account Key	The account key you specify here will determine the appropriate G/L accounts transactions relating to sales are posted. For example, ERL for sales Revenue, ERS for Sales Deductions, and so on.
G/L Account	The account in FI that transactions from SD are posted for accounting purpose.

When assigning G/L Accounts to SD, you have to determine the sequence to use. In SAP, you have five access sequences:

- Cust. Grp/Material Grp/Acct Key.

- Cust. Grp/Acct Key.

- Material Grp/Acct Key.

- General.

- Account Key.

Access sequence allows us to specify different GL accounts for different Sales organizations. Based on your settings, the system will go through the settings in your configuration to find out if a GL account is assigned to an account key. For example, the system will check the first item **Cust *GrpMaterialGrpAccKey.*** If a G/L Account is assigned, then the system will use the G/L account for revenue posting. If no G/L account is assigned, the system will go to the next item on the table in a sequence, and so on. Until the system finds an account key that a G/L account is assigned to. It will use it for posting SD transactions to the G/L accounts in FI.

Note   You are the one that will determine the level that you may want to maintain for your GL Account.

Now let's go through the steps involved customizing the integration of SD to FI.

Problem: Using Account Key (Acct Key), assign GL Account to Sales Revenue (ERL) and Sales Deductions (ERS).

You can access the menu path for Integrating of FI with SD either in FI or SD:

1) *IMG: Financial Accounting (New) ➤ General Ledger Accounting (New) ➤ Periodic Processing ➤ Integration ➤ Sales and Distribution ➤ Prepare Revenue Account Determination*

2) *IMG: Sales and Distribution ➤ Basic Functions ➤ Account Assignment/Costing ➤ Revenue Account Determination ➤ Assign GL Accounts*

The ***Assign G/L Accounts*** screen is displayed. On the Assigned G/L Account Table, select item **5-Account Key** (circled in Figure 13-11) by clicking on it to select it and click Choose at the top left of the screen to go to the next screen.

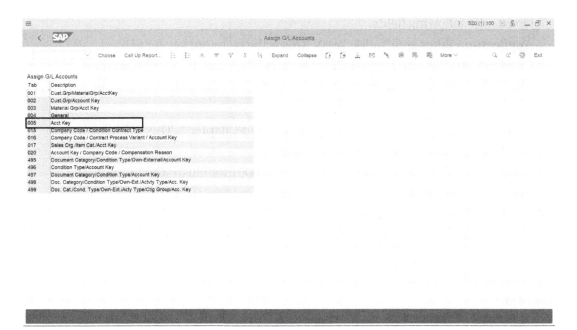

Figure 13-11. *List of items to assign to G/L accounts in SD customizing*

The ***Change View Acct Key Overview*** screen comes-up. Choose New Entries at the top left of the screen. The New Entries: Overview of Added Entries screen (Figure 13-12) comes up.

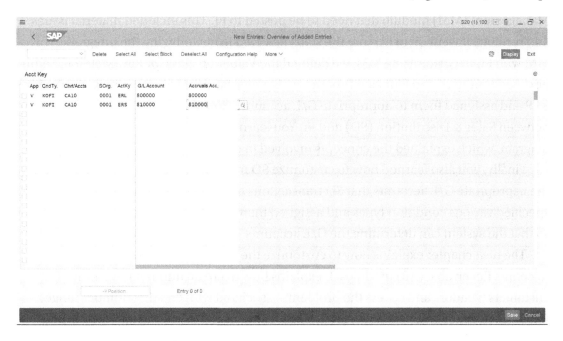

Figure 13-12. *Assign G/L Accounts to Account Key*

Update the following fields:

Application: Enter application key V. This is the standard key for SD.

CndTy.: Enter condition type KOFI. This condition type is used for account determination without posting CO (Controlling). If you want to be able to post to FI and CO, use the condition type KOFK.

ChAc: Enter the chart of accounts you defined in Chapter 2. This will allow you to use the G/L accounts in your chart of accounts.

SOrg: Enter sales organization 0001. We used 0001 for illustration purposes.

ActKy: Enter account key ERL (Sales revenue) and ERS (Sales deductions). The account key will allow the system to distinguish between transactions.

G/L Account: Enter the G/L account you want sales revenue to be posted to in the FI. This activity uses 800000 as the G/L account for illustration purposes.

Provision Acc.: Enter the G/L account you want to post sales deductions to in this field.

Summary

This chapter explained the processes involved in integrating FI with other modules in SAP ERP. It briefly discussed material movements that take place in the Material Management (MM) module that need to be posted to FI. This included material issues and receipts. It went on to explore the steps involved in customizing the integration of MM with FI. In customizing MM, we defined the Valuation class for Raw Material, Semi-Finished Products, and Finished Products using the standard valuation keys supplied by SAP and assigned them to appropriate G/L accounts. You also looked at the relationship between Sales & Distribution (SD) and FI. You learned about this through a flow diagram, which explained the concepts involved in configuring SD with FI.

Finally, you also learned how to customize SD in order for the system to determine the appropriate G/L accounts that SD transactions are posted to. In doing so, you specified various condition types and assigned them to G/L accounts. This is necessary so that the system can determine the G/L accounts that SD transactions are posted to.

The next chapter explains how to customize the Accounts Payable (AP) and Accounts Receivable (AR) modules. It explains how to create number ranges for customers/vendors and covers the problems associated with creating number ranges. It defines account groups with screen layouts, explains the use of payment terms and various instalment plans, and covers how to configure manual and automatic outgoing payments in SAP ERP. It also looks at how to define adjustment accounts for receivables and payables by maturity, and adjustment posting/reversal of documents using negative postings methods.

CHAPTER 14

Accounts Receivable and Accounts Payable

In this chapter, we explain what accounts receivable and payable are, and also look at the steps involved in customizing accounts receivable and accounts payable.

At the end of this chapter, you will be able to:

- Understand what accounts payable/receivable is.

- Describe an account group and understand its importance.

- Maintain the Field Status group for general data about customer account groups.

- Define account groups with screen layout.

- Define payment terms in SAP.

- Maintain terms of payment for an installment plan.

- Define document types for enjoy transactions.

- Maintain settings for manual outgoing payments.

- Define automatic outgoing payments.

- Maintain tolerance groups for employees, customers/vendors, and G/L accounts.

- Define sort methods and adjustment accounts for regrouping receivables/payables.

- Specify adjustment accounts for receivables/payables by maturity.

- Define adjustment posting/reversal using negative posting methods.

- Understand reasons for reversal.

© Andrew Okungbowa 2023
A. Okungbowa, *SAP S/4HANA Financial Accounting Configuration*,
https://doi.org/10.1007/978-1-4842-8957-0_14

Accounts Payable and Accounts Receivable

Accounts Receivable and Accounts Payable simply stands for Customer and Vendor Accounts, respectively. Additionally, a customer is usually referred to as a Debtor and a vendor as a Creditor.

Customer: A business partner from whom receivables are due. In order words, these are business partners owing you money for Goods delivered or services rendered. A customer falls under the category of Sales. In the SAP S4 HANA system, a customer must have a master record. A customer master record contains information about a customer account held in the database, which is applied to accounting transactions in the system.

Vendor: Likewise, a vendor is a business partner to whom payable are due. They are those you owed money for goods and services received. Like customers, vendors come under the category of purchases and have a master record in the SAP system. Likewise, a vendor master record contains information about a vendor account held in the database, which is applied to accounting transactions in the system.

To configure Accounts receivable and Accounts Payable several steps are involved. We will be going through these steps systematically in this activity.

Customizing accounts receivable and accounts payable entails several steps and can be confusing if care is not taken. Firstly, we will start with the configuration of customer accounts and then you will also go through the configuration of vendor accounts.

Note   There is no restriction on which to configure first. The decision to start first with the configuration of Customer Accounts instead of Vendor Accounts is purely a matter of choice.

Customer Accounts

What is Customer Account Group?

Customer Account group allows the classification of customers to a business partner function that best fits the nature of business transaction involved. The customer account groups controls the customer hierarchy containing the customer master record. When a customer account is created, you must assign it to an account group. Account group is a control mechanism that determines the relevant screens and fields to be displayed for input based on individual customer's different business functions. Account group is maintained in IMG.

The importance of Account Group

It Controls:

- Which fields in the customer master are Required, Optional, Display, etc.

- Number Range assignment.

There is a list of account groups supplied by SAP in the system you choose from for your configuration. For example:

It is also possible to create your own account group to meet your requirements.

Note   You can also Define Screen Layout:
- Per Company code (customer).
- Per Activity (customer).

This is outside the scope of this lecture. Simply because SAP standard settings are sufficient.

In this activity, you will be defining Customer Account Groups Screen Layout for Domestic and Foreign Customers, respectively.

Defining Accounts Groups with Screen Layout (Customer)

Problem: Company C100 plc classifies customer account groups into three partner business functions:

1. Domestic Customer,

2. Foreign Customer, and

3. One-time Customer.

Your task is to maintain an account group that will reflect these partner's functions in the system.

In this activity, you will define an account group with appropriate business partner functions and maintain the field status group for its general data. To customize the account groups for your customer based on business partner function, follow this menu path: *IMG: Financial Accounting ➤ Accounts Receivable and Accounts Payable ➤ Customer Accounts ➤ Master Data ➤ Preparations for Creating Customer Master Data ➤ Define Accounts Groups with Screen Layout (Customers).* The *Change View Customer Account Groups Overview* screen is displayed. This is where you will define the account groups for your customers. To go to the screen where you will specify your account group, choose the New Entries at the top of the screen (this is the third function from the left side of the screen). The New Entries: Details of Added Entries screen comes up (Figure 14-1).

Note   you can create as many account groups as you need, such as Foreign Customers, Domestic Customers, One-Time Customers, and so on.

To avoid confusion we will be using DC and two digits for Domestic Customers, FC for Foreign Customer, and OT for One-time Customers in this activity.

Figure 14-1. *Initial screen for account groups specification with screen layout (customer)*

The Customer Account group screen is divided into three sections:

- The section where you specify your account group ID.

- **General data:** Allows you to enter your customer account group name.

- **Field status:** Allows you to specify if a field should be surprised, required, optional, or display.

Tip   *If you are creating a one-time customer group, remember to tick the One-time account check box in* ***General data section*** *in the Account group entries screen.*

Update the following fields:

Account group: Enter your customer group ID in this field. In this activity, we used DC01 (Domestic Customer-01).

General data: In the Meaning field, enter a description for your customer account group.

Once you have updated the screen click the Save button at the bottom right side of the screen. Upon saving the system will notify you on the status bar at the bottom of the screen that your data was saved.

Note   There is no hard rule for the name you use as account group. Account group name is a matter of choice. It is based on how your client wants to classify their customer groups. The Domestic Customer Account Group used in this activity is purely for illustration purposes. It is not a standard.

Before continuing with this activity, create two more customer account groups for Foreign Customer and One-time Customer, using the data in Tables 14-1 and 14-2.

Table 14-1. *Foreign Customer Account Group*

Account Group	Meaning
FC01	Foreign Customer – C100

Table 14-2. *One-time Customer Account Group*

Account Group	Meaning
OT01	One-time Customer – C100

Maintaining the Filed Status Group for General Data of the Customer Account Group

In the **Field Status section,** you can maintain field status group for the following items:

- General data.

- Company code data.

- Sales data.

First, let's look at how to maintain the field status group for general data:

In the **Field status** section of the screen (Figure 14-1), double click **General data** from the list of field status. The *Maintain Field Status Group: Overview* screen is displayed. Select the item you want to define the field status for from the **Select Group** list (e.g., Address, communication, etc.), select *Address* from *Select Group* list by clicking it and click choose function at the top left side of the screen.

The *Maintain Field Status Group: Address* screen is displayed (Figure 14-2). This screen is where you will maintain the Field Status for Address. The specifications you carry out here will determine the field input status, whether a given field should be suppressed, required, or optional. The settings here are based on your client's requirement. In this activity, we set the less important to optional and the important items to required entry. Since we consider the field status group for address less important, make sure that all the optional entry radio are selected.

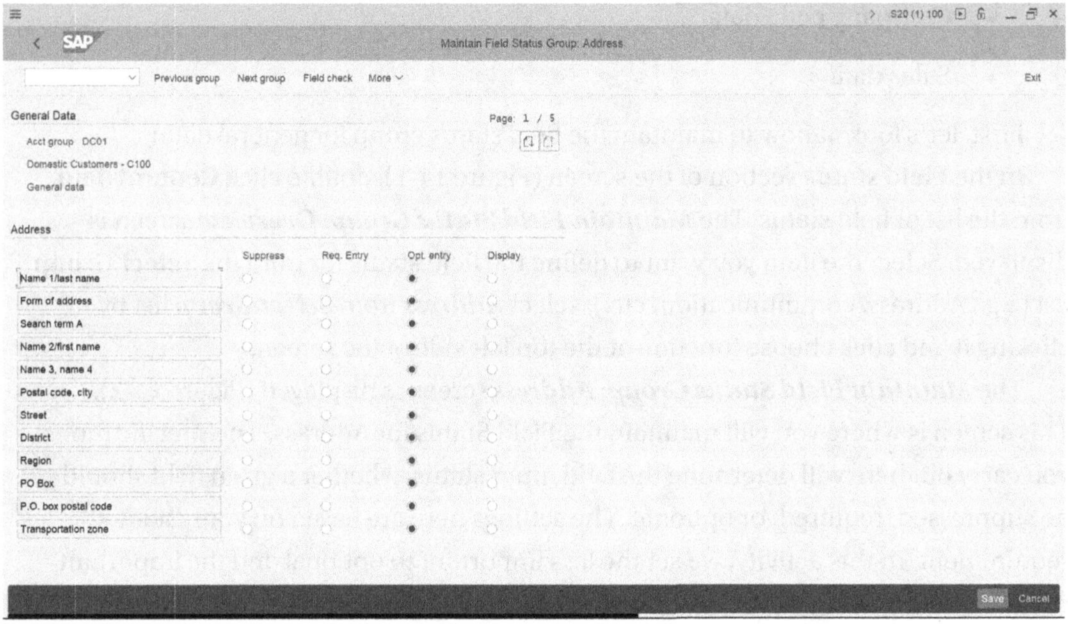

Figure 14-2. *Maintain Field Status Group for customer address*

Click save at the bottom right of the screen to save your specifications.

Note The items you specified as optional gives the account users the option to either enter data in the field or not, but the items you specify as required entry will force the account users to enter data in the field.

Problem: To ensure that users enter important information during document entry, you have been asked to make specifications that will make Reconciliation **account** field and **Sort key** compulsory input entry fields.

The specification of Reconciliation Account and Sort key are carried out in **Company code data** in the *field status* section of the *Change View "Customer Account Group": Details* screen (Figure 14-1). This is where you will specify the field status groups for *Company code data.*

Double click *Company code* in the Field status section on the *Change View "Customer account group": Details* screen. The *Maintain Field Status Group: Overview* page comes up. Select *Account management* from the Select Group list and click the Choose function at the top left side of the screen or press F2 on your keyboard. The *Maintain Field Status Group: Account Management* screen is displayed; set

Reconciliation and Sort key to **Required entry** and all other items to **Optional**. This means that during data entry, the system will request for reconciliation account and the Sort key as required entry.

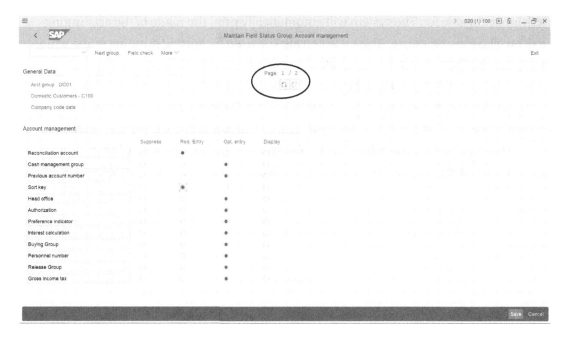

Figure 14-3. *Maintain Field Status Group – Account Management*

1. Select **Reconciliation account** and **Sort Key** as Required Entry fields for Account management and set every other item on the list to optional as they are less important.

Tip   *Do not save your work yet, because you will learn how to use the Next Page Button on this screen.*

To go to the next page of **Account management**, click the Next Page button (Circled in Figure 14-3).

Save your customer account group.

Before moving on, define two more account groups for your foreign customer and one-time customer groups.

Enter Accounting Clerk Identification Code for Customers

In this activity, we will be looking at how to define the Accounting Clerk name under an Identification code (ID). This ID can be entered in the customer/master record, which the clerk is responsible for. The system will automatically print the name of the accounting clerk on all correspondence. This code can also be used for sorting dunning and payment proposal lists. The following menu path will take you to the initial screen where this customizing is carried out: **IMG:** *Financial Accounting* ➤ *Accounts Receivable and Accounts Payable* ➤ *Customer Accounts* ➤ *Master Data* ➤ *Preparations for Creating Customer Master Data* ➤ *Enter Accounting Clerk Identification Code for Customer.*

The *Change View "Accounting Clerks" Overview* screen is displayed. Click at the top of the screen to go to the screen where you will enter your accounting clerks' details (Figure 14-4).

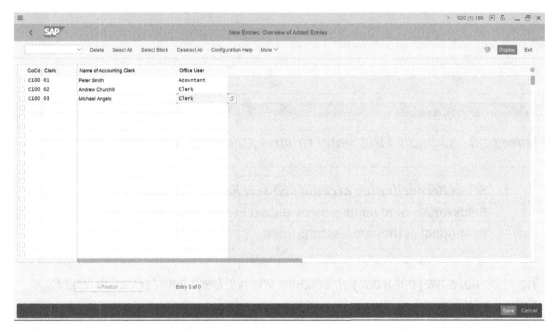

Figure 14-4. *Initial Screen for Accounting Clerk Identification Code for Customer*

The *New Entries: Overview of Added Entries* screen comes up. Update the following fields:

Cod: Enter your company code in this field.

Clerk: Enter two characters identifier ID for your clerk.

Name of Accounting Clerk: Enter the name of your accounting clerk in this field.

Office User: You can also enter the position of your accounting clerk in this field.

After you have updated your New Entries: Overview of Added Entries screen, save your work.

Creating Number Ranges for Customer Account Groups

Number ranges were covered in depth in Chapter 3, so we will only be looking at the basic steps involved in how to create number ranges for customer accounts in this activity. Number ranges for customer accounts are created using a two-character key.

When creating number ranges for your customer account, you should specify:

- The number interval which will be used as the account number for your customer accounts.

- If number assignment is internal or external.

If you select the internal number range indicator, the system will automatically assign number range intervals to your documents during document postings.

On the other hand, if external number range indicator is selected, during document postings, the users will have to enter number intervals manually based on a predefined format during configuration.

Note   Number range assignment can either be internal or external. For internal number range assignment, the system assigns the number assignment automatically. Whereas the external number range assignment is entered manually by the users during document entry.

You may likely encounter a number range overlap problem when creating number ranges. The SAP system does not allow number interval overlap when creating number ranges for customer accounts. So, make sure that your number interval is not overlapping. If your number interval is overlapping, the system will issue a warning **"Interval already available."** Then use another number range until you can find one that is not over lapping.

It is also possible to choose from existing number range intervals in the system instead of creating your own.

Now let's create number ranges for the Domestic and Foreign customer Account Groups you created earlier.

To go to the screen where you will define the number ranges for your customer account group, follow this menu path: *IMG: Financial Accounting ➤ Accounts Receivable and Accounts Payable ➤ Customer Accounts ➤ Master Data ➤ Preparations for Creating Customer Master Data ➤ Create Number Ranges for Customer Accounts.* The Edit Intervals: Customer, Object DEBITOR initial screen is displayed (Figure 14-5).

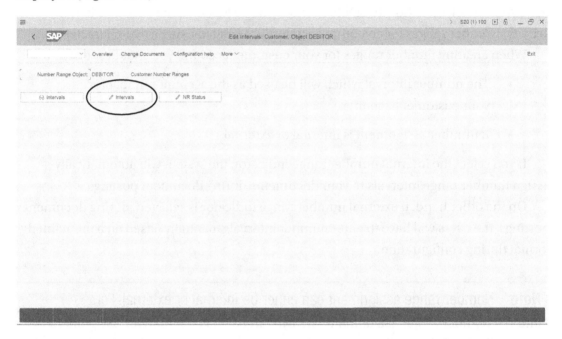

Figure 14-5. *The Edit Intervals: Customer, Object DEBITOR initial screen*

On the *Edit Intervals: Customer, Object DEBITOR* initial screen, click the Intervals button Circled in Figure 14-5. The *Edit Intervals: Customer, Object DEBITOR* second screen comes up (Figure 14-6). This is the screen where you can maintain your customer number ranges, displaying a list of number ranges already in the system. You have a number of options here. First, you can either decide to use an existing number range in the system by simplifying assigning it you're your customer account group, or second, editing an existing number range and then assign it to your customer number range or third, you can create your own customer account group number range from scratch. The choice is entirely up to you. However, in this activity, we will be creating our own number ranges we will be assigning to our customer account group.

Note   The system will not allow number interval overlapping (for example, the number interval 01 is already in the system; therefore, we will not be able to use this number interval again). So, we must use a number that is not already in the system.

Click Insert Line function (this is the fourth item from the left top of the screen) on the ***Edit Intervals: Customer, Object DEBITOR*** (Figure 14-6) to create addition line(s) for your number range intervals. You will notice that a blank line will be inserted at the top of the displayed list of number intervals in the system.

Number Range No.	From No.	To Number	NR Status	External
03	0100000000	0199999999	0	
01	ZZZZZ00000	ZZZZZ09999	0	✓
02	0000001600	0000001800	1609	
04	4000000000	4999999999	4000000029	
05	5000000000	5999999999	5000000009	
07	0000001500	0000001599	1504	
08	0000080000	0000089999	0	
6	0000001001	0000001499	0	✓
90	0000090000	0000099999	90009	
BP	0000000001	0000001000	104	
CT	0000054000	0000054999	0	✓
MC	SH00000000	SH99999999	0	✓
SD	0200000088	0200000099	0	✓
XG	CM0001	CM9999	0	✓
YP	BA000001	BZ999999	0	✓
Z1	1000000001	1999999999	0	
Z2	0000100000	0000299999	0	
ZC	6900000001	9999999999	6900000005	
ZE	A0001	AZZZZ	0	✓
ZN	6800000000	6900000000	6800000004	

Figure 14-6. *Maintain number ranges for Customer Account group*

Since 03 number interval is not in the list of number intervals displayed in the system, we decided to use 03 as our number interval, as in Figure 14-6.

Update the following fields:

Number Range No.: Enter the number such as 03 in this field. Number range sequences are maintained using two digits.

From No.: Enter a start number range such as 0100000000 in this field.

To Number: Enter the end number range such as 0199999999 in this field.

Note   You can create as many number range intervals as desired. The number range interval you define depends on your requirements.

Tip   *For more information on creating number ranges refer to Chapter 3 for a detailed explanation on how to create number ranges.*

*If you are having a problem making your own number range intervals because of number range overlap. Skip this section and go to the next section – **Assign Number Ranges to Customer Account Groups** below and assign any existing number range in the system to your customer account groups. This action will allow you to carry on with your configuration.*

Save your number range intervals.

Note   Transport number range intervals screen will pop up. Ignore the message and confirm your number range intervals by clicking the enter button below.

Transport number range interval screen pops up with a message. Ignore message and click Insert Enter button to confirm your number range intervals.

Note   You can create as many number range intervals as desired. The number range interval you can define depends on your client's requirements.

Assigning Number Ranges to Customer Account Groups

Finally, in this activity on customer account group, you have to assign the number ranges you have created to your customer account groups.

The system will automatically use the number range you have assigned to the customer account group when you create a customer account. The system does this by systematically selecting the next available number from the number range you have assigned. To assign a number range to a customer account group follow this menu path: ***IMG Financial Accounting ➤ Accounts Receivable and Accounts Payable ➤ Customer Accounts ➤ Master Data ➤ Preparations for Creating Customer Master Data ➤ Assign Number Ranges to Customer Account Groups.***

The ***Change View "Assign Customer Acct Groups >> Number Range:" Overview*** screen is displayed. Search for your Customer Account Group using the Position button at the bottom of the screen. In this activity, we used customer account group – DC01-Domestic Customer key and 03 as our number range interval.

Assign your number to your customer Account Group as in Figure 14-7.

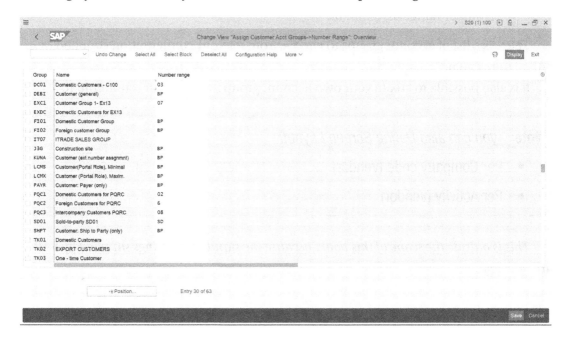

Figure 14-7. *Assign number range intervals to customer account groups*

Save your number range assignment.

Vendor Accounts

What is Vendor Account Group?

Vendor Account group like Customer Account Group allows the classification of vendors to a business partner function that best fits the nature of business transaction involved. The vendor account group controls the vendor hierarchy containing the vendor master record. When a vendor account is created, you must assign it to an account group. Account group is a control mechanism that determines the relevant screens and fields to be displayed for input based on individual vendor's business functions. Account group is maintained in IMG (Implementation Guide).

The importance of Vendor Account Group

It Controls:

- Which fields in the vendor master are Required, Optional, Display, etc.

- Number Range assignment.

There is a list of account groups to choose from for your configuration supplied by SAP in the system.

It is also possible to create your own account group to meet your requirement.

Note   *you can also Define Screen Layout:*

- Per Company code (vendor).
- Per Activity (vendor).

This is outside the scope of this book, because the standards settings supplied by SAP are sufficient.

In this activity, you will be defining Vendor Account Groups Screen Layout for Domestic and Foreign Vendors, respectively.

Defining Account Groups with Screen Layout (Vendors)

Problem: Company C900 plc classifies vendor account group into three categories:

1. Domestic Vendor,

2. Foreign Vendor, and

3. One-time Vendor.

You are to maintain an account group that will reflect these classifications in the system.

In this activity, you will define an account group with appropriate business partner functions and maintain the field status group for its general data. To customize the account groups for your supplier (Vendor) based on business partner function, follow this menu path: *IMG: Financial Accounting* ➤ *Accounts Receivable and Accounts Payable* ➤ *Vendor Accounts* ➤ *Master Data* ➤ *Preparations for Creating Vendor Master Data* ➤ *Define Accounts Groups with Screen Layout (Vendors).* The *Change View Vendor Account Groups Overview* screen is displayed. This is where you will define the account groups for your vendors. To go to the screen where you will specify your account group, choose the New Entries at the top of the screen (this is the third function from the left side of the screen). The New Entries: Details of Added Entries screen comes up (Figure 14-8).

Note   You can create as many account groups as you need, such as Foreign Vendors, Domestic Vendors, One-Time Vendors, and so on.

To avoid confusion, we will be using DV and two digits for Domestic Vendors, FV for Foreign Vendors, and OV for One-time Vendors in this activity.

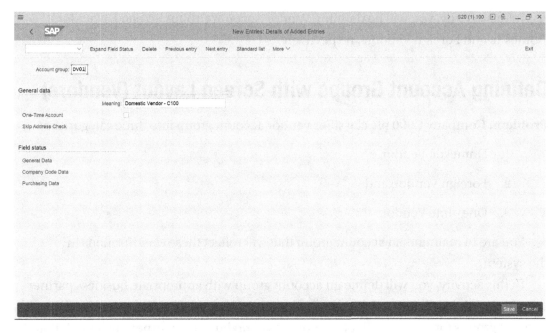

Figure 14-8. *Initial screen for account groups specification with screen layout (vendor)*

The Vendor Account group screen is divided into three sections:

- The section where you specify your account group ID.

- **General data:** Allows you to enter your vendor account group name.

- **Field status:** Allows you to specify if a field should be surprised, required, optional, or display.

Tip   *If you are creating a one-time vendor group remember to tick the One-time account check box in the **General data section** in the Account group entries screen.*

Update the following fields:

Account group: Enter your Vendor group ID in this field. In this activity, we used DV01 (Domestic Vendor-01).

General data: In the Meaning field, enter a description for your vendor account group.

Once you have updated the screen click the Save button at the bottom right side of the screen. Upon saving, the system will notify you on the status bar at the bottom of the screen that your data was saved.

Note   There is no hard rule for the name you use as account group. Account group name is a matter of choice. It is based on how your client wants to classify their vendor groups. The Domestic Vendor Account Group used in this activity is purely for illustration purposes. It is not a standard.

Before continuing with this activity, create two more vendor account groups for foreign vendor and One-time vendor using the data in Tables 14-3 and 14-4.

Table 14-3. *Foreign Vendor Account Group*

Account Group	Meaning
FV01	Foreign Vendor – C100

Table 14-4. *One-time Vendor Account Group*

Account Group	Meaning
OV01	One-time Vendor – C100

Maintaining the Filed Status Group for General Data of the Vendor Account Group

In the **Field Status section,** you can maintain the field status group for the following items:

- General data.
- Company code data.
- Purchasing data.

First, let's look at how to maintain the field status group for general data:

In the **Field status** section of the screen (Figure 14-8), double click **General data** from the list of field status. The *Maintain Field Status Group: Overview* screen is displayed. Select the item you want to define the field status for from the **Select Group** list (e.g., Address, communication, etc.), select *Address* from *Select Group* list by clicking it and click choose function at the top left side of the screen.

The *Maintain Field Status Group: Address* screen is displayed (Figure 14-9). This screen is where you will maintain the Field Status for Address. The specifications you carried out here will determine the field input status, whether a given field should be suppressed, required or optional. The settings here are based on your client's requirement. In this activity, we set the less important to optional and the important items to required entry. Since we consider the field status group for address less important, make sure that all the optional entry bubbles are selected.

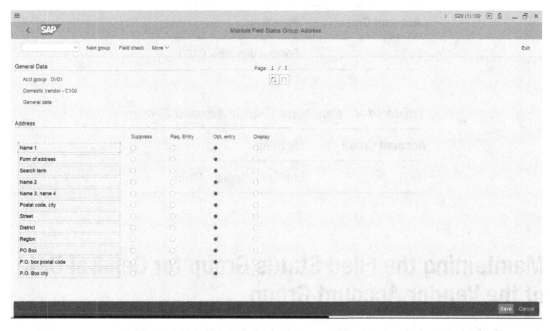

Figure 14-9. *Maintain Field Status Group for vendor address*

Click save at the bottom right of the screen to save your specifications.

Note   The items you specified as optional gives the account users the option to either enter data in the field or not, but the items you specify as required entry will force the account users to enter data in the field.

Problem: To ensure that users enter important information during document entry, you have been asked to make specifications that will make the ***Reconciliation account*** field and ***Sort key*** compulsory input entry fields.

The specification of Reconciliation Account and Sort key are carried out in **Company code data** in the *field status* section of the ***Change View "Vendor Account Group":*** ***Details*** screen (Figure 14-8). This is where you will specify the field status groups for ***Company code data***.

Double click ***Company code*** in the Field status section on the ***Change View "Vendor*** *account **group": Details*** screen. The ***Maintain Field Status Group: Overview*** page comes up. Select ***Account management*** from the **Select Group** list and click the Choose function at the top left side of the screen. The ***Maintain Field Status Group: Account*** ***Management*** screen is displayed; set **Reconciliation** and **Sort key** to ***Required entry*** and all other items to ***Optional***. This means that during data entry, the system will request for reconciliation account and the sort key as required entry.

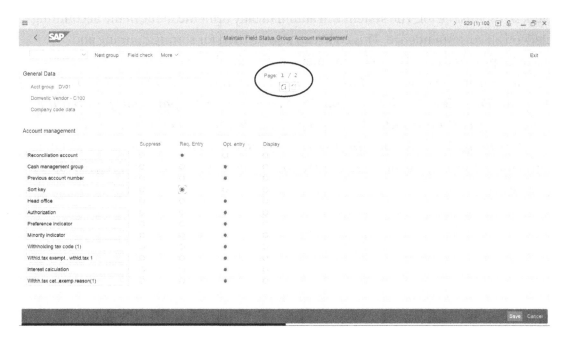

Figure 14-10. *Maintain Field Status Group – Account Management*

1. Select **Reconciliation account** and **Sort Key** as Required Entry fields for Account management and set every other item on the list to optional, as they are less important.

Tip   *Do not save your work yet because you will learn how to use the Next Page Button on this screen.*

To go to the next page of **Account management**, click the Next Page button (circled in Figure 14-10).

Save your vendor account group.

Before moving on, define two more account groups for your foreign vendor and one-time vendor groups.

Enter Accounting Clerk Identification Code for Vendors

In this activity, we will be looking at how to define the Accounting Clerk name under an Identification code (ID). This ID can be entered in the Vendor/master record, which the clerk is responsible for. The system will automatically print the name of the accounting clerk on all correspondence. This code can also be used for sorting dunning and payment proposal lists. The following menu path will take you to the initial screen where this customizing is carried out: **IMG:** *Financial Accounting* ➤ *Accounts Receivable and Accounts Payable* ➤ *Vendor Accounts* ➤ *Master Data* ➤ *Preparations for Creating Vendor Master Data* ➤ *Enter Accounting Clerk Identification Code for Vendor.*

The **Change View "Accounting Clerks" Overview** screen is displayed. Click at the top of the screen to go to the screen where you will enter your accounting clerks' details (Figure 14-11).

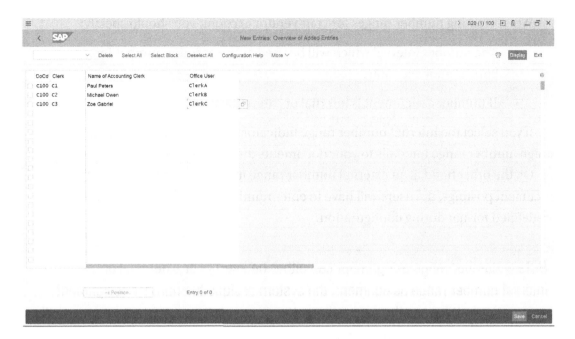

Figure 14-11. *Initial Screen for Accounting Clerk Identification Code for Vendor*

The ***New Entries: Overview of Added Entries*** screen comes up. Update the following fields:

Cod: Enter your company code in this field.

Clerk: Enter two characters identifier ID for your clerk.

Name of Accounting Clerk: Enter the name of your accounting clerk in this field.

Office User: You can also enter the position of your accounting clerk in this field.

After you have updated your New Entries: Overview of Added Entries screen, save your work.

Creating Number Ranges for Vendor Account Groups

Number ranges were covered in depth in Chapter 3, so we will only be looking at the basic steps involved in how to create number ranges for vendor accounts in this activity. Number ranges for vendor accounts are created using a two-character key.

When creating number ranges for your vendor account, you should specify:

- The number interval which will be used as the account number for your vendor accounts.

- If number assignment is internal or external.

If you select the internal number range indicator, the system will automatically assign number range intervals to your documents during document postings.

On the other hand, if an external number range indicator is selected, during document postings, the users will have to enter number intervals manually based on a predefined format during configuration.

Note   Number range assignment can either be internal or external. For internal number range assignment, the system assigns the number assignment automatically. Whereas the external number range assignment is entered manually by the users during document entry.

You may likely encounter a number range overlap problem when creating number ranges. The SAP system does not allow number interval overlap when creating number ranges for vendor accounts. So make sure that your number interval is not overlapping. If your number interval is overlapping, the system will issue a warning **"Interval already available."** Then use another number range until you can find one that is not over lapping.

It is also possible to choose from existing number range intervals in the system instead of creating your own.

Now let's create number ranges for the Domestic and Foreign vendor Account Groups you created earlier.

To go to the screen where you will define the number ranges for your vendor account group, follow this menu path: *IMG: Financial Accounting* ➤ *Accounts Receivable and Accounts Payable* ➤ *Vendor Accounts* ➤ *Master Data* ➤ *Preparations for Creating Vendor Master Data* ➤ *Create Number Ranges for Vendor Accounts*. The Edit Intervals: Vendor, Object KREDITOR initial screen is displayed (Figure 14-5).

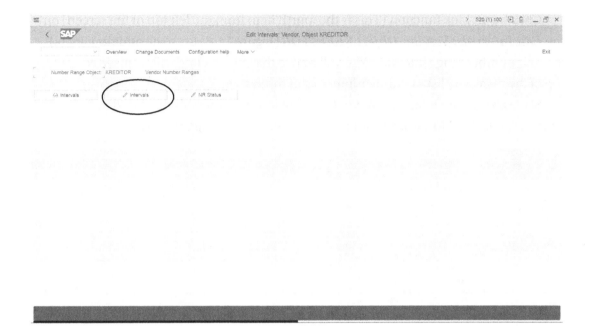

Figure 14-12. *The Edit Intervals: Vendor, Object KREDITOR initial screen*

On the ***Edit Intervals: Vendor, Object KREDITOR*** initial screen, click the Intervals button (circled in Figure 14-5). The ***Edit Intervals: Vendor, Object DEBITOR*** second screen comes up (Figure 14-12. This is the screen where you can maintain your vendor number ranges) displaying a list of number ranges already in the system. You have a number of options here. First, you can either decide to use an existing number range in the system by simplifying assigning it you're your vendor account group, or second, editing an existing number range and then assign it to your vendor number range or third, you can create your own vendor account group number range from scratch. The choice is entirely up to you. However, in this activity, we will be creating our own number ranges we will be assigning to our vendor account group.

Note   The system will not allow number interval overlapping (for example, the number interval 01 is already in the system; therefore, we will not be able to use this number interval again). So, we must use a number that is not already in the system.

Click Insert Line function (This is the fourth item from the left top of the screen) on the ***Edit Intervals: Vendor, Object KREDITOR*** (Figure 14-6) to create addition line(s) for your number range intervals. You will notice that a blank line will be inserted at the top of the displayed list of number intervals in the system.

Since 03 number interval is not in the list of number intervals displayed in the system, we decided to use 03 as our number interval, as in Figure 14-13.

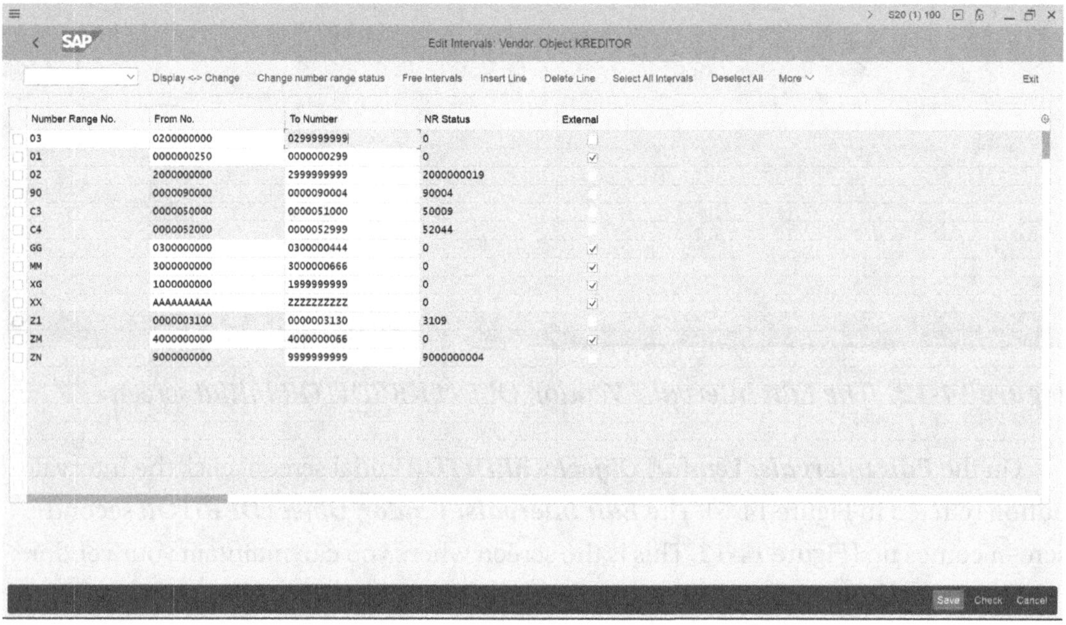

Figure 14-13. *Maintain number ranges for Vendor Account group*

Update the following fields:

Number Range No.: Enter the number such 03 in this field. Number range sequence are maintained using two digits.

From No.: Enter a start number range such as 0200000000 in this field.

To Number: Enter the end number range such as 0299999999 in this field.

Note   You can create as many number range intervals as desired. The number range interval you define depends on your requirements.

> **Tip**   *For more information on creating number ranges refer to Chapter 3 for a detailed explanation.*
>
> *If you are having problem making your own number range intervals because of number range overlap. Skip this section and go to the next section – **Assign Number Ranges to Vendor Account Groups** below and assign any existing number range in the system to your vendor account groups. This action will allow you to carry on with your configuration.*

Save your number range intervals.

> **Note**   The transport number range intervals screen will pop up. Ignore the message and confirm your number range intervals by clicking the enter button below.
>
> You can create as many number range intervals as desired. The number range interval you can define depends on your client's requirement.

Assigning Number Ranges to Vendor Account Groups

Finally, in this activity on vendor account groups, you have to assign the number ranges you have created to your vendor account groups.

The system will automatically use the number range you have assigned to the vendor account group when you create a vendor account. The system does this by systematically selecting the next available number from the number range you have assigned. To assign a number range to a vendor account group, follow this menu path: ***IMG Financial Accounting ➤ Accounts Receivable and Accounts Payable ➤ Vendor Accounts ➤ Master Data ➤ Preparations for Creating Vendor Master Data ➤ Assign Number Ranges to Vendor Account Groups.***

The ***Change View "Assign Vendor Acct Groups >> Number Range:" Overview*** screen is displayed. Search for your Vendor Account Group using the Position button at the bottom of the screen. In this activity, we used vendor account group – VC01-Domestic Vendor key and 03 as our number range interval.

Assign your number to your vendor Account Group, as in Figure 14-14.

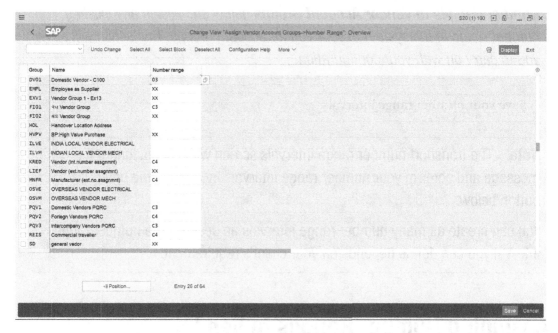

Figure 14-14. *Assign Number Range Intervals to Vendor Account Groups*

Terms of Payment

Cash Discounts

It is a normal business practice for business partners to enter into some form of payment agreement that governs their business relationship on invoice payment and cash discounts awards. This type of agreement is referred to as Terms of Payment. Terms of Payment are conditions agreed with business partners for goods sold or services offered in relation to payment of invoices. The terms of payment defines invoice due date and cash discounts offered for payment of invoice within a specified period.

The terms of payment you defined during configuration are assigned to business partners' master record. Once terms of payment key is assigned to business partner's master record, the system will automatically default the terms of payment during entry. Otherwise the user have to enter it manually.

The SAP system comes with pre-defined standard terms of payment that users can use, but it is also possible to create new terms of payment if necessary.

The purpose of terms of payment is to allow the system to determine invoice due date and cash discount to be awarded to business partner when specified conditions are met (i.e., prompt payment of invoice).

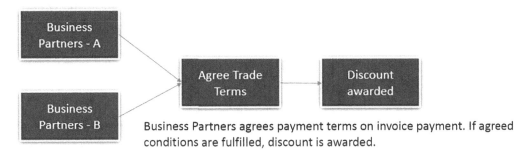

Figure 14-15. *Terms of Payment flow*

When customizing terms of payment, you need to define settings for the following items:

Payment Terms: This is a four-digit identifier key for payment terms. It determines the basis on which discount is granted. This includes the percentage rate used in the calculation of cash discount granted or received.

Day Limit: This is optional. The day limit is used to specify the calendar day that terms of payment are valid.

Account type: Specify whether payment terms relate to customer or vendor and allow the system to post business transactions to appropriate accounts.

Baseline Date: This covers the date for which the terms of payment applies. This is the date used by the system to determine the invoice due date. For the system to default baseline date for payment, you should specify the date to be used.

If you want the system to default a baseline date during document entry, you should set the appropriate indicator from a choice of three default dates:

- Document date.

- Document posting date.

- Document entry date.

On the contrary, if you want to enter the baseline date manually by yourself during document entry, set No default indicator.

Payment terms: The basis on which discount is granted. This includes the percentage rate used in the calculation of cash discount granted or received.

Let's see how terms of payment are maintained in the system.

Note   It is advisable to use separate terms of payment for vendor and customer. This is important because changes may occur in customer payment terms which may not necessarily be relevant to the payment agreement with vendors.

Maintaining Terms of Payment (Customer)

Problem: Company C100 plc offers discounts to customers on the following Terms of payment:

1.   5% for immediate payment.

2.   2% for payment made within 15 days.

3.   No discount for payment in 30 days.

As FI consultant, you are to specify these terms of payment in the system.

To maintain terms of payment for customers, follow this menu path: *IMG: Financial Accounting (New)* ➤ *Account Receivable and Accounts Payable* ➤ *Business Transaction* ➤ *Outgoing Invoices/Credit Memos* ➤ *Maintain Terms of Payment.*

The *Change View "Terms of Payment": Overview* screen is displayed. Choose New Entries function at the top of the screen. This will take you to the *New Entries: Details of Added Entries* screen where you will carry out your terms of payment settings.

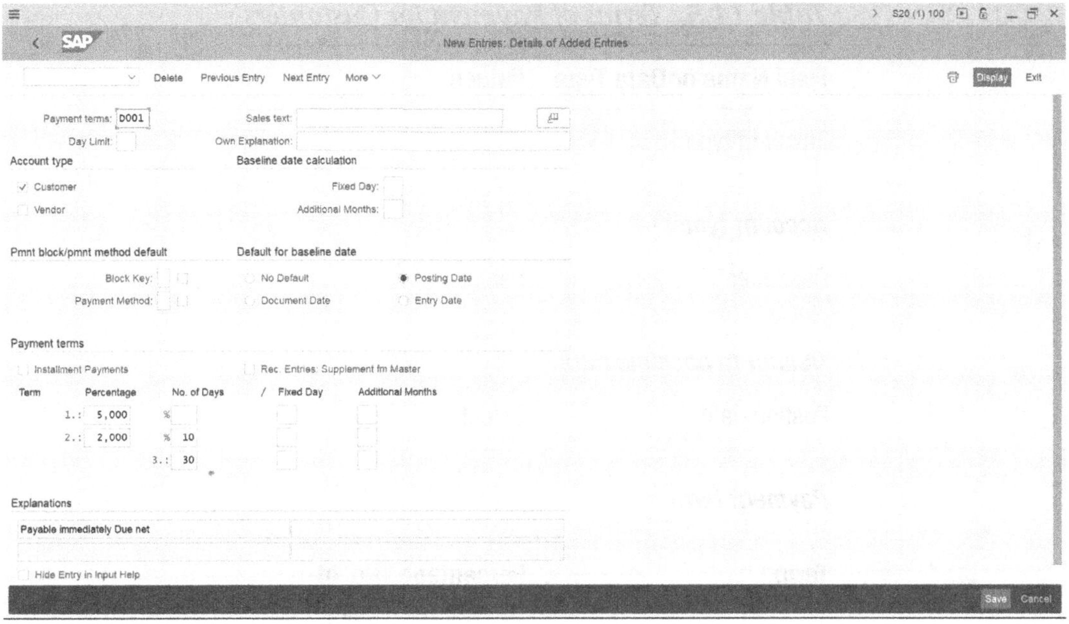

Figure 14-16. *Screen where terms of payment are maintained*

Using the data in Table 14-5 update the following fields.

Table 14-5. *Terms of Payment for Customers*

Field Name or Data Type	Values
Payment type	D001

Account type

Customer	Select

Default to baseline date

Posting date	Select

Payment terms

Term	Percentage	No. of days
1.	5%	Blank
2.	2%	10
3.		30

Save your terms of payment.

Tip   *It is important to define separate terms of payment for Customer and Vendor because it is most unlikely that the terms of payment for customer and vendor will remain the same.*

Payt Terms: This is defined using up to a maximum of four-digit key. This key is entered in the master records of customers/vendors.

Day Limit: Here you specify a given date of the month that you want the payment term to apply to a corresponding payment.

Own explanation: This is where you specify your own special description relating to your payment terms. The description you specify here will replace the system generated explanation by the system.

Account type: This will allow you to specify the account type that your payment term applies to. This could be either Customer or Vendor. It is also possible to set your payment term to both account types by selecting the checkbox for both Customer and Vendor, but we advise that you use one account type per payment term, as changes in one account type may not necessarily affect the other account type.

Default for baseline date: You have a number of options here that you can select from to use as the date applicable to the terms payment. The date you selected will be used by the system to determine permitted cash discount amount or invoice due date.

You have the choice of setting the baseline date for payment that the system will use as:

No default: You use No default if you do not want the system to default a date during document entry. This means during document entry the user has to manually specify the baseline date that is applicable to the terms of payment.

Document date: This is the date on the document or the date you entered during document entry as the document date.

Posting date: This is the date a document is posted or the date you specified as the posting date when posting a document.

Entry date: This is the date the document is entered into the system.

Payment terms: The specification done here will allow the system to award a cash discount if invoice amount is paid within specified days. For example, on immediate payment 5%, within 15 days 3% cash discount, and within 45 days due net.

When *Installment payment* is set. The system will automatically break the invoice amount into partial payments with different due dates specified in your customization.

Now define another terms of payment for Vendor

To maintain terms of payment for customers, follow this menu path: ***IMG: Financial Accounting (New) ➤ Account Receivable and Accounts Payable ➤ Business Transaction ➤ Outgoing Invoices/Credit Memos ➤ Maintain Terms of Payment.***

The ***Change View "Terms of Payment": Overview*** screen is displayed. Choose New Entries function at the top of the screen. This will take you to the ***New Entries: Details of Added Entries*** screen where you will carry out your terms of payment settings for vendor using the data in Table 14-6.

Table 14-6. *Define Terms of Payments for Vendors*

Field Name or Data Type	Values
Payment Type	V001
Account Type	
Customer	Select
Default to baseline date	
Posting Date	Select
Payment Terms	

Term	Percentage	No. of days
1.	5%	Blank
2.	3%	15
3.		45

Tip   *Select Vendor as your Account Type.*

Save your term of payment.

Installment Plan

Another important aspect of payment terms is the installment plan. This is the payment terms where business partners agree for an invoice amount payment to be spread out systematically over a specified period. The total invoice amount is divided into partial amounts and paid at different dates until the invoice amount is cleared or paid off in full. For example, your company agrees with a customer to pay 20% of an invoice amount of $4000 USD monthly over a five-month period. Thus, the installment plan will allow your company to receive $800 USD monthly for the agreed five-month period until the amount is paid in full.

When customizing an installment payment plan, you specify the following terms:

- The number of installments for your payment terms. This is the number of payments needed to pay off the outstanding amount.

- The percentage rate that will be applied to clear the outstanding invoice amount (the percentage rate specified must be equal to 100%).

- Define the terms of payment for individual instalments for each percentage rate applicable to your installment plan.

The system will automatically carry out the instalment split once instalment payment is defined in the system and assigned to the business partner's master record. Secondly, the system will also create a line item for each instalment automatically.

Problem: You have been asked to create a terms of payment for an installment plan, where 10% of the invoice amount is paid immediately, 40% is paid within 60 days, and the balance is paid within 90 days.

Maintaining Terms of Payment for an Installment Plan

Maintaining Terms of Payment may seem to be a complicated exercise, but this is not truly so. To help you understanding how to customize terms of payment for your instalment plan, we have decided to break this activity into a sequence using steps 1-4.

To go to the screen where you will maintain your terms of payment for an installment plan, follow this menu path: *IMG: Financial Accounting ➤ Account Receivable and Accounts Payable ➤ Business Transaction ➤ Incoming Invoices/Credit Memos ➤ Maintain Terms of Payment. The Change View "Rem of Payment": Overview* screen is displayed.

Choose the New Entries button; this will take you to the *New Entries: Detail of Added Entries* screen where you will carry out your terms of payment settings.

Define terms of payment for your instalment plan using a suitable four-character identification key.

Update the screen, as in Figure 14-17.

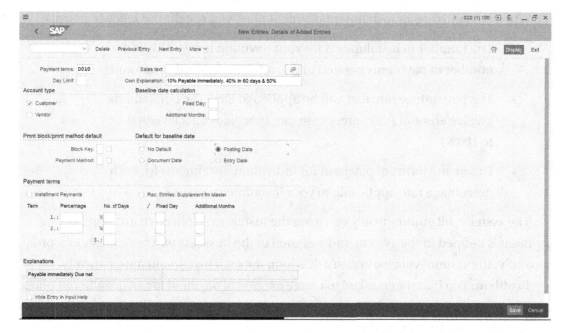

Figure 14-17. *The initial where Installment plan is maintained*

Using the information in Table 14-7 below, update the following fields:

Table 14-7. *The Data to Update the Payment Terms*

Field Name or Data Type	Values
Payment Terms	D010
Own Explanation	10% Payable immediately, 40% in 60 days & 50%
Account Type	
Customer	Select
Default to baseline date	
Posting Date	Select
Payment Terms	

Term	Percentage	No. of days
1.		
2.		
3.		

Payment Terms: Enter four-characters. This key allows you to store payment conditions in your payment terms and identify your terms of payment when you have more than one terms of payment in the system. In this activity, we used DC01 as our payment terms (this is a freely defined key). The terms of payment you have defined here is applicable to all terms of payment. We will be looking at this in depth in the next activity when defining payment terms.

Own Explanation: Describe the payment terms for your installment plan. Enter the description in this field.

Account Type: Specify the account type you want to apply to your payment terms. Since you are maintaining payment terms for your customers, click the Customer checkbox.

Default to Baseline Date: The date you select here will determine the default baseline date. In this activity, we used the posting date as our baseline date. Activate the Posting Date checkbox.

Terms: Specify the terms, percentage rates, and number of days for your payment terms. For this activity, leave this section blank.

At this stage, save your terms of payment.

We advise that you follow the steps in this exercise carefully, without trying to jump a step, unless you are quite good in this area.

The next step in this activity is to define individual payment terms for each percentage rate you are using as a basis of instalment payment. In this exercise, you will be defining payment terms for 10%, 50%, and 40%, respectively.

Tip   *Your total payment terms percentage rate must be equal to 100%.*

Click Next Entry at the top of the screen to go to another blank ***New Entries: Details of Added Entries*** screen.

Step 1

Using the information in Table 14-8, update the following fields.

Table 14-8. *The Data to Update the Payment Terms – Step 1*

Field Name or Data Type	Values	
Payment Type	P010	
Own Explanation	10% Payable Immediately	
Account Type		
Customer	Select	
Default to baseline date		
Posting Date	Select	
Payment Terms		
Installment Payment	Select	
Term	**Percentage**	**No. of days**
1.		
2.		
3.		

Save your terms of payment.

Step 2

Define payment terms for no. of days – 60 days.

Click Next Entry at the top of the screen to go to another blank ***New Entries: Details of Added Entries*** screen.

Update the following fields using the information in Table 14-9.

Table 14-9. *The Data to Update the Payment Terms – Step 2*

Field Name or Data Type	Values	
Payment Type	P040	
Account Type		
Customer	Select	
Default to baseline date		
Posting Date	Select	
Payment Terms		
Term	**Percentage**	**No. of days**
1.		60
2.		
3.		

Save your terms of payment.

Step 3

Define payment terms for no. of days – 90 days.

Click Next Entry at the top of the screen to go to another blank *New Entries: Details of Added Entries* screen.

Update the following fields using the information in Table 14-10.

Table 14-10. *The Data to Update the Payment Terms – Step 3*

Field Name or Data Type	Values	
Payment Type	P050	
Account Type		
Customer	Select	
Default to baseline date		
Posting Date	Select	
Payment Terms		
Term	**Percentage**	**No. of days**
1.		90
2.		
3.		

Payt Terms: Enter a four-character key – P050.

Own explanation: Enter a description for your instalment plan – 50% payable in 90 days

Account type: Set customer indicator.

Default for baseline date: Set ***Posting date*** indicator.

Save your terms of payment.

Now let's define Instalment Payments for the Terms of Payment you created above.

Defining the Payment Terms for Instalment Payments

To define the payment terms for installment payments, follow this menu path: ***IMG: Financial Accounting➤ Account Receivable and Accounts Payable ➤ Business Transaction ➤ Incoming Invoices/Credit Memos ➤ Define Terms of Payment for Instalment Payments.***

The **Change View Terms of Payment for Holdback/Retainage" Overview** screen is displayed. Click the New Entries button at the top of the screen. The **New Entries: Overview of Added Entries** screen is displayed. Use the search function to call up the **Terms of Payment** list.

Search for the installment plan and terms of payment you have created above and use them to update the fields in the **New Entries: Overview of Added Entries** screen (Figure 14-18) using the information in Table 14-11.

Table 14-11. *The Data to Update the Payment Terms*

Terms of payment	Installment	Percent	Payment term
D010	1	10	P010
D010	2	40	P040
D010	3	50	P050

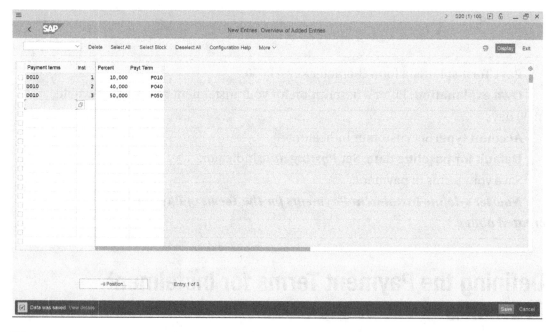

Figure 14-18. *Setting up payment terms for Installment payments*

Save your terms of payment.

Defining Cash Discount Base for Incoming Invoices

A cash discount base is calculated either as net value or gross value depending on your country's regulation.

The specification you make in this activity per company code will determine whether tax amount is considered in the base amount calculation for cash discount by the system. To go to the screen where you will specify your cash discount base for incoming invoices, follow this menu path: ***IMG: Financial Accounting ➤ Account Receivable and Accounts Payable ➤ Business Transaction ➤ Incoming Invoices/Credit Memos ➤ Define Cash Discount Base for Incoming Invoices.***

The ***Change View "Cash Discount Base": Overview*** screen is displayed. Use the scroll bar at the right side of the screen search for your Company Code or you can use the Position button at the bottom of the screen to search for your company code.

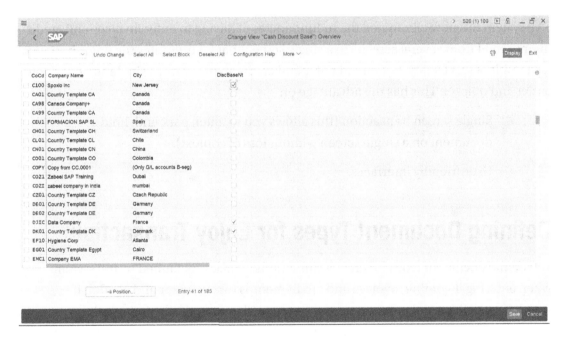

Figure 14-19. *Cash Discount Base for Incoming Invoices*

Activate The DiscBaseNt checkbox.

Save your cash discount base.

> **Note**   By **selecting Discount Base Net** checkbox, you are instructing the system to calculate your cash discount excluding taxes (net value). If the check box is left blank, the system will automatically assume that you want your cash discount amount to be based on gross value. This is part of the global parameter settings in your company code.

Incoming Invoices Credit Memos /Credit Memos – Enjoy

Enjoy Transaction

SAP system has now eliminated the redundancies of having to enter invoices and credit memos in FI from several screens to a single screen that incorporates the enjoy initiative. As a result of this facility, document entry and credit memos from a single screen is now easier and quicker. This has the advantage of:

- Single screen transaction (this allows you to enter, park and, hold a document on a single screen without loss of context).

- User-friendly interfaces.

Defining Document Types for Enjoy Transaction

You define document types for enjoy transactions, which is defaulted by the system when entering incoming invoices and credit memos for customer and vendor. If you did not define a document type, the system will automatically propose the document type that was used in the previous document entry. You can overwrite the proposed document type. Follow this menu path to go to the screen where you will define document types for enjoy transaction: *IMG: Financial Accounting➤ Account Receivable and Accounts Payable ➤ Business Transaction ➤ Incoming Invoices/ Credit Memos ➤ Incoming Invoices/Credit Memos – Enjoy ➤ Define Document Types for Enjoy Transaction.*

The ***Change View Document Types for Enjoy Transaction Overview*** screen is displayed. Click New Entries at the top of the screen. Update the ***New Entries: Overview of Added Entries*** screen using the information in Figure 14-20. The settings carried out here will allow the system to automatically propose a document type during document entry.

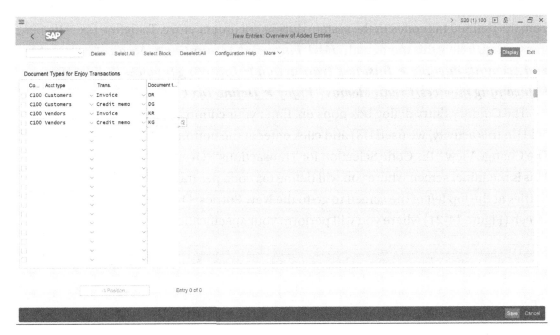

Figure 14-20. *Document types for Enjoy Transaction*

Update the following fields:

Company: Enter your company code (100) in this field. This will apply the settings to your company code.

Acct Type: Enter the account type you want the system to use as the default during document entry. For example, Customers/Vendors.

Trans.: Using the pull-down arrow next to the field to display the predefined transactions list supplied by SAP, enter the transaction description that fits the account type you want to apply the default setting to.

Document: Enter the document type to use as the default. For example:

DR-Invoice (Customers)

DG-Credit Memo (Customers

KR-Invoice (Vendors)

KG-Credit Memo (Vendors)

Save your work.

Defining Tax Code per Transaction

This setting in the Define Tax Code per Transaction section allows you to select a subset from the tax codes (Tax codes where created in chapter 10). As part of this definition, you specify a tax code per transaction and per country key and then you can select a subset from the defined tax codes in the system during document entry. To define tax code per transaction, follow this menu path: *IMG: Financial Accounting➤ Account Receivable and Accounts Payable ➤ Business Transaction ➤ Incoming Invoices/Credit Memos ➤ Incoming Invoices/Credit Memos – Enjoy ➤ Define Tax Code per Transaction.*

The Country Entry dialog box pops up. Enter your country code in the Country Key field (in this activity, we used US) and click enter at the bottom right of the dialog box. The Change View "Tax Code Selection for Transactions": Overview screen is displayed. This is the initial screen where you will define tax code per transaction. Click New Entries at the top left of the screen to go to the New Entries: Overview Added Entries screen (Figure 14-21) where you will perform your specifications.

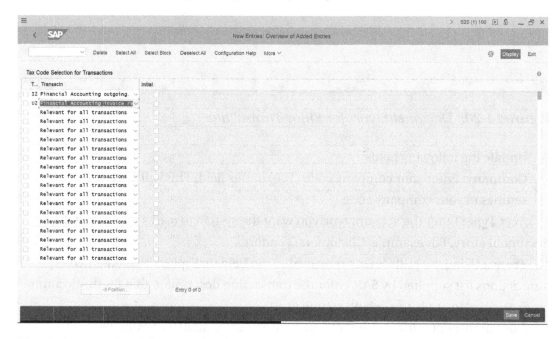

Figure 14-21. *Specifying tax codes per transaction*

Update the following fields:

Tax Code: Enter your output tax code in the first field and input tax code in the next field.

Transaction: Enter the transaction for your tax code in this field. For example, for output tax, select Financial Accounting outgoing and for input tax, select Financial Accounting Invoice.

Save your setting for tax code per transaction.

Cash Discount

Cash Discount Granted

This is the cash discount you give to a customer for complying with an agreed terms of payment. Discount granted reduces the total invoice amount by an agreed percentage of the total invoice amount. Based on the settings you made in this activity, when clearing open items, the system will post cash discount granted to the accounts you defined for cash discount granted.

Note   We advise that you should first create the G/L account 880000 that cash discount granted will be posted to before proceeding with this customizing. Please refer to Chapter 5 where we covered in detail how to customize G/L accounts.

Defining Accounts for Cash Discount Granted.

Cash discount granted is the cash discount you give to a customer for complying with agreed terms of payment. The cash discount granted reduces the total invoice amount by an agreed percentage. Based on the settings you make in this activity; the system will post discount granted amount to the G/L account you assigned to cash discount granted. Use this menu path to go to the screen where you will assign a G/L account for cash discount granted: *IMG: Financial Accounting➤ Account Receivable and Accounts Payable ➤ Business Transaction ➤ Incoming Payments – Incoming Payments Global Settings ➤ Define Accounts for Cash Discount Granted.*

The *Enter Chart of Accounts* dialog box pops up. Enter your Chart of Accounts – CA10 in the *Chart of Accounts* field and click the enter button at the bottom right of the dialog box.

The *Configuration Accounting Maintain: Automatic Posts – Rules* screen is displayed. Click the Save bottom at the bottom left of the screen. The *Configuration*

Accounting Maintain: Automatic Posts – Accounts screen is displayed. Assign the GL Account for Clearing Cash discount Granted – **880000** to Automatic Posting – Accounts and Save your work.

Note   If you have not created a G/L Account for Cash Discount Granted, the system will notify you on the status bar below that your G/L account is not created in the chart of accounts. You can force the system to accept the G/L account temporarily and you can create the G/L account later by hitting the enter key on your keyboard several times and the system will allow you to save your configuration.

Define Account for Cash Discount Taken

This is the cash discount you receive from a vendor for complying with payment conditions. Discount taken will reduce the total invoice amount by an agreed percentage of the total invoice amount. Based on the settings you made in this activity, when clearing open items, the system will post cash discount taken to the accounts you defined for cash discount taken.

Note   Again, just like Cash Discount Granted above, create the appropriate G/L account – 276000 for cash discount taken.

Use this menu path to go to the screen where you will assign a G/L account for cash discount taken: *IMG: Financial Accounting➤ Account Receivable and Accounts Payable ➤ Business Transaction ➤ Outgoing Payments ➤ Outgoing Payments Global Settings ➤ Define Accounts for Cash Discount Taken*.

The *Enter Chart of Accounts* dialog box pops up. Enter your Chart of Accounts – CA10 in the *Chart of Accounts* field and click the enter button at the bottom right of the dialog box.

The *Configuration Accounting Maintain: Automatic Posts – Rules* screen is displayed. Click the Save bottom at the bottom left of the screen. The *Configuration Accounting Maintain: Automatic Posts – Accounts* screen is displayed. Assign the GL Account for Clearing Cash discount taken – **276000** to Automatic Posting – Accounts and

Save your work. The system will notify you on the status bar at the bottom of the screen that changes have been made.

Defining Account for Overpayments/Underpayments

This allows the system to make postings to revenue and expense accounts if the following conditions are present:

- Payment difference arises as a result of either overpayment or underpayment.

- It is not possible to post difference through cash discount adjustment.

- The difference falls within tolerance limits for an automatic adjustment posting.

Note   Again, just like Cash Discount Granted above, create the appropriate G/L account – 276000 for Account for overpayments/underpayments

---

Use this menu path to go to the screen where you will assign a G/L account for Accounts for overpayments/underpayments: *IMG: Financial Accounting➤ Account Receivable and Accounts Payable ➤ Business Transaction ➤ Outgoing Payments ➤ Outgoing Payments Global Settings ➤ Define Accounts for Overpayments/ Underpayments.*.

The *Enter Chart of Accounts* dialog box pops up. Enter your Chart of Accounts – CA10 in the *Chart of Accounts* field and click the enter button at the bottom right of the dialog box.

The *Configuration Accounting Maintain: Automatic Posts – Rules* screen is displayed. Click the Save bottom at the bottom left of the screen. The *Configuration Accounting Maintain: Automatic Posts – Accounts* screen is displayed. Assign the GL Account for Clearing overpayments/underpayments – **881000** to Automatic Posting – Accounts and Save your work. The system will notify you on the status bar at the bottom of the screen that changes have been made.

Defining Accounts for Bank Charges (Vendor)

Bank Charges are posted to an expense account. Here you define the account for bank charges and assign an expense account to it. The system will then automatically post bank charges to your expense account during posting.

Note   Create the G/L Account for Bank Charges (vendor) before proceeding with this customizing. Otherwise, you can force the system to accept the G/L account you are using for this activity and then create it later.

Again, just like Cash Discount Granted above, create the appropriate G/L account – 276000 for Account for overpayments/underpayments.

To go to the screen where you will assign a G/L account for Accounts for Bank Charges (Vendor) follow this menu path: *IMG: Financial Accounting* ➤ *Account Receivable and Accounts Payable* ➤ *Business Transaction* ➤ *Outgoing Payments* ➤ *Outgoing Payments Global Settings* ➤ *Define Accounts for Bank Charges (Vendor)*.

The *Enter Chart of Accounts* dialog box pops up. Enter your Chart of Accounts – CA10 in the *Chart of Accounts* field and click the enter button at the bottom right of the dialog box.

The *Configuration Accounting Maintain: Automatic Posts – Rules* screen is displayed. Click the Save bottom at the bottom left of the screen. *Configuration Accounting Maintain: Automatic Posts – Accounts* screen is displayed. Assign the GL Account for Clearing Bank Charges – **470100** to Automatic Posting – Accounts and save your work. The system will notify you at the status bar at the bottom of the screen that changes have been made.

Defining Payment Block Reasons

When defining reasons for blocking payments, there are a few specifications you need to consider. You can specify whether payment blocks can be changed in payment proposals or during manual payment. You can also specify whether documents defined with block keys can be cleared during manual payment processing or if changes are not allowed.

The reasons you define in this exercise allow you to differentiate why invoices are not to be paid. Standard block reasons are supplied by SAP, which you can use if you do not want to define your own.

Payment block reasons are valid for all company codes. This means all company codes within the client or in the system can use the payment block reasons in the system without having to define payment block reasons that are company code specific. When customizing payment block reasons, you need to update the following fields:

Block Ind.: This is a block indicator key that is defined with a one-digit character key. This key contains reasons for blocking payments. It's entered in a document to block an invoice from being paid for a specified reason.

Description: Enter a short description stating why this payment is being blocked.

Block Indicators: Allows you to specify how you want the payment block reason you defined to function. You have three options to choose from:

> **Change in Payment Proposal:** When you want changes to be carried out during the payment proposal. It is possible to remove a payment block when processing the payment proposal, but when you set this proposal, changes cannot be made during payment proposal processing.

> **Manual Payment Block:** If you do not want documents assigned with a block key to be cleared during manual payment clearing, then choose this option.

> **Not Changeable:** Changes cannot be made during payment proposal processing or during manual payment.

This step allows us to define the reason for blocking invoice(s) for payment. Standard block reasons are supplied which you can use. It is also possible to define additional block reasons if there is any need for it.

Note   Since Payment block reasons are valid for all company code, you can use block reasons already defined in the system.

Now let's define a payment block reason. Follow this menu path to go to the screen where you will define payment block reasons: ***IMG: Financial Accounting*** ➤ *Account Receivable and Accounts Payable* ➤ *Business Transaction* ➤ *Outgoing Payments* ➤ *Outgoing Payments Global Settings* ➤ *Payment Block Reasons* ➤ *Define Payment Block Reasons.*

The ***Change View Payment Block Reasons Overview*** screen is displayed, click New
Entries at the top of the screen and the ***New Entries: overview of added Entries*** screen
is displayed (Figure 14-22).

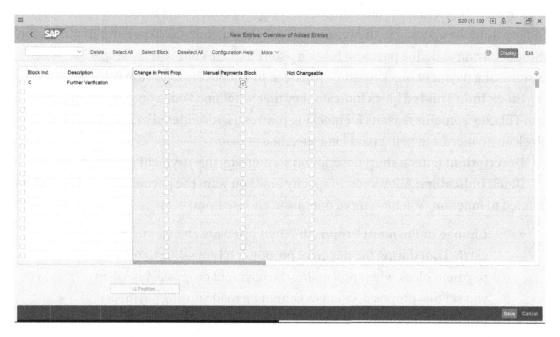

Figure 14-22. *Defining payment block reasons*

Update the following fields:

Block Ind.: Enter your payment block reason key in this field. This is usually defined
using a single-digit character. In this exercise, we used K as our payment block reason
key for illustration purposes. This key is a freely definable payment block reason key. You
can use any key of your choice.

Description: Enter a meaningful short statement describing your payment block
reason. As an example, we used Payment Block C900 as our payment block reason. You
can use any meaningful description of your choice.

Change in Pmnt Prop.: When you select the change in payment proposal checkbox,
the payment block cannot be removed during an automatic payment program run.

Save your block reason.

Manual Outgoing Payments

The settings you carry out here allow end users to manually post vendor payment and clear open items on vendor's account. In order for end users to be able to perform manual outgoing payments in the system, you will need to carry out settings in the following areas in your configuration:

- Tolerances for vendors.

- Reason codes for manual outgoing payments.

- Define account for payment differences.

Defining Tolerances for Vendors

In SAP S4 HANA FI, three tolerance groups are maintained:

- Employees Tolerance Group,

- GL Accounts Tolerance Group, and

- Customers/Vendors Tolerance Group.

Tolerances define acceptable tolerance during posting. Tolerance provides the control mechanism that allows management to restrict the amount accounting clerks are permitted to post. It also serves as a control measure for discounts granted, payment differences, and tolerances for payment advice.

The advantage of setting tolerances is to impose restrictions to avoid major posting errors by clerks or end users.

You have already covered Employees Tolerance Groups and GL Accounts Tolerance Groups earlier in Chapter 9. Hence, you will only be looking at Customers/Vendors Tolerance groups. The settings in this activity are valid for both customers and vendors tolerance groups.

As part of your configuration exercise, you will provide specifications for the following items:

- Clearing transactions.

- Permitted payment differences.

- Posting residual items from payment differences.

- Tolerances for payment advice notes.

The following settings are necessary for Tolerance Groups (Vendor) configuration:

1. **Tolerance group**: This is defined with a four-digit group key (group key is defined with a four-digit ID).

Note   *Blank group key is the standard tolerance group, and it is required as the minimum tolerance group.*

---

2. Once the tolerance group is defined, you then assign it to the right object. In this activity, your tolerance group will be assigned to the Vendor/Customer master record.

Problem: You have been asked by your team leader to create two tolerance groups – one with a group key and the second one without a group key – to satisfy the minimum tolerance group requirements

First, let's define tolerance group with ID:

Follow this menu path: ***IMG: Financial Accounting➤ Account Receivable and Accounts Payable ➤ Business Transaction ➤ Outgoing Payments ➤ Manual Outgoing Payments ➤ Define Tolerances (vendors).***

The ***Change View Customer/Vendor Tolerances Overview*** screen is displayed. Click New Entries, the second item at the top left of the screen, and the ***New Entries: Details of Added Entries*** screen (Figure 14-23) comes up.

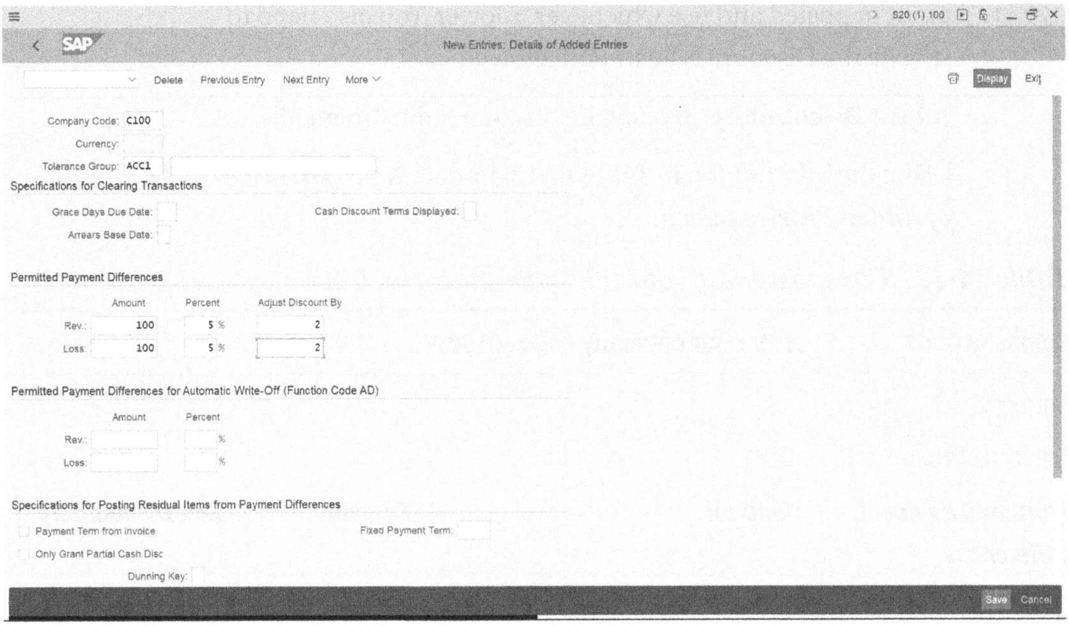

Figure 14-23. *Defining tolerance group*

Update the following fields in the ***New Entries: Details of Added Entries*** screen:

Company code: Enter the four-digits of your company identification key is in this field.

Currency: This is your Company Code Currency. The system will automatically default your company code currency during document entry.

Tolerance group: This is defined with a four-digit ID as your tolerance group key. This ID will be assigned to your tolerance group relating to vendors.

In the Permitted Payment Difference section of the screen, update the following fields:

Rev/Loss: The permitted payment differences that a user is permitted to post in Amount and in percentage are entered in these fields, respectively. When posting a document, the system will check the amount and the percentage of the document amount posted and use whichever is lower. You also need to specify the Discount adjustment allowed.

Adjust Discount By: Specify the discount adjustment allowed.

Using the information in Table 14-12, update *New Entries: Details of Added Entries* screen:

Table 14-12. *Data to update your tolerance group with ID*

Company Code	Enter our company code (C100)		
Currency			
Tolerance Group	CLK1		
Permitted Payment Differences	*Amount*	*Percent*	*Adjust Discount By*
Gain	100	5	2
Loss	100	5	2

Save your tolerance group.

The second step in this activity is to create another tolerance group without a tolerance group ID.

Note   Since you have created a group key for Customer/Vendor tolerances, you also need to create a blank group key, which is for the minimum standard tolerance group.

Follow this menu path to go to the screen where you will define tolerance group without an ID for minimum standard tolerance group: *IMG: Financial Accounting➤ Account Receivable and Accounts Payable ➤ Business Transaction ➤ Outgoing Payments ➤ Manual Outgoing Payments ➤ Define Tolerances (vendors).*

The *Change View Customer/Vendor Tolerances Overview* screen is displayed, click New Entries the second item at the top left of the screen, the *New Entries: Details of Added Entries* screen (Figure 14-24) comes up.

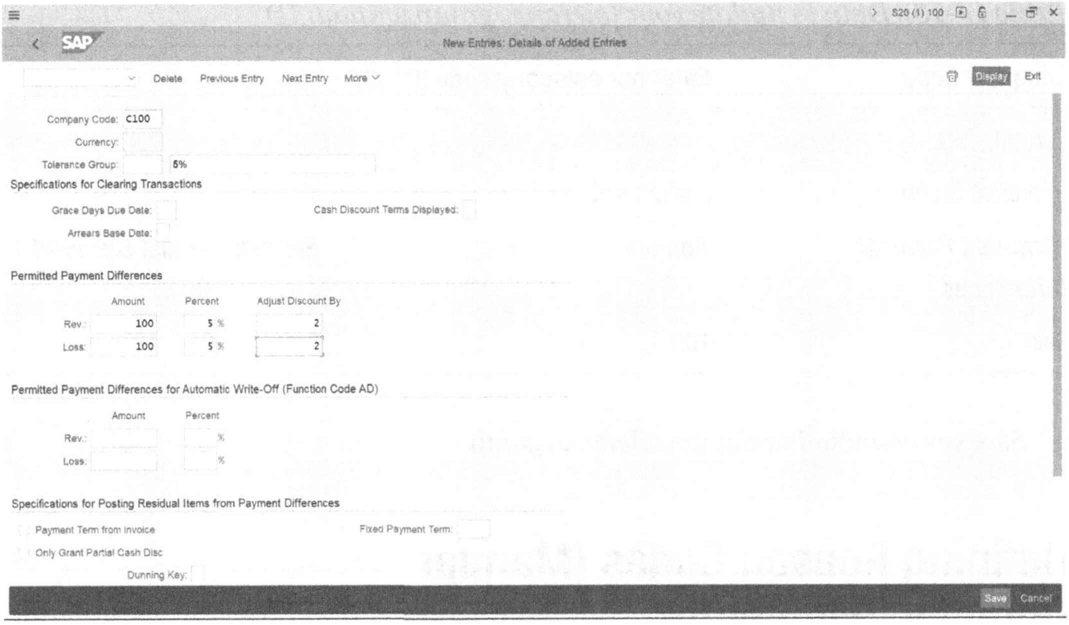

Figure 14-24. *Defining the standard minimum tolerance group (with a group ID)*

Company code: Enter the four-digits of your company identification key in this field.

Currency: This is your Company Code Currency. The system will automatically default your company code currency during document entry.

Tolerance group: Leave this field blank

In the Permitted Payment Difference section of the screen, update the following fields:

Rev/Loss: The permitted payment differences that a user is permitted to post in Amount and in percentage are entered in these fields, respectively. When posting a document, the system will check the amount and the percentage of the document amount posted and use whichever is lower. You also need to specify the Discount adjustment allowed.

Adjust Discount By: Specify the discount adjustment allowed.

Using the information in Table 14-13, update the ***New Entries: Details of Added Entries*** screen:

Table 14-13. *Data to update your tolerance group without ID*

Company Code	Enter our company code (C100)		
Currency			
Tolerance Group	Leave blank		
Permitted Payment Differences	*Amount*	*Percent*	*Adjust Discount By*
Gain	100	5	2

Save your standard minimum tolerance group

Defining Reason Codes (Manual Outgoing Payments)

Payment differences would normally arise when clearing open items against payments. The difference is compared to the tolerance limit allocated to the employee making the posting. If the difference is deemed to be immaterial, the payment is done automatically and the system will adjust the cash discount up to the amount specified in the configuration for cash discount adjustment or the system can write it off to a special account. Otherwise, the payment has to be processed manually.

If payment difference is outside the tolerance limit, such payment has to be processed manually, in one of the following ways as:

- **Partial Payment:** You enter the partial payment against the open item and assign a reason code. When a partial payment is posted, all documents remain in the account as open items.

- **Residual Item:** You assign the residual item and assign reason code. The system will clear the original net amount and the payment, whilst the residual item remains in the account as open item.

- **Payment on account:** All item remains as open items.

Reason Codes

There are several reasons for payment differences. It is important to specify reasons for payment differences when posting partial payments or residual items. SAP has the flexibility to assign more than one reason codes to a payment difference. To do this click on distribute difference push button option on the top right hand side of the payment screen.

Reason code is part of overpayment/underpayment. It is defined per company code. You specify which correspondence type is assigned to the following items when posting payment and clearing open items manually:

- Partial Payments.

- Residual Posting.

- Posting on account.

By setting further indicators during configuration you can include the following optional functions to your reason code:

- **Charge off Difference:** When this indicator is set for a reason code, the payment difference arising will be posted to a separate GL account automatically.

- **Disputed Item:** The Disputed item indicator allows disputed items to be excluded from credit checks.

- **Do not copy text:** When this indicator is set, you will have to enter reason code text into the segment text field of the residual item or the partial payment manually. If the indicator is not set, the system will automatically copy the reason code text you defined in your configuration into the segment text of residual item or partial payment.

Let's go to the screen where you will customize reason codes for your manual outgoing payments. Follow this menu path: ***IMG: Financial Accounting ➤ Account Receivable and Accounts Payable ➤ Business Transaction ➤ Outgoing Payments ➤ Manual Outgoing Payments ➤ Overpayment/Underpayment ➤ Define Reason Codes (Manual Outgoing Payments).***

The ***Determine Work Area: Entry*** dialog box pops up. Enter your Company Code in the ***Work Area*** field (in this activity, we used C100 as our company code). Click enter (the green circle button at the bottom of the dialog box). A warning screen pops up telling you that "All fields which define the area have initial value". Ignore the warning and click the Continue button, which is the top button on the screen. The ***Change View Classification of Payment Differences Overview*** screen is displayed. Click New Entries (this is the first item from the left at the top of the screen) to call-up ***New Entries: Details of Added Entries*** screen where you will define your reason codes.

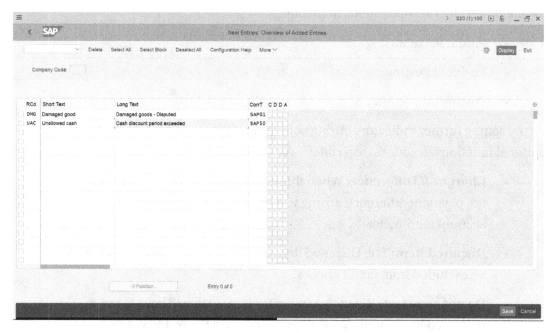

Figure 14-25. *Assigning reason codes to manual outgoing payments*

1. Update the following fields:

   RCd: Enter a three-digit character code in this field. It represents your reason code. This code will allow you to store text and the correspondence type for your reason code.

   Short Text: Enter a short description of your reason code in this field. For example, in this exercise, we used Damaged Goods.

   Long Text: Enter a full description of your reason code in this field. For example, we used Damaged Goods – Disputed.

CorrT: Specify the correspondence type for your reason code in this field. SAP comes with standard predefined correspondence types you can choose from.

Click the pull-down arrow next to the Correspondence Type field to display the list of correspondence types supplied by SAP. Select the correspondence type that best meets your requirement. For example, the code for payment notice with line items is SAP0l and the code for difference 050 payment notice is SAP50.

Note   SAP01 – Payment notice with line items.

SAP50 – Difference 050 Payment notice.

You can create as many reason codes as you want. We advise that you take a look at the reason codes for company code 1000 before defining your own reason codes.

Save your reason codes.

The next step is to define accounts for Payment Differences (Manual Outgoing Payments). The settings you make will allow the system to automatically post payment differences to the accounts you specify.

Defining Accounts for Payment Differences (Manual Outgoing Payments)

Payment differences are posted to a special account in SAP S4 HANA. In this activity, you assign payment differences by reason to your G/L account. You have already created the GL account required for this configuration. Your payment difference will be assigned to unallowed customer discounts and a G/L Account.

Note   You have already created the G/L account (Unallocated Customer Discount 881000) required for this customizing in a previous activity. So you don't need to define it again; all you need to do is simply assign it to the payment differences.

To assign your account to payment difference, follow this menu path: ***IMG: Financial Accounting ➤ Account Receivable and Accounts Payable ➤ Business Transaction ➤ Outgoing Payments ➤ Manual Outgoing Payments ➤ Overpayment/ Underpayment ➤ Define Accounts for Payment Differences (Manual Outgoing Payments).***

The ***Enter Chart of Accounts*** dialog box pops up. Enter your chart of account ID in the Chart of Accounts field and click the Continue button at the bottom right of the screen. The ***Configuration Accounting Maintain: Automatic Posts – Rules*** screen is displayed. Click save at the bottom right of the screen and the Configuration Accounting Maintain: Automatic Posts – Accounts screen is displayed (Figure 14-26). This is the screen where you will assign a G/L Account to your payment differences reason.

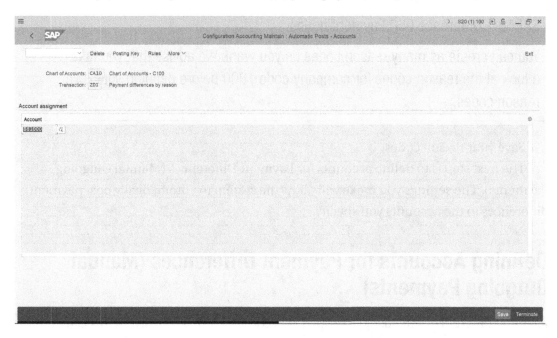

Figure 14-26. *Account determination for automatic posting of payment differences*

Enter the appropriate GL account for payment differences in the ***Account*** field and save your work.

Automatic Outgoing Payments

Automatic Outgoing Payments is a payment management tool in the SAP S4 HANA system that manages payments of multiple open invoices, posts payment documents, and prints payment media using EDI (Electronic Data Interchange) or DME (Date Medium Exchange) simultaneously.

Payment Program can be accessed from the User Side (Easy Access) and IMG. It is recommended that you perform your configuration in IMG. It is very important that you work from top down during configuration to ensure that your settings are complete. Several levels and steps are involved when customizing a payment program in SAP S4 HANA.

Payment program configuration allows you to specify the settings for the following items for Payment Transactions:

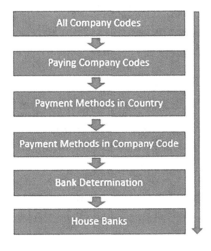

Ok let's begin Automatic Payment Program configuration.

All Company Codes

Specifying the company code you want to include in your automatic payment program is important when the payment process is centralized. For example, when one company code makes payments for other company codes. At this level, you make settings for all the company codes that you want to include in your payment program.

Note   All Company Codes are the company codes you want to include in your payment transactions.

The following specifications are essential for All Company Code configurations:

- The paying company code (this is the company code responsible for processing outgoing payments). This setting is applicable where payments are made centrally by one company code for several company codes.

- The Sending Company code (the company code payment is being made on its behalf to a business partner by another company code). If the sending company is not specified, the system will automatically assume that the paying company is also the sending company.

- You can specify if Separate payment per business area is to be made and use payment method supplements.

- If your business partner normally allows certain days of grace for invoice payment, you can enter it in ***Tolerance days payable*** field. The system will automatically delay payment of the appropriate due items until the next payment run as long as it is within the allowed days of grace in order not to lose cash discounts.

- You can also specify Special GL transactions for vendors and customers settlement using the following special GL indictors from the pull-down lists supplied by SAP in the system (see List below).

Indicators	Description
3	< Text missing >
7	Down payment for current assets
9	Down payment request
A	Down payment on current assets
B	Financial assets down payment
D	Discount
E	Unchecked invoice
F	Down payment request
G	Guarantee received
H	Security deposit
I	Intangible asset down payment
M	Tangible asset down payment
O	Amortization down payment
P	Payment request
S	Check/bill of exchange
V	Stocks down payment
W	Bill of exch. (rediscountable)
X	< Text missing >
Z	Dwn Pmt for Order/Project

To set up all company code codes for your payment transactions, follow this menu path: *IMG: Financial Accounting ➤ Account Receivable and Accounts Payable ➤ Business Transaction ➤ Outgoing Payments ➤ Automatic Outgoing Payments ➤ Payment Method/Bank Selection for Payment Program ➤ Set Up All Company Codes for Payment Transactions*.

The *Change View "Company Code" Overview* screen is displayed. Click New Entries (this is the second item at the top left of the screen) to go to the *New Entries:*

Details of Added Entries (Figure 14-27) screen where you will carry out all company code specifications for your payment program.

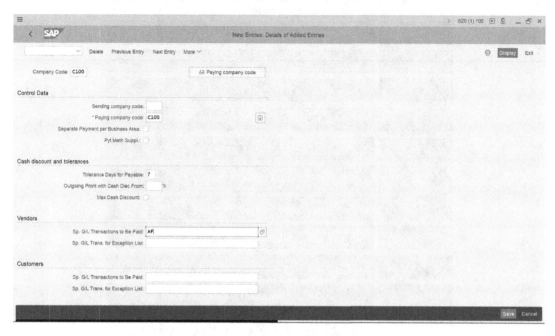

Figure 14-27. Defining payment program for all company codes

Update the following fields using the information in Table 14-14

Table 14-14. Data to update your payment program for all company codes

Fields	Values
Company code	Enter our company code (C100)
Control Data	
Sending Company	
Paying Company	Enter our company code (C100)
Cash Discount and Tolerances	
Tolerance Days for Payable	7
Vendor	
Sp. GL Transactions to be paid	AF

Save your setting for all company codes by clicking the save button at the bottom right of the screen.

Paying Company Codes

The paying Company Code is the company that is assigned with the task of processing payment transactions on behalf of other company codes. This is the case where a centralized payment system is in place. Invoices arising from transactions by other company codes are sent to one Company code within the group company who makes payments on behalf of other company codes centrally. A good example of this is an environment where the head office makes payment for other company codes (i.e., branches). The company code making payment on behalf of other company code is referred to as the paying company code, and the company to whom payment is being made is referred to as the sending company code.

When customizing this section, three options are important:

- **Minimum amount for incoming payment:** This determines the minimum amount that will be allowed by the system to go through the automatic payment program for an incoming payment. Any amount lower than this amount will not be allowed as an automatic payment, it will have to be performed manually instead.

- **Minimum amount for outgoing payment:** The amount specified as the minimum amount for outgoing payments relates to invoice payments. Any amount below the· minimum amount will not be included by the system in the payment run. Amounts below this have to be performed manually. For example, if the minimum amount specification for an outgoing payment is $0.50 USD, any invoice amount less than $0.50 USD on will be excluded from the payment run.

- **Forms:** SAP comes with standard payment program forms in SAPScript. SAPScript defines the form layout that meets certain country specific and international payment methods. You can choose from several standard forms when defining your paying company code. The benefit of using the standard forms defined in SAPScript is that it saves you from using the wrong print program. There are two types of forms in this activity – forms for printing a payment advice and the EDI accompany sheet form.

- **Sender details**: Specify the texts you want to use for your letter header, letter footer, and your company code sending address.

Now let's look at how to setup a paying company code for payment transactions. To do this, follow this menu path: *MG: Financial Accounting* ➤ *Account Receivable and Accounts Payable* ➤ *Business Transaction* ➤ *Outgoing Payments* ➤ *Automatic Outgoing Payments* ➤ *Payment Method/Bank Selection for Payment Program* ➤ *Set Up Paying Company Codes for Payment Transactions*.

The *Change View "Paying Company Codes": Overview* screen is displayed. Click New Entries at the top left of the screen. The *New Entries: Details of Added Entries* screen comes up. This is the screen where you will specify the minimum account for incoming payments and minimum amount for outgoing payment for your paying company code.

Update the following fields:

Paying company code: Enter your paying company code in this field. In this activity, we used C100 as our company code

Minimum Amount for Incoming Payment: Enter the minimum incoming payment you want to include in your payment program in this field. In this activity, we used $0.50USD.

Minimum Amount for Outgoing Payment: Enter the minimum outgoing payment you want to include in your payment program in this field. In this activity, we used $2.50USD.

The next step is to assign SAPScripts, which are country specific to your paying company code (the form for payment advice and EDI accompany sheet form).

Click the Forms button at the bottom Left of the screen in Figure 14-29 to expand the forms section where you will assign payment form to payment advice and EDI accompany form.

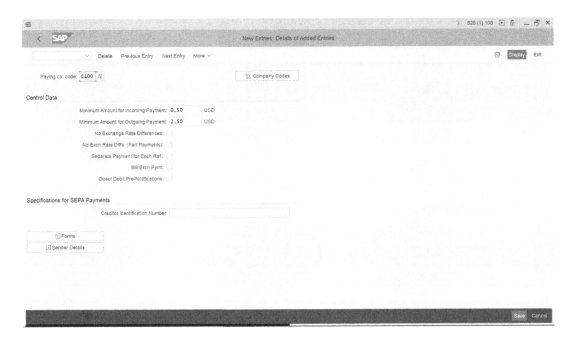

Figure 14-28. *Setting Minimum Amount for Outgoing Payments/Incoming Payments*

Note   SAP comes with several predefined payment forms you can use for your payment advice and EDI. In this activity, you will be using International Script form – F110_IN_AVIS for Payment Advice and Script form – F110_EDI_01 for EDI accompanying Sheet form. You can use any other form of your choice. In practice, you should use your country specific SAPScript or what your company recommends.

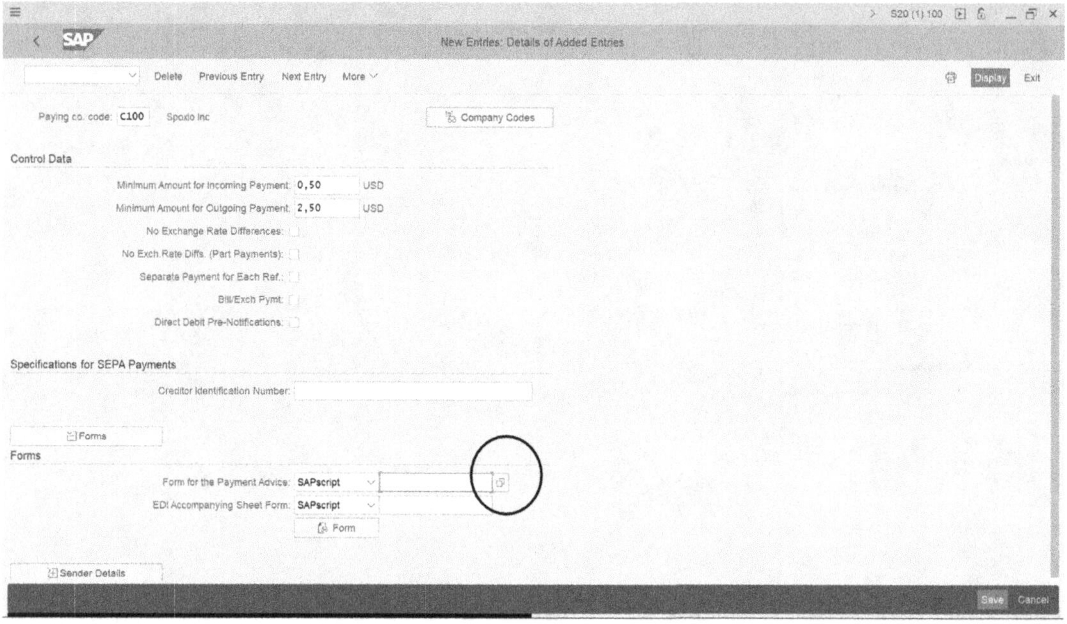

Figure 14-29. *Specifying the Form for Payment Advice/EDI Accompanying Sheet Form using the search function*

Click the search function button by the SAPscript circled in Figure 14-29 to display SAPscript Form Tree (Display Mode) with a list of payment advice versions for countries represented in the system that you want to use in your payment program. Under Payment Medium, choose **International** from the payment medium list. The Payment Medium Workbench comes up with a list of forms represented in the system. Select Payment Advice Note (international), the Form F110_IN_AVIS (AVIS (international)) screen is displayed. Click Form F110_IN_AVIS. This will copy the F110_IN_AVIS to your form for the payment advice – SAPscript, as in Figure 14-30.

The next step is to also assign EDI accompany sheet form to your EDI accompany sheet form.

Click the function by EDI Accompany Sheet Form – SAPscript. Choose **International** from the payment medium list. The Payment Medium Workbench comes up with a list of forms represented in the system. Select EDI Accompany Sheet, the Form F110_EDI_01 (EDI-Begleizettel) screen comes up. Select Language EN Actv from the displayed list and form F110_EDI_01 is copied to your form for the EDI Accompany Sheet Form – SAPscript, as in Figure 14-30.

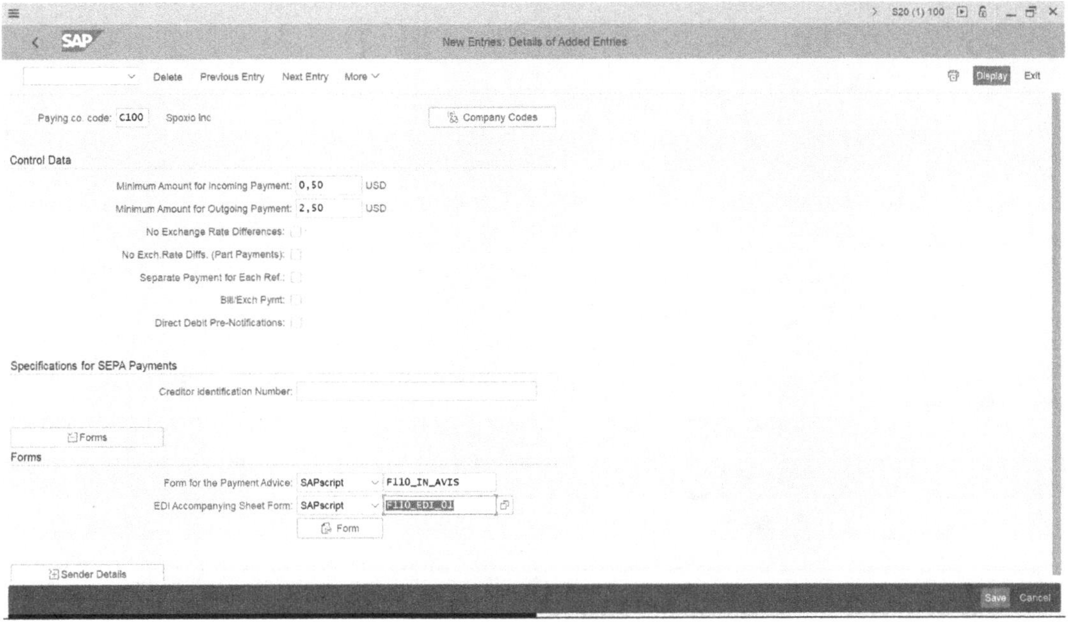

Figure 14-30. *Specification of Payment medium for your payment program*

The final step in payment paying company code customizing is to assign senders details to the paying company code. The value you enter will determine how the sender details are displayed in correspondence. At the bottom right of the screen click the Sender Details button at the bottom left of the screen to expand sender details for your SAPscript form field, as in Figure 14-31.

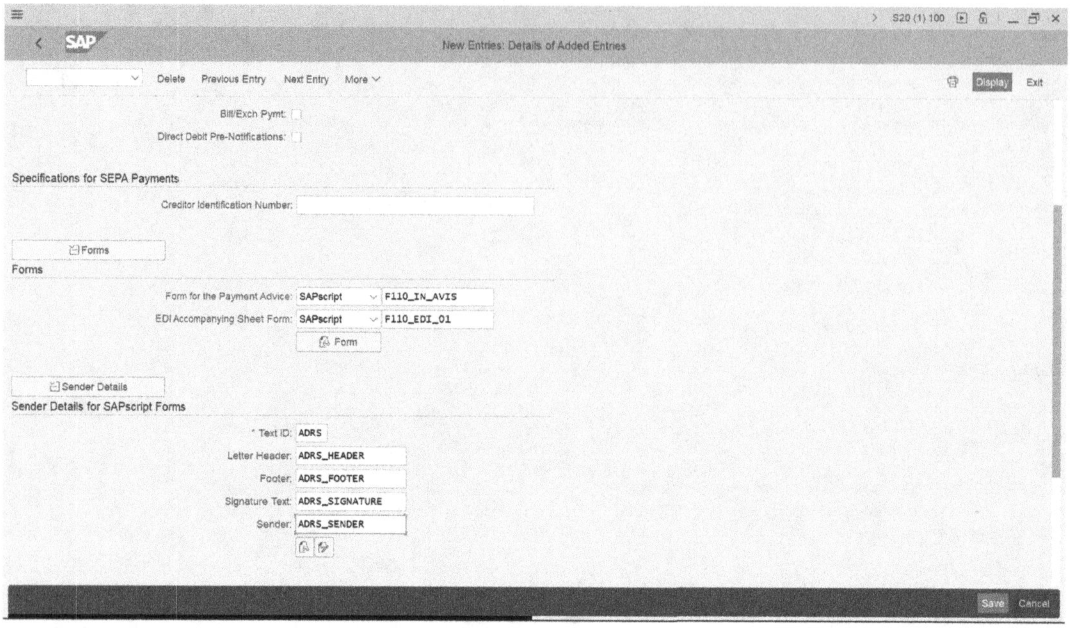

Figure 14-31. *Specification of Sender details*

Save your configuration.

In the next activity, we will be looking at how to customize payment method per company codes.

Payment Methods per Company Codes

The Payment Methods per Company Codes are obtained from Country Payment Keys defined in Payment Methods per Country. It is not compulsory that a Company Code must use the entire payment Methods per Country in the system. In practice, it is possible for a company code to use some or all available payment methods in the system. The specifications you make here will determine the payment methods the system will use in the automatic payment program for your company code when making payments.

You need to specify the following items here:

- The Paying company code (this is the company code responsible for processing outgoing payments).

- The Payment method, for example check, bank transfer, etc.

- Amount limits (minimum and maximum) applies to your payment method(s). Any payment amount below or above specified limits will be excluded from the payment run for your payment transaction.

- Other specifications under this activity includes:

  ➢ Grouping items.

  ➢ *Foreign payments/foreign currency payments for foreign currency transactions:*

  The payment method will allow the system to process foreign currency payments and receipts. Make payments to/from business partner's bank abroad.

- *Bank Selection control:*

  This allows the use of optimization either by bank group or by postal order. When you want the payment program to make payment from bank within the same clearing house, choose *optimize by bank group* indicator in your configuration. Funds are transferred more quickly and easily from your house bank within the shortest possible time to the business partner's bank account. This is possible only if you assign your bank in the master record to the bank group that you have defined. On the other hand, if optimized by postal code is specified, the house bank selection that is closer to the business partner bank postal code is used.

Let's look at how to set up payment method per company code. Follow this menu path to proceed to the screen where the setting is carried out: *IMG: Financial Accounting* ➤ *Account Receivable and Accounts Payable* ➤ *Business Transaction* ➤ *Outgoing Payments* ➤ *Automatic Outgoing Payments* ➤ *Payment Method/Bank Selection for Payment Program* ➤ *Set Up Payment Methods per Company Code for Payment Transactions.*

The *Change View "Maintenance of Company Code Data for a Payment Method" Overview* screen is displayed. Click New Entries at the top left of the screen to go to New Entries: Details of Added Entries screen (Figure 14-32) where you will specify the maximum amount and maintain form data for payment program.

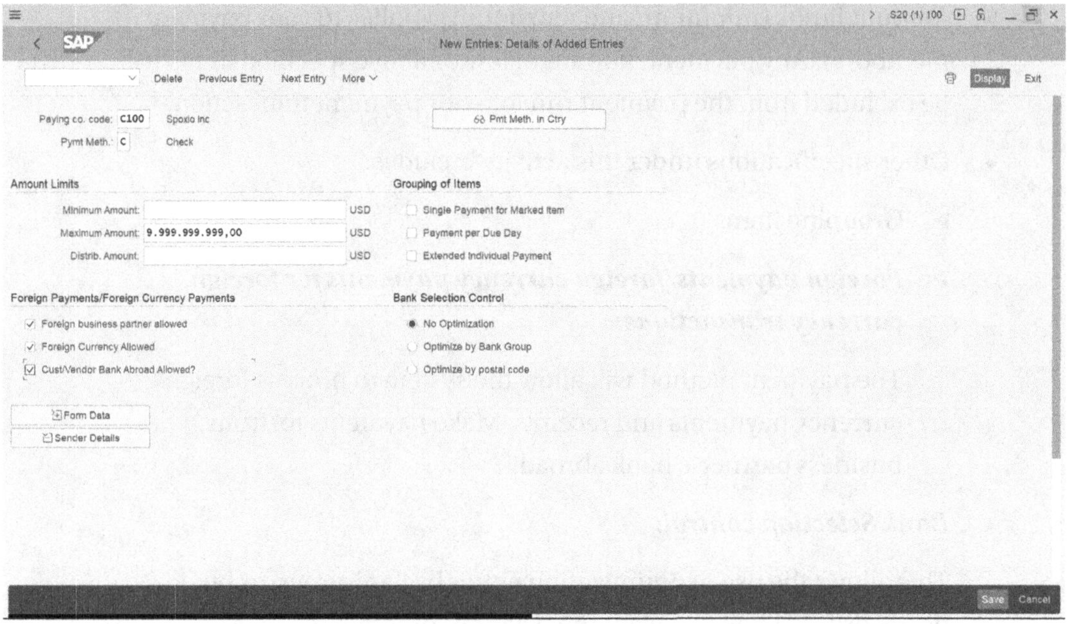

Figure 14-32. *Maintaining paying company code data for a payment method*

Update the following fields:

Paying co. code: Enter the company code that you want to use for transaction payment in your configuration for your payment run.

Payment method: Specify payment method (For example, Check – C and Bank Transfer – T).

Minimum Amount: Enter the minimum amount limit. Any amount below the minimum amount specified will be omitted from the payment run. If the field is left blank, there will be no amount limit restriction.

Maximum Amount: Enter the maximum amount limit in this field. Any amount in the payment transaction in excess of the maximum amount limit will be automatically excluded from the payment run.

Foreign business partner allowed: When indicator for foreign business partner allowed is set, the system will include foreign business partners in the payment run for a payment transaction.

Foreign Currency allowed: Specified foreign currencies are allowed in the payment run.

Cust/vendor bank abroad allowed: When the indicator for foreign business partner allowed is set, the system will allow payments from business partners' bank accounts from abroad to be included in the payment run for a payment transaction

Form data: This is the Form for payment Advice version that you want to use for your payment program.

1. Maintain paying company code Data for a Payment Method for Check payments. Using the information in Table 14-15, update the input field.

Table 14-15. *Data to Update your Paying Company Code for a Payment Method*

Fields	Values
Paying co. code	Enter our company code (C100)
Pymt Method	C
Amount Limits	
Minimum Amount	Blank
Maximum amount	9.999.999.999,00
Foreign payments/foreign currency payments	
Foreign business partner allowed	Select
Foreign currency allowed	Select
Cust/vendor bank abroad allowed/	select
Bank Selection control	
No Optimize	Select

The next step in this activity is to specify a standard payment form in SAPscript to your company code payment method using the international version and check (with check management) to your print checks. Click the Form button at the bottom left of the screen to expand the form page for further entries where you will assign SAPscript form for the paying company code.

Note   Use International Script form for Check (with Check management) in your setting.

Click the search function button by the SAPscript circled in Figure 14-32 to display SAPscript Form Tree (Display Mode) with a list of payment advice versions for countries represented in the system that you want to use in your payment program. Under Payment Medium, choose **International** from the payment medium list, select Check (With Check Management) and the Form F110_Premium Medium screen pops up. Double click Language EN Activ and select F110_Premium to copy it into the Form for Payment Medium field.

The Payment Medium Workbench comes up with a list of forms represented in the system. Select Payment Advice Note (international), the Form F110_IN_AVIS (AVIS (international)) screen is displayed. Click Form F110_IN_AVIS. This will copy the F110_ IN_AVIS to your form for the payment advice – SAPscript, as in Figure 14-30.

The next step is to enter senders' details in in your payment method.

To expand sender details for Drawer on the form section, click the Sender Details button at the bottom of the screen, as in Figure 14-32.

Using the information in Table 14-16, update the **Drawer on the form** section and **Sorting of the** section of the screen.

Table 14-16. *Data to Update your Drawer Form*

Fields	Values
Drawer on the form	Enter your Company's details in this field. For this activity we used
	Spoxio Inc.
	1551 Ferry Avenue
	New Jersey
Sorting of the	
Correspondence	K2 (Name)
Line items	E2 (Date)

Finally, Click the Pyt adv.ctrl button to call up ***Payment Advice Control*** in order for you to specify appropriate items in the ***Payment advice note control*** section. That is vital for your payment program.

Set the following items in the ***Payment advice note control*** section. Select the **as many as req.** radio button and select the NoPytAdv radio button.

Save your work.

1. The next step in this activity is to maintain paying Company Code Data for a Payment Method for Bank Transfer. Follow this menu path to go to the screen where you will specify payment method for bank transfer: ***IMG: Financial Accounting ➤ Account Receivable and Accounts Payable ➤ Business Transaction ➤ Outgoing Payments ➤ Automatic Outgoing Payments ➤ Payment Method/Bank Selection for Payment Program ➤ Set Up Payment Methods per Company Code for Payment Transactions.***

The ***Change View "Maintenance of Company Code Data for a Payment Method" Overview*** screen is displayed. Click New Entries at the top left of the screen to go to New Entries: Details of Added Entries screen (Figure 14-25) where you will specify the maximum amount and maintain form data for payment program.

Using the data in Table 14-17, update the following fields.

Table 14-17. *The Data to Update your Payment Program for Bank Transfer*

Fields	Values
Paying co. code	C900
Pymt Method	T
Amount Limits	
Maximum amount	9.999.999.999,00
Foreign payments/foreign currency payments	
Foreign business partner allowed	Select
Foreign currency allowed	Select
Cust/vendor bank abroad allowed/	Select
Bank Selection control	
No Optimize	Select

The next step is to update the form data.

Click on the Form Data button at the bottom of the screen to expand the form for further entries. Enter your company's details in the ***Drawer in the form*** section.

1. In the ***Payment advice note control*** section select ***None*** and save your work.

To see how your Company Code Payment Method looks, click Back at the top left of the screen to return to ***Change View Maintenance of Company Code Data for a Payment Method*** screen (Figure 14-33).

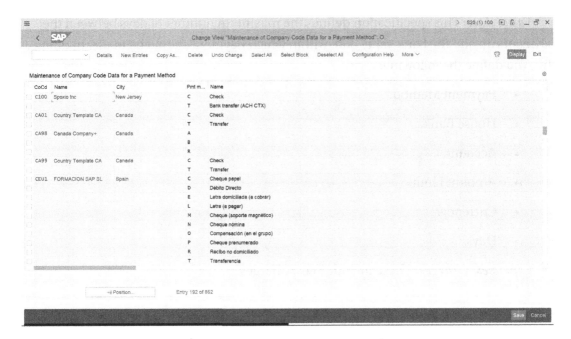

Figure 14- 33. *Company Code Data for Payment Method*

Bank Determination for Payment Transactions

The settings you make in *Bank Determination for Payment Transactions* will allow the payment program to determine which bank account to make payment from based on the ranking order you defined in your configuration.

Define the following specifications in your configuration:

Ranking Order: Payments are made in order of ranking from your house bank by the payment program. The system will check the bank account with the highest priority for sufficient funds. If there are enough funds, payment will be made from the first house bank. If there are not sufficient funds in the first house bank, the system will check the second house bank for sufficient funds and make payment from that house bank, if there are sufficient funds, and so on.

Bank Accounts: The settings made here allow you to specify which bank account the payment program will use for payment.

Available Amounts: For each of the house banks included in your payment program, you should specify the amount available for incoming and outgoing payments. This specification also helps the system to determine which bank accounts to include when making payments.

Value date: This specification defines the maximum number of days between the payment run and the bank value date within which payment should be made. In doing this, you define the following:

- Payment Method.

- House Bank.

- Account.

- Amount Limit.

- Currency.

- Days.

Expenses/Charges: These include Fees/Charges.

Note   Before configuring Bank Determination for Payment Transactions, you should ensure that the House Banks you are applying to your payment transaction have been defined. See how to define House Bank in Chapter 9.

To start with the customizing of Bank Determination for payment transactions, follow this menu path: *MG: Financial Accounting ➤ Account Receivable and Accounts Payable ➤ Business Transaction ➤ Outgoing Payments ➤ Automatic Outgoing Payments ➤ Payment Method/Bank Selection for Payment Program ➤ Set Up Bank Determination for Payment Transactions*.

The *Display View "Bank Selection": Overview* screen comes up. Make sure the *Bank selection* folder on the *Dialog Structure* is open. Work through the folders under the *Bank* selection folder from top down systematically to ensure that there is nothing missing from your configuration.

Ranking Order

Payments are made in order of ranking from the house bank by the payment program. This system will check for the bank account with the highest priority for sufficient funds. If there are enough funds, payment will be from the first bank in order of ranking. If there are insufficient funds in the first house bank, the system will check the second house bank for sufficient funds and make payment from the house bank, if it has sufficient funds.

Using the Position button at the bottom of the screen, look for your company code from the Bank Selection list.

First, select your company from the **Bank selection** list and then Double click on the Ranking Order fold on the left side of the screen in the Dialog Structure. The **Change View Ranking Order Overview** screen is displayed; click New Entries at the top left of the screen and define the Ranking Order for your payment in the **New Entries: Overview of Added Entries** screen.

Update the flowing fields:

Payment Method: Enter the payment method you want to use in your payment transaction and in the appropriate order. (For example, you want payment to be made by check or bank transfer, enter C for cheek payment and T for bank transfer in the payment method field). During payment run, the system will automatically apply the payment method that you entered in the payment method to your payment transaction.

Currency: Enter the currency key that you want to apply to payment transaction. If this field is blank, this will allow the payment program to carry out payment in any currency. If currency is specified, only the currency that you specified will be used by the payment program.

Ranking order: Enter the ranking order that you want the system to make payment from your house bank. For example, ranking order 1, 2, etc.

House Bank: Enter the house banks you want to use for your payment transaction in ranking order in this field.

Using the information in Table 14-18, specify the Ranking Order:

Table 14-18. *Specification of Ranking Order for your Payment Program*

Payment Method (PM)	Currency (Crcy)	Bank Ranking	House Bank
C	Leave blank	1	Bank of America
T	Leave blank	1	Bank of America
C	Leave blank	2	HSBC
T	Leave blank	2	HSBC

Save your payment program ranking order.

Note   Leave currency blank. This will allow the payment program to carry out payment in any currency. If a currency is specified, only the currency that you specified will be used by the payment program.

Assuming you have more than one House Bank, since Barclays Bank is ranked 1, the second bank will be ranked 2, the third bank will be ranked 3, and so on. Ranking is based on priority.

Bank Accounts

Bank accounts allow you to specify which house bank the payment program can make payment from and where outgoing payments are posted during a payment run. Payments are posted to subaccounts based on payment method. For example, an outgoing payment made with a check is posted to the subaccount for checks. Likewise, payments made with bank transfer are posted to the subaccount for bank transfer.

Note   You have already created the bank accounts needed for your configuration in Chapter 9 in House Bank configuration. Make sure that you have created the appropriate GL account for your bank account. Otherwise, you have to create them by referring to Appendix – A, Chapter 9.

Double click the Bank Account folder on the *Dialog Structure*. The *Change View Bank Accounts Overview* screen is displayed. Click the New Entries button and define the Ranking Order for your payment in the *New Entries: Overview of Added Entries* screen.

1.   Update the flowing fields:

   House Bank: Enter the house banks you want to use for your Bank account in this field in payment ranking order. (For example, you want payment to be made first from your Barclays Bank Account. However, if there are not sufficient funds in Barclays Bank Account, then use HSBC Bank Account, and so on).

Payment Method: Enter the payment method you want to use in your payment transaction and in the appropriate order. (For example, you want payment to be made by check or bank transfer, enter C for check payment and T for bank transfer in the payment method field). During payment run, the system will systematically apply the payment method that you entered in the payment method to the represented Bank Subaccounts, respectively.

Currency: Enter the currency key that you want to apply to payment transaction. If this field is blank, this will allow the payment program to carry out payment in any currency. If currency is specified, only the currency that you specified will be applicable to Bank Subaccount in your payment program.

Account ID: Enter your Bank Account ID in this field. This Account ID was created earlier during House Bank configuration in Chapter 9.

Bank Subaccount: Enter the GL account you created earlier for Check Account and Bank Transfer Account in Chapter 9.

Using the information in Table 14-19, specify the Banking Accounts for Paying Company Code.

Table 14-19. *Data for Specifying the Bank Accounts for Paying Company Code*

House Bank	Payment Method (PM)	Currency (Crcy)	Account ID	Bank subaccount
BARC1	C	Leave blank	BARC	111412
BARC1	T	Leave blank	BARC	111414
HSBC1	C	Leave blank	HSBC	113155
HSBC1	T	Leave blank	HSBC	113158

Save bank account setting.

Note   GL account 111412 – Bank of America - Check issued out (the account check payments are posted for Bank of America).

GL account 111414 – Bank of America - Outgoing transfer (the account bank transfers are posted for Bank of America).

GL account 113155 – HSBC Bank - Check issued out (the account check payments are posted for HSBC).

GL account 113158 – HSBC Bank - Outgoing transfer (the account bank transfers payments are posted for HSBC).

The final step in your customizing is to specify the available amount that can be paid out of a bank account.

Available Amounts

The available amounts field holds the funds available in your selected bank accounts. You specify the amount available for incoming and outgoing payments. During payment run, the payment program will check the selected banks based on ranking order to find out whether there are enough funds for payment. If the available amount is insufficient in the first bank, the payment program will automatically check the next bank account for available funds and so on, until it finds a bank account with sufficient funds for payment.

The Payment program does not conduct amount splits, but the system does have the flexibility to check your bank account based on ranking order to find out which bank account has sufficient funds for payment. If none of the bank account assigned to payment have sufficient funds, payment will not be carried out.

It is important that before running the payment program, you ensure that available amounts in the bank accounts assigned to your payment program are up to date.

Double click Available Amounts folder in the *Dialog Structure*. The **Change View "Amount Available": Overview** screen is displayed. When you click the New Entries at the top left of the screen, the **New Entries: Overview of Added Entries** screen comes up.

Update the following fields:

House Bank: Enter your House Bank Identifier key for the bank accounts assigned to your payment program.

Account ID: Enter your Bank Account ID in this field. This Account ID was created earlier during House Bank configuration in Chapter 9.

Days: This facility is only needed if you want to post payments by bill of exchange before due date. Otherwise, enter 999 in this field.

Using the information in Table 14-20, specify the amount available for outgoing payments for each bank account for the Paying Company Code.

Table 14-20. *Data to specify the amount available for outgoing payments for each bank account for the paying company code*

House Bank	Account ID	Days	Currency	Amount available for outgoing payment
Bank of America	BAME	999	GBP	9.999.999.999.999.00
HSBC	HSBB	999	GBP	9.999.999.999.999.00

Note   Use dot (.) to separate the amount in units down to hundreds and comma (,) t o separate the amount in unit of tens. For example the unit amount of 1000 will be represented in the system as 1.000,00

Save your specification.

This brings us to the end of the automatic payment program.

The next Activity is to look at how to customize sort methods and adjustment accounts for regrouping receivables/payables.

Sort Methods and Adjustment Accounts for Regrouping Receivables/Payables

Accounting standards define how companies classify and disclose receivables and payables according to their remaining life. SAP provides the facilities to perform this function in the sort methods and adjustment accounts for regrouping receivables/payable. The remaining life of AR and AP is defined in the sort method. For example, AR remaining life is classified as less than one year or more than one year. Payables' remaining life is classified as less than one year, 1–5 years, and more than five years.

The settings you define here allow you to classify receivables and payables into periods or years. For example, receivables/payables due within a year are classified as receivables/payables due within one year. Likewise, the receivables/payables due after one year, but within five years, are classified as receivables/payables due between one to five years. Other items due outside these periods are classified as receivables/ payables due after five years. It is important to classify transactions arising from receivables and payables in the G/L account based on periods to allow proper disclosure in the financial report.

In this activity, you will define settings that allow you to sort receivables and payables items into periods.

Problem: Spoxio Inc. accounting staff wants to be able to classify receivables and payables in the G/L Accounts in periods for proper disclosure in the financial statement. Your task as FI consultant is to define sort methods and adjustment accounts for regrouping receivables and payables for receivables/payables due within one year and receivables/payables due after one year

Define Sort Methods

To define sort methods for receivables, follow this menu path: *MG: Financial Accounting➤ General Ledger Accounting ➤ Periodic Processing ➤ Reclassify ➤ Transfer and Sort Receivables and Payables ➤ Define Sort Method and Adjustment Accts for Regrouping Receivables and Payables*.

The Change View "Sort Methods": Overview screen is displayed. This is the initial screen where you will start customizing sort methods. Click New Entries at the top left of the screen to go to The New Entries: Overview of Added Entries screen where you will specify the periodic intervals and description for your receivables/payables periodic intervals (Figure 14-34).

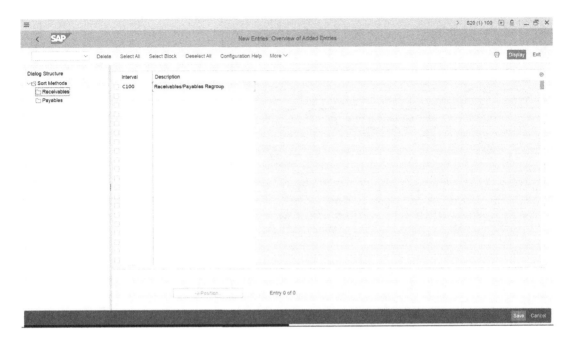

Figure 14-34. *The initial periodic intervals screen for receivables*

Double click the Receivable folder in the Dialog Structure on the left side of the
screen and update the following fields:

Interval: Enter a four-digit ID in this field. We recommend that you use your
company code for ease of identification as especially in an environment where you have
more than one company code. We used C100 as our interval ID in this activity.

Description: Enter a short description for your sort method.

Save your customizing.

Period Interval for Receivables

The next step is to create the periodic intervals for receivables due within one year and
receivables due after one year. To create periodic intervals for receivables, select the
periodic interval (C100) that you have defined in Figure 14-34 (since you are sorting
receivables in this activity) double-click the Receivable folder in the Dialog Structure on
the left side of the screen. The Change View "Receivables": Overview screen is displayed.
Click New Entries at the top left of the screen to go to the New Entries: Overview of
Added Entries screen to specify the periodic intervals for receivables (Figure 14-35).

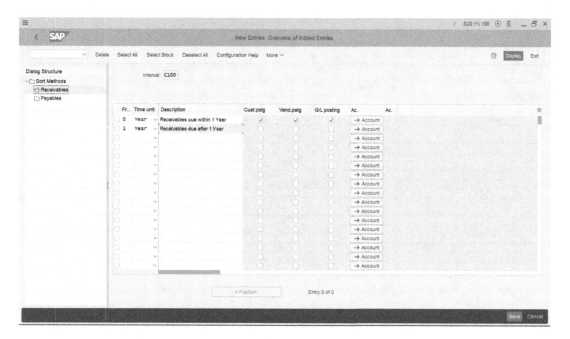

Figure 14-35. *Specifying periodic intervals for receivables*

Update the following fields:

From: Enter 0 for receivables due within one year and 1 for receivables due after one year.

Time Unit: You have three options to choose from: Day, Month, and Year. Using the drop-down arrow, select Year for each field. This will classify the receivables on a yearly basis.

Description: Enter the descriptions for each interval: "Receivables due within 1 year" and "Receivables due after 1 year."

Cust.Pstg: When you click the Customer Posting checkbox, the system will classify receivables based on your interval specifications.

Vend.Pstg: When you click the Vendor Posting checkbox, the system will classify payables based on your interval specifications.

G/L Posting: When you click the G/L posting checkbox, the system will classify postings to the G/L account based on your interval specifications.

Save your work.

Periodic Intervals for Payables

Next, you need to define the periodic intervals for payables due within one year, payables due between one and five years, and payables due after five years. To create the periodic intervals for payables, select the periodic interval (C100) you defined earlier in Figure 14-32 and double-click the Payables folder on the left pane of the screen. The Change View "Payables": Overview screen is displayed. Click the New Entries at the top left of the screen to go to the New Entries: Overview of Added Entries screen, where you'll create the periodic interval specifications for payables. Update the screen using the data shown in Figure 14-36.

Figure 14-36. *Specifying periodic intervals for payables*

Save your work.

Define Adjustment Accounts for Receivables/Payables by Maturity

In this activity, you define adjustment accounts for receivables and payables by maturity. The system will automatically post to the accounts you have assigned for each period interval based on your specifications.

> **Note**   Before defining adjustment accounts for receivables and payables by maturity, we advise that you first create the G/L accounts you will need in your customizing. How to create G/L accounts is covered in Chapter 5).

In this activity, we only covered adjustment accounts for receivables/payables by maturity for foreign receivables/payables. The same procedure is applicable when you create domestic and onetime receivables/payables. We advise that you create accounts for domestic and one-time payables/receivables on your own.

Receivable Due Within One-Year

To maintain automatic posting procedures for adjustment accounts for receivables/payables by maturity accounts due within one year, follow this menu path: *MG: Financial Accounting➤ General Ledger Accounting ➤ Periodic Processing ➤ Reclassify ➤ Transfer and Sort Receivables and Payables ➤ Adjustment Accounts for Receivables/Payables by Maturity.*

The Configuration Accounting Maintain: Automatic Posting – Procedures screen comes up, displaying a list of procedures you can choose from. Click on Receivables <= 1 year from the list of displayed procedures and click Choose at the top left of the screen. The Enter Chart of Accounts dialog screen pops up. Enter your chart of accounts ID in the Chart of Accounts field (in this activity, we used CA10 as our chart of accounts) and click Continue at the bottom of the dialog box. This will take you to The Configuration Accounting Maintain: Automatic Posting – Accounts screen (Figure 14-37) where you will assign accounts to procedures for automatic postings (see Table 14-21).

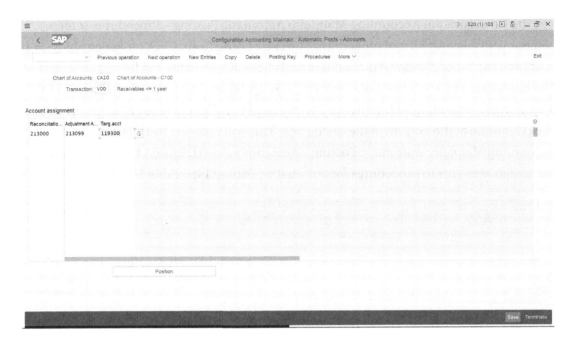

Figure 14-37. *Assignment of G/L accounts to periodic intervals for automatic posting of payables due within 1 year*

Table 14-21. *The Accounts for Posting Receivables Due Within 1 Year*

Reconciliation	Adjustment	Targ. Acct.
213000 – Trade creditors – foreign	213099 – Trade payable – foreign adjustment	119300 – Vendor with a debit balance

Save your work.

Receivables Due After One Year

To maintain automatic posting procedures for adjustment accounts for receivables/ payables by maturity due after one year, follow this menu path: ***MG: Financial Accounting*➤** ***General Ledger Accounting* ➤** ***Periodic Processing* ➤** ***Reclassify* ➤ Transfer and Sort Receivables and Payables* ➤** ***Adjustment Accounts for Receivables/ Payables by Maturity.***

The Configuration Accounting Maintain: Automatic Posting – Procedures screen comes up, displaying a list of procedures you can choose from. Click on Receivables <= 1 year from the list of displayed procedures and click Choose at the top left of the screen. The Enter Chart of Accounts dialog screen pops up. Enter your chart of accounts ID in the Chart of Accounts field (in this activity, we used CA10 as our chart of accounts) and click Continue at the bottom of the dialog box. This will take you to The Configuration Accounting Maintain: Automatic Posting – Accounts screen (Figure 14-38) where you will assign accounts to procedures for automatic postings (see Table 14-22).

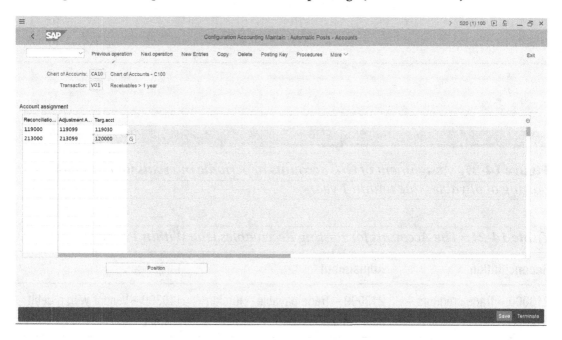

Figure 14-38. *Assignment of G/L accounts to periodic intervals for automatic posting of payables after 1 year*

Table 14-22. *The Accounts for Posting Receivables Due After 1 Year*

Reconciliation	Adjustment	Targ. Acct.
119000 – Trade debtors foreign	119099 – Trade receivables foreign adjustment	119030 – Trade receivables foreign due > 1 yr.
213000 – Trade creditors foreign	213099 – Trade payables foreign adjustment	120000 – other debtors due > 1 yr.

Save your work.

Note   The same procedure is applicable when defining adjustment accounts for receivables/payables by maturity.

Adjustment Posting/Reversal

It is inevitable that during document posting, some incorrect document might be mistakenly entered in the system. An incorrect document entered in the SAP system cannot be deleted; instead it must be reversed. Documents can be reversed in the system using either the normal posting reversal or the negative reversal method.

With normal posting reversal, the debit and credit sides of the total transaction are increased with the adjustment figure. With negative reversal, the adjustment figure is subtracted from the total transaction figure in the account. In other words, the total transaction figure will not be increased with the transaction figures. The transaction figures in the system remain as the original figures before posting. This systematic style of reduction is referred to as negative posting. When you permit negative posting, negative postings will be permitted for your company code. This will allow the system to reduce transaction figures in G/L and in your customer and vendor accounts without actually increasing the total transaction figures.

Permit Negative Postings

Problem: The accounting team in the C900 Pie Company heard that transactions posted to the system can be systematically reversed without having to increase total transaction figures. The team is interested in knowing how this can benefit them. Consequently, your colleagues have asked you to customize the system to allow negative postings for Spoxio Inc.

In this exercise, you will specify a negative posting for your company code. This specification will allow you to carry out negative postings. To activate Negative Postings, follow this menu path: IMG: Financial Accounting ➤ Accounts Receivable and Accounts Payable ➤ Business Transactions ➤ Adjustment Postings/Reversal ➤ Permit Negative Postings.

The Change View "Maintain Negative Postings in Company Code": Overview screen is displayed (Figure 14-39). This is where you specify that you want your company code to be permitted for negative postings.

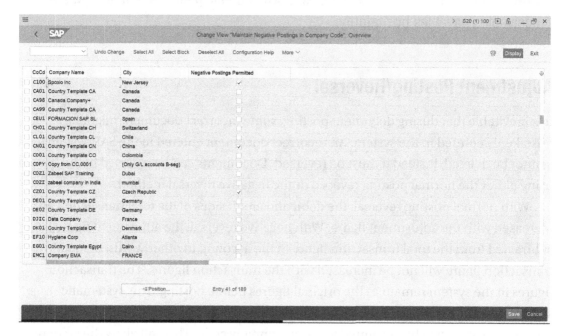

Figure 14-39. Maintaining negative postings by company code

Search for your company code from the list of company codes displayed on the screen using the Position button at the bottom of the screen. Then click tick the check box for Negative Postings and save your settings.

Define Reasons for Reversal

It is mandatory to state the reason for reversing a document in SAP ERP during document reversal. Hence it is important to define reasons for reversing documents. When you're posting document reversal, the reason for the reversal will be copied to the document that is reversed.

Note   You can use standard reversal reasons supplied by SAP or you can define your own reversal reasons.

To define reasons for reversal that will be applied to negative postings, follow this menu path: IMG: Financial Accounting ➤ Accounts Receivable and Accounts Payable ➤ Business Transactions ➤ Adjustment Postings/Reversal ➤ Define Reasons for Reversal.

The Change View "Reason for Reversal Posting" Overview screen is displayed. This screen contains reasons for reversal. For example:

01 – Reversal in current period.

02 – Reversal in closed period.

Click the New Entries at the top of the screen to go to the New Entries: Overview of Added Entries screen (Figure 14-40).

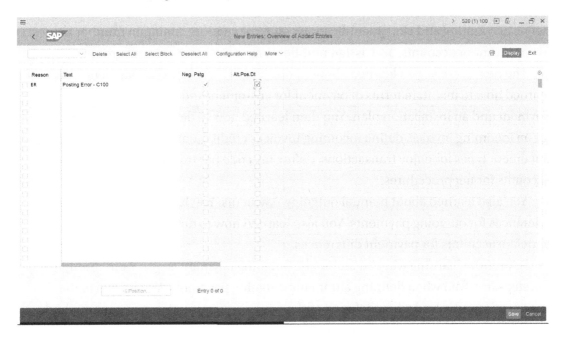

Figure 14-40. *Specifying the reasons for posting reversal*

Update the following fields:

Reason: Enter up to two characters of your choice in this field. This is a freely definable code. For example, we used ER (Error) as our reason code for this activity. This code serves as the identifier code of your defined reason for reversal.

Text: Enter a short text that best describes the reason for reversal in this field, such as Posting Error.

Neg. Posting: When you click the Negative Posting checkbox, you can create negative posting for this reason code.

Alt.Pos.Dt: This checkbox allows alternative posting dates for this reason code.

Summary

This chapter covered account payables and account receivables and explained what a customer account is. It also explained the steps involved in defining account groups with screen layout for customers. You learned how to maintain the field status group for general data for a customer account group. You also learned how to enter an accounting clerk identification code for customers and create number ranges and assign them to your account groups. You learned what a vendor account is and how to customize vendor accounts. You learned how to define account groups with screen layout for vendors, maintain the field status group for general data for a vendor account group, define accounting and clerk identification codes for vendors, maintain number ranges for your vendor accounts, and assign number ranges to end or account groups.

The next exercise you learned about in this chapter was terms of payment. You learned how to maintain terms of payment for customers and how to maintain terms of payment and an installation plan. You then learned how to define a cash discount base for an incoming invoice, define incoming invoices credit memos/credit memos, define document types for enjoy transactions, define tax code per transaction, and define accounts for net procedures.

You also learned about manual outgoing payments. You learned how to define tolerances for outgoing payments. You also learned how to define reason codes and how to define accounts for payment differences.

Apart from learning what an automatic outgoing payment is, you went through the steps involved when defining automatic outgoing payments. You looked at the specifications involved when defining and paying company codes, payment methods per country, and payment methods per company codes.

You learned how to define sort methods and adjust accounts for regrouping receivables/payable. You learned how to define sort methods for accounts receivables and payables by defining periodic intervals for receivables and payables. The next exercise explained how to define adjustment accounts for receivables/payables by maturity based on periods receivable and payables due to enabling automatic postings to the GIL accounts. In so doing, you learned how to define accounts for receivables/payables due in one year, receivables due after one year, payables due between one and five years, and payables due after five years.

Finally, you looked at the difference between the normal reversal and negative reversal posting methods. You learned how to activate the indicator for permitted negative postings and how to define a reason code for negative posting.

In the next chapter, you will learn how to define correspondence in SAP. In doing this, you will define correspondence types, assign programs for correspondence type, define sender details for correspondence form, determine call-up functions, define dunning procedures, specify the special G/L transactions that allow the system to dun special GIL transactions, and learn about the various levels involved when defining dunning.

CHAPTER 15

Defining the Dunning Procedure

This chapter explains what dunning is and covers basic settings involved in customizing the dunning procedure.

At the end of this chapter, you will be able to:

- Define a dunning procedure.

- Defining dunning levels.

- Specify G/L transactions that allow the system to dun special G/L transactions.

- Assign a dunning procedure to customer master data.

Dunning

It is a normal business practice for business partners to sometimes fall behind in invoice payments. Hence a form of reminder mechanism needs to be in place that will remind business partners of overdue invoices.

Dunning is an automatic process of sending reminder notices to customers demanding payment of overdue invoices. This program ensures that the mechanism for sending reminder letters for due invoice payments is in place.

Dunning procedure

The dunning procedure defines how the dunning is carried out. More than one dunning procedure can be defined. There is no restriction to the number of procedures you can define. The account that you want to include in your dunning process must have a dunning procedure assigned to it.

© Andrew Okungbowa 2023
A. Okungbowa, *SAP S/4HANA Financial Accounting Configuration*,
https://doi.org/10.1007/978-1-4842-8957-0_15

A dunning procedure is applicable to both normal and special GL transactions in the SAP system.

Note   SAP comes with standard dunning procedures. These procedures can be adapted and modified to meet your company code specific settings.

Basic Settings for Dunning

In Basic Settings for Dunning, you can define the followings:

- **Dunning Areas:** A dunning area could be defined as a department or a unit within a company code which you may want to use for processing dunning.

- **Dunning Keys:** Are company code independent. The advantage of a dunning key is that it allows you to specify item display separate with dunning key and print dunning key text in the dunning notice.

- **Dunning Block Reasons:** Allow you to exclude an item or account being dun during dunning run. To do this, a block key is entered in the dunning block field in the master record.

Tip   *If you are defining your own dunning, we recommend that you use the Basic settings supplied by the system. Hence there is no need to carry out any settings here.*

Define Dunning Procedures

Problem: Spoxio Inc. wants to have four dunning levels as part of their credit control that will systematically generate reminder letters to customers for overdue invoices. The first letter is to be a courteous reminder, and thereafter subsequent reminders will be a little bit firmer, and so on.

Your task is to define four dunning levels for Spoxio Inc.

When maintaining the Dunning Procedure, you can defined the specifications for the following items:

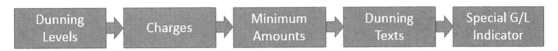

- Dunning Levels.

- Charges.

- Minimum Amounts.

- Dunning Texts.

- Special GL Indicator.

To define the dunning procedure for your dunning program, follow this menu path: ***IMG: Financial Accounting ➤ Account Receivable and Accounts Payable ➤ Business Transaction ➤ Dunning ➤ Dunning Procedure ➤ Define Dunning Procedures***.

The ***Maintain Dunning Procedure: List*** screen comes up displaying a list of existing dunning procedures in the system. Since in this activity we want to create a New Dunning Procedure, click the New Procedure at the top of the screen (this is the second item from the left). The ***Maintain Dunning Procedure: Overview*** screen is displayed (Figure 15-1).

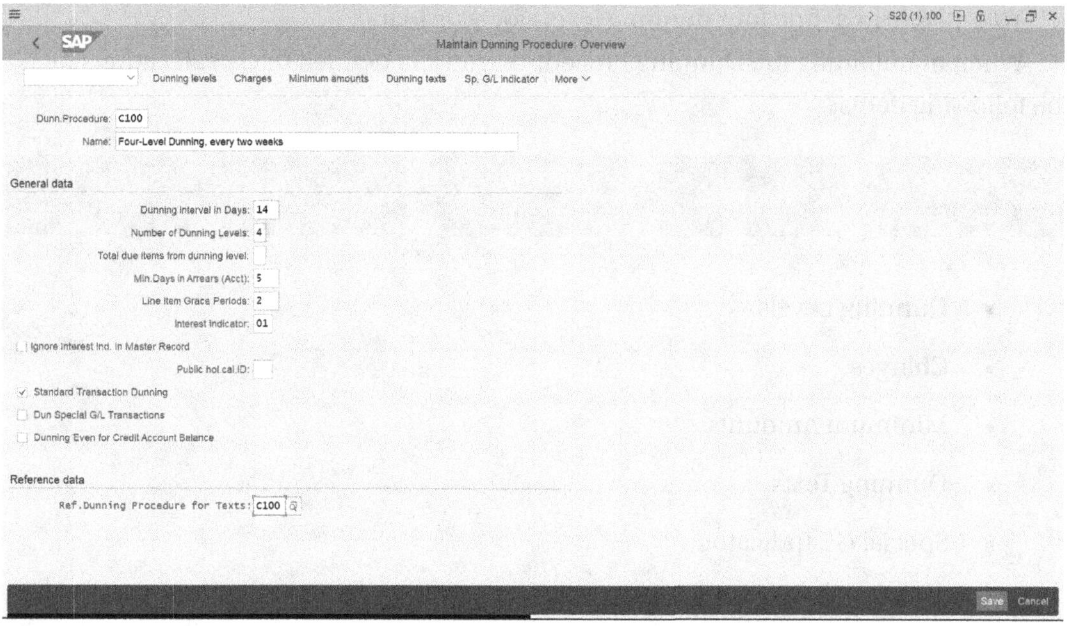

Figure 15-1. *The screen for maintaining a dunning procedure*

Dun procedure: This represents the key for the dunning procedure to be used. The key is company code independent.

Dunning Interval in Days: This specification defines the intervals in days to ensure that the accounts in this procedure are dunned at given intervals. The system checks at every dunning run to see if the number of days specified is greater than the last run day. If this is the case, a new dunning note is issued; otherwise, a new dunning note will not be issued.

No of Dunning Levels: This specification represents the number of dunning levels that are permitted in this procedure. Usually, the system allows up to a maximum of 9 levels.

Min. days in arrears (acct): This is the minimum days an item in the account must have for the account to be dunned. Otherwise, a dunning notice will not be created.

Line item grace period: Is the number of days allowed above an item due day. If the days in arrears is less than or equal to the days of grace, the account will not be considered for dunning during a dunning run.

Interest Indicator: When this indicator is selected, interest will be calculated.

Using the information in the following table, update the *Maintain Dunning Procedure: Overview* screen.

Fields	Values	Description
Dun. Procedure	C900	Enter your Company Code in this field.
Name	Four-level Dunning, every two weeks	Enter a short description for your dunning procedure in this field.

General Data

Dunning Interval in Days	14	The dunning interval entered here will allow the system to checks at every dunning run to see if the number of days specified is greater than the last run day. If this is the case a new dunning note is issued.
No. of dunning levels	4	Enter the number of dunning levels that is permitted in this procedure in this field.
Total due items from dunning level	Leave Bank	
Min. days in arrears (acct)	5	This allows the system to determine the minimum days an item in the account must have for the account to be dunned.
Line item grace period	2	The entry here specify the number of days allowed above an item due day.
Interest indicator	01	When you select this indicate, interest will be calculated on due amount.

(*continued*)

Fields	Values	Description
Reference data		
Ref. Dunning Procedure for Texts	C100	This serves as reference for dunning text for your dunning procedure.

Tip   If you try to save your dunning procedure at this level, the system will notify you on the status bar at the bottom of your screen that "reference dunning procedure has 0 dunning levels." So, we advise you not to save your work yet.

The next step in this activity is to define the dunning levels for your dunning procedure.

Defining Dunning Levels

Dunning level allows you to determine the dunning letter to assign to your dunning notice. As a part of the credit control procedure, several letters are sent out systematically to remind business partners of open items in their account. These letters are categorized into various levels (SAP allows up to nine dunning levels that can be assigned to the dunning procedure). The first dunning level could be a very friendly reminder; the second obviously becomes a lot firmer, and so.

At the top left of the *Maintain dunning Procedure: Overview* screen click Dunning levels (Figure 15-2). This will allow you to apply the following the settings to your dunning levels:

- Days in arrears.

- Interest calculation applicable to your dunning level.

- Print parameter.

- Legal dunning procedure.

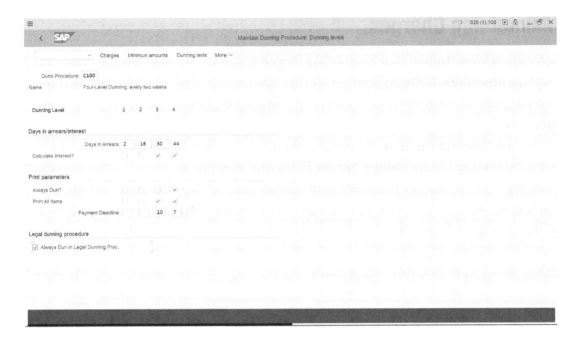

Figure 15-2. *Maintaining dunning levels for dunning procedure*

Update the screen by specifying the following items:

Days in Arrears: The number of days an invoice is in arrears determines the dunning notice level that is created for it. For example, if an overdue item is in arrears for two days, the payment program will create a dunning notice at dunning level 1. Likewise, if an overdue item is in arrears for 16 days, the payment program will create a dunning notice at level 2, and so on.

Calculate Interest: The system calculates interest on the set dunning levels. For example, interests should be calculated on dunning levels 3 and 4.

Always Dun: This allows the dunning program to always dun the overdue item at the last dunning level so that no item is skipped at this level.

Print All Items: This allows you to print an overview of the customer/vendor account balance at the specified level.

Payment Deadline: This determines the new payment deadline printed on the dunning notice. It is best to use a basic 12-month calendar to avoid the payment deadline falling on a weekend.

Always Dun in Legal Dunning Proc.: Selecting this option allows you to print dunning notices using a legal dunning procedure, regardless of whether any changes have taken place in the account or not.

Maintaining Charges

Sometimes a small amount of fee may be charged at certain dunning levels in the dunning procedure. Dunning charges are displayed only in the Dunning letter; no other entry will take place in the system. Dunning charges are entered in the customer account manually.

On the Maintain Dunning Procedure: Dunning levels screen, click Charges at the top left of the screen. The **Dunning Charges** dialog box pops up. Enter your company code currency – USD in the Currency field in the dialog box and click the Continue button at the bottom of the dialog box to go to the screen where you will maintain charges for the dunning program (Figure 15-3).

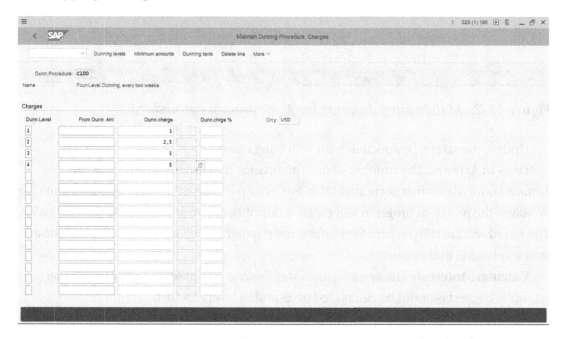

Figure 15-3. *Maintaining charges for you dunning procedure*

Specify the dunning levels and charges you want to apply to each dunning level.

The next step is to specify the minimum amount you want to apply to your dunning levels.

Maintaining Minimum Amounts

You set minimum dunning amounts per dunning level to stop the system from triggering high dunning levels for insignificant amounts. You can do this by specifying a minimum amount or minimum percentage rates for each dunning level. The dunning program will check the open item to see if it is to be dunned. If the amount due on the open item is less than the minimum amount, the dunning program will exclude it from the dunning. But if the open item exceeds the minimum amount or the minimum percentage rate, the system will dun the open item. The system will also check your specifications to determine the minimum amount on which interest is applied.

Note   When you set a minimum as the dunning amount per level for which to charge interest, any amount below the minimum amount you set will not attract charges.

On the Maintain Dunning Procedure: Charges screen, click Minimum amounts on the top of the screen to go to the screen where you will maintain the minimum amount charged at each dunning level. The Minimum Amounts dialog box comes up. Enter your company code country currency key in the Currency field and click Continue at the bottom of the dialog box. The Maintain Dunning Procedure: Minimum amounts screen appears. This is the screen where you will specify the minimum amount that should attract charges.

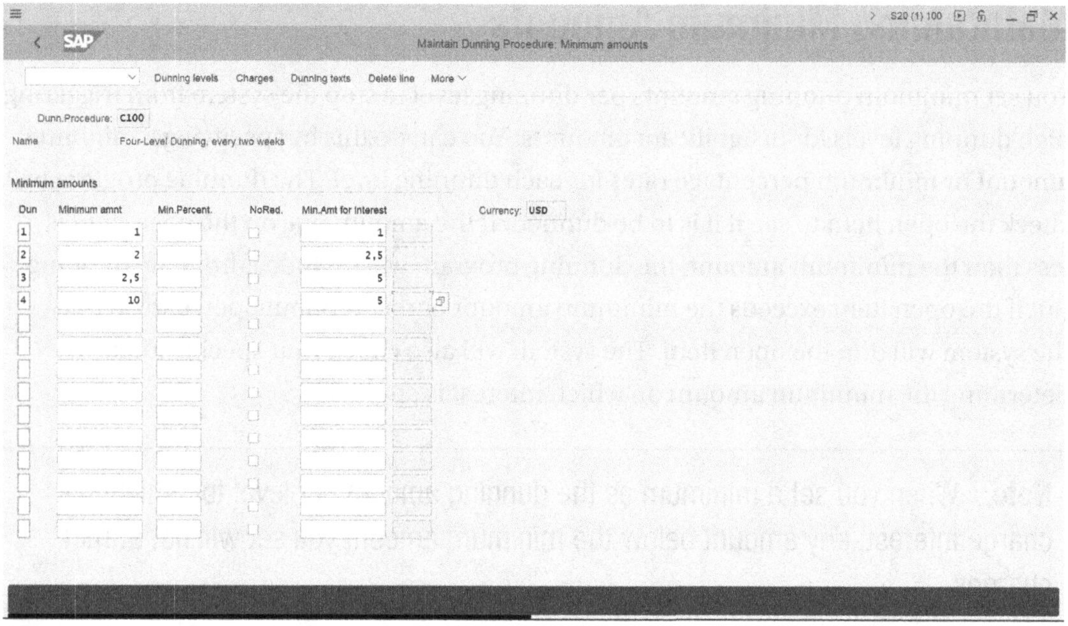

Figure 15-4. *Specifying of minimum amount and minimum amount for interest for each dunning level*

When the minimum amount or percentage is reached or exceeded in respect of all open items, the system will trigger the next upper dunning level. If the specified minimum amount or minimum percentage is not reached, the system will automatically assign the items to the next level and carry out another check.

Note   You can specify either a minimum amount or percentage to your dunning procedure. You cannot use both at the same time.

The next step is to specify the dunning texts you want to use for each dunning level.

Dunning texts

SAP comes with standard forms in SAPscript, which you can use for your dunning procedure. You can maintain the name of the form that you want to use per dunning level. SAPscript defines the layout of the form represented in the system. The dunning program generates payment advice notes, dunning notices, and payment terms.

Click Dunning texts at the top of the screen, the Company Code/Account Type dialog box pops up; enter your company code in the Company Code field (C100). In the Account type section of the screen, you are presented with two account types: Customer and Vendor. Select the account type for your dunning text. In this case, select Customer by activating the radio button in front of it. Then click Continue at the bottom right of the dialog box. The Maintain Dunning Procedure: Company code data screen is displayed. Click New company code at the top left of the screen, the *New Company Code* dialog box pops up, enter your company code (C100) in the Company Code field and click continue to confirm your entry. You will notice that your company code comes on top in the list of company codes list in the Maintain Dunning Procedure: Company code data screen, as in Figure 15-5.

Company code	Dunning by dunning area	Separate notice per dunning level	Ref.comp.code for texts
C100	☐	☐	C100
EPR1	☐	☐	1710
EX13	✓	✓	EX13
EYFR	✓	☐	0001
GR01	✓	☐	0001
GR02	✓	☐	0001
GR06	✓	☐	0001
GRES	✓	☐	0001
JC01	✓	☐	0001
JS01	✓	☐	0001
MC01	✓	☐	0001
MM01	☐	☐	1710
OXOZ	✓	☐	0001
PQRC	☐	☐	PQRC
RECO	✓	☐	0001
REOB	✓	☐	0001
RERF	✓	☐	0001
SD01	✓	☐	0001

Figure 15-5. *Maintaining company code data in your dunning program*

At this level, save your dunning program customizing.

The next thing you need to do is to assign SAPscript forms to each dunning level. Click the Back Arrow bottom at the top left of the screen to return to the previous screen, the Maintain Dunning Procedure: Minimum Amounts screen. The Maintain company code screen pops up with the question "Do you want to save the data?" choose the yes button at the bottom left of the screen to save your configuration.

On the Maintain Dunning Procedure: Minimum amounts screen displayed, click Dunning texts at the top of the screen. The Company Code/Account Type dialog box pops up, defaulting your company code and customer account type. Click continue at the bottom right of the dialog box and Maintain Dunning Procedure: Dunning texts screen appears. This is the screen where you will specify the appropriate SAPscript form for each dunning level, as in Figure 15-6.

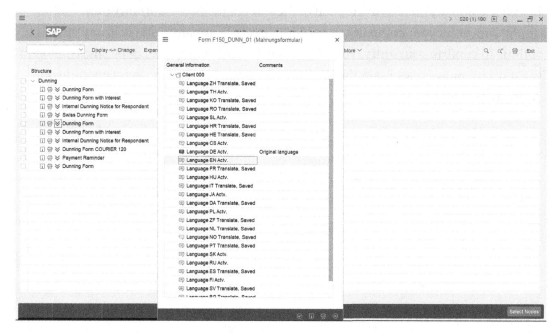

Figure 15-6. *The list of SAPscript forms provided by SAP in the system*

Now specify the appropriate form for each dunning level (Figure 15-7).

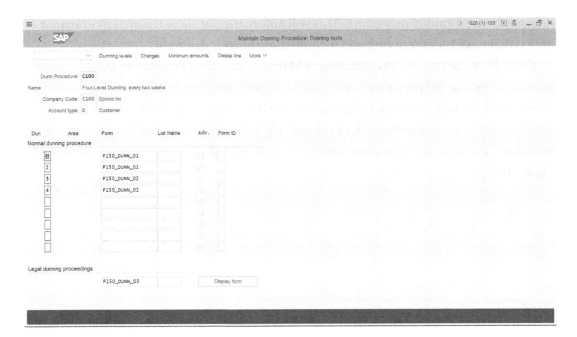

Figure 15-7. *The screen where you specify the appropriate SAPscript form for each dunning level*

SAPscript forms contain the reminder letters you apply to each dunning level. SAP provided dunning forms that you can assign to each dunning level. For Example, F150_DUNN_01, F150_DUNN_02, and F150_DUNN_03. We recommend that you use the SAPscript form F150_DUNN_01 for dunning levels 1 & 2 and F150_DUNN_02 for levels 3 & 4. The SAPscript F150_DUNN_01 content is more cautious than the remaining SAPscript forms.

Tip   You can change the content of the form to meet your requirements.

The final step in customizing the dunning procedure is to specify special G/L indicators for customers and vendors.

Special GL Indicator

This specification will allow special GL transactions to be dunned. You can also include special GL transactions to your dunning by setting the appropriate indicators. For example, if you want Down payment request to be dunned, you must set the special GL indicator in the dunning procedure. This will automatically allow the system to search for due down payment requests and include them in your dunning.

Click the Back arrow at the top right of Maintain Dunning Procedure: Dunning texts screen to return to the previous screen, the Maintain Dunning Procedure: Overview screen. Click Sp. G/L indicator at the top right of the screen to go to the screen where you will carry out the specification of special G/L indicator(s) for your dunning procedure. The Maintain Dunning Procedure: Special G/L indicator screen is displayed (Figure 15-8).

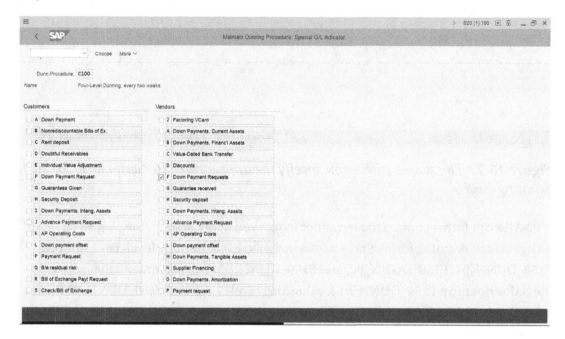

Figure 15-8. _Special G/L indicators specification_

Click the Back arrow at the top left of the screen to return to the previous screen, the Maintain Dunning Procedure: Overview screen, and save your dunning procedure.

You have just completed the configuration for automatic dunning. The next activity in this chapter is to look at how to configure correspondence in SAP S4 HANA.

Assigning Dunning Procedure to Customer Master Data

As we mentioned earlier, dunning is an automatic process of sending reminder notices to customers demanding payment of overdue invoices. This program ensures that the mechanism for sending reminder letters for due invoice payments is in place.

To assign a dunning procedure to customer master data follow this menu path: *Easy Access: Financial Accounting* ➤ *General Ledger* ➤ *Master Data* ➤ *Change.* The Customer Change: Initial screen pops up, search for the customer you want to assign dunning. The Customer's details will be displayed, click Correspondence at the top right of the screen and assign dunning.

Summary

This chapter explained what dunning is and talked a bit about how to define a dunning area. You learned how to define a dunning procedure. You also learned how to specify dunning levels, charges, and minimum amounts for your dunning procedures. You learned how to assign text to the dunnings and how to specify the G/L indicators for each dunning procedure.

The next chapter looks at configuring special G/L transactions. As part of this customizing activity, you will learn how to define various types of down payments, define tax clearing accounts, and use various special G/L transactions, including guarantees (automatic offsetting entry (statistical), down payments (free offsetting entry), and bills of exchange (noted items).

CHAPTER 16

Special GL Transactions

Objective

In this chapter, we look at Special GL Transactions and how to disclose Special GL transactions in SAP R/3 using alternative reconciliation accounts.

At the end of this activity, you will be able to:

- Configure Special GL Transactions.

- Define various types of Down Payments (i.e., Down payment Made, Received, and Requested).

- Define Tax Clearing Account for Down payments.

- Explain various Special GL Transactions, including Down Payments (Down payment request, down payment made, and down payment received), Other Special GL Transactions such as Guarantees, noted items, Free Offsetting Entry, and Automatic Offsetting Entries.

Special G/L Transactions

Before looking at special GL transactions in detail, it is important to first look at what are General Ledger (GL) and GL Reconciliation Accounts?

GL accounts strictly adhere to the basic accounting principle of Debit and Credit – double entry bookkeeping. In SAP, transactions relating to Account Receivables (AR) and Account Payables (AP) are posted to sub-ledgers defined in the system. The totals of sub-ledgers are automatically posted to reconciliation accounts. The advantage of a reconciliation account is to provide a quick snapshot of subledger balances as totals in order to be able to draw-up a financial/income statement easily. Secondly, to also be

© Andrew Okungbowa 2023
A. Okungbowa, *SAP S/4HANA Financial Accounting Configuration*,
https://doi.org/10.1007/978-1-4842-8957-0_16

able to determine the totals of receivables and payables for a given period, the balances of reconciliation account can be quickly called up, instead of having to go through numerous subledgers, which may be time consuming.

Therefore, reconciliation accounts are summaries of subledger accounts. It is important to specify the reconciliation account to be posted during the creation of payables/receivables in customers/vendors master record in the company code segment.

Special GL transactions are part of AR and AP transactions. Due to their nature and disclosure in the financial report, they are displayed separately in the general ledger and subledgers.

Reconciliation account is defined in the subledger account. This links the subledger to the General ledger. Subledger accounts with special GL transactions are assigned using a special GL indicator; this makes postings to alternative reconciliation accounts (special GL accounts) possible. Hence separate disclosure.

Special G/L transactions include down payments, bill of exchange, and other transactions. In SAP S4 HANA, special G/L transactions can be distinguished between business relationships and technical factors. This is represented in Figure 16-1.

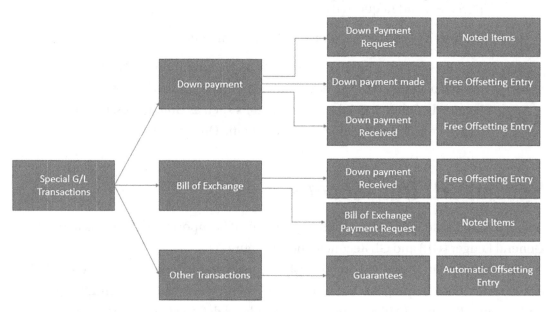

Figure 16-1. *The distinctions between the special G/L transactions according to their relationships and technical factors*

Special GL transactions include:

1) Down payments.

2) Bill of exchange.

3) Other Transactions (Guarantees).

Special GL - General Ledger types

Special GL transactions can be looked at under three headings based Special GL types and variability according to their relationship with the main ledger:

1. Automatic Offsetting Entry

A typical example of Automatic Offsetting Entry is guarantee of payments. They are termed as statistical postings because they are not displayed in the financial statements. They are only displayed as notes to the financial statements. Since they form part of automatic offsetting entries, entries are made in the same offsetting account. The offsetting entries account is defined in IMG; this makes it possible for the system to make automatic offsetting entries. Once an open item is cleared in the account, the system will carry out automatic clearing to clear related items simultaneously in the offsetting account.

2. Noted Items

Examples of noted items are down payment requests, bill of exchange payment requests, etc.

Noted items have no impact on the GL because no posting is made to the GL. It is purely for information purposes, which serves as a reminder. When a down payment request exists on an account, during payment posting, the system will automatically reminds the user that a down payment request exists on the account. No open item balance check is made with noted items and offsetting entry is not needed. Only one line item is updated when a noted item is created.

A noted item is treated as an open item in the system, hence line item should be activated. It is also possible for the payment program and dunning program to access noted items for further processing.

3. Free Offsetting Entry

An example of free offsetting entry is down payment received. Depending on the type of posting involved, free off setting entry generates a proper posting in the general ledger since is it part of accounts receivable/payable. Special GL transactions relating to Free Offsetting Entry will automatically debit or credit special GL reconciliation accounts once it occurs.

Configuration of Special GL Transactions.

In this activity, you will only be looking at down payment made, down payment received, and guarantees.

No further configurations are needed for bill of exchange and other special GL transactions. The settings for these items supplied by SAP in the system relating to country specific settings are sufficient.

Down Payments

Introduction

There are typically two types of down payments:

- Down payment made.

- Down payment received.

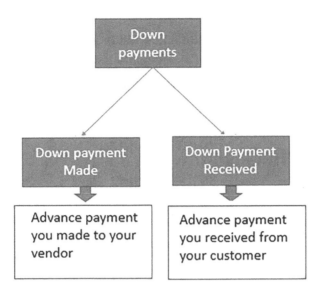

Figure 16-2. *Types of down payments represented in SAP S4 HANA*

Down payments are short-term finance. This is a usual business practice for either a customer or vendor to obtain a short-term finance without having to pay interest on down payment. This is normally the case in a situation where, for example, a manufacturer may not be able to finance production alone and as a result may request down payment before a production begins or during, after or after partial completion of production.

It is an accounting practice to separate down payments from the normal business receivables and payables balances and display them separately in the balance sheet.

There are several factors that give rise to down payments during a normal course of a business. For example, payable or receivable arising from either the purchase of an asset or from providing a service.

Down payments are disclosed on the balance sheet either as assets or liabilities. If the transaction is a receivable, it is treated as an asset and debited accordingly. On the other hand, if the down payment is payable, it is a liability and it is credited on the balance sheet.

Upon the delivery of goods or the performance of services of which down payment were made, the accounts involved needs to be cleared and the down payment will no longer be displayed on the balance sheet.

Note   Before you commence with the integration of Down Payments, it is advisable to create the appropriate G/L Accounts that will be needed in your configurations. To do this, please refer to Chapter 5 on how to create G/L accounts.

Down Payment Received

This an advance payment made to you by your customer for the provision of goods or services. As mentioned earlier, down payment is a sort of financing.

Reconciliation Accounts for Customer Down Payments

In this activity, you will define customer down payments that are managed in GL. The settings you specify will make it possible for the system to automatically post down payment transactions to a special GL reconciliation account instead of the normal receivable GL reconciliation account.

Problem: As part of accounting policy, Company C900 plc wants to be able to post Customer Down Payment to a special Reconciliation Account, instead of the normal Customer Reconciliation Account. You are to define Reconciliation Accounts for Customer Down Payment for Spoxio Inc.

To define the reconciliation accounts for sown payments, follow this menu path: *IMG: Financial Accounting➤ Accounts Receivable and Accounts Payable ➤ Business Transactions ➤ Down Payments Received ➤ Define Reconciliation Accounts for Customer Down Payments.*

The *Maintain Accounting Configuration: Special G/L List* screen is displayed. Containing the list of possible Special G/L Transactions (Figure 16-3).

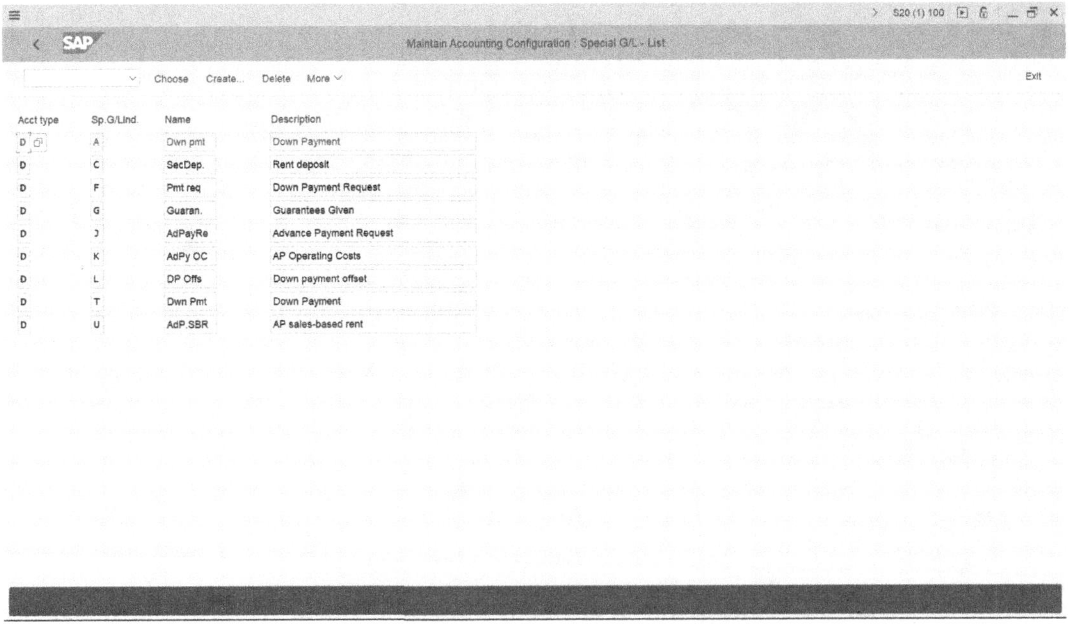

Figure 16-3. *List of special G/L transactions provided by SAP in the system*

Select **Down Payment (SP.G/Lind. A)** from the list by clicking on it to select it and click Choose at the top left of the screen. The Chart of Accounts Entry dialog Box pops-up. Enter your Chart of Accounts ID (CA10) in the *Chart of Accounts* field and click Continue at the bottom right of the dialog box.

The *Maintain Accounting Configuration: Special G/L - Accounts* screen is displayed (Figure 16-4). Enter G/L Account – 119000 in the Reconciliation Account field and enter the Special G/L Account – 170000 in the Special G/L Account field. Enter Output tax type – **A** in the Output tax clearing field.

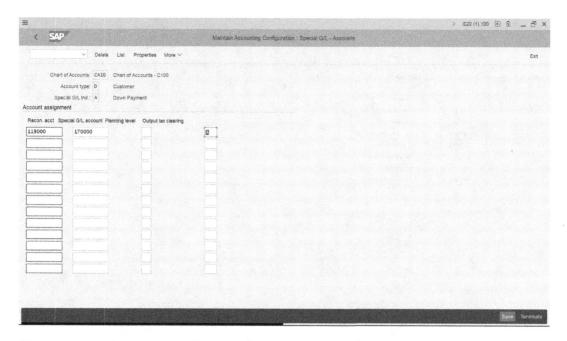

Figure 16-4. *Assignment of reconciliation accounts for customer down payments*

Update the following fields:

Recon. acct: Enter the G/L reconciliation account for clearing down payment (we used 119000 as our reconciliation account in this activity) in this field.

Special G/L account: Enter the G/L for advance customer payment (we used 170000 in this activity) in this field.

Output tax clearing: Enter A (output tax type) in this field. This specification allows the system to post tax elements arising from down payments to the output clearing account. SAP comes with two tax types: A for output tax and V for input tax. You can access these tax types by using the match code or search function that appears when you click on the Output tax clearing field.

The next step is to check the defaulted specifications in the system for your Special G/L payment properties to see if the setting meets your requirement. To do this, click Properties (this is the third item from the top left of the screen).

Note   SAP normally comes with preconfigured settings for Special G/L properties. Check the Special G/L specifications provided by the system to make sure that it meets your need.

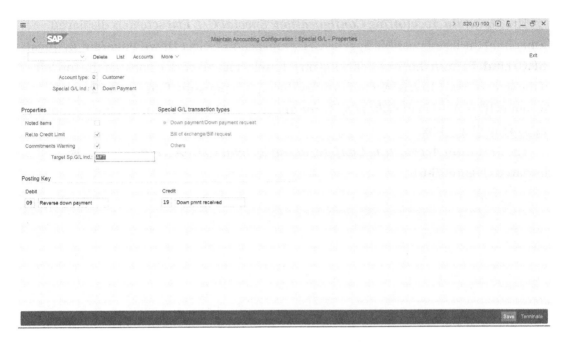

Figure 16-5. *The standard properties for customer down payments*

Save your work.

The next step in this activity is to define down payment request for customers.

Down Payment Requests (Customer)

As mentioned above, Down Payment is a form of short-term finance, and it could also engender commitment from customers, especially in a situation where the integrity of the customer is in question. Down payment request is a normal business practice where an advance payment is requested in full or partially prior to commencement of a business transaction.

Defining Reconciliation Accounts for Customer Down Payments Request

To define the reconciliation accounts for customer down payment request, follow this menu path: ***IMG: Financial Accounting*** ➤ ***Accounts Receivable and Accounts Payable*** ➤ ***Business Transactions*** ➤ ***Down Payments Received*** ➤ ***Define Reconciliation Accounts for Customer Down Payments***.

The ***Maintain Accounting Configuration: Special G/L List*** screen is displayed.
Containing the list of possible Special G/L Transaction. Select **Down Payment Request**
(SP.G/L Ind. F) from the list by clicking on it to select it and click Choose at the top left
of the screen. The Chart of Accounts Entry dialog Box pops-up. Enter your Chart of
Accounts ID (CA10) in the ***Chart of Accounts*** field and click Continue at the bottom
right of the dialog box.

The ***Maintain Accounting Configuration: Special G/L - Accounts*** screen is
displayed (Figure 16-6).

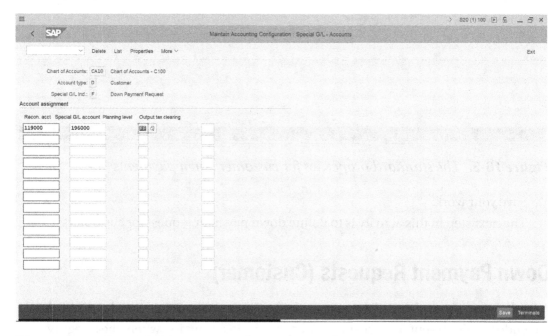

Figure 16-6. *Special G/L accounts for customer down payment request*

Enter G/L 119000 in the Reconciliation Account field and Payment requests
(Customer) – 196000 in the Special G/L account field. Enter planning level FF (Down
Payment Request) in the Planning level field.

Click the Properties function at the top of the screen to check the defaulted
specifications in the system for your Special G/L payment properties to see if the setting
meets your requirement. To do this, click Properties (this is the third item from the top
left of the screen).

Save your settings.

The final step in defining customer down payments is to define the tax clearing
account.

Defining Account for Tax Clearing (Down payments Customer)

The tax entered for down payment will be posted to the tax clearing account you defined in this activity and the tax rate typically depends on your company code country's legal specifications. To define the account for tax clearing, follow this menu path: ***IMG: Financial Accounting➤ Accounts Receivable and Accounts Payable ➤ Business Transactions ➤ Down Payments Received ➤ Define Account for Tax Clearing.***

The ***Configuration Accounting Maintain: Automatic Posts – Procedures*** screen comes up, displaying a list of procedures provided by SAP in the system. From the Procedure list, Select **Output tax clearing on down payments – MVA** by clicking on it and click Choose at the top left of the screen. The ***Chart of Accounts Entry*** dialog screen pops up. Enter your Chart of Accounts ID (CA10) in the ***Enter Chart of Account*** field and click Continue at the bottom right of the dialog box. The ***Configuration Accounting Maintain: Automatic Posts – Rules*** comes up. Select the **Output tax clearing** checkbox in **Accounts are determined based on** section of the screen and then click the Save button at the bottom right of the screen.

The ***Configuration Accounting Maintain: Automatic Posts – Accounts*** screen is displayed (Figure 16-7).

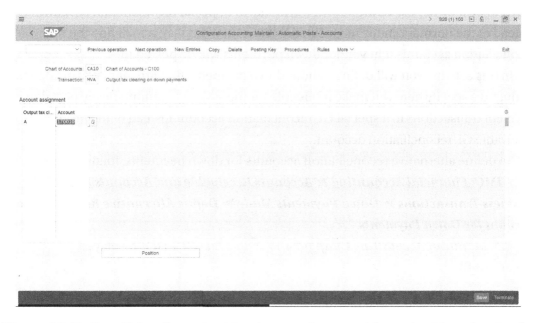

Figure 16-7. *Specifying the output tax type and account for output tax clearing for customer down payments*

Enter Output Tax type – **A** in the ***Output Tax type*** field and enter the appropriate G/L Account for Output tax clearing on down payments (We used 170010 as our G/L account in this activity) in the ***Account field***.

Save your work.

Down Payment Made

Down payment made is an advance money you pay to your vendor as a down payment in anticipation of receiving goods or services at a future date. For example, you might make a down payment on your current assets.

Note   Before you carry out the customization of down payment made, make sure that you have created the appropriate G/L Accounts for Alternative Reconciliation Account for Down Payments.

Reconciliation Accounts for Vendor Down Payments

Problem: As part of Spoxio Inc. accounting policy, the Spoxio Inc. accounting team wants to be able to post vendor down payments to a special reconciliation account, instead of the normal vendor reconciliation account. Your task is to define the reconciliation accounts that vendor down payments will be posted in.

In this activity, you will define Vendor down payments that are managed in GL. The settings we specify here will make it possible for the system to automatically post down payment transactions to a special GL reconciliation account instead of the normal receivable GL reconciliation account.

To define alternative reconciliation accounts for down payments, follow this menu path: ***IMG: Financial Accounting ➤ Accounts Receivable and Accounts Payable ➤ Business Transactions ➤ Down Payments Made ➤ Define Alternative Reconciliation Account for Down Payments***.

The ***Maintain Accounting Configuration: Special G/L List*** is displayed (Figure 16-8).

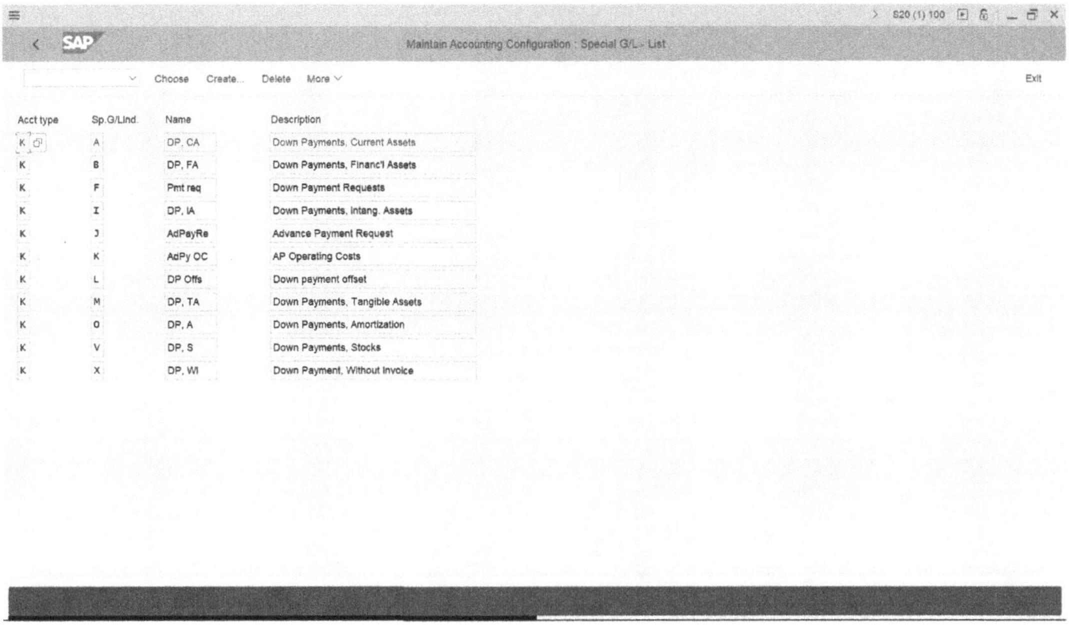
S20 (1) 100
Maintain Accounting Configuration : Special G/L - List
Choose
Create...
Delete
More
Exit
Acct type
Sp.G/Lind.
Name
Description
K A DP, CA Down Payments, Current Assets
K B DP, FA Down Payments, Financ'l Assets
K F Pmt req Down Payment Requests
K I DP, IA Down Payments, Intang. Assets
K J AdPayRe Advance Payment Request
K K AdPy OC AP Operating Costs
K L DP Offs Down payment offset
K M DP, TA Down Payments, Tangible Assets
K O DP, A Down Payments, Amortization
K V DP, S Down Payments, Stocks
K X DP, WI Down Payment, Without Invoice

Figure 16-8. *Possible list of special G/L transactions provided by SAP*

To specify the special G/L account that down payment transactions will be posted in, select **Down Payments Current Assets (SP.G/Lind. A)** from the list by clicking on it to select it and click Choose at the top left of the screen. The Chart of Accounts Entry dialog Box pops up. Enter your Chart of Accounts ID (CA10) in the ***Chart of Accounts*** field and click Continue at the bottom right of the dialog box.

The ***Maintain Accounting Configuration: Special G/L - Accounts*** screen is displayed (Figure 16-9).

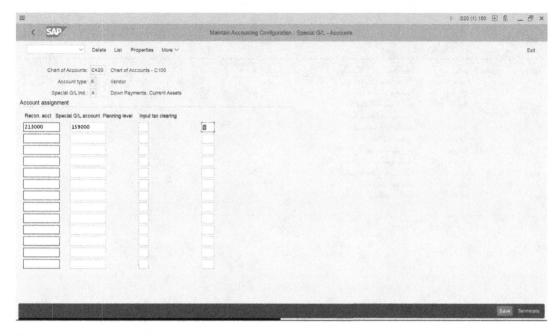

Figure 16-9. *Special G/L accounts for vendor advance*

Update the following fields:

Recon. acct: Enter the G/L reconciliation account for clearing down payment for vendor (we used 213000 as our reconciliation account in this activity) in this field.

Special G/L account: Enter the G/L for advance vendor payment (we used 159000 in this activity) in this field.

Output tax clearing: Enter V (input tax type) in this field. This specification allows the system to post tax elements arising from down payments to the input clearing account.

Save your settings.

The next step is to check the defaulted specifications in the system for your Special G/L payment properties to see if the setting meets your requirement. To do this, click Properties (this is the third item from the top left of the screen). The Maintain Accounting Configuration: Special G/L – Properties is displayed. You don't need to adjust any settings here, this exercise is just to check your settings and make sure that they are okay.

Your screen should look like the one in Figure 16-10.

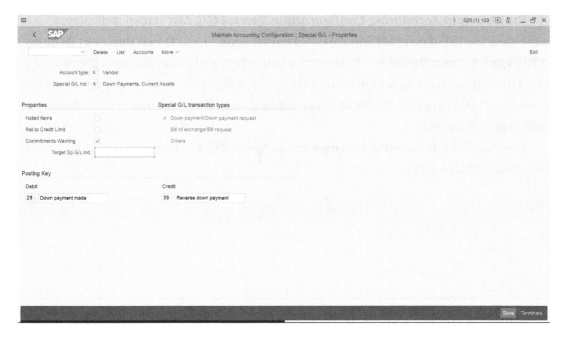

Figure 16-10. *Standard Special G/L properties settings*

Note   SAP normally comes with preconfigured settings for Special G/L properties. Check the Special G/L specifications provided by the system to make sure that they meet your needs.

Down Payment Request for Vendors

This is when a vendor requests partial or full advance payment from you before commencing a business transaction.

Note   Down Payment Request is a noted item.

To customize down payment request for vendors, follow this menu path: **IMG: Financial Accounting➤ Accounts Receivable and Accounts Payable ➤ Business Transactions ➤ Down Payments Made ➤ Define Alternative Reconciliation Account for Down Payments.**

The ***Maintain Accounting Configuration: Special G/L List*** screen is displayed, containing the list of possible Special G/L Transactions. Select **Down Payment Request (SP.G/Lind. F)** from the list by clicking on it to select it, and click Choose at the top left of the screen. The Chart of Accounts Entry dialog Box pops up. Enter your Chart of Accounts ID (CA10) in the ***Chart of Accounts*** field and click Continue at the bottom right of the dialog box.

The ***Maintain Accounting Configuration: Special G/L - Accounts*** screen is displayed (Figure 16-11).

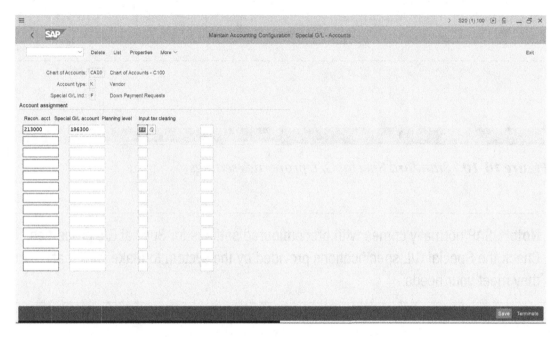

Figure 16-11. *Special G/L accounts for vendor down payment request*

Enter G/L 213000 in the Reconciliation Account field and Payment requests (Vendor) – 196300 in the Special G/L account field. Enter planning level FF (Down Payment Request) in the Planning level field.

Click the Properties function at the top of the screen to check the defaulted specifications in the system for your Special G/L payment properties to see if the setting meets your requirement. To do this, click Properties (this is the third item from the top left of the screen).

Save your settings.

The final step in defining vendor down payments is to define the tax clearing account.

Defining Account for Tax Clearing (Down payments – Vendor)

Depending on your country's legal specifications, the tax entered for down payment will be posted to the tax clearing account you defined in here.

Problem: Your client wants a tax clearing account that will enable the Spoxio Inc. accounting team to display gross down payments in the vendor accounts in order to meeting legal requirements. Your task is to define a clearing account for down payments made that will enable the Spoxio Inc. accounting team to achieve this objective.

To define account tax clearing for vendor down payments, follow this menu path: *IMG: Financial Accounting* ➤ *Accounts Receivable and Accounts Payable* ➤ *Business Transactions* ➤ *Down Payments Made* ➤ *Define Account for Tax Clearing*.

The *Configuration Accounting Maintain: Automatic Posts – Procedures* screen comes up, displaying a list of procedures provided by SAP in the system. From the Procedure list Select **Input tax clearing on down payments – VVA** by clicking on it, and click Choose at the top left of the screen. The *Chart of Accounts Entry* dialog screen pops up. Enter your Chart of Accounts ID (CA10) in the *Enter Chart of Account* field and click Continue at the bottom right of the dialog box. The *Configuration Accounting Maintain: Automatic Posts – Rules* comes up. Select **Input tax clearing** checkbox in **Accounts are determined based on** section of the screen and then click the Save button at the bottom right of the screen.

The *Configuration Accounting Maintain: Automatic Posts – Accounts* screen is displayed (Figure 16-12).

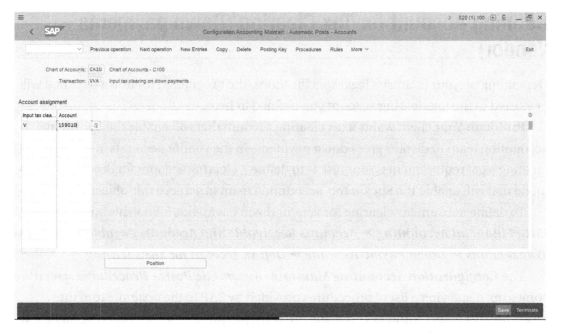

Figure 16-12. *Specifying the Input tax type and account for Input tax clearing for customer down payments*

Enter Output Tax type – **V** in the ***Input Tax type*** field and enter the appropriate G/L Account for Input tax clearing on down payments (we used 159010 as our G/L account in this activity) in the ***Account field***.

Save your work.

Guarantees

Bank Guarantee is a legally binding document issued by the banks or other financial institutions on behalf of their client to a third party (supplier) to enable the client to obtain goods or services from a supplier on credit for an agreed time period. Bank guarantee is a kind of short-term borrowing. It is a formal assurance by the bank to make payment to a supplier in an event where their client fails to keep their part of the debt obligation for goods or services received within the specified period.

It is a normal business practice for banks to request some form of collateral or security from their clients before issuing them a letter of credit in order to safeguard the assets of the bank.

Note   Before you proceed with this activity, you have to first create the GL accounts that you would need to assign to your settings for Guarantee during your configuration. Please refer to Chapter 5 on how to create G/L accounts.

Defining Alternative Reconciliation Accounts for Vendors (Guarantees)

Problem: It is mandatory to disclosure the requirement for Spoxio Inc. to maintain separate special G/L accounts where guarantees are posted, instead of the normal vendor reconciliation accounts. Your task is to define alternative reconciliation accounts that will enable posting guarantees to G/L special accounts.

To go to the screen where you will define alternative reconciliation accounts for customers (guarantees), follow this menu path: *IMG: Financial Accounting ➤ Accounts Receivable and Accounts Payable ➤ Business Transactions ➤ Postings with Alternative Reconciliation Account ➤ Other Special GL Transactions ➤ Define Alternative Reconciliation Account for Vendors.*

The *Maintain Accounting Configuration: Special G/L List* screen is displayed (Figure 16-13), containing the list of possible Special G/L Transactions.

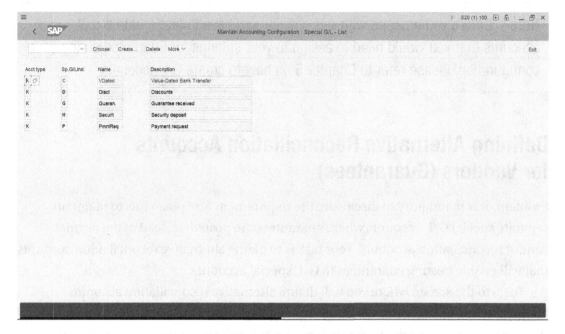

Figure 16-13. *List of special G/L transactions provided by SAP in the system (Guarantee)*

Select **Guarantee (SP.G/Lind. G)** from the list by clicking on it to select it and click Choose at the top left of the screen. The Chart of Accounts Entry dialog Box pops up. Enter your Chart of Accounts ID (CA10) in the ***Chart of Accounts*** field, and click Continue at the bottom right of the dialog box.

The ***Maintain Accounting Configuration: Special G/L - Accounts*** screen is displayed (Figure 16-14). Enter G/L Account – 213000 in the Reconciliation Account field and enter the Special G/L Account – 196400 in the Special G/L Account field.

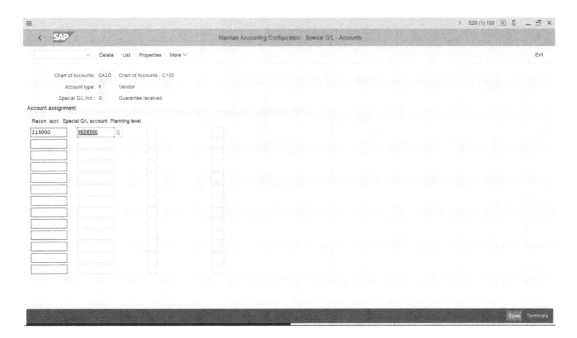

Figure 16-14. *Assignment of reconciliation accounts for Guarantees*

Update the following fields:

Recon. acct: Enter the G/L reconciliation account for clearing down payment (we used 213000 as our reconciliation account in this activity) in this field.

Special G/L account: Enter the G/L for advance customer payment (we used 196400 in this activity) in this field.

The next step is to check the defaulted specifications in the system for your Special G/L payment properties to see if the setting meets your requirement. To do this, click Properties (this is the third item from the top left of the screen).

Note   SAP normally comes with preconfigured settings for Special G/L properties. Check the Special G/L specifications provided by the system to make sure that they meet your needs.

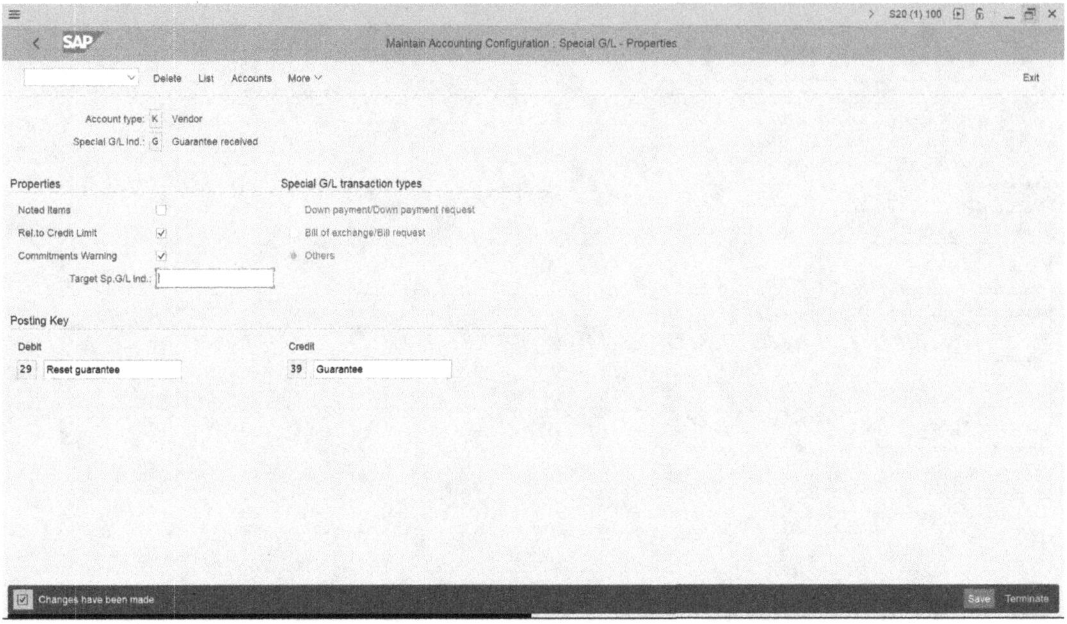

Figure 16-15. The standard properties for guarantee received settings

Save your work.

The last step in our guarantee customizing is to define accounts for automatic offsetting entry. By defining accounts for automatic offsetting entries, you are simply specifying the G/L accounts that the system will post the offsetting entries to for special G/L transactions.

Defining Accounts for Automatic Offsetting Entry

Accounts determination for automatic offsetting Entry for special GL transactions are based on account type, special G/L indicator, chart of accounts, and reconciliation account.

Problem: Your task is to define Accounts for Automatic Offsetting Entries for the following Accounts:

- DG – Customer – Guarantee.

- DS Customer – Check/bill of exchange.

- KG – Vendor Guarantee.

- KS – Vendor – Check/bill of exchange.

To define accounts for automatic offsetting entry, follow this menu path: ***IMG: Financial Accounting ➤ Accounts Receivable and Accounts Payable ➤ Business Transactions ➤ Postings with Alternative Reconciliation Account ➤ Other Special GL Transactions ➤ Define Accounts for Automatic Offsetting Entry.***

The ***Enter your Chart of Accounts*** dialog box pops up. Enter your Chart of Accounts ID (CA10) in the Chart of Accounts field. Confirm your entry by clicking Continue at the bottom right of the dialog box. The ***Configuration Accounting Maintain: Automatic Posts – Rules*** screen comes up. Set ***Account type/sp.G/L ind*** checkbox. On the Automatic Posting Rules in **Accounts are determined based on** section of the screen, click the Save button at the bottom right of the screen.

The ***Configuration Accounting Maintain: Automatic Posts – Accounts*** screen where you will assign the G/L accounts for automatic Offsetting postings is displayed (Figure 16-16).

Using the information below, update fields following: Account type/special G/L Indicator and Account.

Table 16-1. *List of Account Types/Special G/L Indicators and Accounts*

Account type/sp.G/L Ind	Account
DG – *Customer – Guarantee*	196110
DS *Customer – Check/bill of exchange*	196210
KG – *Vendor Guarantee*	196410
KS – *Vendor – Check/bill of exchange*	196210

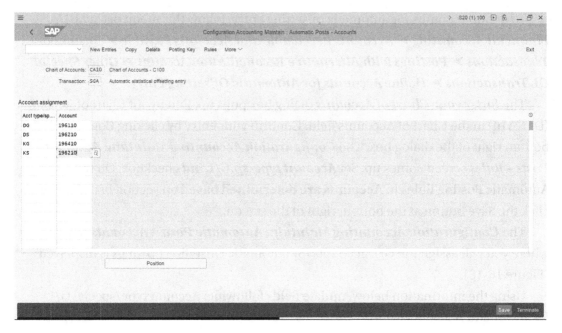

Figure 16-16. *Assigning account types to G/L accounts for automatic statistical offsetting entries*

Save your customizing.

Summary

This chapter looked at special G/L transactions in detail by comparing special G/L transactions with the normal G/L transactions. It explained various forms of special G/L transactions covered in SAP ERP, such as down payments, bills of exchange, and guarantees. You learned about the technical factors they belong to (noted items, free offsetting entry, and automatic offsetting entry). You also learned how to configure down payments (down payment made, down payment received, and down payment request) and how to check the properties of standard down payment settings supplied by SAP to see if they meet your requirements. You also learned how to define tax clearing accounts for down payments and learned about the specifications of the accounts special G/L transactions are posted to.

Finally, you learned what a guarantee is. You learned about alternative reconciliation accounts for customers/vendors and defined accounts for an automatic offsetting entry.

The next chapter explains Ledgers by looking at how to define accounting principles, assigning defined principles to ledger groups, defining settings for ledgers and currency types, and assigning accounting principles to ledger groups.

CHAPTER 17

Ledgers

In most cases, global organizations usually operate various accounting standards such as group accounting standard, local accounting standards, tax accounting standards, and so on. As a result, it may be important for large organizations to set up parallel accounting. SAP recommends to use separate ledgers for each accounting principle. For example, one ledger with US GAAP assigned to it and another with local accounting principle, and so on.

These forms of accounting standards need to be represented in the system. Ledgers in SAP HANA are an attempt to map parallel accounting business transactions in the G/L accounting as it gives you the flexibility to maintain various parallel ledgers that meet different accounting principles.

Since financial reporting requirements have increased significantly in recent times, and the primary responsibilities of organizations are to meet legal reporting requirements such as IFRS, GAAPs, IAS, and so on, the accounting principles mapped in ledgers allows organizations to generate financial statements to meet accounting standards requirements.

Parallel ledgers are maintained in general ledger accounting to represent several accounting principles such as IFRS for the leading ledger at the group level and local accounting standards such as Local GAAP in the extension ledger.

SAP comes with standard tables for saving and analyzing values based on total tables. For example, in ECC, the table is FAGLFLEXT, and in SAP S4 HANA, the line item table is ACDOCA.

SAP S4 Featured two types of ledgers in the system.

1. Standard ledgers:

    Leading ledger is represented as – 0L in SAP S4 HANA. This standard ledger is a minimum requirement. Leading ledger stores accounting documents based on different accounting principles from a group point of view.

© Andrew Okungbowa 2023
A. Okungbowa, *SAP S/4HANA Financial Accounting Configuration*,
https://doi.org/10.1007/978-1-4842-8957-0_17

Non-Leading Ledger is a parallel ledger that allows reporting requirements to meet local accounting principles. Table ACDOCA stores the records created in the Leading Ledger in the Non-Leading Ledger.

2.   Extended Ledger. This is a non-standard ledger

The idea of Extended Ledger is to be able to create parallel ledgers not as part of Standard Ledgers for local accounting principles. The primary purpose of extended ledger is that it serves as an underlying ledger. Therefore, postings made in the underlying ledger are applicable to the extended ledger. Hence, records relating to leading ledger in ACDOCA are not transferred to the extended ledger.

Now let's look at how to define accounting principles under ledgers in SAP S4 HANA.

Defining Accounting Principles

Accounting principal configuration is part of Parallel Accounting in the SAP S4 HANA system. The Accounting principles that you defined in this activity will makes it possible for the system to perform various accounting treatments in one entry like valuations and closing preparations for your company code according to defined accounting principles for IAS/US GAAP for the group and for other accounting principles for local accounting principles.

Warning   Do not delete the accounting principles that you have defined because of the relationship accounting principles have with other accounting functions like currency valuation and others.

In this activity, you will defined Accounting Principles and assign the accounting principles you have defined to appropriate ledger groups.

To define accounting principles in SAP S4 HANA, follow this menu path: ***IMG: Financial Accounting ➤ Financial Accounting Global Settings ➤ Ledgers ➤ Parallel Accounting ➤ Define Accounting Principles***.

The Change View "Accounting Principles": Overview screen comes up, displaying accounting principles presented in the system (Figure 17-1). This is the screen where you define your accounting principles such as GAPP, IFRS, IAS, and so on, that you can assign to ledger.

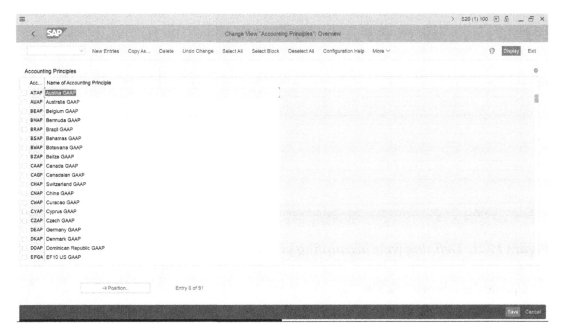

Figure 17-1. *List of accounting principles represented in the system*

Note   SAP have provided some of accounting principles in the system (Figure 17-1) which you can use, so you don't have to create them again. However, we are just going to create accounting principles for local report.

Click New Entries at the top left of the screen to go to the screen where you will specify the settings for your accounting principle, as shown in Figure 17-2.

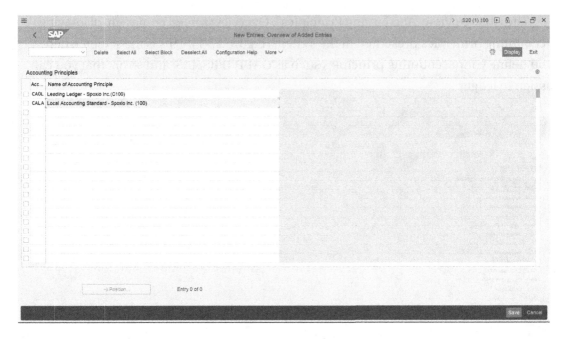

Figure 17-2. *Defining your accounting principles*

Update the following fields:

Accounting Principle: Enter a key for your local accounting principle in this field. In this activity, we used CA0L for our leading ledger and CALA for our local accounting standard.

Name of Accounting Principle: Enter description for your accounting principles in this field.

Save your accounting principle.

Note   You cannot use an accounting principle key that has already been assigned to a ledger group in the system; if accounting principle keys C10, C20 C30 have been used, you will not be able to use them again. So, when defining accounting principle keys, try and use keys that have not been used already.

The next step in this activity is to define a ledger group that will be assigned to the accounting principles you have defined in this activity.

Defining Ledger Group

The Ledger group is the bringing together of several ledgers in a given group in order to simplify specific functions that are stored in the system relating to G/L accounting.

The ledger group is important in the sense that it allows you to specify the ledger group that the system can post to in the ledgers relating to the group you have specified in your customizing.

To Assign accounting principle to ledger groups, follow this menu path: ***IMG: Financial Accounting ➤ Financial Accounting Global Settings ➤ Ledgers ➤ Ledger ➤ Define Ledger Group.***

The Change View "Ledger Group": Overview screen is displayed. Click New Entries at the top left of the screen. The New Entries: Overview of Added Entries screen comes up (Figure 17-3).

Figure 17-3. *Defining ledger group for your accounting principles*

Enter keys for your ledger groups and a description. We used 0L as our leading ledger group and SO for our local accounting standard.

Save your work.

The next step is to assign the accounting principles you defined in Figure 17-2 to the target Ledger groups you created in Figure 17-3.

Assigning Accounting Principle to Ledger Groups

To define ledger groups for your accounting principles, follow this menu path: ***IMG:
Financial Accounting ➤ Financial Accounting Global Settings ➤ Ledgers ➤ Parallel
Accounting ➤ Assign Accounting Principle to Ledger Groups***.

The Change View "Assignment of Accounting Principles to Target Ledger Group"
Screen is displayed. Click New Entries at the top left of the screen to go to the New
Entries: Overview of Added Entries screen (Figure 17-4) where you will assign your
accounting principles to target accounting group.

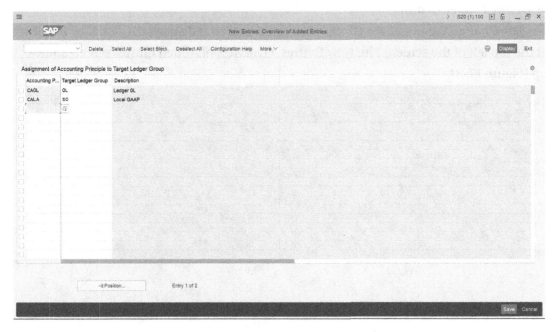

Figure 17-4. *Assignment of Accounting Principle to Target Ledger Group*

Enter the accounting principles you defined in Figure 17-2 in the Accounting
Principle fields. Using the search function or the match code to search for the accounting
principles in the Target Ledger Group fields, as in Figure 17-4. In this activity, we used
CA0L as our leading ledger and assigned it to a target group – 01. For local accounting
standard, we used CALA as our accounting principle key and used SO as our non-
leading ledger.

Save your work.

The next step in this activity is to define settings for ledgers and currency types.

Defining Ledger Settings for Ledgers and Currency Types

To define a Ledger for your accounting principle, follow this menu path: ***IMG: Financial Accounting ➤ Financial Accounting Global Settings ➤ Ledgers ➤ Ledger ➤ Define Settings for Ledgers and Currency Types***. Change View "Ledger": Overview screen is displayed. Click on the Ledger folder in the Dialog Structure on the left side of the screen and choose New Entries at the top left of the screen. The New Entries: Overview of Added Entries screen is displayed (Figure 17-5). This is the screen where you will carry out your customizing of the ledger for accounting principles.

Figure 17-5. *Defining ledgers for accounting principles*

Update the following field:

Ledger: Enter the ledger group keys you defined (in Figure 17-3) in this field. You can also use the search function to search for your ledger group key.

Ledger Name: Enter the name of the ledger group in this field. Such as 0L-Leading 0L and S0-Local GAAP.

Leading: Specify the leading ledger by ticking the checkbox in this field.

Ledger Type: Using the arrow by the side of the field, specify whether your ledger is a Standard Ledger or Extended Ledger. The ledger you activated as the leading ledger here will be used by the system as your leading ledger.

Standard Ledger: This ledger holds the contents of journal entries relating to the business transactions represented in the system.

Extension Ledger: This ledger is a new concept in SAP S4 HANA. This ledger use to be referred to as Appendix ledger in earlier versions. The extension ledger plays an important role in the sense that it helps to eliminate journal entries duplication, especially in an environment where several business transactions are valid for both standard and extension ledgers and minimum adjustments are required in the extension ledger at the end of each month.

Save your ledgers specifications.

Define Settings for Ledgers and Currency Types

SAP S4 HANA comes with a list of currency types that supplement the standard SAP currency types such as document currency – 00, company code currency – 10, controlling area – currency – 20, group currency – 30, and so on. The system also gives you the flexibility to create your currency types if you need to do so. However, we consider the currency types supplied by SAP in the system to be enough for your accounting.

SAP S4 HANA allows you to use up to 10 parallel currencies per ledger. The purpose behind this concept is to allow you to manage, check, and monitor balances and line items represented in different currencies based on your company's requirements.

It is important to note that the minimum requirement is that all company codes must be assigned to at least a leading ledger. Two leaders are represented in SAP S4 HANA.

To define Settings for ledgers and currency types, follow this menu path: Menu: **IMG Financial Accounting ➤ Financial Accounting Global Settings ➤ Ledgers ➤ Ledger ➤ Define Settings for Ledgers and Currency Types**. The Change View "Ledger": Overview screen is displayed (Figure 17-6).

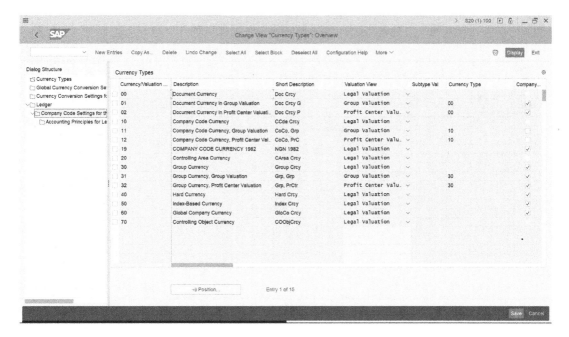

Figure 17-6. *The initial screen for defining company code settings for ledger*

Since we are only defining accounting principles for ledger and company code in this activity, double click the Company Code Settings for the Ledger folder in the Dialog Structure on the left side of the screen. The Determine Work Area: Entry dialog box pops up. Enter your leading ledger key (01) in the Ledger filed and click the enter (the green circle) button at the bottom of the screen. The Consistency Check: Display messages screen comes up with a list of warnings; ignore the warning and X the screen. The Change View "Company Code Settings for Ledger": Overview screen with a list of company codes in the system is displayed. Using the Position button at the bottom of the screen or you can use the scroll bar at the right side of the screen, click on your company code (C100) to select it and click Details at the top left of the screen. The Change View "Company Code Settings for Ledger" Details screen is displayed (Figure 17-7).

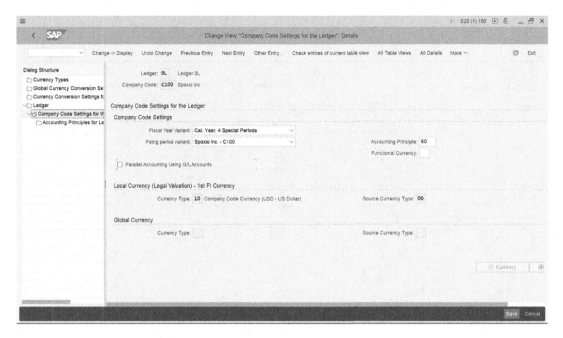

Figure 17-7. *The screen where you define settings for ledgers*

The system automatically defaults the Fiscal Year Variant, The Posting period variant, and your company code currency type – 10. Enter your accounting principle key (60) in the Accounting Principle field. If you activate the Parallel Accounting Using G/L Accounts by ticking the checkbox, this will allow additional data when assigning more than one accounting principle to a combination of ledger and company code.

You can also assign up to 8 freely defined currencies. To do this, click the circled + sign at the bottom right of the screen to extend the screen.

Note   The Global currency type will be automatically defaulted if you have defined your controlling area and assign your company code to the controlling area.

Tip   Do not save your work yet.

The next step is to define the accounting principle for ledger and company code. At the Dialog Structure on the left pane of the screen, Double click The Accounting Principles for Ledger and Company code (This is the last items under Company Code Settings for the Ledger).

The Change View "Accounting Principles for Ledger and Company Code": Overview screen is displayed. Click New Entries at the top left of the screen. The New Entries: Overview of Added Entries screen comes up (Figure 17-8).

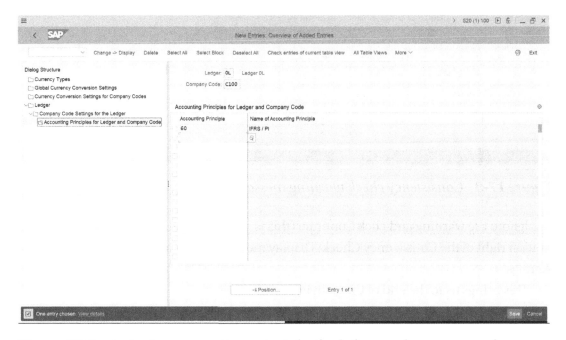

Figure 17-8. *Assigning accounting principles for ledger and company code*

Use the search function of the match code at the side of the Accounting Principle field to call up the list of accounting principles in the system. Assign your company code, and hit enter on your keyboard for the system to assign your accounting principle. Click the Save button at the bottom left of the screen. The Consistency Check: Display messages screen pops up, as in Figure 17-9, containing a list of warnings.

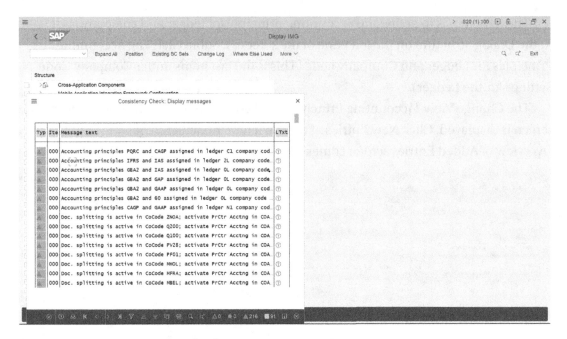

Figure 17-9. *Consistency check warning message*

Ignore the warning and click Continue (this is the green tick circle button) at the bottom right of the Consistency Check: Display messages screen and then save your settings.

This brings us to the end of this activity.

Summary

This chapter briefly explained what ledgers are and briefly looked at the types of ledgers in SAP S4 HANA, namely Standard ledger and extension ledgers. We then took you through various steps involved in defining accounting principles and how to assign accounting principles to a ledger group. You also learned other customizing steps such as defining a ledger group, and how to assign accounting principles to a ledger group.

Finally, you proceeded to learn how to define ledger settings for ledger and currency types. This brings us to the conclusion of this book.

Now that you have completed the customizing activities covered in this book, we are optimistic that you can apply what you learned in this book to real-world scenarios. This was our primary objective for writing this book. Good luck, we wish you the very best in the world of SAP FI consultancy.

APPENDIX A

Some Useful Transaction Codes

FI

Organizational Structure

Description	Transaction Code
Display IMG	SPRO
Company Code	OX15
Change View "Company Code" Overview	OX02
Assign Company Code to Company	OX16
Business Area	OX03
Fiscal Year Variant	OB29
Assign Company Code to Fiscal Year Variant	OB37
Posting Periods Variant	OBBO
Assign Posting Periods Variants to Company Code	OBBP
Open and Closing Posting Periods	OB52

Master Data

Description	Transaction Code
Edit Chart of Accounts List	OB13
Assign Company Code to Chart of Accounts	OB62
Define Account Group	OBD4
Define Retained Earnings Account	OB53

© Andrew Okungbowa 2023
A. Okungbowa, *SAP S/4HANA Financial Accounting Configuration*,
https://doi.org/10.1007/978-1-4842-8957-0

Document Control

Description	Transaction Code
Define Document Number Ranges for Entry View	FBN1
Define Field Status Variants	OBC4
Assign Company Code to Field Status Variant	OBC5

Tolerance Groups

Description	Transaction Code
Define Tolerance Groups for G/L Accounts	OBA0
Define Tolerance Groups for Employees	OBA4
Assign Users to Tolerance Groups	OB57

General Ledger

Description	Transaction Code
Create G/L Account Centrally	FS00

Clearing Open Item

Description	Transaction Code
Automatic Open Item Clearing	OB74
Create Accounts for Clearing Differences	OBXZ

Maximum Exchange Rate Difference

Description	Transaction Code
Define Maximum Exchange Rate Difference per Company Code	OB64
Company Code Global Data	OBY6
Define Valuation Methods	OB59
Prepare Automatic Postings for Foreign Currency Valuation	OBA1

Foreign Currency Valuation

Description	Transaction Code
Define Valuation Methods	OB59
Prepare Automatic Postings for Foreign Currency Valuation	OBA1

Currencies

Description	Transaction Code
Define Standard Quotation for Exchange Rates	ONOT
Enter Prefixes for Direct/Indirect Quotation Exchange Rate	OPRF
Define Translation Ratios for Currency Transaction	OBBS
Enter Exchange Rates	OB08

GR/IR Clearing Account

Description	Transaction Code
Define Adjustment Accounts for GR/IR Clearing	OBYP

Bank

Description	Transaction Code
Define House Bank	FI12
Make Global Settings for Electronic Bank Statement	OT83
Manual Bank Statement – Create and Assign Business Transaction	OT52
Define Variants for Manual Bank Statement	OT43
Create and Assign Business Transactions for Check Deposit	OT53
Define Variants for Check Deposit	OT45

Tax Sales/Purchase

Description	Transaction Code
Check Calculation Procedure	OBYZ
Assign Country to Calculation Procedure	OBBG
Define Tax Codes for Sales and Purchases	FTXP
Define Tax Accounts	OB40
Assign Taxable Codes for Non-Taxable Transactions	OBCL

Cash Journal

Description	Transaction Code
Define Number Range Intervals for Cash Journal Documents	FBCJC1
Define Number Range Intervals for Cash Journal Documents	FBCJC1
Set up Cash Journal	FBCJC0
Create, Change, Delete Business Transactions	FBCJC2
Set Up Print Parameters for Cash Journal	FBCJC3

FSV

Description	Transaction Code
Define Financial Statement Version	OB58

Integration of FI with Other Modules

Description	Transaction Code
Define Accounts for Material Management	OBYC
Prepare Revenue Account Determination	VKOA

Accounts Receivable and Accounts Payable

Description	Transaction Code
Define Accounts Groups with Screen Layout (Customers)	OBD2
Create Number Ranges for Customer Accounts	XDN1
Define Account Groups with Screen Layout (Vendors)	OBD3
Create Number Ranges for Vendor Accounts	XKN1
Assign Number Ranges to Vendor Account Groups	OBAS
Maintain Terms of Payment	OBB8
Define Terms of Payment for Instalment Payments	OBB9
Define Document Types for Enjoy Transaction	OBZO
Define Tax Code per Transaction	OBZT
Define Account for Net Procedure	OBXA
Define Accounts for Cash Discount Granted	OBXI
Define Accounts for Cash Discount Taken	OBXU
Define Accounts for Lost Cash Discount	OBXV
Define Accounts for Overpayments/Underpayments	OBXL
Define Accounts for Bank Charges (Vendor)	OBXK
Define Tolerances (Vendors)	OBA3
Define Reason Codes (Manual Outgoing Payments)	OBBE
Define Accounts for Payment Differences (Manual Outgoing Payment)	OBXL
Customizing: Maintain Payment Program	FBZP
Define Correspondence Types	OB77
Assign Programs for Correspondence Types	OB78
Define Sender Details for Correspondence Form	OBB1
Determine Call-Up Functions	OB79
Define Dunning Procedures	FBMP

Special GL Transactions

Description	Transaction Code
Define Alternative Reconciliation Account for Customers	OBXY
Define Alternative Reconciliation Account for Vendors	OBXT
Define Accounts for Automatic Offsetting Entry	OBXS

Down Payments

Description	Transaction Code
Define Reconciliation Accounts for Customer Down Payments	OBXR
Define Account for Tax Clearing (Customer)	OBXB
Define Alternative Reconciliation Account for Down Payments	OBXY
Define Account for Tax Clearing (Vendor)	OBXD

Define Sort Method and Adjustment Accts for Regrouping

Description	Transaction Code
Define Sort Method and Adjustment Accts for Regrouping Receivables/Payables	OBBU
Adjustment Accounts for Receivables/Payables by Maturity	OBBV

Easy Access

Customer

Description	Transaction Code
Customer Master Record – Create	FD01
Customer Master Record – Change	FD02
Customer Master Record – Display	FD03
Customer Master Record – Block/Unblock	FD05
Customer Master Record – Set Deletion Indicator	FD06
Customer Invoice	FB70
Customer Credit Memo	FB75
Park/Edit Invoice	FV70
Display Parked Document	FBV3
Incoming Payment	F-28
Down Payment Request	F-37
Down Payment Received	F-29
Down Payment Clearing	F-39
Customer Balance Display	FD10N
Display/Change Line Items	FBL5N
Change Line Items	FB09
Invoice – General	F-22
Manual Outgoing Payment	F-53

Correspondence

Description	Transaction Code
Correspondence Request	FB12
Print Correspondence As per Requests	F-61
Dunning	F150

Vendor

Description	Transaction Code
Vendor Master Record – Create	FK01
Vendor Master Record – Change	FK02
Vendor Master Record – Display	FK03
Vendor Master Record – Block/Unblock	FK05
Vendor Master Record – Set Deletion Indicator	FK06
Vendor Invoice	FB60
Invoice – General	F-43
Post Parked Document	FBV0
Display Balances	FK10N
Balance Confirmation - Print Letters	F-18
Down Payment Request	F-47
Down Payment	F-48
Down Payment Clearing	F-54
Invoice Clearing	F-44
Incoming Payment	F-28

Automatic Payment

Description	Transaction Code
Check Lots	FCHI
Automatic Payment Program	F110
Cash Journal	FBCJ

Index

A

© Andrew Okungbowa 2023
A. Okungbowa, *SAP S/4HANA Financial Accounting Configuration*,
https://doi.org/10.1007/978-1-4842-8957-0

F

Printed in the United States
by Baker & Taylor Publisher Services